De Cella in Seculum

Religious and Secular Life and Devotion in Late Medieval England

De Cella in Seculum

RELIGIOUS AND SECULAR LIFE AND DEVOTION
IN LATE MEDIEVAL ENGLAND

An Interdisciplinary Conference
In celebration of the eighth centenary
Of the Consecration

Of St Hugh of Avalon
Bishop of Lincoln

20-22 July, 1986

Edited by Michael G. Sargent

D. S. BREWER

© Contributors 1989

First published 1989 by D.S.Brewer, Cambridge

D.S.Brewer is an imprint of Boydell & Brewer Ltd
PO Box 9, Woodbridge, Suffolk IP12 3DF
and of Boydell & Brewer Inc.
Wolfeboro, New Hampshire 03894-2069, USA

ISBN 0 85991 268 X

British Library Cataloguing in Publication Data
De Cella in seculum.
1. England. Christianity, 1200-1500
I. Sargent, Michael G.
209'.42
ISBN 0-85991-268-X

Library of Congress Cataloging-in-Publication Data
De cella in seculum : religious and secular life and devotion
in late medieval England : an interdisciplinary conference
in celebration of the eighth centenary of the consecration
of St. Hugh of Avalon, Bishop of Lincoln, 20-22 July,
1986 / edited by Michael G.Sargent.
    p.   cm.
  ISBN 0-85991-268-X
  1. Hugh, of Lincoln, Saint, 1140-1200—Congresses.
2. England—Church history—1066-1485—Congresses.
3. Carthusians—England—History—Congresses.
I. Sargent, Michael G.
BR754.H83D4 1989
282'.0942—dc19   88-6066
                                                   CIP

∞   The paper used in this publication meets the minimum
requirements of American National Standard for Information
Sciences – Permanence of Paper for Printed Library Materials,
ANSI Z39.48–1984.

Printed and bound in Great Britain by The Camelot Press PLC, Southampton

CONTENTS

ILLUSTRATIONS

CONTRIBUTORS

Canon John Nurser	Chancellor, Lincoln Cathedral
Michael G. Sargent	Queens College, The City University of New York
David Hugh Farmer	University of Reading
Richard W. Pfaff	University of North Carolina at Chapel Hill
Richard Loomis	Nazareth College of Rochester
H. E. J. Cowdrey	St Edmund Hall, Oxford
Rev. Gordon Mursell	Salisbury and Wells Theological College
James Hogg	Universität Salzburg
Gordon Whatley	Queens College, The City University of New York
Sarah M. Horrall (†)	University of Ottawa
S. S. Hussey	University of Lancaster
Nicholas Watson	
George R. Keiser	Kansas State University
Vincent Gillespie	St Anne's College, Oxford
Sr M. Teresa Brady	Pace University
Rev. Robert A. Horsfield	
Ann M. Hutchison	York University
Martha W. Driver	Pace University

It is with regret that the editor and collaborators in this volume announce the death of their colleague Sarah Horrall on July 27, 1988.

PREFACE

Canon John Nurser

Dr Sargent, Ladies and Gentlemen

I would like to welcome you to Lincoln. There will be an opportunity tomorrow for the Mayor to welcome you and show you some of our rather remarkable civic treasures. I suppose that the structures of all our present-day corporate life at the town level date back – as evidenced by such cities as Lincoln and London – to the generation immediately following St Hugh. It gives me considerable pleasure to see the flags of that family of cities – London's the St George's Cross with the sword of the Cathedral of St Paul, Lincoln's with the fleur-de-lys of the Cathedral of the Blessed Virgin Mary.

But my role is to welcome you on behalf of my colleagues of the Chapter of that Cathedral, and indeed of the churches in this place generally. I am glad to say that our Lincoln Council of Churches is genuinely comprehensive and includes Roman Catholics and members of charismatic 'house churches', both of whom in England are often only content to sit with other churches as observers.

I have been privileged to serve as chairman of the national committee that was established four years ago in order to celebrate the eight hundredth anniversary of the first Carthusian to be canonised, Hugh of Avalon, coming in 1186 from the first Charterhouse in the British Isles, at Witham in Somerset, to be elected, consecrated and enthroned as Bishop of Lincoln. For virtually the whole of his remembered life before that he had been a member of a religious community. For the overwhelming proportion of that time he had been a Carthusian monk, a leader within a group consciously dedicated not only to a specially stringent ascetic life but to solitary meditation. Almost overnight he became - in a country whose common language was foreign to him – one of the senior officers of church and state in the prime of the Angevin empire; the pastor – not only in the sense of shepherding but also of ruling – of what was perhaps the largest diocese in Western Europe; and a bishop whose *cathedra* was buried under a pile of rubble after the collapse of Remigius' Romanesque cathedral in an earth tremor. It was indeed a story of *De Cella in Seculum*. His story has inspired our committee to organise and welcome a very great range of events, and it has almost demanded that they be of their very nature planned as ecumenical events. None of the events of this year, therefore, are more welcome than this annual international conference of work in progress associated with *Analecta Cartusiana*, for nothing is more ecumenical than scholarship.

On reflexion, that is not true. For it would be misleading – spectacularly so this year – to allow to scholarship the ecumenical crown. The highest form of ecumenicity must remain the practice of holiness.

More than once in our committee we have had Thomas Merton's title, *Contemplation in a World of Action*, come to our mind as a phrase that we could, if necessary, volunteer to those who might enquire what it was about the memory of Hugh of Avalon's life that caused us to honour him. I have a particularly vivid recollection of a story that I tell, not against Irish Catholicism in the English-speaking world, but against virtually all of us.

I served for a time in the centre of Canberra, the capital of Australia. We were accustomed to numerous visitors from the countries of South and East Asia. A librarian from Sri Lanka, who was a Buddhist, came to work for a year as an associate of the university library. He was commended to us after he had already been in Canberra for some months, and we invited him to our house. He was unhappy. He missed his family. Indeed, within a couple of weeks of our meeting, he decided to cut his time short and go back home. The reason, fundamentally, was that he saw no prospect of growing or learning in spiritual things while he was with us. In Sri Lanka it was his practice to go home after work, change into comfortable clothes, cycle to the local temple and discuss religion for an hour or two, then cycle back to his family for dinner. In Canberra, he put himself into what he thought *mutatis mutandis* would be a comparable lifestyle and would enable him to get the benefit of our foreign experience in the common spiritual enterprise. So he asked for the place where he might meet the local holy men, and was directed to the presbytery of the nearest Roman Catholic Church. He rang the bell, and spoke of his eagerness to participate in spiritual dialogue with the largely Irish fathers. He was most courteously invited in and asked to sit and wait in the hall. Father X came by and passed the time of day on his way to a parent-teachers evening at the church school. Father Y rushed out to take a wedding interview. Father Z was clearly in a terrible state because the only car they had was not firing properly and he had to drive two hundred miles to Sydney next morning to a conference. This or something like it happened every evening, and my friend from Sri Lanka came sadly to the conclusion that he never would get a chance to talk with Christians about anything important.

Hugh seems to have had an unusual capacity – like Jesus of Nazareth – to relate directly to people he encountered. He could suddenly say something important to them. He put on one side the fact of their being lepers, or foresters or Jews or kings. Perhaps it was this directness, expressed in affairs of the world as perception and will, that enabled him to achieve such an extraordinary variety of practical and political tasks so successfully. It is not a novel idea to suggest it was a quality of Hugh the bishop that owed almost everything to those years alone in his cell and garden as Hugh the Carthusian monk.

There is little doubt that it was Hugh's reputation for holiness in his own lifetime that contributed greatly to the powerful influence he exerted on virtually every aspect of the life of his time. He was energetic, capable, and incorruptible, but it was his spiritual force that made the difference. For a church like mine that talks a lot about politics and justice, and *Faith in the City*, that is a practically useful observation.

INTRODUCTION

Michael G. Sargent

The papers in this volume represent the proceedings of a conference held at Edward King House, Lincoln, 20-22 July, 1986, as part of the celebration of the eighth centenary of the consecration and enthronement of Hugh of Avalon as bishop. St Hugh's vocation to both the monastic or heremitic cell and to the public world – one of the most remarkable aspects of his religious life – determined the theme of this conference: *de cella in seculum*. Born in the French Dauphiné in the second quarter of the twelfth century, Hugh became a canon regular in his youth and was appointed to the cure of a small local parish. At the age of twenty-three, he chose to withdraw from the world to the mountain 'desert' of the Chartreuse; after ten years of the heremitic austerity of the Carthusian life, Hugh was appointed procurator of the Grande Chartreuse, responsible for the governance of the lay brothers and the temporal affairs of the house. Six years later, at the request of England's King Henry II, he was made prior of the newly-founded but languishing first English Charterhouse at Witham – one of the religious houses, according to Carthusian tradition, that Henry had founded in the partial expiation for his responsibility in the death of Thomas à Becket. As prior, Hugh secured and enhanced both the monastic buildings and the spiritual life of Witham Charterhouse; from this post he was nominated to the see of Lincoln by his king, canonically elected by the chapter, and commanded by his religious superior, the prior of the Grande Chartreuse (he refused to accept until the latter two conditions were met).

As bishop of a major see, with a close personal relationship to the king of England, Hugh's career also involved him in political and ecclesiastical affairs on the national and international level, yet he found time to return to Witham for several weeks every year, to live simply as a Carthusian choir monk. At his death in 1200, the man who was to be the first Carthusian canonised a saint was born to his grave by a funeral party including the kings of England and Scotland, the archbishops of Canterbury, York and Ragusa, and numerous magnates and prelates.

Reflecting this double vocation to the cell and the world, the papers of the St Hugh conference all dealt with the ecclesiastical, historical or literary aspects of the adaptation to secular ends or audiences of what was originally or primarily monastic or heremitic. The first four papers in the present volume deal with the details of this transformation in Hugh's own life. Dr David Hugh Farmer, drawing upon his and Decima Douie's edition of Adam of Eynsham's *Magna Vita Sancti Hugonis*,[1] demonstrates the balance of various ideals in Hugh's sanctity. As a secular canon in his youth, and as a bishop in his maturity, he was drawn to monasticism; as a Carthusian monk, he was entrusted with worldly responsibilities and positions of authority. He dealt as equals with those of all social levels, from common labourers to bishops and kings. He was both the first Carthusian and the first bishop of Lincoln to be canonised. Professor Richard Pfaff, whose particular area of expertise is medieval liturgical history,[2] describes the evidence for the devotional practices of a man translated from the monastic to the secular *milieu*. Drawing upon the remaining records of the liturgical practices of the Carthusian Order and of the cathedral chapter at Lincoln in the later twelfth century, and comparing this with the descriptions of Hugh's own practice in the *Lives* of Adam of Eynsham and Gerald of Wales, Professor Pfaff details a regular practice impeded occasionally by episcopal duties, but with strongly idiosyncratic elements particularly with regard to the chanting of the psalms (which Hugh seems to have performed alternately standing and sitting in a way that may be reflected in modern Carthusian practice, but does not seem to be demonstrated for the twelfth century), the reading of the Gospels through the year at matins and mealtimes, and Hugh's particular devotion to the services for the dead.

Professor Richard Loomis, who presents the third paper, recently published a critical edition and translation of Giraldus de Barri's (Gerald of Wales') *Life of St Hugh*,[3] which predates that of Adam of Eynsham. Where earlier historians have questioned Giraldus' appropriateness as Hugh's biographer, Professor Loomis points out that we may see in the *Life* the portrayal of a man who represents those ideals to which Giraldus aspired but never attained. Hugh was portrayed as a man of highest moral character, whose virtue was rewarded with ecclesiastical preferment culminating in his elevation to a prominent episcopal see, while the onetime *soi-disant* 'electus of St Asaph' was an envious and contentious man who found himself continually blocked from the advancements he so eagerly sought. Viewed in this way, Giraldus' homage to Hugh of Avalon was singularly appropriate.

Professor H. E. J. Cowdrey is a noted expert in eleventh and twelfth century monastic history, and particularly in the relationship between the hierarchy and the reforming orders and movements.[4] In his study of Hugh

[1] Adam of Eynsham, *Magna Vita Sancti Hugonis: the Life of Hugh of Lincoln*, ed. Decima L. Douie and Hugh Farmer, 2 vols. (London, 1961-62; 2nd edn 1985).
[2] Pfaff, *New Liturgical Feasts in Later Medieval England* (Oxford, 1970); *Medieval Latin Liturgy: A Select Bibliography* (Toronto, 1982); articles in *Studies in Philology, Speculum, Journal of Ecclesiastical History, Scriptorium, Revue de théologie ancienne et médiévale*. Cf. also *Montague Rhodes James* (London, 1980).
[3] Loomis, ed., *Giraldus Cambrensis. The Life of St Hugh of Avalon*, Garland Library of Medieval Literature, ser. A, vol. 31 (New York and London, 1985).
[4] Cowdrey, *The Cluniacs and the Gregorian Reform* (Oxford, 1970); ed. and trans., *Gregory VII: The Epistolae Vagantes* (Oxford, 1972); *The Age of Abbot Desiderius: Montecassino, the Papacy and the Normans in the Eleventh and Early*

of Avalon, Carthusian and bishop, Professor Cowdrey demonstrates the reconciliation of the ideals of this most heremitic of religious orders with the episcopal vocation. First, he shows the close relationship between the Grande Chartreuse and the see of Grenoble – a relationship that saw the metropolitan bishop as the protector of the privacy and discipline of the Order, and the Order as the provider of candidates for the episcopacy, particularly in the Dauphiné throughout the twelfth century: in Grenoble itself, in Belley, Maurienne, Die, Geneva and Valence, Arles, Tarentaise and Embrun. It is in the context of this close relationship between the Chartreuse and the episcopacy that the events leading to Hugh of Avalon's elevation to the see of Lincoln and his zeal as bishop there, are to be seen.

The next two papers both deal with early Carthusian spiritual writers. Rev. Gordon Mursell points out in his presentation that the proper relation of the Carthusian monk to the world, as seen in the influential *Meditations* of Guigo I, fifth prior of the Grande Chartreuse, is not rejection, but an ordered love that sees man as the intermediary between God and his creation. Professor James Hogg, editor of the *Analecta Cartusiana*, treats next of the *De Quadripartito Exercitio Cellae* of Adam of Dryburgh, the former Premonstratensian abbot, later a Carthusian at Witham and a friend of St Hugh. Professor Hogg traces the history and evidence for attribution of this important work of monastic spirituality, describes the circumstances of its composition, and assesses its evidence for late-twelfth-century Carthusian life and devotion.

The next pair of papers deal with questions of spirituality and the common man in England in the high and later Middle Ages. The first is presented by Professor Gordon Whatley, whose edition and translation of the twelfth-century *Miracula Sancti Erkenwaldi Episcopi* is forthcoming.[5] Beginning with an introductory review of the kinds of historical evidence that miracle collections can yield, Professor Whatley describes some of the results of an analysis of the miracles of St Erkenwald, focusing primarily on a story of divine retribution visited upon a workman who refused to honour the saint's feast day. Of particular interest is the layman's defence against priestly remonstrance, couched not in the terms of normal medieval anticlericalism – that clerics fail to live up to the ideals that justify their social status – but rather in open defiance of clerical ideals in general. Professor Sarah Horrall, the general editor of the southern version of the *Cursor Mundi*,[6] presents the next paper. Noting the intention of the author

Twelfth Centuries (Oxford, 1983); cf. also 'The Carthusians in England' in B. Bligny, ed., *La Naissance des chartreuses. VIe Colloque internationale d'histoire et de spiritualité cartusiennes* (Grenoble, 1984), pp. 345-56.

[5] Whatley, ed., *The Saint of London: The Life and Miracles of Saint Erkenwald*, Medieval and Renaissance Texts and Studies (Binghamton NY: at press); cf. 'The Uses of Hagiography: The Legend of Pope Gregory and the Emperor Trajan in the Middle Ages', *Viator* 15 (1984), pp. 25-63; 'Heathens and Saints: *St Erkenwald* in its Legendary Context', *Speculum* 61 (1986), pp. 330-63.

[6] Horrall, ed., *The Southern Version of Cursor Mundi*, vol. 1 (Ottawa, 1978); other volumes forthcoming; cf. also 'An Old French Source for the *Genesis* section of *Cursor Mundi*', *Mediaeval Studies* 40 (1978), pp. 361-73.

of the *Cursor* to popularise theological teaching 'for the commun at understand' for northern Englishmen who lacked appropriate literature for this purpose, Professor Horrall demonstrates this work's relationship to its sources and models – particularly such French works as the *Bible* of Herman of Valenciennes, the *Bible des sept états du monde* of Geoffroi de Paris, and the *Traduction anonyme de la Bible entière* – and describes the probable provenance of the *Cursor*.

The remaining eight papers all concern themselves with the implied and actual audiences for contemplative and devotional literature in England in the later Middle Ages, and thus deal with the transition from the cell to the world of writings rather than people. The first of these is a paper by Professor S. S. Hussey, the editor for the Early English Text Society of the second book of Walter Hilton's *Scale of Perfection*.[7] In his study, Professor Hussey examines the evidence concerning the audience for the writings of Richard Rolle, the author of the *Cloud of Unknowing*, Hilton, Julian of Norwich, and Margery Kempe, first by examining the actual dedications of some of these works, next by considering the implied readers both for single texts and for a given authorial *corpus*, and finally by identifying groups of known fifteenth- and early-sixteenth-century readers. The next paper, by Nicholas Watson, considers Rolle's *Judica me Deus* for evidence of the author's attitude toward his audience.[8] Rolle, Watson points out, is a complex character in this regard: he claims to write for the uneducated – but most of his works are in Latin; he stresses the singularity of the heremitical life – yet some of his works survive in large numbers of copies. Although he wrote the *Judica me Deus* with the double purpose of providing a friend with pastoral instruction while also defending his own irregular life, these two disparate aims may be seen as representing a single impulse founded in charity, and they achieve interesting harmonies in their literary realisation.

The next three papers consider the use of contemplative writings in didactic and devotional compilations, and the audiences which they found in this form. Professor George R. Keiser, who has written on the Thornton manuscript and on the use of the *Scala Claustralium* of Guigo II, ninth prior of the Grande Chartreuse in the Middle English *Ladder of Foure Ronges* and the *Holy Boke Gratia Dei*,[9] has here combined these two

[7]   Cf. Hussey, 'An Edition, from the Manuscripts, of Book II of Walter Hilton's Scale of Perfection' (diss. University of London, 1962); 'Latin and English in *The Scale of Perfection*', *Mediaeval Studies* 35 (1973), pp. 456-76; 'The Text of *The Scale of Perfection*, Book II', *Neuphilologische Mitteilungen* 65 (1964), pp. 75-92; 'Editing the Middle English Mystics', in James Hogg, ed., *Spiritualität Heute und Gestern*, Analecta Cartusiana 35:3 (Salzburg, 1983), pp. 160-73.
[8]   Cf. Watson, 'The Methods and Objectives of Thirteenth-Century Anchoritic Devotion', in Marion Glasscoe, ed., *The Medieval Mystical Tradition in England: Exeter Symposium IV* (Cambridge, 1987), pp. 132-53.
[9]   Keiser, 'A Note on the Descent of the Thornton Manuscript', *Transactions of the Cambridge Bibliographical Society* 6 (1976), pp. 347-49; 'Lincoln Cathedral Library MS. 91: The Life and Milieu of the Scribe', *Studies in Bibliography* 32 (1979), pp. 158-79; 'The Holy Boke Gratia Dei', *Viator* 12 (1981), pp. 289-317; 'More Light on the Life and Milieu of Robert Thornton', *Studies in Bibliography* 36

interests. Illustrating his analysis with other examples of didactic and contemplative literature, Professor Keiser details the alterations in tone and audience implied in the changes in text from the *Scala* to the *Ladder* and the *Holy Boke*, substantiating these observations with the evidence of actual provenance and early ownership of the surviving copies of these works – among the more famous of which is the Thornton manuscript now in the possession of the library of the Dean and Chapter of Lincoln Cathedral.

The primary field of expertise of Dr Vincent Gillespie, who presents the next paper, is in the creation and transmission of such major didactic compilations as the *Speculum Christiani*.[10] In his study of the *cura pastoralis in deserto*, Dr Gillespie details first the responsibilities of Carthusian priors and procurators for the spiritual care of their subordinates: the choir monks, lay brothers and familiar servants of each community. Showing the development of these responsibilities through the legislative documents of the order, Dr Gillespie then demonstrates the coincidence of aims in this kind of spiritual care and the creation of the *Cibus animae*, from which the Latin, and much of the vernacular, material of the *Speculum Christiani* was drawn. Although ultimately the evidence of provenance is sparse, Dr Gillespie makes a strong case that the *Cibus animae* could have taken shape in a specifically Carthusian *milieu*.

Not all such transformations of contemplative literature to didactic ends stopped at this point, however: some continued on into contexts unsympathetic to the heremitic and monastic ideals that had informed the original works. Like the *Speculum Christiani*, the *Pore Caitif* is a major didactic treatise containing some contemplative materials which Sr Mary Teresa Brady, the editor of the *Caitif*,[11] has traced back to the works of Richard Rolle. In her paper on Lollard interpolations and omissions in manuscripts of the *Pore Caitif*, Sr Brady points out that although there are a number of alterations made to the more specifically didactic portions of the text, which she catalogues according to the doctrinal points that they

(1983), pp. 111-19; '"To Knawe God Almyghtyn": Robert Thornton's Devotional Book', in James Hogg, ed., *Spätmittelalterliche geistliche Literatur in der Nationalsprache*, Analecta Cartusiana 106:2 (Salzburg, 1984), pp. 103-29.

[10]   Gillespie, '*Doctrina* and *Predicacio*: The Design and Function of Some Pastoral Manuals', *Leeds Studies in English* ns 11 (1980), pp. 36-50; 'The Literary Form of the Middle English Pastoral Manual, with Particular Reference to the *Speculum Christiani* and Some Related Texts' (diss. Oxford University, 1981); 'The *Cibus Anime*, Book 3: A Guide for Comtemplatives?' in James Hogg, ed., *Spiritualität Heute und Gestern*, Analecta Cartusiana 35:3 (Salzburg, 1982), pp. 90-119; '*Lukynge in haly bukes*: *Lectio* in some Late Medieval Spiritual Miscellanies', in James Hogg, ed., *Spätmittelalterliche geistliche Literatur in der Nationalsprache* vol. 2, Analecta Cartusiana 106:2 (Salzburg, 1984), pp. 1-27.

[11]   Brady, 'The Apostles and the Creed in Manuscripts of *The Pore Caitif*', Speculum 32 (1957), pp. 323-25; '*The Pore Caitif*: An Introductory Study', *Traditio* 10 (1954), pp. 529-48; 'The Pore Caitif, edited from MS Harley 2236 with Introduction and notes' (diss. Fordham University, 1954); 'Rolle's *Form of Living* and *The Pore Caitif*', *Traditio* 36 (1980), pp. 327-38; 'Rolle and the Pattern of Tracts in *The Pore Caitif*', *Traditio* 39 (1983), pp. 456-65.

exemplify, there are no such alterations to the more devotional 'short sentences inciting men to heavenly desire'.

The final three papers deal with the continuing audience for contemplative and devotional literature on the eve of the Reformation in England, and particularly with the literary connections of Sheen Charterhouse, at Richmond in Surrey, and the Brigittine convent of Syon, immediately across the Thames at Isleworth. The first of these three is by Rev. Robert Horsfield, and describes the *Pomander of Prayer*, a tract written for a lay audience by a Carthusian of Sheen and printed, with an opening exhortation by a monk of Syon, no fewer than four times between 1528 and 1532. Fr Horsfield details the provenance of the *Pomander*, various ascriptions of authorship, and the work's aim and content. Dr Ann Hutchison, who is presently working on an edition of *The Myroure of oure Ladye*, presents the second of this final group of papers, which deals with devotional reading in the monastery and in the late medieval household. Using evidence drawn from the legislative documents governing the discipline at Syon as well as its library catalogue and the history of its contacts with London printers, Dr Hutchison describes the practice of devotional reading there, and goes on to point out the similarities to this practice of the regime adopted by such ladies as Margaret, Duchess of Clarence, Margaret Beaufort, and Elizabeth of York. The final paper is presented by Professor Martha Driver, and deals with the functions of page layout and illustration in late-fifteenth- and early-sixteenth-century English religious books for lay readers. Observing in detail the *mise-en-page* of a number of early printed books, several specifically associated with Syon, Dr Driver describes the contribution of illustration in such books to the devotional purposes of the text.

In sum, the papers of this conference recapitulate its theme: they begin in the Chartreuse in the twelfth century, and end in the world on the brink of the Reformation.

I would like finally to add a note of thanks to several people and agencies whose assistance and presence contributed to the above proceedings: first of all, to Rev. Dr John S. Nurser, Chancellor of Lincoln Cathedral, who invited me to organise our conference in the name of the International Committee, St Hugh 1986, and the *Analecta Cartusiana*, and to Professor James Hogg, general editor of the *Analecta* and organiser himself of a series of conferences on the history and spirituality of the Carthusian Order, on whom I depended for advice and support; also to the Hon. Councillor John Plant, Mayor of Lincoln, who graciously received us and demonstrated the fine hospitality of the city; to Miss Joan Williams, Librarian of Lincoln Cathedral Chapter Library, and Dr Rodney Thomson, who was then cataloguing its manuscript collection, to Dr Anne Hudson, Professor Derek Pearsall and Dr Mary C. Erler, who enriched the conference with their contributions and comments; and, not least, to Mrs Margaret

Mitchell, Bursar of Edward King House and her staff, who made our stay there so enjoyable. Finally, I would like to record my personal debt to Queens College of the City University of New York, and Dean John H. Reilly in particular, for supporting me in organising the St Hugh conference and compiling this present volume of its proceedings.

HUGH OF LINCOLN, CARTHUSIAN SAINT

David Hugh Farmer

Hugh, bishop of Lincoln, died on 16 November 1200. The strong, spontaneous and widespread conviction of many that a saint had died is witnessed by contemporary writers. He was formally canonised by Pope Honorius III twenty years later. His contemporary biographer and the Canonisation Report both emphasise in slightly different ways that he was a saint because he was a monk, faithful to his vocation to prayer and solitude as a Carthusian while at the same time faithful to his vocation as a pastoral bishop, a role he had never sought and did his best to avoid. The steps taken to canonise him were initiated by the church of Lincoln and there is no surviving record of the Carthusians being consulted. But two Carthusian monks of Witham, both formerly Benedictines, had invited Adam of Eynsham to write Hugh's Life. This Life is a remarkably full, accurate and reliable testimony to Hugh's monastic way of life and ranks high among medieval hagiographical writings.[1]

Dauphiné in Burgundy, Witham in Somerset and Lincoln itself were all places where he spent important periods of his life. His aristocratic origin as the son of a Burgundian knight, whose castle of Avalon was the key one in a series of border fortifications, was a significant and lasting element of his personality. It enabled him to withstand Angevin kings and talk to them in a way which they understood but did not always relish. In his early twenties, Hugh left the small Augustinian priory of Villarbenoit, which he had joined with his aged father as a boy and joined the Grande Chartreuse on the other side of the impressive mountain range, whose powerful presence accompanied his earlier years.

Chartreuse was then a comparatively small but fervent community of hermits, established in their mountain home by St Hugh of Grenoble, the reforming diocesan bishop. When Hugh joined it, it was famous for its solitude, poverty and fine library. There were a maximum of fourteen choir monks and about sixteen lay brothers. The sheep which grazed on the mountain slopes were used to provide wool for their clothes and

[1] The *Magna Vita S. Hugonis* (hereinafter *MV*) is the principal source (ed. D. L. Douie and D. H. Farmer, 2 vols., 2nd edn, Oxford Medieval Texts, 1985). The Life by Gerald of Wales (ed. R. M. Loomis, New York, 1985) is also contemporary and authentic. D. M. Smith has recently published the Acts of St Hugh: *English Episcopal Acta, vol. IV: the charters of St Hugh and of William of Blois* (1986). See also C. Garton, *The Metrical Life of St Hugh* (1986). The contemporary chroniclers such as William of Newburgh and Roger Howden also mention Hugh several times.

parchment for their books. The monks' perpetual abstinence ensured that the meat was sold. Fruit, vegetables, eggs and cheese made up their monotonous diet, while gifts of fish were accepted occasionally. The original cells, habits and regime closely resembled those of the local shepherds.

Hugh's biographer, writing about the bishop's early life after he himself had visited Chartreuse and Grenoble near the end of Hugh's life in 1200, stressed his master's early commitment to the austere way of life in all its details. The severe regime was intended to provide the necessary element of asceticism in a life whose final goal was mystical contemplation. Knowledge, instruction and reading were necessary integral elements. So too was the writing of books (regarded by Guigo I as in some ways providing an alternative to preaching). All these elements were found also in Hugh's life when he was a bishop.

As a Carthusian monk he expected to pass the rest of his days in his mountain solitude. He was ordained priest after a few years and was deputed to look after the aged St Peter of Tarentaise, a Cistercian bishop who used to visit the Grande Chartreuse. From him, it may be credibly conjectured, he acquired not only further knowledge of the Fathers and of the spiritual life, but also an attitude of independence towards secular rulers and deep compassion for the needs of the oppressed.

Some years later Hugh was promoted to the office of procurator, which was the most important of all in his monastery save that of prior. He took charge of the lay brothers, the guests and the temporal administration. This was a taxing responsibility for one devoted so deeply to prayer and the contemplative life. Day by day he had to care in a practical way for matters which he had previously renounced: this was his new service to the community. The care of guests however eventually led to his arrival in England. Henry II's ambassadors on marriage negotiations with the count of Maurienne spoke so warmly of Hugh that the king asked for him to be sent to his first Carthusian foundation in England at Witham in Somerset, as prior. This had been begun as part of Henry's commuted penance for the murder of Thomas Becket, archbishop of Canterbury. It had been founded directly by the Grande Chartreuse, but the first choice of a superior was not a happy one: the king had not implemented his promises of funds necessary for its consolidation and it seemed to be in imminent danger of complete failure. Hugh's departure from Chartreuse was in fact to be permanent, apart from his last visit in 1200.[2]

Many details concerning Witham can be gleaned from the *Magna Vita*. The initial difficulties of creating a 'desert' like the Grande Chartreuse, whose foundation charter forbade hunting, roads and building rather like a nature reserve of our own day, involved the removal of the former inhabitants on the edge of Selwood Forest to other settlements some miles away. This was accomplished by Hugh in close collaboration with the king, from whom he negotiated the most favourable terms possible. A beginning on the buildings could then be made (with the lay brothers'

[2]   *MV* I, 24-44; II, 162-72.

house at some distance from the main monastery), but this was again delayed by the king's failure to provide the necessary funds. Hugh agreed to take with him to see Henry the redoubtable lay brother Gerard, whose outspoken condemnation of the king's parsimony (to Hugh's acute embarrassment) makes one of the most vivid episodes in his Life. So too years later does his skilful handling of the veteran brother Einard, who wished to take French leave and return to the Grande Chartreuse unauthorised and unannounced. Both these incidents form rare contemporary and authentic evidence about Carthusian lay brothers, of whom little is generally known. The latter also shows Hugh's continued care for Witham after he was a bishop. He used to visit it for a month or two at harvest time in order to refresh and re-direct his spiritual ideals.[3]

During the years 1180-86 Hugh experienced as prior of Witham for the first time in his life an independent command. He and he alone was responsible for the well-being of his small community in matters spiritual and temporal. The siting and completion of the buildings, the acquisition of a library (helped again by the king), the pastoral care of his small community of between twenty and thirty all contributed to his further development as a person and as a saint. This pastoral care which added to his very early experience as a deacon at far-away Saint-Maximin before he became a Carthusian, prepared him for the unexpected task of ruling the enormous diocese of Lincoln from 1186 until his death. News reached him at Witham of his promotion; he stayed there while the election was contested; there too he received the final call to accept the charge which came from the prior of the Grande Chartreuse. Although his promotion to an English see was a unique event without precedent or repetition, Carthusian monks had become bishops of Grenoble and Belley before him. The bishop of Grenoble who had intervened at the Grande Chartreuse in favour of his going to England was in fact a Carthusian himself.[4]

This is not the place to relate in detail the many achievements of his episcopate, which has often been done before.[5] But when the commission for his canonisation was set up, its members were understandably more interested in his pastoral than his monastic life. They did however underline both his membership of the Carthusian Order and his excellence within it as well as his procuratorship and his priorate. So high was the esteem of the papacy for Chartreuse that his reputation as a Carthusian monk seemed a strong element in his claim to sanctity.

The duties of his state as bishop of Lincoln were very different from those as a Carthusian monk, but there was no diminution of his commitment to his profession or to the fundamental elements of his monastic life. If the rebuilding of his cathedral on a larger scale than before seemed out

[3]   *MV* I, 60-79; II, 49-54, 62-69.
[4]   *MV* I, 92-101 and 54-55. This was John of Sassenage (d.1219). The prior of the Grande Chartreuse who sent Hugh to England was Guigo II, the spiritual writer (d.1188); the one who told him to accept the episcopate was Jancelin (d.1233).
[5]   Lives of St Hugh have been written by G. C. Perry (1869), H. Thurston (1898), R. M. Woolley (1927), J. Clayton (1931) and D. H. Farmer (1985). See also H. Mayr-Harting, ed., *St Hugh of Lincoln* (Oxford, 1987).

of scale with the small buildings characteristic of Carthusians, both were set up as worthy settings of the Church's liturgy. If his provision for the education of his clergy through the lectures and writings of William de Montibus, a local scholar whom he recalled from Paris, was a new activity, it proceeded nonetheless from a deep appreciation of the value of *lectio divina* in the spiritual life. Neither Hugh nor the Carthusians made a virtue out of ignorance. Hugh's esteem for his canons can also be seen as an extension of his esteem for his monastic community, even though his fifty-six canons, or at least some of them, were more sophisticated and better educated than many Carthusians.[6]

His skill in legal matters was famous and unexpected. He had the rare ability of being able to apply his wisdom to sometimes abstruse questions of conflicting rights. His care for the oppressed and his independence of the powerful were seen not only in cases which he judged in the king's court, but also in celebrated church cases in which he was the judge delegate of the papacy. The archbishops of Canterbury and York as well as their chapters, not to mention the bishops of Coventry and of Durham were all litigants in cases judged by Hugh. Whether the cases involved the tithes of fish disputed by the canons of Grimsby and of Bridlington or the rights of the monks of Canterbury likely to be infringed by the archbishop's plan to build a rival church, Hugh showed the same impartiality and prudence to such an extent that when asked on his deathbed if he had ever given judgment for favour or partiality, he was able to reply in the negative without hesitation.[7]

As far as ecclesistical liberties were concerned Hugh's contribution was considerable. This was recognised both in his lifetime and in the canonisation report. It was also a principal theme both of Gerald of Wales' Life as well as the *Magna Vita*. Three Angevin kings in turn, Henry II, Richard I and John, all recognised his spiritual power, his resolute defence of his church's rights and his sheer holiness which enabled him to speak to kings with all the freedom and authority of the classic holy man of antiquity. Whether it was the preferment of a royal candidate to Lincoln canonry or the provision of knight-service abroad by the church of Lincoln or the secondment (unpaid) of Lincoln canons to the royal diplomatic service, all these kings met with determined and effective resistance. In addition Richard and John both received homilies on simony, infidelity and the king's duties of state in this world, neglect of which would lead them to share the fate of the reprobate kings depicted on the west front of Fontevrault abbey church. However, Hugh had a unique gift of making his victims laugh, which made his reproofs acceptable even to these harsh and grasping

---

[6] Hugh was reputed a learned man and a patron of scholars by contemporaries. His chancellor, William de Montibus, although seemingly old-fashioned compared to the great scholastics of the thirteenth century, enjoyed a high reputation for about two hundred years. See H. Mackinnon in *Essays … presented to Bertie Wilkinson*, ed. T. A. Sandquist and M. R. Powicke (1969), pp. 32-45 and D. H. Farmer, *St Hugh of Lincoln Exhibition Catalogue* (Bodleian Library, Oxford, 1986), pp. 5-7.

[7] *MV* II, 194-5; see also D. H. Farmer, *St Hugh of Lincoln* (1985), pp. 57, 73-83.

kings. At Hugh's funeral King John (and William the Lion, king of Scotland) did him the supreme honour of carrying his coffin.[8]

While Hugh's relationship with kings was seemingly unique, something must also be said of his relationships with bishops. Towards St Peter of Tarentaise his attitude was one of filial and studious respect. The same qualities characterised his attitude to successive priors of the Grande Chartreuse. But there was development and difference in his relationship with two archbishops of Canterbury. Baldwin, the Cistercian archbishop of Canterbury, helped Hugh considerably in his difficult early years of episcopate. The help took the form not only of advice but also of the gift (if the word may be used) of two of his best curial clerics for the service of the diocese of Lincoln. In return Hugh gave Baldwin excellent advice not to proceed with the controversial building of a new chapel in Canterbury: his fears of loss of reputation, resources and prestige were realised to the letter. Baldwin was a learned man, but Gerald of Wales (who knew both men well) esteemed Hugh as the more learned as well as the wittier of the two: Baldwin's leadership of the Church, also according to Gerald, was weak and vacillating. It may well be that Gerald's view was incomplete, but he clearly blamed Baldwin for not consolidating or extending the advantages brought to the Church from St Thomas of Canterbury's resistance to royal power. Baldwin's successor however, Hubert Walter, was a royal cleric with similar ideals to those of the younger, unconverted Thomas Becket: a State in which high office would be held by the same clerics as those who exercised the highest office in the Church. Hubert Walter in fact combined the two functions in a way which seems to anticipate the achievements of Cardinal Wolsey. Hugh however did not share these ideals. To him the independence of the Church was essential and those who seemed to wish to subject churchmen to the State in ecclesiastical matters were not appreciated. In addition there seems to have been some personal antipathy between Hugh and Hubert.

Several times they had clashed over the issues already mentioned. On Hugh's deathbed Hubert came to remind him how often he had provoked him and to ask for an apology. The answer was stark and uninhibited: 'I should not repent of angering you but rather grieve that I did not do so more often ... My sin was that I preferred to offend God rather than offend you ... If I am spared, I am resolved not to fail in this way again.' Few dying men would be so sure of themselves to speak in this way to their metropolitan archibishop at the point of death.[9]

After Hugh died at his London house, his coffin was carried to Lincoln and buried there in the cathedral he had rebuilt and enriched with his collection of relics. From the time of the funeral can be detected evidence of the beginning of a popular cult. Records of cures were kept at his tomb

[8] *MV* II, 225; I, 68-72; II, 102-14, 139-42.
[9] *MV* II, 188-89. After Hugh's death Hubert visited Witham, where he seems to have experienced a conversion and received the discipline from Adam of Dryburgh; see A. Wilmart, 'Maitre Adam ... devenu chartreux à Witham', *Analecta Praemonstratensiana* ix (1933), 207-37, and C. R. Cheney, *Hubert Walter* (1967).

and in 1219, following requests from the English bishops, the Lincoln diocese and the king, a papal commission was set up to examine the possibility and desirability of his canonisation. This commission was small, able and representative: it consisted of the archbishop of Canterbury, the bishop of Coventry and the abbot of Fountains. North, south and midlands were all represented, so were the centres in which Hugh had acted as papal judge-delegate. Both bishops and monks served on this commission, so also did other clergy on sub-committees to investigate particular miracles.[10]

It is noteworthy that some of these had been so striking that they were not forgotten twenty years after their accomplishment. It was also fortunate that both the Dean of Lincoln, Roger of Rolleston, and Hugh's biographer Adam, now Abbot of Eynsham, were still alive to testify to Hugh's sanctity and various achievements. The commission, having satisfied itself both that Hugh's life was worthy and that his virtue was proved by miraculous cures, sent back a positive recommendation to the Holy See. The canonisation was made formal and official in 1220. From that day to this Hugh, the first Carthusian monk to be canonised and the first bishop of Lincoln to achieve this distinction, has been formally invoked as a saint. His feast in the calendar is 17 November: after his translation in 1280, this event was commemorated in another feast (confined to the Lincoln diocese) on 6 October. His shrine was much visited thereafter, but it seems that the number of pilgrims and the offerings were not so considerable as those of England's principal shrines at Canterbury, Westminster or Durham. However it was always noteworthy and continued to flourish up to the time of the Reformation.[11]

Thus far the official verdict: what of the inner reality of Hugh as Carthusian saint? His fidelity in private prayer and his diligence in the Liturgy were famous, so too were his asceticism and his care for the poor and the handicapped. Among the latter the lepers were prominent: Hugh, following his mother's example, used to wash their sores and kiss their limbs. With regard to the poor, his biographer claimed that he gave away a third of his income to their service. This exceeded Gregory's instruction to Augustine to devote a quarter of his revenues to this purpose. The income of the Lincoln diocese can be deduced from the payments made to the royal Exchequer during a diocesan vacancy. Lincoln in the late twelfth century was probably the fifth richest in the country, producing a revenue of over £1000, a sum exceeded only by Canterbury, York, Winchester and Durham. His almsgiving seems to have been both institutional (as to his leper hospital at Newark) and individual, distributed at least in part through his chaplain who was also his biographer.[12]

[10] See D. H. Farmer, *St Hugh of Lincoln*, pp. 97-107; the Canonisation Report is printed in *Lincs. Architectural and Archaeological Society Papers* vi (1956), 86-117.
[11] See R. M. Woolley, *op. cit.*, appendix: the shrine contained a chained book of St Hugh's Life. The Canonisation Report (based partly on Gerald) formed the basis of the Lessons in the Breviary: these were translated into English for Caxton's edition of *The Golden Legend*.
[12] See Margaret Howell, *Regalian Right in Medieval England* (1962), pp. 32-48

Even more significant was the help he gave through spiritual comfort to innumerable individuals, clergy and laity. Few examples have been documented, but some of his sayings have been recorded. These combine pithiness with depth and provide thought for all ages, our own included.

> The kingdom of God is not restricted to monks, hermits and anchorites. When God finally judges each individual, he will not hold it against him that he has not been a monk or a hermit, but to each of the reprobate rejection will come if he has not been a true Christian. A Christian is expected to possess three virtues: if one of them is lacking, the name of Christian without the reality will profit him nothing. The name without the reality convicts of falsehood one who claims to follow the truth. From each will be required both truth and virtue: always to have charity in the heart, truth in the mouth and chastity in the body.

Again he would receive women to his table and exhort them to follow in the footsteps of the women saints. He would encourage them by saying: 'Almighty God certainly deserves to be loved by women for he did not disdain to be born of a woman ... To no man was it granted to be called the father of God, but to a woman alone was it granted to be God's mother.'

When people seemed inconsolable for the death of a friend, he would say: 'It would be very hard for us if we were never allowed to die.' This came, not from neglect of the dead in whose care he was exemplary, but rather from a deep sense of the fulfilment of human life in eternity.[13]

Hugh was not perfect. Sometimes he seemed harsh, at other times he showed pepperish temper in quarrelling with his canons. It seems likely that he was sometimes mistaken in claiming certain rights for his Church. But all in all he manifested a personality transformed by Christ in and through the Carthusian way of life which made him what he was. Appropriately he was the first canonised Carthusian saint, venerated as such not only in Lincoln but also throughout the Carthusian Order from 1220 until the present day.

and 211ff. Several of England's rural bishoprics had incomes of £300 or less; Carlisle had only £52.19.6.
[13] *MV* II, 46-48, 223.

DE CELLA IN SECULUM:
THE LITURGICAL ASPECTS*

Richard W. Pfaff

In moving from a Carthusian monastery to the bishopric of Lincoln, St Hugh changed his liturgical context drastically. I want to try to explore some of the dimensions of that change of context. This will be done, not surprisingly, on the basis of relevant evidence from the sources for Hugh's life, for the liturgy of the Carthusians in his day, and (a scanty amount this) for that of the cathedral church at Lincoln. We may find, however, that the information yielded by these sources is insufficient both in quantity and, so to speak, in quality: that is, that we can ask more questions than can be answered. Yet the mere asking of these questions may be seen as part of what we are seeking; and so it may not be out of place to close with some misgivings about where we seem to be left by what we have learned.

Not that the nature of the subject itself furnishes any warrant for flabbiness or imprecision. We have a clearly focused question: what were the dimensions of Hugh's life as a liturgical person? Our sources will, of course, go some ways towards answering that question. But if the dimensions of the question outstrip what the sources tell us, that does not invalidate the question. To take a perhaps apt parallel, the interest of a number of modern historians in *alimentation* has opened a path for historical investigation of one of the most fundamental aspects of human life. Deeply obvious as the limitations of the evidence are, the importance of asking questions about something as basic as the nourishment by which human beings live is clear – even when it is also clear that many of the questions most likely cannot be answered.

So with St Hugh. To be sure, the historian of *alimentation* might well, thanks to the numerous references to diet in the *Magna Vita*, find him a fascinating case study; but it is by no strained analogy that we approach thinking about Hugh's liturgical life in this way. The contexts in which he lived make it axiomatic that liturgical worship must have been a prime element in his existence; and we can infer from our knowledge of the finished product – St Hugh as revealed to us by his biographers – that this

* I should like to express gratitude for assistance at various points to David Farmer, Rodney Thomson, and Joan Williams. All citations from Adam of Eynsham's *Magna Vita Sancti Hugonis* are to the edition of D. L. Douie and (D.) H. Farmer (2nd edn, 1985), whose translation has also been used. This edition is referred to by volume and page numbers in parentheses.

was at least to a certain extent the case. But what can be said beyond this axiom and this inference?

Hugh's liturgical formation was in a small community of regular canons, where he was sent at the age of eight. There were at least seven of these canons, so the *Magna Vita* tells us; almost certainly they used the liturgy of the diocese of Grenoble in which they were located. After some eleven years there Hugh, having been ordained deacon, was put in charge of a parish church run by the same canons. This meant that he went from a fairly small to a tiny liturgical context. He soon imported another canon, who was a priest;[1] what liturgical life there was, was solely up to the two of them.

The case here seems almost like the classical one of the promising young cleric just out of seminary, shocked at the loneliness and isolation of church life in a small parish. Indeed, this may help to explain why Hugh was so overwhelmed by his visit to La Grande Chartreuse.[2] The apparent sanctity of the monks and the fascinating combination of eremetic and coenobitic elements in which they lived aside, we may suppose that Hugh's spiritual imagination was kindled at the prospect of a regular and splendid, if predictably austere, liturgical life. It was as a Carthusian that he was ordained priest. At that point he could have expected to spend the rest of his life functioning as a monk-priest in a medium-sized context, probably somewhat larger than that of the canons' community at Grenoble but not exceeding two or three dozen choir monks at most.

When Hugh entered the Charterhouse in about 1160, its liturgy seems to have been quite clearly fixed. The Constitutions of Guigo I were some thirty years old, and had been reinforced by the directive of the 1142 Chapter General that all Carthusian houses should worship in the same way.[3] Subsequent amplifications of custom had imported hymns into the divine office, made possible the more frequent celebration of mass, and in general brought the Carthusian rite within the normal range of western liturgical practice of the twelfth century – at the simple end of the range, to be sure, but by no means on a lunatic fringe of austerity: plain chasubles were worn by the celebrant at mass, but chasubles nonetheless.

These were the liturgical norms Hugh would have carried with him to Witham. Despite its royal foundation it was not an immediate success; nonetheless, after he arrived as its third prior, in 1179, it is likely that its worshipping life soon approximated that of the Great Charterhouse. And, in the absence of any sources for Witham itself, it seems safe to take the liturgical usages of that mother house as representing what Hugh was accustomed to at the time of his election as unwilling bishop of Lincoln in 1186.

[1] Whether this is the same man as the 'simple priest' referred to in *MV* I.vi (1.20) (*simplici quodam sacerdote*) is not clear.

[2] It may also be that Hugh's reaction to Cluny when he visited it late in his life (*MV* V.xv (2.175): 'Truly, if I had seen this place before I fell in love with Chartreuse, I should have become a Cluniac monk') reflects sympathetic admiration for its complex liturgical life.

[3] *Patr. Lat.* 153.1126.

At Lincoln the situation was of course very different. Whereas Witham had been a new, uncertain, and relatively small foundation, the establishment at Lincoln Minster was of reasonable age, very sure (and proud) of itself, and undeniably large. Monastic bishops were no particular rarity in the twelfth century – certainly not in England – and several recent bishops of Grenoble had been drawn from the ranks of the Carthusians. Nonetheless for the prior of the Witham Charterhouse to become bishop of Lincoln was, so to speak, an enormous jump liturgically. This jump was not only from a monastic to a secular liturgy. Equally drastic, I suggest, were the aspects of size and of *persona*: henceforth Hugh as a liturgical person would be functioning when at Lincoln in a very large context, when travelling in a national (and even international) context; and, save for intervals of respite back at Witham and La Grande Chartreuse, always as a bishop.

There is a key question here to which, though purely factual, no definite answer seems at this point possible: how often did Hugh participate in the liturgy of his cathedral church?[4] There are some bits of evidence, but only partial ones. On the one hand, he is in Lincoln on a Good Friday when the miracle of the hod takes place;[5] and he celebrates there on a St Stephen's day, when another wondrous event occurs.[6] On the other, he is away from the Minster on an Easter Eve[7] as well as at other great feasts. Of course, as a bishop (and a tenant-in-chief) he frequently had to subordinate any purely personal priorities he might have felt to the demands of other duties; so it behoves us to be somewhat cautious about assuming that what he did is in every case what he would like to have done.

Let us begin to consider the transition he made – summed up as it is by the overall title of our Conference as *de cella in seculum* – by looking at three specific examples. The first has to do with the rhythm of the divine, or daily, office. The normal Carthusian practice was that vespers, matins, and lauds (to use the normative later medieval terminology) were said in choir, the other offices privately in each monk's cell.[8] At Lincoln of course this was not the case. In theory – and we would do well to remember that at Lincoln theory was probably a good deal further removed from practice than at a Charterhouse – all clerics in residence met for all of the hours in the Cathedral choir. In practice, of course, this must have meant, besides much absenteeism, a good deal of running of separate hours together, but the theory was a more completely corporate one than the Carthusian.

Another obvious difference that would have been apparent to Hugh in the rhythm of the divine office is that in the shape of its largest component,

[4] Indeed, in the absence of a full itinerary for Hugh as bishop, the question will most likely always remain unanswered; certainly no consecutive account of his movements can be derived from the existing biographical materials.
[5] H. Farmer, ed., 'The Canonization of St Hugh of Lincoln: the text of Cotton Roll xiii.27', *Lincolnshire Archit. and Archaeol. Soc. Jnl* 6.ii (1956), 86-117, at p. 97.
[6] *MV* V.ii (2.80).
[7] This seems to be the correct inference from the story in *MV* IV.v (2.21).
[8] Guigo I, *Consuetudines Cartusiae* xxix.6, ed. un Chartreux, *Coutumes de Chartreuse*. Sources chrétiennes 313 (Paris, 1984), 230.

matins. Whereas the Carthusian office was an adaptation of the monastic (Benedictine), Lincoln of course followed secular practice. While both forms divided the service into three nocturns, monastic use allocated the psalms quite differently from the secular distribution, and arranged the lessons in units usually of four (or, in ordinary summertime, one) compared with three for the secular. And – probably the most noticeable contrast to one experiencing both forms – great feasts have twelve lessons in monastic use as opposed to nine in secular. Though any difference in aggregate duration must depend on how long the individual lessons are, in general it is likely that to one accustomed to the fullness of a monastic matins of twelve lessons, its secular counterpart containing a third fewer seemed somewhat sparse. Certainly the balance is different.[9]

All indications are that Hugh was scrupulous in observing the hours of the daily office; yet a personal devotional practice referred to in detail by Adam of Eynsham suggests that either he found the spiritual nourishment imparted by matins inadequate or that the demands of his own life made the regular observance of that hour impossible (we shall return to this point later).

Occasionally there are signs of what seems to be almost a casual attitude towards the daily office. This is shown in the story Adam tells of Hugh's prevision of the death of his almoner, the Templar Morinus, which led him to order horses to be prepared so that he could meet Morinus's corpse. His vision had caused him to rise earlier than usual, and perhaps it took a while to prepare the horses; in any case, as Adam puts it, 'Whilst the horses were being got ready, the bishop and his clerks were chanting the Prime hymn.'[10] The impression one gets is that the waiting time was put to good use; someone – was it Hugh? – must have said something like, 'At least we can get Prime out of the way.'

Similarly with Compline, which Hugh's entourage were chanting as he died: here Adam explains that, though unwilling to leave the dying man at such a time, they nonetheless withdrew (where, he does not say) to recite the hour.[11] In neither case is any connection suggested between the office and either the church or the cell. In short, the attitude is much more like that of the cleric reading his breviary on the subway than like that which ostensibly, anyhow, characterised the canons of Lincoln, not to mention the monks of Witham.

This question of how liturgical observances are conceived, as well as how they are performed, leads us to the next area of investigation: roughly, how the psalms are understood. By this I do not mean how they are interpreted but how the psalms as (in a rough phrase) liturgical

[9] One obvious factor is that not only are there more lessons by one third, but responsories after each lesson to match; since responsories often took longer to sing than lessons to read, the cumulative musical effect of a twelve-lessons matins would have been much fuller than that of nine.

[10] *MV* V.xviii (2.213). Prime, like compline, could easily be said from memory by those familiar with it; the story does not necessarily imply the possession of breviaries.

[11] *MV* V.xvi (2.198).

artifacts lend themselves to being used. Partly this is a matter of some factors we have just noticed. There is a different allocation of psalms for the divine office in the monatic use than in secular, so that in most cases individual psalms appear at different points in the week's *cursus*.[12] But of course the psalms are used extensively also in the liturgy of the mass (not, however, as whole and identified psalms) and of the occasional or pastoral offices; and they were the staple of the accretions that grew around the basic core of liturgy from Carolingian times onwards.

So it is not surprising that there are apparent in Hugh's liturgical contexts some peculiarities – we might be tempted to call them eccentricities – in the use of the psalms. This is evident in a passage from the *Magna Vita* which is either unclear or, or taken at face value, astonishing. During Hugh's last days, Adam says,

> As long as he was strong enough, he kept to the custom of alternately sitting and standing for the psalms and made his clerks to do the same. Thus, whilst one sat down to rest his weary limbs, another stood up to show his respect for the presence of God and the angels.[13]

What can Adam mean here by *vicissitudinem standi et sedendi inter psallendum*? Hugh would have been familiar with the practice prescribed in the *Consuetudines Sancti Antelmi* (pre-1170) by which there was quite a lot of shifting of positions during responsories, especially on greater feasts;[14] and there was the usual quota of bowing at various points in the recitation of the invitatory at matins and in other parts of the office.[15] But nothing like the jack-in-the-box effect Adam seems to describe appears as a Carthusian custom.

When, however, Hugh was at Lincoln – and properly even when he was not – he might have taken part in an equally odd practice involving the psalms. This is the custom of dividing the psalter among the cathedral clergy for daily extra-liturgical recitation. This parcelling out of the psalms goes back at least to the 1130s. In Lincoln Cathedral MS 1, the Great Bible, there is a list headed, *Hi sunt ad psalterium canendum*, which lists the psalms allotted to forty-three cathedral clergy.[16] This list itself seems to be a late twelfth-century copy; but since forty-three is the number of clergy – bishop, dignitaries, and prebendaries – known to have existed at the Minster in 1132, it seems likely that the practice referred to in the list dates from that earlier period.

[12] An obvious example is Sunday matins, which in all secular uses includes many of the first twenty psalms but in the monastic distribution employs pss. xx-xxxi.
[13] *MV* V.xvi (2.188). We may wonder whether it is possible that Adam was speaking of the use of misericords. That would be the case only if Hugh invariably observed his offices in a choir – which is what we have just seen he did not do.
[14] *Consuetudines Antelmi* cap. vi, ed. James Hogg, *Die ältesten Consuetudines der Kartäuser*. Analecta Cartusiana 1 (Berlin, 1970; Salzburg 1973), 110.
[15] Cap. vii; *op. cit.* p.111.
[16] Fol. 207ra; printed in D. E. Greenway, ed., *Fasti Ecclesiae Anglicanae 1066-1300* III: *Lincoln* (London, 1977), 151-3, and less accurately in *Lincoln Cathedral Statutes* (see note 20) III.788-92.

The principle on which the list works is purely numerical – the bishop says the first four psalms, the dean the next four, and so on, with the final eight assigned to an unidentified prebendary William – and the rationale for the practice must be simply that it is in some way a good thing to get through the psalter in a day. That is of course an ancient ascetical practice at what we may call the championship level; St Benedict alluded to it in explaining his own allocation of the psalms into a weekly *cursus* suitable to the 'tepid' monks for whom his Rule was intended.[17] The notion of a daily psalter split forty-three ways can scarcely be considered a championship-level practice. Even less is this true from c.1187 (the year after Hugh became bishop), by which time we know from a second list in the same Bible that the number of members of the chapter has grown to fifty-six, a figure which becomes standard for Lincoln throughout the rest of the middle ages; and this figure does *not* include the bishop.[18] Though there are some difficulties about this list, it is almost certain that the expanded list also related to the allocation of the psalms – as witness the fifty-six stall-back plates with the psalm-incipits on them in the Minster choir.[19] If this is the case, that the second list lacks the bishop's name may be of special importance. The natural inference from that fact is that he was no longer included in the allocation of psalms; and the obvious question is, why not? Could this exclusion, somewhere between Alexander the Magnificent (bishop 1123-48) and Hugh, from participation in the shared-out daily psalter have been the result of a disinclination on Hugh's part to cooperate in a practice he found strange or even incomprehensible?

That suggestion is pure speculation. A likelier answer is that during the seventeen years when the see was effectively vacant – from the death of Robert de Chesney in 1166 through the inconclusive episode of Geoffrey Plantagenet to the accession of Walter of Coutances in 1183 – the combination of the lack of a bishop to take a part plus what is clearly a considerable growth in the number of prebends resulted in the bishop's quota being taken away in the general reassignment of psalms. Whatever the reason, it is curious that in the copy of this list in no less a source than the *Liber Niger* – the great hodge-podge of Minster documents originally collected about 1300 and, with the rest of the cathedral statutes, edited exhaustively but almost incomprehensibly by Henry Bradshaw and Christopher Wordsworth in 1892[20] – calls the document 'Antiqua constitucio pro psalterio et pro missa singulis diebus dicendis'. The headnote further specifies,

Provisum est ab R. decano[21] adiunctis ei discretis iuris de capitulo et institutum in capitulo presente Domino Hugone Lincolniensi

[17] *Reg. Ben.* xviii; ed. and tr. J. McCann (London, 1960), 66.
[18] Fol. 207rb; ptd Greenway, pp. 162-5.
[19] J. F. Wickenden, 'The Choir Stalls of Lincoln Cathedral', *Archaeological Journal* 38 (1881), 42-61, esp. 49-53.
[20] H. Bradshaw and C. Wordsworth, ed., *Statutes of Lincoln Cathedral*, 3 vols (Cambridge, 1892-7), I.300.
[21] Either Richard fitz Neal, dean probably from Dec. 1183 until 1189, or just

Episcopo et confirmante ut psalmi hoc ordine dicantur ab Episcopo
et Decano atque canonicis.

In the arrangement there recorded the bishop had been restored to the
rota, pss.i-iii being assigned to him. This list is arranged not by the canons'
names but by the titles of their prebends, again fifty-six. By the end of
the thirteenth century,[22] then, it was believed that St Hugh was the founder
of a practice we have seen reason to think he took no part in. But he
cannot have helped knowing about it, and perhaps knowing that some of
his predecessors had shared in it. Again, we wonder how it must have
struck him.

This basic question of ours recurs also in the third general area we want
to look at, that of contrasts between the sanctorale of the Carthusians and
of Lincoln. To say 'contrasts in the liturgical year' between the two would
be putting it too strongly, because of course the main outlines of that year
were standard throughout western Christendom long before the twelfth
century. But the contrasts we seek now are not wholly confined to the
observance of saints' days. Most notably, when Gerald of Wales tells us
that Hugh was conspicuous among his brother prelates for his strict
keeping of solemn feasts, and instances specifically Ascension, Pentecost,
and Trinity Sunday, we take note;[23] because (if this witness of Gerald's is
accurate – a point to be returned to later) Hugh probably never observed
Trinity Sunday until he became bishop. It was not included in the
Carthusian calendar until much later; as is well known, its popularity
spread from England as a by-product of the cult of Thomas Becket, who
had been consecrated bishop on that day.

For the sanctorale in the strict sense – in full phrase, the *proprium
sanctorum* – the differences between Carthusian and Lincoln use were not
all that great. On balance the Carthusian calendar – we take that of c.1134
as normative[24] – was, as would be expected, sparer than that which we can
postulate for Lincoln (no more than postulate: no Lincoln calendars of
anything like that period survive).[25] But the Carthusian calendar of Hugh's
time included no English saints, not even Oswald, widely culted on the
Continent. Did it therefore seem to Hugh strange to be the head of a
liturgical unit which observed many distinctively English feasts – among
which would almost certainly have been Alban, Augustine of Canterbury,
Cuthbert, Etheldreda, Swithun, Botulf, Guthlac, Edmund King of the

conceivably Roger de Rolleston c.1195-1223 (Greenway, p.9).

[22] This list was completed after 1290 when the fifty-sixth prebend, Milton Ecclesia,
was re-established; there had during most of the century been only fifty-five.

[23] Giraldus Cambrensis, *Opera* VII, ed. J.F.Dimock (Rolls Series, 1877), 100;
cf. R.Loomis, ed., *Giraldus Cambrensis. The Life of St Hugh of Avalon*, Garland
Library of Medieval Literature, ser. A, vol.31 (New York and London, 1985),
pp.22-3.

[24] Printed in Hansjakob Becker, *Die Responsorien des Kartäuserbreviers. Untersuchungen zu Urform und Herkunft des Antiphonars der Kartause*, Münchener
Theologische Studien, ser. II.39 (Munich, 1971), 42-5.

[25] Indeed, what scanty evidence there is for a Lincoln 'use' as a whole also comes
from much later.

East Angles, perhaps also Ethelbert King of the East Angles, Edward the Martyr, Dunstan, Alphege, and Edward the Confessor, with maybe one or two others like Aidan or Aethelwold?

Of discrepancies the other way round – feasts observed by the Carthusians but not at Lincoln – there would probably have been fewer, though it is possible that a couple of primarily monastic occasions would not have been present in a secular calendar – Paul the first hermit on 10 January and Hilarion on 21 October (and possibly Antony on 17 January). But since on the whole the early Carthusian calendar is no more than that of the fully developed sacramentaries of the same sort as would have underlain the Lincoln calendar also, it is less likely that Hugh would have been struck by any very glaring omissions than by what must have seemed to a Carthusian the filling up of the calendar with a dozen or so of local saints.

A few more pieces of information need to be laid out before we try to sum up this attempt to get inside St Hugh's 'liturgical sensibility'. One further bit concerns his attitude towards celebrating the mass. By his time it had become normal for Carthusian monk-priests to celebrate frequently, and it seems safe to assume that the daily celebration recorded as his practice during his retreats at Witham represents his personal preference.[26] But what were the parameters of that liturgical action for him? This question arises in connection with the episode of Easter Monday of 1199.[27] Leaving Richard's court in Normandy he goes to La Flèche and is there about to say mass when he is told that his wagons and horses have been impounded by the garrison and the pack animals seized by robbers; whereupon his clerks (and, Adam adds, even the bishop of Rochester, who was also on the trip) urge Hugh to give up the idea of a celebration and instead merely to read the Gospel! Hugh refuses, insisting instead on donning full pontifical vestments and adding a pontifical blessing. In the circumstances it might have seemed sensible to postpone the celebration altogether and flee forthwith; what is astonishing is the alternative suggestion, the very making of what presupposes that it was at least within the realm of possibility. Would we have thought that a twelfth-century Carthusian bishop would even remotely consider a reading of the liturgical Gospel to be in any way an adequate alternative, or even substitute, for the celebration of the eucharist, especially on so solemn a day as Easter Monday?

The continuation of that story provides us with another piece of valuable information about one of Hugh's liturgical attitudes. As he proceeds on to Le Mans the danger has not disappeared; nonetheless he declines to permit the lessons at matins to be shortened, insisting, Adams says, 'on having long lessons recited as was his custom'.[28] This suggests that he put a premium on that element of the night office which may be termed basic nourishment, the lessons from scripture, patristic homilies, and the lives of the saints. Yet we are told twice in the *Magna Vita* of his practice of

---

[26] *MV* IV.x (2.49, 50).
[27] *MV* V.xii (2.146).
[28] *Ibid.* (p.147: *longas more solito recitari facit lectiones*).

24

having read to him at mealtimes very much the same sort of literature as he would have heard during the nocturns. In the first mention Adam implies that Hugh somehow found the night office readings inadequate, and devised a systematic plan for supplementing them:

> At mealtimes he had the scriptures read to him with such assiduity that at matins and dinner he managed to cover practically all the Old and New Testaments (with the exception of the four gospels) ... and in addition to this the passions of some of the martyrs, certain lives of the saints, and the best known sermons of the fathers for the great festivals.[29]

The second mention explains his *schema* for the gospels:

> Whilst every year he had the other canonical books read to him at the appointed times both at Matins and at meal times, he caused the four books of the gospels to be read in the four seasons of the year at Prime after the Martyrology. He never neglected these readings even when journeying on horseback.[30]

Note that this is not the bishop exercising his *ius liturgicum*; it is Hugh's own private devotional practice we are dealing with, one which we must put into the general category of para-liturgical.

The same word, para-liturgical, could almost be applied also to Hugh's attitude to one of the pastoral offices. This concerns his curious propensity for taking part in funerals, apparently almost at random.[31] Even when he was not officially involved in the funeral, he would, if a book were available, take the priest's part – that is, interject himself into the rite otherwise performed by (so we assume) the parish priest. So great was this propensity that we are told of a book Hugh almost always had with him, *orationes cum psalmis*,[32] which must have been either a separately bound office of the dead or more likely a manual, alias ritual. Since one of these episodes takes place in Normandy we cannot suppose that Hugh's rationale was that as chief liturgical officer of his diocese it was fitting that he should function at any ecclesiastical rite he encountered; rather, his habit of intruding himself into funerals must be seen as an expression of a private, perhaps somewhat morbid, spirituality – and as a practice which he could follow only because he had during his lifetime acquired a great reputation for sanctity and authority.

His liturgical preparations for his own death both show the intensity of his concern for the rites associated with dying and give the one specific bit of light that we have concerning his own awareness of the liturgical dimension of his transition *de cella in seculum*. As he returns from the Continent to England in the late summer of 1200, sensing himself to be fatally ill and realising that his fellow-prelates were all at the session of the Great Council, meeting (as it happened) at Lincoln, Hugh, by this time at

[29]   *MV* III.xiii (1.126).
[30]   *MV* IV.xvi (2.194).
[31]   E.g., *MV* V.i (2.77).
[32]   *MV* V.ii (2.79).

his London residence, asked for seven or eight monks from Westminster and choir clerks from St Paul's to attend him:[33] that is, he requested a mixed force representing both the monastic tradition from which he had come and the secular element into which he had been thrust. Surely this was not accidental; indeed, having lingered longer than was expected, and still at London, the day before he died he sent to the abbot of Westminster and the dean of St Paul's for the same mixture of monks and clerks. It seems clear that this gesture of his is meant to reflect the mixed liturgical context in which the final fourteen years of his life had been led.

As we reflect on these bits of evidence about St Hugh as a liturgical person, one impression comes through with surprising clarity: that to a large extent the liturgical attitudes we have ascribed to him are those we customarily associate not with the high but with the later middle ages. Among these are the idea of liturgical equivalency (let some action stand for some other, like the reading of the Gospel for the mass); a sense of corporate worship as less vivid than private forms of religiosity (his creation of what is virtually his own lectionary system, supplementing to the point of supplanting that of matins); and the kind of individualism that we see reflected in his idiosyncratic intrusions into funerals, the urgency of rites for the dying somehow cancelling all ordinary notions of liturgical propriety and good sense.

Beyond that conclusion, this brief and *faute de mieux* superficial attempt to get inside Hugh's liturgical sensibility has some ramifications of wider significance than the admittedly rather small number of instances deployed here would seem to suggest. In ascending order, perhaps, of relevance to the business of this conference, they may be termed ascetical, psychological, and historiographical. The ascetical belongs to the theologian's province – which may indeed be that of other papers here. My brief will stretch only so far as to pose a single question, one which those with some experience of a structured liturgical life may want to ponder: is the modern presumption that a liturgically-based spirituality is in general the most normative and healthiest just that, a modern presumption? When every caution has been expressed about the limits of our evidence and so on, it remains true that the spirituality of this great Carthusian saint, as conveyed primarily through the eye of a Benedictine biographer, comes through to us as much less informed by the liturgy than we might have imagined.

And this leads to the second ramification of our story, the psychological or (at the risk of jargon) psycho-historical. Whether or not we are surprised that on the ascetical level the liturgy does not bulk larger than it seems to do in what we know of Hugh's life, on the level of trying to understand the inner workings of a late twelfth century man we are faced with a different kind of enigma. In saying this I am thinking of the interest of many contemporary historians not this time in *alimentation* but in what has come to be called *mentalités*. A sentence from George Duby's recent life of William the Marshal sums up this approach eloquently: 'I

[33]   *MV* V.xvi (2.191).

want to try to see the world the way these men saw it.'[34] Thus expressed, our problem is that from the prevailing impression we have of his age, the way Hugh saw the world *should* have been considerably, perhaps even primarily, based on the liturgy. That we cannot with confidence affirm this to be the case makes for a certain uneasiness. If what we had supposed to be one of our lynch-pins in building up a picture of the past proves weak, what else may totter?

Of course, a shaking of received assumptions is no bad thing. It is, however, distressing historiographically – our final ramification – when sources we thought would provide us with a certain kind of information fail to do so. This point is fundamental to my concern (speaking as an historian) because I am aware that it may be not so much that there is something amiss in what we would have thought made Hugh tick (the psycho-historical) nor in what the judgment of prescriptive theologians might suggest ought to have made him tick (the ascetical), as that our sources just do not add up to a believable picture. We have to deal with the factors of both incompleteness and exaggeration. Gerald the Welshman's account of Hugh's faithfulness in keeping Trinity Sunday may be an example of the latter. I think it quite possible that Hugh never kept Trinity Sunday at all and that Gerald either did not know that fact or had no qualms about improving on the existing state of affairs. Similarly, it may be merely the incompleteness of our evidence which accounts for the impression we have of Hugh as a bit liturgically quirky, and that if we had more – some sort of Parson Woodforde-like diary, say, recording with tedious fidelity each liturgical obligation met – we would realise that some of the more or less juicy bits we have been considering were of interest to Hugh's biographers just because they were atypical.

Still, we can only make the best use of what evidence we do possess. If, as promised at the beginning, this paper has raised more questions than it has answered, it does perhaps fill what would otherwise be a sizeable gap in a conference devoted to the life and legacy of Hugh of Avalon, the Charterhouse, Witham, and Lincoln: for no even remotely complete assessment of him will ever be possible without the liturgical dimension's being taken fully – if never quite satisfactorily – into account.

[34]   G. Duby, *William Marshal. The Flower of Chivalry*, tr. Richard Howard (New York, 1985), 38.

GIRALDUS DE BARRI'S HOMAGE
TO HUGH OF AVALON

Richard Loomis

Dom David Knowles questions whether Giraldus de Barri was the man to appreciate Hugh of Avalon, echoing the opinion of Giraldus's Rolls Series editor, James Dimock (Rolls Series 21, 7: liii). In *The Monastic Order in England, 940-1216*, Knowles describes Giraldus's *Life of St Hugh* as 'very meagre and disappointing' (381). Giraldus was certainly not Hugh's equal in virtue, nor does his short life match the voluminous and persuasive detail of the *Magna Vita Sancti Hugonis* attributed to Adam of Eynsham. But there are grounds for recognising Giraldus as a man capable of appreciating Hugh of Avalon and for judging his *Life of St Hugh* a sensitive tribute to the Bishop of Lincoln that contributed significantly to his public cult.

One must first make a distinction between Giraldus the historian and Giraldus the man of letters. That such a distinction would have had meaning to men of the twelfth century is suggested by the fact that the author of the *Magna Vita* apologises that he is not a man of letters, as he also apologises for recounting personal details of Hugh's behaviour that might seem trivial or even denigrating. These details are the very thing prized by modern readers, and if being literary meant no more than producing the rhetorical flourishes with which Adam encumbers his biography, one would be happy to dispense entirely with all merely literary achievements.

Literary critics have paid Giraldus less attention than have historians, but they could render a useful service by helping readers recognise his literary artistry and judge him in terms of the artistic aims he may address in a particular work. They might even help readers appreciate Giraldus's obtrusive persona, that vain and garrulous literary man bristling with resentments who, though autobiographical in origin and hence more sadly actual, is worthy to belong in the gallery where the Wife of Bath vents her ire and the Pardoner celebrates his chicanery. Giraldus dramatises his material, including his own life, in several poetic and rhetorical modes, turning history, for example, into moralised tragedy (as in his account of Henry II in *De Principis Instructione*) or a legal dispute into a rhapsody of aggrieved old age (as in *Speculum Duorum*).

C.R.Cheney in *From Becket to Langton: English Church Government, 1170-1213* speaks of Giraldus as being 'of all our sources of illumination the brightest if not the steadiest light' (3). The unsteadiness of Giraldus de Barri is revealed not only in his fluctuating assessments of such figures as

Henry II or Richard I (who provoke mixed responses in most observers) or in the inaccuracy of some of his reporting, but principally in the emotional vehemence and self-absorption that frequently surface in his writing. When he is not dully pilfering a *florilegium*, his writing can have troubled depths. In his critical study, *Gerald of Wales*, Robert Bartlett draws attention to the 'rich and dark' imagery of the dream-visions recounted by Giraldus in his depiction of the fall of Henry II: 'Images of filth and convulsive, violent action predominate' (89). After Giraldus withdrew from ecclesiastical administration in 1203, he wrote three volumes reviewing his aborted career as an elected but never consecrated Bishop of St David's, for which see he had sought metropolitan status independent of Canterbury. He recounts some thirty visions relative to the case, with interpretations (these are printed in *De Invectionibus*, Rolls Series 21, 1: 156-78). A nun at St David's sees Giraldus lying on the high altar of the cathedral; his body suddenly grows immense, and his limbs are extended throughout Wales. This could prefigure how great his fame would become, observes Giraldus. In another vision, Giraldus stands before the high altar at St David's and opens a book that gives out such brilliant light that pilgrims from all over Wales can see the entire country, including gardens and houses, as if close up. This, notes Giraldus, could refer to his having made St David's famous, or to his four popular books on Ireland and Wales. A priest sees the sun rising in the west; many think that unusual western light symbolises Giraldus and his works. A lion, a dragon, a star are all interpreted as representing Giraldus and his right to be bishop, just as his enemies may be represented by beasts and monsters that attack him in dreams. Though frustrated on earth, Giraldus can yet hope for spiritual success and a reward in heaven. He is seen by one visionary as ascending from a pit and by another as swimming against the current in a deep river and finally reaching land. Many years before, one of his own masters in Paris had told him of a dream in which he saw Giraldus rising from a sick bed and affirming that he had been seriously injured in the head but had recovered with the help of God. This injury to the head, says Giraldus, could represent persecution or perhaps a wound to his conscience; from either, Giraldus trusted he would recover. A last vision shows Giraldus lying in a black cape on the ground, on a bare plank. Told to get up, he answers that he cannot get up for a while but that by God's grace he will in time rise again. This could mean, writes Giraldus, that he cannot by his own efforts rise from the depth of earthly cupidity and hunger for pleasure but that he will rise through grace. All the other dreams that had seemed to promise Giraldus victory and magnificence – now that Giraldus has lost the battle for St David's and chosen scholarly retirement – could be seen as prefiguring a happy end to his life, if his death matches these dreams of recovery. Such dreams, Giraldus had always said, are either revelations from God foretelling the future or – no less remarkable – they are the devil's illusions meant to ensnare.

The account of these dream-visions is typical of Giraldus. He is presenting evidence for his being worthy of eminence in the church, but in so doing displays an inordinate vanity that would seem to disqualify him for spiritual leadership. He knows he has failed to win eminence of office but seeks to build victory out of that defeat, as many a beaten politician has done in his memoirs. Exploring one stark dream, Giraldus honestly admits that earthly attachments hold him down, but he later also admits that all the visions he has so seriously been interpreting could be the devil's impostures. His is indeed an unsteady light. There is nonetheless pleasure for the modern reader in this catalogue of twelfth-century dreams, and there is instruction in what these dreams suggest of medieval minds and what they show of medieval dream literature. There is historical truth, too, and even some accurate prophecy. Giraldus did in fact make a heroic try for St David's, and his failure was not absolute. He is honoured today as a champion of Welsh nationalism, and the fame of his books has steadily grown. If he does not sprawl like Gulliver across Wales, he is a luminary that has risen impressively from that western land.

A careful examination of all of Giraldus's observations on Hugh of Avalon reveals, to quote my introduction to the *Life of St Hugh*, that Giraldus's testimony in Hugh's behalf was 'early, intelligent, and generous' (liv).

In the years 1193 and 1194, Giraldus was engaged in an effort to secure the benefice of Chesterton in Oxfordshire. He had been named to the benefice by a former sheriff of Lincoln, Gerard of Camville, but Bishop Hugh delayed instituting Giraldus because the royal court had challenged Gerard's right to present to that living. Giraldus saw the case as another instance of interference by the royal government in the administration of the church. A settlement was finally reached by which Giraldus would be rector but would have a vicar named by the court party to be paid some twenty marks a year, leaving only about four and a half marks as income for Giraldus. Giraldus subsequently addressed a letter to Hugh (Rolls Series 21, 1: 259-68) complaining that he had never received all of that amount, nor did he know from whom to request payment. He scarcely even knew the vicar. The letter is a remonstrance, reminding Hugh of the glorious exmple of Beckett and adopting the pose of Job. Giraldus will be patient, he will even resign the rectorship if Hugh prefers to give in to the court. But one would not expect Hugh to give in. The letter is evidence of Hugh's reputation as a defender of the church. The Bishop of Lincoln, writes Giraldus, is now the island's only hope in the struggle between church and state. Who could restrain the court if he should weaken? He reminds Hugh that after Giraldus presented his case at a diocesan synod in Oxford – as briefly as he could, but with not a point omitted – Hugh had secretly told him that he was trying by a single payment to cancel the tax of the *pallium* (the donation of a mantle made to the king by earlier bishops of Lincoln) and could not risk offending the court. Once the *pallium* was settled, he would attend to Giraldus's business. The outcome was that Giraldus did remain in possession of Chesterton. Indeed, our only record of his death is the entry in the register of the bishop of Lincoln three decades later that the church of Chesterton was vacant through the death of Master Giraldus de Barri (*Life of St Hugh*, Garland edition, xxiii; this edition is cited hereafter as *Life*).

Giraldus retired from service as a royal clerk at the time of the Chesterton dispute. Since fresh hostilities between Richard I and Philip Augustus prevented his going to Paris, he chose, after spending some time at Oxford, to settle in Lincoln. His reason was that Hugh had assembled there a group of scholars distinguished for learning and virtue. Among these was a theologian with whom Giraldus had studied during his earlier years in Paris, Master William de Montibus. While at Lincoln, Giraldus was commissioned to write the life of the first bishop of the Norman diocese of Lincoln, Remigius. He supplemented this with an account of the bishops who succeeded Remigius, down to the present incumbent, Hugh of Avalon. Hugh is regarded as the foremost successor to Remigius, writes Giraldus, 'if his end should agree with his beginning' (*Life* xxvii). Giraldus then presents an essay on three pairs of twelfth-century English bishops in which he links Hugh of Avalon with Baldwin of Ford, both of whom had been contemplative monks before becoming bishops. Here is my translation of his comparison of these men, each of whom he knew personally:

> The king arranged for two men to be promoted bishops from the ranks of monks, one a Cistercian, the other a Carthusian. One became the bishop of Worcester and afterward archbishop of Canterbury; and the other, bishop of Lincoln. The first had been abbot of Ford, and the other, prior of Witham. In his last years – though it seemed more from a concern for opinion and show than out of piety – King Henry II had resolved to bestow cathedral sees upon members of these two monastic orders, to redeem his reputation thus, since he had previously made many unworthy men bishops. These two seemed to be equally good and religious, but they were quite different in the style of their virtues. Each was learned enough, but the second [Hugh] was very learned. The first [Baldwin] was slow to speak and brief; the other was full of wit and playful talk. The first was almost always rather sad and apprehensive; the other, good-humored, with nearly constant cheerfulness and assurance. The first was a Diogenes, the other a Democritus; the first was cautious and restrained in anger, as in nearly everything; the other was provoked by even a slight occasion. The first was mild, lukewarm, and slack; the other, keen, ardent, and strict. (*Life* xxxi)

Giraldus was called upon to write a life of Hugh after the bishop's death in 1200. The commission probably came from the Dean of Lincoln, Roger of Rolleston, whom Giraldus names as having urged him to add a summary of miracles that occurred at the saint's tomb after the interdict was imposed in 1208 (*Life* 68). The resulting work, the *Vita Sancti Hugonis*, is extant in one manuscript, Corpus Christi College, Cambridge, MS 425, in which it follows the *Vita Sancti Remigii*. A case can be made that this manuscript is in Gerald's own hand. The Rolls Series editor, James Dimock, who examined many Giraldus manuscripts, would go no further than to indicate the possibility of its being an autograph (Rolls

Series 21, 7: ix-x). In parallel fashion, the editors of *Speculum Duorum* observe that 'unfortunately it is not possible to say whether Giraldus wrote these additions [to a passage in *Speculum Duorum*] himself, although it is likely that he did so in some cases' (lxiii). The additions they think likely to have been entered by the author are stylistic touches that suggest an author's embellishing, rather than a copyist's correcting, a manuscript. There are similar embellishments in the *Vita Sancti Hugonis*. In the table of contents on page 2 of my edition, the title of chapter 4 has an added *pariter* that does not appear in the title on page 16. Similarly, on page 14, an *amplior* is added to the text that echoes the title of chapter 3 as given, not on that page, but in the table of contents on page 2. Both of these emendations reflect an author's stylistic concerns. They are in the same hand as the entire manuscript, including all emendations, such as these substantive additions on page 38 of my edition of *Vita Sancti Hugonis*: *post transitum eiusdem*; *ex condicto*; *Anselmus*. The conclusion that Giraldus is the scribe is supported by the likeness of this hand to one of the hands of the *Speculum Duorum* manuscript (see *Speculum Duorum*, figure 3, p. lxii). That manuscript is evidently a working manuscript prepared under the author's direct supervision; it shows abundant emendations and additions, some of which probably were entered by the author himself (*Speculum Duorum*, lvii-lxvi).

The lives of Remigius and Hugh are dedicated to Stephen Langton. The manuscript was evidently completed in the spring of 1214 (*Life* lii), when Langton was beginning in a limited way to exercise his functions as archbishop of Canterbury and when his long conflict with King John was drawing towards its dramatic conclusion in the struggle over Magna Carta. Giraldus gives space in these lives of the bishops of Lincoln for pointed tributes to Thomas Becket, whose heroic resistance to royal government he recommends to Langton, as he had earlier to Hugh of Avalon. Giraldus was about sixty-eight years old and was crowning a busy lifetime with several literary ventures that show him to be in touch with the political and intellectual life of his age. Unlike his larger tomes, the *Life of St Hugh* is an *opusculum*, a summary suitable for reading aloud, though substantive enough to contribute to the cause of Hugh's canonisation and to provide material versified by Henry of Avranches in his *Metrical Life of St Hugh* (see *Life* 83-95). The focus is on Hugh's character as manifested through deeds. Giraldus omits the conventional apparatus of a saint's life; there are no portents at birth, no miracles or prophecies during the saint's lifetime, no death-bed scene. His treatment is dignified and restrained. He does not tell of Hugh's worldly wit, as in that remark of Hugh's he includes in *Gemma Ecclesiastica* – a professional manual for priests – to the effect that ordination is a cure for impotence (see *The Jewel of the Church: A Translation of Gemma Ecclesiastica*, translated by John J. Hagen, 190). Nor is he autobiographical, though we might wish he had told us more of his own life in Lincoln. For that we must turn to *Speculum Duorum*, which for all its turbidity is rich in details of the literary life in Lincoln in the early thirteenth century. Giraldus is too often perfunctory in the *Life of*

St Hugh, not developing topics on which we know from his other writings that he was well supplied with information and opinions. It is this which must have disappointed Dimock and Knowles. But the *Life of St Hugh* is a tribute of praise, not a scientific demonstration. Happily, its focus on characteristic actions of St Hugh does lead Giraldus to present interesting details, many of them unique to this work.

Most famous are the animal stories. Giraldus is circumstantial and precise in telling these. When Hugh was a young monk at the Grande Chartreuse, says Giraldus, he tamed birds and squirrels so that they would join him at dinner as table-companions (*Life* 10). We should remember the Carthusian cell – not a prison lock-up, but a two-storey cottage with its own garden and an upper floor where the monk slept, prayed, studied, and copied manuscripts. Here he had a kitchen and a small table where he took his solitary meals during the week. It would have been at this table that Hugh welcomed his animal guests. His prior came to know of this, Geraldus adds, and Hugh was told to stop, lest the practice disturb his devotions. Presumably, Hugh himself is Giraldus's source; the *Magna Vita* relates that Hugh was fond of sharing reminiscences (*Magna Vita* 1: 6; and elsewhere). Giraldus, though he does not say so, might have visited Hugh at Witham, the scene of the next animal story he tells. As prior of this struggling Carthusian foundation in south-western England, Hugh persisted in cultivating the friendship of wild animals. In his cell at Witham, Giraldus reports, Hugh had a bird as regular dinner guest – a *burneta*, perhaps a hedge-sparrow (*Life* 12-13). This little bird would dine with Hugh except during her annual periods of bearing young. When that was over, she would present her chicks to him as her lord. This lasted for three years and was ended not by anyone's prohibition but by the little bird's death, which caused Hugh great sorrow.

After Hugh left Witham to become bishop of Lincoln, he acquired a new animal friend, his celebrated swan at Stow. This bird Giraldus had seen himself. 'It would stand beside its lord to defend him against the approach of others,' writes Giraldus, 'as I have often seen with amazement' – *sicut aliquociens cum admiracione conspexi* (34-35). Giraldus's description permits us to identify the bird as a whooper swan, distinguished from the smaller mute swan. The description had first appeared in Giraldus's account of Hugh that supplemented the *Life of Remigius*; it is also quoted in the *Magna Vita*. His memorable words helped fix the swan as St Hugh's chief iconographic emblem, and Giraldus's concern for naturalistic detail heightens the realness of the description. What attracted animals to Hugh was his gentle kindness, Giraldus notes. To account for the bird's restive behaviour whenever Hugh was about to visit the manor, Giraldus speculates that the swan could tell from the stir of preparations that Hugh was coming to Stow. He marvels at the prodigy of this friendship but looks for natural explanations of the bird's responses.

Hugh's devotion was not impaired, as his prior at the Grande Chartreuse had feared, by his love for wild animals. On the contrary, Hugh was remarkable for the spirit of faith with which he observed the sacramental rites of the church. Giraldus tells several incidents illustrative of this. Hugh of Coventry, for example, a much more political bishop, always ready to accommodate Henry II, hurries through his mass so as not to keep the king waiting. But Hugh of Avalon takes his time, singing the chants properly, for the sake of the king of kings (20). An old man wants to be confirmed; when Hugh gives him the ritual slap on the cheek, he does so briskly – *fortiter* – because the old man had so long postponed receiving that important sacrament (16). Another man wants his son confirmed a second time to give him a luckier name. Hugh refuses the request and imposes a severe penance as punishment for so superstitious an attitude (16). Several times Giraldus tells how Hugh would take time to bury bodies found lying along the roads he travelled. As David Hugh Farmer points out in his recent biography of the saint, the bishop was thereby showing a concern for the dispossessed, since these neglected corpses would be the bodies of outcasts not thought by others to be worthy of burial (46).

Among the most affecting anecdotes Giraldus tells of Hugh are ones showing the saint's compassion toward the afflicted. These incidents are well told by Giraldus; concisely and freshly, they convey a sense of Hugh's distinctive, often unconventional, personality. Here are two, in my translation:

> He had such holy compassion, always so free of coveting earthly things, that when his officers had brought him the ox of a certain deceased man as his heriot – being the dead man's best possession owed to the lord by custom of the land – the man's wife came to the bishop and begged him with tears to let the ox go, since only that ox remained to her and her poor family for the support of her children, now without a father. The steward of the place saw this and said to him, "My lord, if you concede these and similar legal claims of yours in this way, you will not be able to hold land." When he heard this, the bishop slipped from his horse to the ground, which was very muddy at the time, and filling both his hands with clay, said, "I am holding land now, but I concede to the woman her poor little ox." And he threw the clay from his hands. Looking up, he added, "Because I am seeking not to hold land below, but rather heaven above. This woman had only two workers. Death took away the better one, and shall we take the other from her? Far be that greed from us, for she deserves comfort at a time of so much grief, not more affliction." (17)

The second is an incident which Giraldus says was reported by his former master, William de Montibus:

> Master William [de Montibus], whom the bishop installed in his church at Lincoln as canon and chancellor, testified that in the town of Newark the holy Bishop Hugh kissed a certain leper. Lest the bishop think he had done something great in this, rather to make him conscious of his limitation in not curing the leper with a kiss,

William (who was very much his friend and favorite) said to him, "Martin cleansed a leper with a kiss." Understanding what prompted the remark, the bishop answered, 'Martin, by kissing the leper, cured him in body, but the leper with a kiss has healed me in soul." (31)

Balancing these instances of Hugh's concern for the poor is Giraldus's account of how Hugh resisted the exactions of Richard I and his ministers (26-31). Hugh's weapons were independence of judgment, patience, and good humour. He refused to supply troops for Richard's overseas warfare with Philip Augustus in Normandy. Richard responded by ordering the bishop of Lincoln stripped of the temporal possessions he held as a feudal tenant-in-chief to the king. Hugh journeyed to Richard's new fortress, Château Gaillard, built on the Seine midway between Paris and Rouen. In the chapel there, Hugh forced the king to accept his embrace, but the king replied that he had obliged him only out of good humour, his complaint against Hugh being unchanged. Hugh insisted that the king had no just cause for complaint against him and that this could be demonstrated. During the mass that the king's chaplain then celebrated, the king came to the bishop in choir and gave Hugh the kiss of peace. He also ordered that the bishop, who abstained from meat, be given a large pike. After mass, Hugh shifted from defence to attack and, with fatherly concern, upbraided Richard for certain excesses of his, which appear to have included infidelities to his wife and the sale of offices (see *Magna Vita* 2: 104, n. 4).

Henry II had initially brought Hugh to England to build the Carthusian community at Witham. Hugh was a builder both of buildings and of communities, affirms Giraldus, speaking of Hugh's rebuilding of the cathedral and chapter at Lincoln. He expresses his own eye-witness response to the renovated cathedral, noting its 'wonderful stone roofing' – *miro lapideo tabulatu* (still to be observed in the choir vault) – and the harmony as though painted of the alternating small columns of white stone and black marble (18). To build the community at Lincoln, Hugh not only recruited persons of learning and virtue but offered humane hospitality. This is articulated in an elegant aphorism quoted by Giraldus (30-31): 'He often used to say to his people, "Eat well, and drink well, and serve God well and faithfully" (*Bene comedatis, et bene bibatis, et bene ac devote Deo serviatis*).'

Giraldus concludes his life of St Hugh with an incident in the chapter house at Lincoln that probably took place in the latter half of the year 1213 (76-81). A paralysed boy had recovered the power to walk after a vigil at Hugh's tomb. When this cure was announced in the chapter house, a man arrived unexpectedly who reported yet another miracle attributed to Hugh's intercession; this one had occurred at a cell of Worksop Priory. Giraldus regards the unexpected report of this second miracle, accomplished far away and providentially multiplying the saint's glory, as itself a kind of miracle – *pro miraculo quodam reputari potuit* (80). He names officials of the church who were present – Geoffrey the precentor, Reimund the archdeacon of Leicester, William the archdeacon of Stow – 'and many canons and clerks of the church and many laymen as well' (80-81). The details and tone suggest that Giraldus was there, too. Both miracles include dream-visions regarding St Hugh. It is characteristic of Giraldus, as I have noted earlier, to pay attention to dreams. We may be reminded in this instance of Giraldus's account of that earlier dream in which he himself was seen as paralysed and needing the grace of God to rise. Here is my translation of his story of how through a dream St Hugh provoked a paralysed boy to stand up:

> When morning came, after he had slept a little, it seemed to him in his sleep that two clerks wearing white stoles were properly preparing the adjoining altar, that of St John the Baptist, as if for celebrating mass. Then a bishop, mitred and appropriately clothed in episcopal vestments, handsome in both face and stature, passed by him on his way to the altar and said to him, "Rise." He answered, "And how shall I rise, since I cannot move from where I am lying?" But the bishop went on to the altar, celebrated mass there, and when it was done, returned with his ministers past the same sick man. Bending his head towards him and breathing upon his face, he said to him, "Rise, I say to you, rise." And with that he vanished. But the paralytic woke up at these words and felt his legs pierced as by a sword. Though in anguish with the pain, like that of fresh wounds, yet longing to obey such a great man's commands, he tried with all his might to get up. After stretching his legs out, he drew himself immediately into a standing position. He tottered at first and staggered, then sank forward onto the ground. Getting up again on his own, he stood more steadily. The sisters of the hospital of Lincoln who had ministered to him in his sickness were also there at the time in vigils and prayers. When they saw him upright and walking on his own feet, they rejoiced with great joy. Crying out and celebrating as women do, they and everyone there who had seen these things magnified God with praise, who is wonderful in his saints and glorious in all his works. (77-79)

Throughout his career, Giraldus de Barri maintained close relations with the cathedral chapter at Hereford. Located on the River Wye, Hereford is a border city not far from the Welsh town of Brecon near which, at Llanddew, Giraldus had a residence while he was archdeacon of Brecon. 'The mistaken assumption,' writes M. T. Clanchy in *England and its Rulers, 1066-1272*, 'is to think of Herefordshire as a backwater .... A more appropriate metaphor for such regional centres is that of a transmitter or transformer. Herefordshire was a meeting place of languages (Welsh, English, French and Latin) and of cultures (Celtic, Anglo-Saxon, Anglo-Norman and cosmopolitan)' (177). A few years after writing the *Life of St Hugh*, Giraldus addressed a letter to the chapter at Hereford (Rolls Series 21, 1: 409-19). The ostensible purpose is to ask them to return to him the copy of his last book, *Speculum Ecclesiae*, which he had lent them and which he wishes to revise. Giraldus develops the letter as his literary apologia, listing and commenting on his books. He admits that his saints' lives are minor works, *opuscula*, while associating them with saints' lives by such celebrated authors as St Ambrose and St Bernard. He is acting as his own editor, determining his canon. From the list one can see how industrious his late years were, and his comments reveal his perception of his literary achievement. This he offers partly by indirection, through quoting a commission which he says Archbishop Baldwin had given him after hearing Giraldus read his *Topographia Hiberniae* (in the course of their trip through Wales to recruit crusaders in 1188). Remembering Giraldus's sketch of Baldwin in that comparison with Hugh that spoke of Baldwin as 'slow to speak and brief ... rather sad and apprehensive ... cautious ... lukewarm', one may be surprised at Baldwin's speech in this letter. He is eloquent, impassioned, and unequivocal. But of course, this is Giraldus composing a fine address for the slack archbishop, as, in imitation of classical historians, he had composed heroic speeches for leading figures in his epic narrative of the conquest of Ireland. This work of yours which we have just heard, says Baldwin, deserves great praise. It is adorned throughout with elegant words and pithy sentences (*verborum flosculis ... sententiarum medullulis*) so well fitted that the whole work – beginning, middle, and end – holds together flawlessly. More than earthly riches, you should love and value the grace of style the Lord has given you, and you should never fail to put it to use. We give you a prelate's injunction always to exercise your literary gift for the good of many and to end your life engaged in this work of love (*in caritatis opere tali vitalia complere tempora non desistas*). Giraldus tells the canons of Hereford that he has obeyed the archbishop, by not ceasing to engage in literary as well as theological, philosophical, and historical studies (*in litteralibus studiis, et tam theologiciis quam philosophicis et historicis*). Yet a writer cannot escape calumny. Today as always, writing is subject to envy, especially the work of one who mints new things (*nova cudentis*). Giraldus characterises himself as an innovative writer attacked by those who envy him. His old-fashioned rhetoric and his extensive borrowings from school-anthologies may seem anything but innovative. In fact, like other shaping spirits of his age, he is an amphibian, deliberately traditional, but alive to the new. Behind his florid learning squirms an inquiring intelligence; amid the pomp of his treatises, new forms of literature play and grow. For his histories are works of literary imagination. One finds there not only new stuff, as in the ethnography, folklore, and political portraiture he records, but also embryonic foreshadowings of the forms of later British romance, satire, fabliau, epic, and tragedy. The patterns are often inchoate or fragmentary, embedded in a vivid sentence or half-told story; they are sometimes more fully worked out, as in the tragedy of Henry II or the farcical humiliation of William Longchamp. But in Giraldus, one sees how fertile a matrix for poetry history can be when the historian has a poet's sensibility. And one cannot help marvelling at this bustling, creative, self-important master, even while knowing that British literature will need more time and trials before Chaucer can make high comedy of interwoven texts and experience or Shakespeare open many hearts by entering into the heart of history.

Despite his preoccupation with himself and his works, Giraldus is not a cold egotist. In 1215 he addressed a letter to Archbishop Stephen Langton urging him not to resign and enter a monastery (Rolls Series 21, 1: 401-7). Pope Innocent III had joined King John in condemning Langton for his support for the barons who fought for Magna Carta. Remain at your post of leadership, Giraldus tells Langton, you are needed. In his biographical study, *Stephen Langton*, F. M. Powicke describes Giraldus's concern thus: 'How excitable and fussy he was, with his royal Welsh ancestry and his long record of wirepulling and controversy, yet how loyal and affectionate' (133). Giraldus shows himself 'excitable and fussy' in the letter to Langton by asking the archbishop not to let one of the Canterbury monks get his hands on a book of Giraldus's that this monk had denounced as libellous. Keep it away from him, demands Giraldus, he may edit it! Do not let his deletions or his additions corrupt the text. If he wishes, let him listen to it being read. That may do him good. The letter to Langton and the letter to the chapter at Hereford are both preserved in a manuscript at Lambeth Palace, MS 236, which contains the only extant copy of Giraldus's guide for priests, *Gemma Ecclesiastica*. This is a beautifully executed manuscript and has been thought to be the copy Giraldus gave to Pope Innocent III (who, says Giraldus, prized it so much he kept it by his bed and would let none of the cardinals see it). It is more likely to be a presentation copy for the Archbishop of Canterbury, as it is also likely to be a revised edition of the *Gemma* (see my comments in the *Life of St Hugh*, xviii) and hence yet another product of Giraldus's seventh decade.

Loyalty to and affection for Hugh of Avalon are expressed in the last pages of Giraldus's last book, the *Speculum Ecclesiae*. In this survey of the church, Giraldus singles out Hugh's Carthusian Order as being *perfectissimus*, the most perfect of the monastic orders (Rolls Series 21, 4: 259), since their rule keeps Carthusian monks secluded from the world and, while supported by community life, yet also as a community keeps them from accumulating too much property. Giraldus later cites Henry II's choice of Hugh of Avalon to be bishop of Lincoln as a rare happy instance of a secular ruler's involvement in the election of a bishop. Hugh is surely a saint. Archbishop Baldwin had died while on the Third Crusade, but whether he has won a heavenly crown is no more than a probability, writes Giraldus. Of Hugh, one can be certain. For God has verified his triumph *aperte per signa et prodigia multa* – 'openly by many signs and wonders' (Rolls Series 21, 4: 345). This confident allusion to Hugh's sainthood publicly confirmed by miracles may be read as Giraldus' endorsement of the canonisation of Hugh of Avalon. The papal bull of canonisation is dated 17 February, 1220, only a few years before the death of Giraldus was reported to the bishop of Lincoln. At the end of his life, then, Giraldus de Barri is constant in his readiness to celebrate the heroic virtue of Hugh of Avalon.

Works Cited

[Adam of Eynsham.] *Magna Vita Sancti Hugonis: The Life of St Hugh of Lincoln*. Edited and translated by Decima L. Douie and Hugh Farmer. 2 vols. London: Thomas Nelson, 1961-62

Bartlett, Robert. *Gerald of Wales, 1146-1223*. Oxford: Clarendon Press, 1982

Cheney, C. R. *From Becket to Langton: English Church Government, 1170-1213*. Manchester: Manchester University Press, 1956

Clanchy, M. T. *England and its Rulers, 1066-1272: Foreign Lordship and National Identity*. Oxford: Basil Blackwell, 1983

Farmer, David Hugh. *Saint Hugh of Lincoln*. London: Darton, Longman and Todd; Kalamazoo: Cistercian Publications, 1985

Giraldus Cambrensis. *Opera*. Edited by J. S. Brewer, James F. Dimock, George F. Warner. Rolls Series, no. 21. 8 vols. London, 1861-91

_____. *Speculum Duorum, or A Mirror of Two Men*. Edited by Yves Lefèvre and R. B. C. Huygens; translated by Brian Dawson; general editor, Michael Richter. Cardiff: University of Wales Press, 1974

_____. *The Jewel of the Church: A Translation of Gemma Ecclesiastica*. Translated by John J. Hagen. Davis Medieval Texts and Studies, no. 2. Leiden: E. J. Brill, 1979

_____. *The Life of St Hugh of Avalon*. Edited and translated by Richard M. Loomis. Garland Library of Medieval Literature, Series A, Volume 31. New York and London: Garland Publishing, Inc., 1985

Knowles, Dom David. *The Monastic Order in England, 940-1216*. 2nd edn Cambridge: The University Press, 1963

Powicke, F. M. *Stephen Langton*. Oxford: Clarendon Press, 1928

HUGH OF AVALON, CARTHUSIAN AND BISHOP

H. E. J. Cowdrey

In May 1186, and so just eight hundred years ago, Hugh of Avalon was elected bishop of Lincoln, and on 21 September he received consecration.[*] He occupied the see until his death on 16 November 1200, as the last of the truly great and saintly foreigners who, in the wake of the Norman Conquest of 1066, ruled medieval English dioceses. Hugh was not only a foreigner, born at Avalon in Burgundy not far from the frontier with Savoy, but also a Carthusian monk and so a member of the strictest and most withdrawn monastic family of the twelfth-century western church. The purpose of this paper is to inquire how a Carthusian, born not far from Chartreuse, could become a diocesan bishop in far-distant England, and do so in a manner that, in his own eyes as well as those of contemporaries, fulfilled rather than contradicted his Carthusian vocation.

I

The Carthusians had been founded in 1084 by St Bruno, and between 1121 and 1128 Prior Guigo I had written down the Customs that governed their life.[1] Many features of the Carthusian order made it prima facie

[*] The following abbreviations are used:

Colloque	La Naissance des Chartreuses. VIe Colloque Internationale d'Histoire et de Spiritualité Cartusiennes, 1984 (Grenoble, 1986)
Coutumes	Guigues Ier, Coutumes de Chartreuse, ed. by a Carthusian, SC 313 (Paris, 1984)
Lettres	Les Lettres des premiers Chartreux, 1: St Bruno, Guigues, St Anthelme, 2: Les Moines de Portes, ed. by a Carthusian, SC 88, 274 (Paris, 1962-80)
Magna vita s. Hugonis	The Life of St Hugh of Lincoln, edd. D. L. Douie and H. Farmer (2 vols., London, etc., 1961-2; repr. with corrections, Oxford, 1985)
PL	Patrologia Latina
Recueil	Recueil des plus anciens actes de la Grande-Chartreuse (1086-1196), ed. B. Bligny (Grenoble, 1958)
SC	Sources chrétiennes
Vita s. Hugonis	Guigo I, Vita sancti Hugonis Gratianopolitani, PL 153. 761-84

[1] *Coutumes.* Bruno's own conception of the eremitical life is stated in his letters

unlikely that it would develop into what it quite rapidly became – a
nursery of outstanding diocesan bishops. It was founded and grew up in the
context of the *crise du monachisme* to which, at the end of the eleventh
and the beginning of the twelfth centuries, proximity to the world had
brought the black monks, including the Cluniacs. A number of new foundations, including the Carthusians' younger sister-order the Cistercians,
removed themselves from the habitations of men to a distant *eremus*, or
desert place; but the Cistercians, for example, acquired extensive lands
and far-flung granges. The Carthusians, by contrast, carried the search for
seclusion to its practicable limit. In a memorable phrase, Dom David
Knowles commented upon their 'logical formality and uncompromising
strength', in which he saw a quintessential expression of the French genius.[2]
The Carthusian *eremus* was to be as complete and as uncompromising as
human resourcefulness could make it.

It would be wrong to envisage the *spaciosa heremus* which Prior Bruno
established in the high mountains behind Grenoble,[3] as if it were a piece of
the Sahara incongruously transported into France, or a mere hankering
after the fourth-century Egyptian desert of St Antony. It was a solitude
which here and now could provide all the spiritual and material necessities
of a small and austere community of men who were single-mindedly
dedicated to penitence and meditative prayer. Chartreuse, and in principle
its first five dependent Charterhouses which were founded under Guigo I
– in 1115 Portes, and in 1116 Les Écouges, Durbon, la Sylve-Bénite, and
Meyriat – are each set in a high mountain valley which forms a natural
cul-de-sac. The sole, easily controlled entry leads first to a lower house of
the *conversi* or lay brothers, and only then to an upper house of the
monks themselves. From the very beginning the Carthusians were anxious
to set strict boundaries (*termini*) to the patrimony of their houses. Those
of Chartreuse itself were established by stages between 1084 and 1129.[4]
Within their *termini* – here, Knowles's 'logical formality' is particularly
evident – the Carthusians possessed everything; outside them they were to
possess nothing. As nearly as possible the *termini* were to be impervious

to Ralph *le Verd* (1096/1101) and to the Carthusian community (1099/1100):
Lettres, 1.66-89.
[2] D. Knowles, *The Monastic Order in England*, 2nd edn (Cambridge, 1963),
pp.375-391, at p.380. I have also particularly used the following: B. Bligny,
L'Église et les ordres religieux dans le royaume de Bourgogne aux xiᵉ et xiiᵉ siècles
(Paris, 1960); *ibid.*, 'Les chartreux dans la société occidentale du xiiᵉ siècle', in
Aspects de la vie conventuelle aux xiᵉ-xiiᵉ siècles (Lyons, etc., 1975), pp.29-58. A
Carthusian and J. Dubois, 'Certosini', in *Dizionario degli Istituti di Perfezione*, 2
(Rome, 1975), cols. 782-821. J. Dubois, *Histoire monastique en France au xiiᵉ siècle*
(London, 1982), nos. VII-X; *ibid.*, 'Le désert, cadre de vie des chartreux au
Moyen-Age', *Colloque*, pp.15-35.
[3] *Recueil*, no.1, pp.1:8; see also Guibert of Nogent, *De vita sua*, 1.11, Guibert de
Nogent, *Histoire de sa vie*, ed. G. Bourgin (Paris, 1907), pp.32-6, and Peter the
Venerable, *De miraculis*, 2.28, *PL* 189. 943-5, esp. col.944BC.
[4] i. 1084: *Recueil*, no.1, pp.1-8. ii. Before 1103: *ibid.*, no.8, pp.22-4. iii. 1103:
ibid., no.9, pp.24-7. iv. 1107/9: nos.10-11, pp.27-30. v. c.1112: *ibid.*, nos.12-14,
pp.30-4. 1129: *ibid.*, nos.15-17, pp.35-45.

in both directions. They were to contain no habitations save those of the monks and the *conversi*. Women and armed men were strenuously excluded from entry, as were hunters, fishers, and graziers. When some iron miners tried to resume their operations at Chartreuse, a former land-owner who had given them leave to do so was speedily made to repent and to affirm that henceforth he would grant no more concessions, even if not just an iron mine but a gold mine were discovered there![5] In his Customs, Guigo prescribed the complement to this so far as the monks were concerned: 'To exclude so far as possible every occasion of greed, we order that those who dwell in this place shall possess absolutely nothing outside the boundaries of their desert (*extra suae terminos heremi*) – no fields, no vines, no gardens, no churches, cemeteries, oblations, tithes, or anything of that kind.'[6]

To ensure physical sustenance in the high mountains even for a manner of life marked by *vilitas et asperitas*,[7] the Carthusians strictly limited numbers within their houses: Guigo allowed only thirteen or fourteen monks and, normally, sixteen *conversi*.[8] Guests were bluntly warned to expect no provender for their horses; above all, Guigo ruled out the monastic almsgiving that elsewhere was a universal obligation. He explained himself with further Gallic directness: 'We did not flee to the solitude of this desert in order to undertake the material care of other men's bodies; we did so to seek the eternal salvation of our own souls. Therefore let no one marvel if we offer greater friendship and solace to those who come here rather for the good of their souls than of their bodies. Were it otherwise, we would have done better from the start to have established ourselves somewhere by a public highway, not in a savage, remote, and well-nigh inaccessible place.' For, as Guigo insisted, the Carthusians followed the way of Mary, not that of Martha.[9]

Indeed, they took the way of Mary almost, but not quite, to the extreme, practising a form of eremitical life tempered by a little common life.[10] The ideal of the Carthusians was the *vita solitaria*; the place of its habitual conduct, whether in prayer, work, or recreation, was the individual cell. Of the daily offices, only Matins and Vespers were recited in community; the remainder were said in the cell. In the early decades there was not even a daily mass. Social recreation and conversation were allowed only occasionally. Except on Sundays and greater festivals, meals were taken alone in the cell, though here as so often Carthusian austerity was applied with good sense; on the day when a Carthusian was buried, his brethren were not bound to keep to their cells, but to provide solace (*consolationis gratia*), unless it were a major fast they twice ate together.[11] Thus, occasional meetings for prayer, meals, or recreation punctuated the prevailing

[5] *Ibid.*, nos. 6, 18, pp. 16-20, 45-7.
[6] *Coutumes*, cap. 41.1, p. 244.
[7] *Ibid.*, cap. 22.1, p. 212.
[8] *Ibid.*, caps. 78-9, pp. 284-6.
[9] *Ibid.*, caps. 19-20, pp. 204-10.
[10] Cf. *Lettres*, p. 20.
[11] *Coutumes*, cap. 14.2, p. 194.

solitude. But the strongest bond of common life was the vow of stability and obedience that bound the Carthusian to the direction of his prior, as the head of Chartreuse was called.[12] Guigo prescribed for the novice that from the time of his profession 'he should consider himself so alien from all things of the world, that without the prior's leave he has power over nothing whatever, not even his own self. Although [Guigo commented] obedience should be maintained with great zeal by all who have under-taken to live under a monastic rule, it should be practised the more devotedly and carefully by those who have embraced a stricter and more severe vocation.'[13]

One might think that a final commitment to a life of solitude and seclusion, lived under obedience within the carefully drawn boundaries of a Charterhouse, could not be more categorically stated, nor could a progression to the episcopate be more categorically debarred. But there was another side to the Carthusian monasticism into which Hugh of Avalon was admitted c.1163. From its very beginning and increasingly as time went on, Chartreuse inevitably interacted with the surrounding church and world much as did other parts of western monasticism. It owed an incalculable debt to succeeding bishops of Grenoble – Hugh I (1080-1132), Hugh II (1132-48), and then, after the transient Othmar, Geoffrey (1151-63) and John I of Sassenage (1163-1220). Their advice and protection were essential for the establishment and protection of Chartreuse's *eremus*, which lay entirely within their diocese. In his Life of Hugh I, Prior Guigo recalled how the bishop had helped Bruno with the foundation of his house.[14] The early Carthusian *acta* document the continuing debt. Thus, in 1086 at a diocesan synod, Hugh confirmed the gift of the original *spaciosa heremus* by a number of local lords and by Abbot Seguin of la Chaise-Dieu, one of whose priories, Saint-Robert-du-Mont-Cornillon, had certain rights there. In 1090, after Bruno's departure to Italy had led to the dispersal of the community and the return of its lands to Seguin, Pope Urban II charged Archbishop Hugh of Lyons and Bishop Hugh of Grenoble to reinstate them. It was Bishop Hugh who, some ten years later, by a mandate to the clergy and laity of his diocese, prohibited the circulation within Chartreuse's *termini* of women and of armed men.[15] Again, it was Bishop Hugh who warded off the intrusion of iron miners and haymakers.[16] As the *termini* were gradually extended between 1099 and 1129, almost every stage took place through donations made in the bishop's presence and fortified by his confirmation.[17] Even a matter so domestic to the order as the emergence of the Carthusian general chapter took place under close episcopal guidance. In 1141, when Prior Anthelme convened the first true general chapter of himself and five other priors besides himself, he did so upon Bishop Hugh II's advice; the bishop

[12] *Ibid.*, cap. 23.1, p. 214; cf. *Magna vita s. Hugonis*, 1.7, 10, vol. 1.22-4, 31-4.
[13] *Coutumes*, cap. 25.2, p. 218.
[14] *Vita s. Hugonis*, 2.11, cf. 5.23, *PL* 153.769-70, 778.
[15] *Recueil*, nos. 1, 3, 4, 6, pp. 1-8, 11-14, 16-20.
[16] *Ibid.*, nos. 18-19, pp. 45-50.
[17] As n. 4; the exception is nos. 10-11.

was present and himself received the priors' promise of obedience to the chapter. In 1155 under Prior Basil, when general chapters assumed settled form and became regular occasions, Bishop Geoffrey fulfilled a similar role as guardian of the Carthusian order.[18] As late as 1196, Bishop John of Sassenage could allude to the 'good customs' which by agreement had admitted himself and his predecessors to a place in Carthusian affairs; only if a bishop of Grenoble were persistently to transgress these customs should the Carthusians' papally conferred exemption be invoked against him.[19]

For during the first hundred years of Carthusian history the papacy, too, had become deeply concerned and reinforced Chartreuse's liberty. Its involvement began as early as with Pope Urban II, who in 1090 remedied the problems that Bruno's departure had occasioned by persuading Abbot Seguin of la Chaise-Dieu to restore Chartreuse to its returning monks so that it might remain *in libertate pristina*; in 1091 he took it under papal protection and approved the election of Landuin, the second prior whom Bruno had designated.[20] In 1133 Pope Innocent II followed (as he said) the example not only of Urban II but also of his successors Paschal II, Calixtus II, and Honorius II, by approving Carthusian constitutions and customs as well as by giving papal protection to all Carthusian possessions both present and future; his bull included a detailed description and guarantee of the *termini* of Chartreuse, with the observation that the *sacer ordo eremeticus Cartusiensis ... ad honorem sacrosanctae Romanae ecclesiae ... omnino devotus est*.[21] It was particularly after 1163, when Bishop Geoffrey of Grenoble was deposed for having adhered to the Emperor Frederick Barbarossa and his antipope – an episode by which the Carthusians themselves were not directly compromised – that the popes frequently and comprehensively protected the Carthusians and their interests. Their acts protected the Carthusians' lands and privacy, developed their exemption, and confirmed the statutes of their general chapters.[22] The papacy became more important than the bishops in giving the Carthusians the protection that they needed; inevitably they themselves reciprocated by sharing papal aspirations and by being drawn into papal service and papal affairs.

They began to be so involved from very early days. Bruno, the first prior, had formerly been *scholasticus* of the cathedral of Reims where Odo of Châtillon, the future Pope Urban II, had been his pupil. Urban remem-

---

[18] *Ibid.*, nos. 21-2, pp. 53-64.
[19] *Ibid.*, no. 67, pp. 180-1. The bishop of Grenoble's part in Carthusian deliberations is illustrated by the discussions that preceded Hugh of Avalon's departure for Witham: *Magna vita s. Hugonis*, 2.3-4, vol. 1.53-9.
[20] *Recueil*, nos. 2-5, pp. 9-16.
[21] *Ibid.*, no. 20, pp. 50-3. No *acta* of Paschal II, Calixtus II, or Honorius II survive, but for a reference to a lost papal letter, see *Magna vita s. Hugonis*, 1.10, vol. 1.33.
[22] Alexander III: *Recueil*, nos. 25 (1164), 29-30 (1173/6), 31 (1176), 32 (1177), pp. 70-2, 83-94. Lucius III: *ibid.* nos. 37-9 (1184), 40-2 (1185), pp. 103-20. Urban III: *ibid.*, nos. 44-5 (1186/7), pp. 126-8. Clement III: *ibid.*, nos. 46-7 (1188), 51-2 (1190), pp. 129-36, 144-7. Celestine III: *ibid.*, 53-7 (1192), 58 (1193), pp. 147-64.

bered his master and c.1090 he called him to the service of the apostolic see; although Bruno, having refused the pope's offer of the archbishopric of Reggio/Calabria, quickly withdrew to found a new eremitical community at La Torre. There, in 1100, his successor at Chartreuse, Landuin, came to consult him; on his return journey he died while a captive of the antipope Clement III's partisans.[23] A generation later, like Bernard of Clairvaux, Prior Guigo I of Chartreuse became deeply committed to Pope Innocent II and his cause in the Anacletan Schism of 1130-9. As early as 1131 he wrote to Innocent and exhorted him to steadfastness in the afflictions of the Roman church. He strongly condemned the leader of the French Anacletans, Bishop Gerard of Angoulême, and he pleaded with Duke William X of Aquitaine to abandon his support of Bishop Gerard. Most important was his cordial contact with the papal chancellor, Cardinal Haimeric, to whom he wrote after the cardinal had recently visited Chartreuse. Guigo deplored the *cruenta scissio* which rent the Roman church. He traced its spiritual origins to pride in the mind and indulgence in the body (*elatio in mente et voluptas in corpore*); the consequence had been the arming of Christian against Christian. Guigo proceeded to his most considerable discussion that survives of how Christians should interact with the rulers of this world. With an allusion to the dangers that lurked in the notion of a bishop's *regalia* to which the concordat of Worms (1122) had given prominence, he urged that it was better that churches should give laws to kings' palaces than that palaces should give laws to churches. Kings should receive sackcloth from churchmen, rather than churchmen receive the purple from kings. 'It better serves them,' Guigo commented, 'to borrow our poverty, fasts, and humility, than it serves us to borrow their greed, delicacy, and pride.'[24] Guigo's letters make it clear that Chartreuse had its spiritual and moral message for transmission to churchmen and to kings.

After the Anacletan schism had thus served to extend Chartreuse's horizons of concern far beyond its own *eremus*, the process of dialogue with those outside developed in three especial ways. First, loyalties engendered during the schism led to the Carthusians' maintaining close spiritual and personal contacts, especially through letter-writing and confraternity, with other monastic families – notably the Cluny of Peter the Venerable and the Clairvaux of St Bernard.[25] In 1128 Guigo wrote to Hugh of Payns, grand master of the Templars, exhorting him to spiritual

[23] For the lives of the early priors of Chartreuse, see A. Wilmart, 'La chronique des premiers chartreux', *Revue Mabillon*, 16 (1926), 77-142. For the letter that Landuin was bringing back, *Lettres*, no. 2, vol. 1.82-8.
[24] *Lettres*, nos. 3-5, vol. 1.166-95. The special greeting at the end of no. 5 for Cardinals Matthew of Albano and John of Ostia is further evidence for Guigo's contact with the papal curia.
[25] Peter the Venerable: *Recueil*, nos. 23-4, pp. 64-9; *The Letters of Peter the Venerable*, ed. G. Constable (2 vols., Cambridge, Mass., 1967), nos. 24, 48, 132, vol. 1.44-7, 146-8, 333-4. St Bernard: *S. Bernardi Opera*, 7-8, *Epistolae*, edd. J. Leclercq and H. Rochais (Rome, 1974-7), nos. 11-12, 153-4, 250, vol. 1.52-62, 359-61, vol. 2.145-7.

rather than military valour, but also calling down upon him divine aid *in spiritualibus quam etiam in corporalibus praeliis.*[26] Secondly, the expansion and development of the Carthusian order, which by 1200 numbered some thirty-nine foundations, also fostered its interaction with the world outside. It did so in many ways. When a new house was established at a distance, the goodwill of the local bishop might need to be secured.[27] When monks were dispatched to institute new houses, they might come up against and feel bound to contend for the church's wider needs. Thus, when the Carthusian monk Einhard, who set up many Charterhouses, once heard of the Albigensian heretics' brazen blasphemy (as Adam of Eynsham described it) against all the sacraments of the church, he did not stand idly by. 'White-hot with zeal against such godless men,' Adam wrote, 'he went to the nearest Catholic magnates and aroused them to take up arms against the heretics, slaying many of them, and a preacher of so damnable a heresy never again appeared in the neighbourhood.'[28] Besides the foundation of new houses, the regular holding of general chapters of all Carthusian priors involved Chartreuse in larger expenditure than its infertile *eremus* could sustain. Therefore the Carthusians came to welcome grants of fiscal privileges, rights of pasture, and other benefits from magnates and kings. In 1192 Pope Celestine III vindicated against local 'tyrants' their right to receive testamentary bequests; it is noteworthy that the pope appealed, not to Carthusian traditions and customs, but to natural human justice and the norms of canon and civil law.[29] As a result of such contacts with magnates and kings, Carthusian values were impressed upon kings, as when the future Carthusian *conversus*, Count Gerard of Nevers, shamed the idleness of the French royal court under King Louis VII and showed the Carthusian life to be a better route to Jerusalem than the Second Crusade upon which the king was about to embark.[30] In 1133 Prior Guigo I heard of an attack on the reforming bishop of Paris, Stephen of Senlis, and joined the ageing Bishop Hugh I of Grenoble to write a letter urging the council of Jouarre to deprive perpetually of their benefices the clerks who had been involved.[31] Thirdly, if Chartreuse had its windows to the world, outsiders came to Chartreuse and stayed with its monks. For although it discouraged visits from those seeking merely material alms, it was always welcoming to those who came for their spiritual benefit. Bishops were especially admitted to benefit from, and also contribute to, life at Chartreuse; this is well illustrated by the frequent spiritual retreats there of the Cistercian Archbishop Peter of Tarentaise (1142-75), during which he also instructed Hugh of Avalon when a young monk.[32]

[26] *Lettres*, no.2, vol.1.154-61.
[27] *Lettres*, no.9, to Archbishop Reynald of Reims (1136), vol.1.224-5.
[28] *Magna vita s. Hugonis*, 4.13, vol.2.62-9, esp. 65-6.
[29] Fiscal privileges: *Recueil*, nos.33-5, 61-2, 65-6, pp.94-100, 169-71, 175-9. Gifts: *ibid.*, nos.34, 36, 50, 59, 60, pp.96-8, 100-2, 142-4, 164-9. Celestine III's bull: *ibid.*, no.53, pp.147-9.
[30] *Magna vita s. Hugonis*, 4.12, vol.2.55-8.
[31] *Lettres*, no.6, vol.1.201-2.
[32] Visitors might come on a surprisingly large scale, as during Hugh of Avalon's

In view of Chartreuse's long history of interacting in such ways as these with the world outside, it is not surprising that, from an early date, its priors and monks did not regard the episcopal office as being alien to the Carthusian vocation. On the one hand, bishops who were not themselves Carthusians might so behave as to reflect and propagate Carthusian principles; on the other, a Carthusian vocation might itself lead on to the episcopate.

The figure of Bishop Hugh I of Grenoble was of the utmost importance in leading the Carthusians to adopt this view. Two years after he died in 1132, Pope Innocent II canonised him and imposed upon Prior Guigo I the task of writing his Life. Innocent's stated reasons were that God should be honoured in his saint, and that the clergy who read and the laity who heard his Life might give God glory and have the benefit of Hugh's intercessions.[33] Since Hugh was already canonised, Guigo had no need to rehearse his miracles. He could present him as an exemplary monk-bishop according to a pattern that the Carthusians understood and approved: he was torn between his desire for the monastic or eremitical life at its most demanding, and his zeal for the well-being of his diocese and its people as required by contemporary reforming aspirations and by pastoral necessities. Guigo set out Hugh's Life in six chapters. The first concerned his parents, education, and years as a canon of Valence. It featured Hugh's father, Odo of Châteauroux, a knight of virtuous life who upon his second wife's death entered Chartreuse and became an exemplary Carthusian. At Valence, Hugh attracted the notice of Pope Gregory VII's standing legate in France, Hugh, then bishop of Die and later archbishop of Lyons. Hugh of Die enlisted the young man as his helper against the prime targets in France of the papal reform – laymen who held churches, tithes, and cemeteries; married priests; and simoniacs. Secondly, Guigo described how, in 1080, Hugh became bishop of Grenoble at the age of twenty-seven: at Hugh of Die's council of Avignon, the clergy of Grenoble requested him as its bishop; he refused episcopal consecration from his metropolitan, Archbishop Warmund of Vienne, on grounds of his simony, and received it instead at Rome from Gregory VII himself. Guigo dwelt upon Gregory's pastoral care of the young man when he encountered severe temptation, and upon the continuing favour that he showed him. He described the parlous state of the new bishop's diocese, which arose from its married clergy, the prevalence of simony, the churches, tithes, and cemeteries in lay hands and so subject to secular jurisdiction, and the wasting of church property. Thirdly, Guigo showed how, after becoming a bishop, Hugh experienced a deep longing for the monastic life. In 1082 he completed a noviciate and made his profession at la Chaise-Dieu which he admired for its *paupertas* and *humilitas*; but Gregory VII himself intervened and ordered him to resume his pastoral care. In 1084 when Chartreuse was founded, Hugh was Bruno's adviser and helper, and he

last journey: *Magna vita s. Hugonis*, 5.14, vol. 2.164-6. For Peter of Tarentaise, *ibid.*, 1.13, vol. 1.38-40.
[33] *Vita s. Hugonis*, PL 153.761-2.

always maintained familiarity with the Carthusians. 'He was with them not as lord and bishop,' Guigo wrote, 'but as one of themselves and as a most humble brother.' When he stayed with them, Bruno sometimes had to drive him back to his flock and counsel him to moderate his austerities. Fourthly, Guigo exhibited Hugh as a model in respect of custody of the senses and of the tongue. His fifth chapter concerned his external actions as bishop – his almsgiving, his refusal of gifts for himself and his other virtues, his zeal as peacemaker and preacher, and his services to the papacy in 1111 when the German Emperor Henry V descended upon Rome as well as during the Anacletan schism. Guigo concluded with an account of Hugh's last sickness, death, and burial. Overall he provided the Carthusian model of a saintly bishop, to whom Chartreuse owed a great debt, who aspired to the monastic life and lived by its standards, but who also measured up to the spiritual, moral, and political demands of Gregory VII, his agents, and successors, no less than to the standards of the Carthusians.

Because the Carthusians had so clear a model of the episcopal life and office, it is not surprising that Chartreuse and other Carthusian priories became an important source of bishops for the provinces that lay in their vicinity.[34] At Grenoble, Guigo's Life of Bishop Hugh I relates that, in his declining years, a monk of Chartreuse became his coadjutor, and in due course succeeded to the see as Bishop Hugh II.[35] The remaining twelfth-century bishops of Grenoble – Othmar, Geoffrey, and John of Sassenage – were all Carthusians.[36] In 1148, Pope Eugenius III translated Hugh II to the archbishopric of Vienne, although after a troubled period he withdrew in 1155 to the Charterhouse of Portes. It was the Charterhouse of Meyriat which, in 1121, had provided the first Carthusian bishop in Pons II of Belley; this see for most of the remainder of the twelfth century had Carthusian bishops, chief among whom was the subsequently canonised Anthelme (1164-78) who had been prior of Chartreuse itself (1139-51) and then of Portes. Between 1130 and 1200 the see of Maurienne had three Carthusian bishops, as did Die; Geneva and Valence each had one. There were also archbishops: Arles received a Carthusian in 1137, Tarentaise in 1174, and Embrun in 1194.

Thus, by 1186 when Hugh of Avalon became bishop of Lincoln, the Carthusian bishop was a familiar figure in the provinces of the church that were adjacent to Chartreuse. One may doubt whether there was any derogation of *Cartusia nunquam reformata quia nunquam deformata*.[37] Without abandoning its original vision, Chartreuse found its place, as new developments in western monasticism have usually done, in the wider context of the church and of society. From the first, Bruno, the friend of

[34] The following details of Carthusian bishops are taken from Bligny, *L'Église*, pp. 310-15, and 'Les Chartreux', pp. 45-6.

[35] *Vita s. Hugonis*, 5.33, *PL* 153.784A.

[36] Upon Hugh II's departure in 1148, Noel, a Carthusian from Portes, was rejected as a candidate for the see of Grenoble on account of objections from Chartreuse itself.

[37] But cf. Bligny's opinion: 'Les Chartreux', p. 38. The Latin citation is, of course, of much later origin.

Pope Urban II, began the process tentatively and somewhat clumsily; especially when the Anacletan schism called so many in the newer orders of monks and canons to the support of Pope Innocent II, Prior Guigo I made it definitive and fruitful. In ideal through Guigo's Life of Bishop Hugh of Grenoble and in practice when Carthusian monks themselves accepted the episcopal office, the monk-bishop became a frequent and characteristic means of Carthusian influence.

II

Hugh of Avalon's own progress from the community of Chartreuse to the see of Lincoln was thus well prepared within the development of the Carthusian order. Hugh's novice-master's prediction that 'now you will become a priest and afterwards, in God's good time, a bishop', and Adam of Eynsham's observation that by his austerities at Chartreuse 'he was being prepared by God for the highest grade of priesthood [that is, the episcopate]', have the ring of *ex eventu* wisdom; yet they are not in-congruous with the outlook at Chartreuse.[38] His eventual monastic office of procurator, with charge of the lower house of the *conversi* and consequent administrative duties that led Guigo I to describe the procurator as the Martha of the Carthusian community, was also a preparation for a more active life.[39]

Hugh's coming to England was facilitated politically by England's place in the Angevin Empire of King Henry II (1154-89), to whose cousin Henry of Blois, bishop of Winchester (1129-71) Chartreuse accorded exceptional liturgical benefits.[40] Henry II's Empire extended so far to the south-east as the county of Auvergne, and in 1172-3 he was negotiating an abortive marriage settlement for his youngest son John with Count Humbert of Maurienne. His interests thus embraced Burgundy and its vicinity. In the 1160s, his quarrel with Archbishop Thomas Becket brought about contacts between the Carthusians and adherents of both parties. They included the dispatch from Chartreuse in 1167 of a reproving letter to the king, and in 1168 Prior Basil of Chartreuse and his predecessor in office Anthelme, now bishop of Belley, visited Henry in France as bearers of a papal letter.[41] According to an unconfirmed Carthusian tradition, Henry's foundation c.1178/9 of the first English Charterhouse at Witham (Somerset) was part of his commutation of a vow of pilgrimage to the

---

[38] *Magna vita s. Hugonis*, 1.11-12, cf. 2.3-4, vol.1.36-7, 54-7.
[39] *Ibid.*, 1.14, vol.1.41-4. For the procurator's duties, *Coutumes*, caps. 16, 18, pp.200-5.
[40] *Recueil*, no.24, pp.67-9; cf. the decree of the Carthusian general chapter of 1156: *PL* 153.1128D-1129A.
[41] *Materials for the History of Thomas Becket*, edd. J.C.Robertson and J.B. Sheppard (7 vols., London: Rolls Series, 67, 1875-85), 6, nos.289, 404, 424, pp.165-6, 394-6, 438-40. See also H.E.J.Cowdrey, 'The Carthusians in England', *Colloque*, pp.345-56.

Holy Land that he made after Becket's murder.[42]

The king himself brought about Hugh's coming to England after the first two priors had proved themselves unequal to the task of setting up the new priory. Henry, who crossed to the continent in mid-1180, there questioned an unnamed *nobilis* from Maurienne about the Carthusians, and received the advice that their procurator Hugh was the only man for the task. He thereupon sent to Chartreuse an embassy headed by Reginald, bishop of Bath, in whose diocese Witham was situated; with Bishop John of Grenoble's strong support he procured Hugh's dispatch.[43] During the next six years or so, Hugh, whom Adam of Eynsham described as Witham's *fundator et institutor*,[44] resolved successfully the problem that had defeated his two predecessors, by establishing Witham's exclusive patrimony within inviolable boundaries. Backed by the king's authority, he offered the peasantry who must be displaced the alternative of receiving lands and habitations comparable with those that they must vacate upon royal manors of their choice, or of emancipation from villeinage; they also received from the king financial compensation for the loss of their homes. The contact with Hugh that was involved in establishing Witham led Henry to adopt him as his especial spiritual counsellor. A belief that Hugh's intercessions saved him from shipwreck reputedly made Henry determined to endeavour to make him a bishop.[45]

Thus Hugh came to the English episcopate. His work as bishop of Lincoln is most fully set out by Adam, monk of Eynsham, who was his chaplain and companion during the last three years of his life. Adam referred to Bishop Hugh I of Grenoble as Hugh of Lincoln's model only once, when he spoke of him as 'the inheritor alike of [Hugh of Grenoble's] name and of his sanctity'.[46] But his principal model was his patron St Martin (c.316-97), whose Life by Sulpicius Severus depicted an ecclesiastical cursus from life as a solitary monk to being abbot of Ligugé and eventually bishop of Tours. St Martin was one of the most powerful influences upon French monasticism during the middle ages and upon conceptions of the monk's place in the episcopate; Hugh of Lincoln saw in him, above all others, a pattern to adopt and imitate.[47]

But literary models were less important for Hugh of Avalon as Adam of Eynsham presents him than the traditions of Chartreuse. His own

[42] C. le Couteulx, *Annales ordinis Cartusiensis ab anno 1084 ad annum 1429*, 2 (Montreuil-sur-Mer, 1888), 449-52.

[43] *Magna vita s. Hugonis*, 2.1-4, vol.1.46-60. Bishop Reynald of Bath had been consecrated in 1174 at Maurienne by Archbishops Richard of Canterbury and Peter of Tarentaise.

[44] *Ibid.*, 1, Prol., vol.1.3.

[45] Hugh's years as prior of Witham are the subject of Adam of Eynsham's second book: *ibid.*, vol.1.45-89.

[46] *Ibid.*, 4.9, vol.2.43-4; but for Hugh's own use of Guigo's Life, see 4.12, vol.2.55.

[47] For references to St Martin, see *ibid.*, 1.7, 4.9, 5.17, 19, vol.1.24, vol.2.43, 199-206, 217, 219, 223-4. The Lives of Martin and Hugh of Grenoble appear together in Lincoln Cathedral MS 107 which may be associated with Hugh of Lincoln: R. M. Woolley, *Catalogue of the Manuscripts of Lincoln Cathedral Chapter Library* (Oxford, 1927), pp.70-1.

commitment to Chartreuse was always strong. He accepted the see of Lincoln only under obedience from its prior, Jancelin;[48] he never ceased to wish to return there, and in 1200 he paid a final, memorable visit.[49] Whenever possible he returned to Witham once or twice a year and shared its life to the full; indeed, he seems to have retained formal authority over it until the end of his life.[50] In his everyday conduct he is reminiscent of Guigo I's admonition to Cardinal Haimeric that churchmen should not borrow kings' greed, delicacy, and pride, for he maintained a Carthusian life-style so far as he could; like Bishop Hugh of Grenoble he kept careful custody of his senses.[51]

By his references to Bishop Hugh of Grenoble's travels with Hugh of Die and to his favour with Pope Gregory VII, Guigo I had established the freeing of churches from lay lordship and jurisdiction as a due part of a bishop's activities. In his dealings with the Angevin kings of England, Hugh of Lincoln strongly asserted it. In 1186 he would not accept the see of Lincoln otherwise than by free election. Throughout his episcopate he championed the freedom of the church in all its forms: 'God forbid,' he once exclaimed, 'that ecclesiastical liberties and privileges should be infringed by decree of any layman!'[52]

Like Hugh of Grenoble, Hugh of Lincoln was also conspicuous for his performance of external good works, for which his duties as procurator at Chartreuse had in some measure prepared him.[53] Adam of Eynsham made much of his assiduousness in ministering to children and in performing confirmations and burials, and he took especial care for lepers and for the sick.[54] He was deeply concerned for the reform of clerical morals and for the edification and instruction of his clergy, both in his cathedral and throughout his diocese.[55] He defended the vulnerable against the rapacity of his own archdeacons and rural deans no less than that of the king's foresters.[56] He was a distinguished papal judge-delegate;[57] yet, just as Guigo I in his letter to Cardinal Haimeric was deeply critical of standards in the papal entourage, so Hugh warned Archbishop Baldwin of Canterbury against recourse to Rome: 'You will be exposed to the pride and aggravation of the Roman curia,' he said, 'and to the host of high and mighty

[48] *Magna vita s. Hugonis*, 3.3-5, vol. 1.98-102.
[49] *Ibid.*, 4.5, 5.13, 14, vol. 2.99, 149, 164-7.
[50] *Ibid.*, 4.9, 10-14, vol. 2.44-5, 49-73. See also A. Wilmart, 'Maître Adam, chanoine Prémontré devenu Chartreux à Witham', *Analecta Praemonstratensia*, 9 (1933), fasc. 3-4, 209-32, at p. 231.
[51] *Magna vita s. Hugonis*, 3.5, 13, 5.16, vol. 1.102-3, 125-7, vol. 2, 195-7.
[52] Lincoln: *ibid.*, 3.1-3, vol. 1.92-8. Freedom of the church: *ibid.*, 2.7, 3.9, 4.7-8, vol. 1.71-2, 114-15, vol. 2.34-7, 39-41.
[53] *Ibid.*, 1.14, vol. 1.41-4.
[54] Children: *ibid.*, 3.14, vol. 1.129-33. Confirmations: *ibid.*, 1.13, vol. 1.127-8. Burials: *ibid.*, 5.1-2, vol. 2.75-85. Lepers and the sick: *ibid.*, 4.3, vol. 2.11-15.
[55] *Ibid.*, 3.11, 5.5, vol. 1.119-21, vol. 2.95-8.
[56] Archdeacons and rural deans: *ibid.*, 4.7, vol. 2.37-8. Foresters: *ibid.*, 3.9, 4.5-6, vol. 1.114, vol. 2.26-8.
[57] *Ibid.*, 3.12, 5.13, vol. 1.121-3, vol. 2.149-52.

men who are to be found there.'[58] Deeply though Hugh venerated Thomas Becket as a martyr, he deprecated his practice during his lifetime of taking monetary fines from spiritual offenders.[59] He reserved his sharpest criticisms for the Angevin kings and their ministers, earning himself the sobriquet 'hammer of kings (*regum malleus*)'.[60] While still prior of Witham he admonished Henry II about the conduct of episcopal and abbatial elections. Throughout his episcopate he spared no words in rebuking Henry's sons Richard I and John, as well as their ministers, amongst whom he especially took to task Archbishop Hubert Walter who was for long the royal justiciar. Hugh was particularly insistent in refusing to provide Richard I with military service beyond the shores of England from the resources of the see of Lincoln.[61] One recalls the strictures of the future Carthusian, Count Gerard of Nevers, upon the court and the Crusading plans of King Louis VII of France. Overall, Hugh's manner of life and his public attitudes and activities as bishop of Lincoln were well grounded in the Carthusian tradition and ran true to it.

Yet Hugh was a bishop of such stature that, in the episcopal office, he was not constrained by that tradition, but was very much his own man. In this respect it would be wrong to eulogise him uncritically. There are sides to his episcopal activity that do not immediately commend themselves to the modern observer. Two examples are his use of his powers of anathema and his conduct as a collector of relics. Adam of Eynsham gloried in how many men and women 'he gave over to a wretched death by the power of his excommunication alone', and how, by contrast with the sanctions deployed by less saintly bishops, the mere threat deterred royal officers from seizing his goods because they dreaded it as quite literally a death sentence. But it was not only the over-mighty whom it struck down. Even an adulterous Oxford girl of burgess origins suffered death for her disobedience:

'As you have refused my blessing and have preferred my curse [said Hugh to her], lo! my curse will seize you.' She went home still defiant, and during the few days that God allowed her for coming to a better mind, her heart became more hardened and impenitent. She was smothered by the devil, and suddenly exchanged her illicit and perishable delights for eternal and just torments.[62]

If Hugh's use of his anathema may seem excessive and vindictive, his zeal in collecting relics was greedy and even deceitful. Thus, when he visited the abbey of Fécamp which possessed a relic of St Mary Magdalen's armbone, he was not allowed to see the relic itself. So he took a knife from one of his notaries, cut the thread that bound it, and himself undid its wrappings. After contemplating it and kissing it he tried to prise a piece

[58] *Ibid.*, 3.12, vol.1.122.
[59] *Ibid.*, 4.7, vol.2.38.
[60] *Ibid.*, 2.4, 5.20, vol.1.56, vol.2.231-2.
[61] Henry II: *ibid.*, 2.7-8, 3.9-10, vol.1.68-74, 114-19. Richard I: *ibid.*, 5.1, 5-6, vol.2.78-9, 98-106. John: *ibid.*, 5.11, 16, 19, vol.2.137-44, 188, 225. Hubert Walter: *ibid.*, 3.12, 5.5, 7, 16, vol.1.123, vol.2.98-100, 110-14, 188-9.
[62] *Ibid.*, 4.4-6, vol.2.19-33.

off for himself with his fingers, but unsuccessfully. So he bit it, first with his front teeth and then with his back ones, breaking off two fragments which he handed to Adam of Eynsham. The abbot and monks were beside themselves: 'What an outrage!' they exclaimed; 'we supposed that the bishop asked to see this relic out of devotion, but look! he has gnawed it with his teeth like a dog!' To calm them, Hugh observed that he had not long before handled the body of the Lord of the saints with his fingers and bitten it with his teeth; for his welfare, why should he not similarly treat the bones of the saints and, when he had a chance, acquire them?[63] In such respects, Hugh was, perhaps, all too much a child of his day and age.

But not in other, far more important respects, in which he rose far above them. He did so because he understood with exceptional clarity that to different men and women, different modes of the Christian life are appropriate. Hermits and monks, clergy and laity, have their several and very different callings. The very austerity of Hugh's Carthusian background, which he well knew that only rare individuals could support, made him aware of this truth, as St Bernard, for example, seems never to have understood it. An elderly Carthusian had put the point of the Carthusians' exceptional vocation to him in unforgettable words when, still a young regular canon, he had first sought admission to Chartreuse. 'My dear boy,' he had said, 'how can you ever think of coming here? The men you see inhabiting these rocks are harder than any stones; they take pity neither upon themselves nor upon those who live with them. This place is dreadful to look at, but our way of life is harder by far. ... The rigour of our discipline would crush the bones of one so tender as you seem.'[64] Hugh never forgot that the Carthusian life is for the very few who are personally fitted to receive it, and that it is not a model even for most monks to copy. Thus, when an abbot went beyond the Rule of St Benedict in compelling his monks to abstain from meat, Hugh was far from praising his zeal; instead, he warned him of the danger of hypocrisy and scrupulosity, saying,

> I do not eat meat, not because of my own judgement, but because that is the decree of the order to which long ago I made myself subject. It has so very few members, because it was not designed for a lot of people, all of them made differently. You, however, have been set over a large community; as your Founder decreed you must take account of many different sorts of men and condescend to many kinds of weakness and human need.[65]

Because Hugh knew exactly where he himself stood as a Carthusian, he could perceive clearly the roles and duties of other kinds of people, and point them out with firmness and charity.

Hugh's perceptiveness, and the maturity and confidence to which it conduced, enabled him, in sharp contrast to Thomas Becket, resolutely to

[63] Hugh and relics: *ibid.*, 5.13, 14, vol. 2.153-4, 167-73.
[64] *Ibid.*, 1.7, vol. 1.23-4.
[65] *Ibid.*, 5.16, vol. 2.196-7; cf. Rule of St Benedict, cap. 2.

defend what contemporary reformers understood by the liberty of the church, and to act as a *regum malleus* in reproving kings, without ever sacrificing his personal relationship with them – even so difficult a line as the Angevins of his time. His sureness of pastoral touch was early manifest in his handling of Henry II, when the king was offended by his refusal, couched in terms reminiscent of Prior Guigo I's letter to Cardinal Haimeric, to collate a royal nominee to a prebend of Lincoln cathedral. 'Ecclesiastical benefices,' Hugh said, 'should not be conferred upon courtiers but upon ecclesiastics, and their holders should not serve the court (*palatium*) or treasury or exchequer but, as Scripture teaches, the altar.' When the king sulked publicly and called for a needle and thread to play at repairing a finger-stall that he was wearing, Hugh impudently mocked him: 'How like you are to your Falaise cousins!' Henry himself explained to his courtiers Hugh's allusion to his own great-great-grandfather William the Conqueror's being the bastard of a supposedly leather-working family at Falaise. Relishing the joke, he came round to Hugh's point of view.[66] Again, Hugh shrewdly made use of the kiss of peace at mass to be reconciled to Richard I after his refusal of overseas military service.[67] Although Hugh fruitlessly drew attention to the sculpture of the Last Judgement over the porch at the abbey of Fontevraud to warn John of his sins, John visited him on his deathbed and at his funeral carried his coffin.[58] Hugh was exceptional in maintaining the highest standards of the episcopal office under such kings, and yet in preserving his friendship with them.

He rose no less far above the generality of his contemporaries in his attitude to women. He differed even from Carthusian tradition. Not only were women rigorously excluded from the *termini* of Chartreuse but, in his Customs, Guigo I drew upon many Old Testament examples to drive home how hard it was to escape their flatteries and deceits. His exemplary bishop, Hugh of Grenoble, always ministered faithfully to them, but only once did he allow his eyes to settle upon a woman's face, and then for an urgent pastoral reason.[69] Hugh, on the other hand, had a profound regard and care for women. He did not hesitate to follow the general custom of bishops by occasionally admitting matrons and widows to eat at his table. His regard for women was based upon his understanding of Christ's Incarnation. 'Almighty God,' he used to say to them, 'well deserves to have women love him, for he did not disdain to be born of a woman. He thereby conferred a splendid and truly fitting privilege upon all women. For to no man was it granted to be, or to be called, the father of God; but a woman was allowed to become the mother of God.'[70]

Above all, Hugh exhibited his personal stature and uniqueness by the

[66] *Magna vita s. Hugonis*, 3.9-10, vol.1.114-19. Cf. E.M.C. van Houts, 'The Origins of Herleva, Mother of William the Conqueror', *English Historical Review*, 101 (1986), 399-404.

[67] *Magna vita s. Hugonis*, 5.5, vol.2.100-02.

[68] *Ibid.*, 5.11, 16, 19, vol.2.138-44, 188, 225.

[69] *Coutumes*, cap. 21.1-2, p.210; *Vita s. Hugonis*, 4.15, PL 153.772-3.

[70] *Magna vita s. Hugonis*, 4.9, vol.2.48.

high value that he set upon the life and witness of ordinary lay Christians. He was far from holding the conventional view, that only a few would be saved, and most of them would be monks. When lay persons praised his own Carthusian style of life and conventionally deplored the hindrances of life in the world, so long as he knew them to have no calling to the monastic life he would assure them of the sufficiency for salvation of their own state:

> Monks, not to mention hermits and anchorites [he used to say to them] will not be the only ones to inherit the kingdom of God. When God comes in judgement upon every man, he will upbraid no one for not being a hermit or a monk; but he will dismiss from himself those who have not been true Christians. Three things are required of every Christian; if one of them is lacking when he meets his judgement, the mere name of Christian will not help him. No, rather, the name without the practice will do him harm, because falsehood is all the more blameworthy in one who makes profession of the truth. A man must bear Christ's blessed name both in fact and in truth; therefore the true Christian carries love in his heart, truth on his lips, and chastity in his body.

And so married people, even though they never changed their state for a single life, had the virtue of chastity and would share an equal heavenly reward with virgins and celibates. In recording this teaching, Adam of Eynsham added that Hugh was no less adept in explaining the Christian life to simple folk than to the learned.[71]

Hugh of Avalon was one of those rare individuals whose personal qualities raise them above whatever background or environment, however admirable, that they may have had. Nevertheless, the foundation of his episcopate was always his Carthusian life and training, and he manifested and built upon its best characteristics of spiritual and human wisdom. For the historian, his significance is, perhaps, threefold. First, he is the supreme example in Angevin England of a model diocesan bishop, ruling his diocese, shepherding all its people, and discharging a bishop's national role resolutely but acceptably to kings and magnates even when he most strenuously reproved them. Secondly, his conduct as a bishop warrants the conclusion that the relationship which the Carthusians from the first began to form with the wider church and world did not contradict or detract from their primary call to the eremitical life; it was a proper and authentic complement to it. Thirdly, Hugh of Avalon, as champion of the liberty of the church and of its moral reform, must be understood within the long sequence of Carthusian links with the episcopate which began with the paradigm figure of Bishop Hugh I of Grenoble, who was himself the favoured disciple of Pope Gregory VII. Tangible links between Gregory and the twelfth century are remarkably few and difficult to observe. Hugh of Avalon, Carthusian and bishop, stands within a living

---

[71] *Ibid.*, 4.9, vol. 2.46-7.

tradition of episcopal spirituality and activity that Gregory was concerned to foster. He continued it until Pope Innocent III, the most effective of all the medieval reforming popes, had ascended the papal throne.

LOVE OF THE WORLD
IN THE *MEDITATIONS* OF GUIGO I

Rev. Gordon Mursell

The *Meditations* of Guigo I, fifth prior of the Grande Chartreuse, have been the subject of much critical interest in recent years, principally as a result of the new edition by Dom Maurice Laporte published as *Sources Chrétiennes* volume 308 (1983), and of the translation and (I hope) forthcoming commentary by Gaston Hocquard published as *Analecta Cartusiana* volume 112 (1984). The attribution of this early twelfth-century text to Guigo is not now seriously in doubt: quite apart from the manuscript history, the similarities in style and content with later writings of Guigo (notably the *Consuetudines Cartusiae* and the *Life* of St Hugh of Grenoble) incontestably point to the same author. Internal evidence suggests a date of c.1115 for the *Meditations*: Guigo would then have been in his early thirties, and had been prior for about six years. As a work of medieval literature, the *Meditations* are unique, which is to say that I know of no other contemporary (or even remotely contemporary) text that is at all similar. The text forms a kind of spiritual journal, combining moral and theological comment with reflection on Guigo's own experience of exceptional acuteness. No one has yet challenged André Wilmart's contention that this text is a masterpiece entirely worthy of comparison with the *Pensées* of Pascal.

Various interpretative hypotheses have been advanced about the central themes of the *Meditations*, and about the extent to which it is legitimate to claim a measure of internal and thematic coherence for a work of this nature. It is the argument of this brief paper that there exists in the *Meditations* a coherent and substantive theology of love which not only underpins the text as a whole, but which is itself the theological basis for the Carthusian life as it was to be described in the *Consuetudines* and advertised (so to speak) in the *Life* of St Hugh. The intention of this paper is simply to outline the main ingredients of this theology, and then to explore briefly their implications for Guigo's view of the world.

The theology of love is grounded in a view of creation as constituting a threefold order, a view which is most fully adumbrated in the final series of *Meditations* (numbers 464-76 in Wilmart's numbering). In Guigo's anthropology, man is the midpoint in creation; above him is God and below him is the world. What is original is not the schema itself, but its application: Guigo writes

The true perfection of a rational creature is to value each thing as it should be valued. However, it must be valued at its true worth, because to assess it at more or less than that is wrong. [M 466]

Happiness, or fulfilment, then, is attainable by means of a proper understanding and love of the threefold order (the indissolubility of love and knowledge is very important). By apprehending man's true place as the midpoint of this order, human beings are free to respond to each of the three levels of that order as they should: God alone is to be loved as an end, disinterestedly and unconditionally; other people can then be loved in a manner that seeks their true good, and without the need to seek dependence on them, or praise from them; and the world can then be used as a means, not an end – or, as Guigo puts it, can be 'brought back' for the 'well-being' of humanity and to the 'honour' of God [M 471].

This analysis is rendered most explicit in *Meditation* 471, where Guigo explains with characteristic economy and precision the implications of his theology:

> Therefore, such a person will have the higher things as his delight, the equal things as his companions, the lower things as his servants. He will be devoted to God, kind to his neighbour, temperate to the world. He will be the servant of God, the companion of man, the lord of the world ... He will take nothing from the lower, nothing from his equals, but everything from the higher things: marked with the imprint of the higher, he will mark the lower with his own imprint; moved by the higher, he will move the lower; swayed by the higher, he will sway the lower; following the higher, he will draw the lower; possessed by the former, he will possess the latter; brought by the former back into their likeness, he will bring the latter back into his.

Man's proper attitude to creation and to Creator is analysed here by means of a series of precise relations. By finding his delight in God, man is able to keep company with his neighbour, and to be served by the world. By being devoted to God, man can be kind to his neighbour and temperate in his attitude to the world. By being the servant of God, man can be the companion of his neighbour and the lord of the world; and by discovering himself to be set beneath God, he can be free from arrogance towards his neighbour and from subjection to the world. The two sins consequent upon a failure to apprehend the threefold order are thus arrogance (setting himself above his neighbour), and enslavement (setting himself beneath the world, or setting the world in God's place). Elsewhere in the *Meditations*, Guigo reflects on the dangers of this enslavement, or idolatry, which is in effect the simple but total reversal of the threefold order inasmuch as it entails the worship of something that should be beneath us. Guigo suggests a simple test whereby we may avert this peril:

> Try having a conversation with the things you delight in – if you can. And, if you can't, be ashamed of yourself, you idolater!

So finding your joy, or delight, in things of the world is disordered love, precisely because it upturns the threefold order and distorts man's relationship with God and with his neighbour. Enslavement to the world therefore diminishes man's true vocation, as Psalm 49 puts it:

> In his riches, man lacks wisdom:
> he is like the beasts that are destroyed. [Ps 49:13]

We might now return to *Meditation* 471. If man apprehends correctly his true place in the threefold order, he is free to relate to the world in the only manner that is appropriate: free to 'bring the world back', 'restore' it (the Latin verb here is 'redigere') to the good of his neighbour and the honour of God. But he can only do that if he learns first to receive everything from God. There is a grammatical point of great significance in the concluding section of *Meditation* 471: in each of the sets of attributes, man is in the active mode with respect to the world and the passive with respect to God. This passivity, or receptiveness, before God alone allows man to be creatively active towards the world ...

> ... marked with the imprint of the higher, he will mark the lower with his; moved by the higher, he will move the lower, &c.

The two principal sins mentioned above are the inversion of this: arrogance implies activity towards God, and enslavement or idolatry implies passivity towards the world. Guigo nowhere makes the connection explicit, but he may have had in mind here the identification of the ascetic monk with the passivity, or passion, of Christ, by which alone the world is redeemed.

What, then, is implied by 'restoring' the world to man's good, and by 'activity' towards the world in this context? It should first be made clear that this in no sense suggests a dilution of monastic asceticism. Some of the *Meditations* reflect Guigo's own uncompromising attitude to the perils of worldly delights:

> Consider how much easier is the way to life through unpleasant things than through pleasant ones. For it is easier to curb lust and other vices when nothing beautiful or seductive has come your way. [M 9]

Guigo elsewhere contrasts love of God with false love of the world:

> God has commanded man to love something that he can never love too much. Man, on the contrary, loves above all else something that he can never, or scarcely ever, love too little. [M 277]

Man's preference for things of the world reflects his lack of trust in God, his reluctance to give himself unconditionally to him. But it also reflects his inability properly to love others:

> It is one thing for us to love something because we need it, so that through it we may be either good or happy – such as loving God; it is quite another to love it because we are good, and not because we need it – such as loving man. For we love man as people who wish him well. Nevertheless, a person is not really good or happy if he is

not good to others. For a misery that is born from separation from God and love for this fleeting song that is the world is what makes us bad to others. [M 239]

This a vital point: an ascetic approach to the world, properly understood, does not cut us off from our neighbour – on the contrary, it frees us from a false dependence in order to love him as we should. In turn, as Guigo elsewhere points out, this frees our neighbour from a false dependence on us. It is therefore not surprising that Guigo, following Ezekiel and Hosea, uses the imagery of adultery to illustrate the dangers of worldly enslavement:

What woman is impudent enough to say to her husband: 'Find me some man for me to sleep with, who attracts me more than you – and, if you don't, I won't give you any peace'? Yet this is the way you treat your husband – in other words, the Lord himself – when, loving something else more than him, you ask that very thing from him. [M 241]

Idolatry is a subtle sin: people will never admit that they do not love what is good for them. Guigo observes that, if you tell an idolater he is not worshipping God, he will at once leap up and swear that he does [M 369]. Indeed there is an even more subtle form of it: when people love you for your own sake, instead of for God's sake, they are committing a form of idolatry; and they deserve the same thanks as fleas do [M 326]. Love of the world, then, is in reality not love at all – and freedom to indulge in transient delights is in reality not freedom but servitude. We might finally consider what this means in practice.

Guigo expresses at two points an appropriate 'activity', or attitude, towards the world:

The greatest value of physical bodies is in their use as signs. For many signs that are necessary for our salvation come from them, such as voices from breath, crosses from wood, baptism from water. Moreover, souls only know each other's feelings by means of physical signs. [M 308]

Bear in mind the different ways of recognising God by reflecting on created things: through established signs, like crosses, words, and so on; and through natural signs, like the way a person's face suddenly blushes or goes pale, and so on. Some of these signs are of physical things, some of spiritual ones. [M 373]

To approach the world in this way is to discover its true value, its usefulness, without becoming enslaved to it. The *Meditations* abound with references to some of the most prosaic and earthy things of the world Guigo has renounced, precisely because he has renounced it, for that alone sets him free to discern their true worth. Here are a few brief examples:

Since nothing could be closer to any particular object than itself, and nothing more readily at hand, it is utterly astonishing that the human soul should be able to know something else better and more intimately than itself. For if someone holds a knife, or some other object, in his hand, and then starts looking for it, he undoubtedly makes everyone watching him laugh. But what is so immediately at hand to the soul as itself? What can it know better, then, than itself. Or, for that matter, how can it know anything at all, if it doesn't know itself? [M437]

While a beetle is flying round looking at everything, it doesn't pick on anything beautiful or wholesome or durable, but immediately settles down on any foul-smelling dung that might be lying around, rejecting so many lovely things.
In the same way, your soul flits around, glancing at heaven and earth and all that is great and precious within them; but it doesn't attach itself to any of these things: despising them all, it gladly embraces all kinds of shoddy and sordid things that come into its thoughts. You should be ashamed of yourself at this. [M 440]

You love foul-smelling goats for their milk, bees for their honey and wax, the dregs of olives for their oil, bunches of grapes for their wine, manure for wheat. So when you love God for the sake of temporal things, you look upon him as a goat, a bee, olive dregs, bunches of grapes, and manure ... [M 414]

Both ordinary things, and ordinary experiences, become parables or signposts for moral or theological reflection. In one of the most famous passages, Guigo recalls his behaviour during one of the monastic offices:

Notice how, when you recently tripped up in front of the brethren by saying one antiphon instead of another, your mind tried to think of a way of putting the blame on something else – either on the book itself, or on some other thing. For your heart was reluctant to see itself as it really is, and so it pretended to itself that it was different, inclining itself to evil words to excuse its sin. The Lord will reprove you, and set before you what you have done; you won't be able to hide from yourself any longer, or to escape from yourself. [M 282]

And it is the Lord, the incarnate life of Christ, who forms the central foundation of Guigo's theology of love. Because we were so blind that we could not see, let alone respond to, the truth of the threefold order and of our place within it, the eternal Word was made flesh, so that through the same flesh the Word might 'teach, accomplish and endure' whatever was necessary to instruct and correct mankind. In Christ alone are found to perfection the attributes already outlined: Jesus was unconditionally devoted to God, loving nothing even remotely as much as him, and setting nothing as his equal. By so doing he was able to love his neighbour perfectly, directing everything towards his neighbour's good ('omnia ad utilitatem proximi convertit', M 475), even to the extent of enduring the implications of such love on every level of physical existence – which include, ultimately, death itself. But towards the things of the world

Jesus's attitude was sternly ascetic: 'Towards the world, however, he showed such moderation and such great contempt that the Son of man had nowhere to lay his head.' [*ibid.*]

Christ is thus our exemplar, but he is also more than that: he is, so to speak, perfect human nature, incarnating in his life, death and teaching the essence of the human vocation. What he did by virtue of his intimate personal union with God, we are now able to do by virtue of the sacraments, the teaching, and the example through which his incarnate life is present to us now. And to do this will mean living as he did, or, more precisely, conforming ourselves to the likeness of God as it is revealed to us in the Word made flesh. This process of conformity is a process at once of understanding and of love: without understanding, and appropriating for ourselves, the threefold order and the place and vocation of man within it, our love will be wrongly directed, and we will succumb either to pride or to lust. But without love our understanding will be empty and speculative cerebration.

This attitude to the world can best be summarised and illustrated by reference to a particularly significant word in Guigo's writings: 'utilitas'. The word means much more than the English 'usefulness', and is perhaps closer to other Latin words relating to 'the good', such as 'prosum' or 'expedire'. Above all, though, it reflects this theologically coherent relationship between the different parts of the threefold order, from which all Guigo's thought derives. The word is used in all of Guigo's works, and in a wide variety of contexts, but it illustrates that interweaving of the eternal and the earthly that is the fruit of a true apprehension of the threefold order whereby man is free to seek only his, and other people's, good. Thus Guigo writes:

> ... only someone who loves God wishes for or loves what is good for him (vult aut diligit utilitatem suam). For God alone is the entire and only good of human nature (tota et sola utilitas est humanae naturae) [M 370]

Elsewhere in the *Meditations*, Guigo tells himself to aspire to being a 'utilis socius', not an arrogant master. 'Your natural place is to be a good companion and friend of people, not a proud master. You should therefore do everything with companionable love, not with overbearing arrogance.' [M 150] In his much later *Life* of St Hugh of Grenoble, in which in my view Guigo presents to the world a model of how this theology of love can direct the life of a Christian bishop 'in the world', Guigo describes the elderly bishop as seeking permission to resign and be replaced by a 'utilior' pastor in Grenoble [*Vita* 25]; and in the *Consuetudines* Guigo writes

> From Easter until the feast of St Michael, they [the lay brothers] may not use their slippers between Prime and Compline. Furthermore, at the dormitory in the upper house, they have beds, skins, and slippers for common use. In all such questions nothing matters other than to protect them from the cold and keep them covered. For they

have shoelaces and belts made of crude hemp, and even their under-clothing is made of hemp. Thus everything is conceived according to the demands, not of vanity or pleasure, but only of necessity or 'utilitas'. [CC 57:3]

Guigo's attitude to the world in the *Meditations*, then, is one of stern and uncompromising asceticism, as might be expected; but it is a means to an end, and can only be seen as part of a larger view when its theological context is made clear. The renunciation of worldly motives sets man free to enjoy God alone, and thus to love man without seeking dependence, or domination – that is, to love man as he should be loved, as God loves him. The process may be put the other way round: by seeking to enjoy God, man discovers freedom to love his neighbour and the world as they should be loved. He is free from the need to seek his happiness or salvation through them, which would only result in enslavement to them; and this alone enables him to love them in a way which is conducive to their good as well as to his. This is not to imply (as I myself first thought) that Guigo has a 'high' doctrine of the created order and its worth. But it is to imply that 'the world', and even our most banal experiences within it, can be conducive to man's good provided he has renounced any kind of enslave-ment to it. Then the monk becomes a part of the redeeming work of Christ: he can, as Guigo puts it, 'restore the world [the lower things] for the well-being of the middle things [man] and the honour of the higher ones [God]' [M 471]. Guigo's theology is very close to the famous text from St Paul's second Letter to the Corinthians – 'poor ourselves, we bring wealth to many; penniless, we own the world' [2 Cor. 6:10]; and it is surely this paradox which Guigo has in mind in his own characteristically pithy summary of the Carthusian's true vocation: to be 'the servant of God, the companion of man, the lord of the world' [M 471].[1]

---

[1] For a much fuller analysis of the theology of the *Meditations* of Guigo, see G. Mursell, *The Theology of the Carthusian Life*, Analecta Cartusiana (Salzburg, 1988).

ADAM THE CARTHUSIAN'S
DE QUADRIPARTITO EXERCITIO CELLAE

James Hogg

Dom David Knowles in his magisterial survey, *The Monastic Order in England*,[1] rated the *De Quadripartito exercitio cellae*, as one of the most influential witnesses of early Carthusian life and spirituality, adding that it enjoyed a 'considerable vogue in medieval charterhouses at home and abroad'. At roughly the same period Sister Bruno Barrier constructed her study *Les activités du solitaire en Chartreuse d'après ses plus anciens témoins*[2] around Adam's treatise. Over the centuries, however, it does not seem to have been popular even within the Order itself. Thus when Dom Sebastian Maccabe, under the pseudonym of 'A Monk of Parkminster', published an abridged translation of it under the title *Eden's Fourfold River*[3] he was totally unaware of who the real author was, though he correctly dated it c.1200. There was, therefore, no living tradition in the English charterhouse on which he could draw identifying the author as Adam of Dryburgh, former Premonstratensian abbot of the Scottish Border abbey of that name, a spiritual writer immersed in the Scriptures,[4]

[1] Cambridge, 1950, p.384.
[2] Analecta Cartusiana 87 (1981).
[3] London, 1927.
[4] For a fairly complete list of his works and a useful bibliography on him cf. James Bulloch, *Adam of Dryburgh* (London, 1958), pp.172-177. The most significant studies are: N.J.Weyns, *Het Premonstratenser Kloosterleven volgens Adam van Dryburgh* (Tongerloo, 1948), and F.Petit's introduction to his edition of *Ad viros religiosos (Quatorze sermons d'Adam Scot)* (Tongerloo, 1934). In 1974 M.J.Hamilton published *Adam of Dryburgh: Six Christmas Sermons*, Analecta Cartusiana 16. He receives a notice in all reference works, and Dom J.Leclercq, Dom F.Vandenbroucke and Louis Bouyer assess his significance in *La Spiritualité du Moyen Age* (Paris, 1961), p.186: 'Tous ces écrits ne sont point d'égale qualité; on y relève des longueurs, et parfois un certain abus de l'allégorie. Dans l'ensemble, pourtant, très bon styliste, entièrement nourri de la Bible, très marqué par l'influence des Pères, surtout de saint Augustin et d'Origène, Adam Scot unit à une poésie intense, à une exquise sensibilité, une pensée ferme et précise au sujet de la vie canoniale et de la contemplation. Par sa doctrine et ses tendances profondes, que reflètent ses modes d'expression, il est plus proche de la tradition monastique, cistercienne ou bénédictine que de la scolastique.' The authors stress the solitary aspect of the life of the early Premonstratensians: 'Issue de la "crise du cénobitisme", elle est érémitique au sens que ce mot revêt souvent alors: il s'agit d'une vie en commun, mais menée dans la solitude, et également loin des villes; ... partout on insiste sur le recueillement, la solitude du coeur, le repos intérieur: ...' (p.187). They are less enthusiastic about his surviving Carthusian treatise: 'Adam

who became Adam the Carthusian of Witham, the friend of St Hugh of Lincoln, and the most significant spiritual writer the English Carthusian province produced, if *The Cloud of Unknowing* is not accepted as of Carthusian provenance.

For centuries the *De Quadripartito exercitio cellae* was attributed to Guigo II,[5] prior of the Grande Chartreuse 1174-1180, often referred to as Guigo the Angelic, author of the *Scala Claustralium*, a work which, to judge by the surviving manuscripts, must have enjoyed a considerable circulation in the Middle Ages and which has continued to be read right up to the twentieth century, and of a series of meditations. The most cursory examination of the *De Quadripartito exercitio cellae* shows clearly, however, that its style is very different to that of the works of Guigo and its preface indicates the circumstances of its composition – circumstances which would be difficult to reconcile with Guigo's supposed authorship. In any event, the attribution of Adam's treatise to Guigo II was tardive. We do not find it before the Jesuit Pierre-François Chifflet edited it for the first time in 1657 along with a collection of Carthusian spiritual texts under the title *Manuale solitariorum e veterum Patrum Cartusianorum cellis deprumptum*, published in Dijon Chavance. Chifflet had studied two manuscripts of the work, one from the charterhouse of Portes, now probably the Grenoble Bibliothèque municipale MS. 397, dating from the thirteenth century,[6] and another from the charterhouse of Parc.[7] The 1677 reprint at Lyons[8] accepted Chifflet's tentative attribution, as did Migne in the *Patrologia Latina* 153.[9] Dom Charles le Couteulx in his *Annales Ordinis*

Scot, devenu chartreux, rédigera, au début du XIIIe siècle, son dernier livre, intitulé: *Les quatre exercices de cellule*; il y déploie les qualités qui faisaient le prix de ses oeuvres de prémontré; mais il ne rend point tout à fait la même note de simplicité que ceux qui ont toujours vécu en solitude.' (p. 196) They also deny that he made any major contribution for the description of contemplative prayer: 'Adam Scot a poussé plus loin les distinctions en ce qui concerne la méditation: il en décrit huit espèces différentes, ce qui ne laisse pas d'être artificiel. Cependant, il s'est abstenu d'analyser avec une égale précision la contemplation elle-même. Il a surtout marqué que celle-ci demeure la fin des autres exercices; on trouve chez lui les éléments d'une doctrine de la "prière méthodique"; heureusement, il a perçu que la contemplation est au-delà de toute méthode.' (p. 201)
[5] Cf. Edmund Colledge and James Walsh, eds., *Guigues II le chartreux: Lettre sur la vie contemplative (L'Echelle des Moines), Douze méditations*, Sources Chrétiennes 163 (Paris, 1970).
[6] Some scholars wish to date it late twelfth century. This seems to me highly unlikely. The manuscript is heavily abbreviated.
[7] It has been generally assumed that the MS. from the charterhouse of Parc was lost in the aftermath of the French Revolution. François Petit, *Ad Viros Religiosos*, p. 52, n. 137, writes, however: '... Les manuscrits connus sont au Mans les numéros 8, 57, 109, 114, 353; Charleville 181; Trèves (Stadtbibliot.) 755.' It is interesting that he omits the Grenoble MS., which has been recorded by numerous scholars, but records no less than five manuscripts at Le Mans, that no one else has ever heard of. The Bibliothèque municipale at Le Mans was unable to throw any light on these manuscripts.
[8] It was contained in vol. 24 of a collection of ecclesiastical texts, col. 1463-1520.
[9] Col. 799-884.

Cartusiensis,[10] compiled late in the seventeenth century, knew no better, and the Abbé F. A. Lefevre[11] repeated the error at the end of the nineteenth century, as did the great Carthusian bibliographer, Dom Stanislas Autore, some years later,[12] even though Dom Ganneron long before had maintained that it was the product of an unidentified Carthusian in his *Antiquités de la Chartreuse du Mont Dieu*.[13]

It was thus left to Dom André Wilmart to resolve the question of the authorship of the treatise, but even he failed in his article 'Les écrits spirituels des deux Guigues'[14] printed in 1924, in which he rejected Guigo's authorship, but attributed the work to his successor as prior of the Grande Chartreuse, Jancelin, to whom currently Erika Bauer is trying to relate the so-called *Letters of St Jerome*.

More or less at the same moment E. Margaret Thompson[15] and Dom André Wilmart studied a text in the London British Library MS. Cotton Vespasian D. IX on f.167v, signed by the Carthusian scribe W. Mede, which has since been known as the Witham Chronicle Fragment.[16] This item not only presents an account of Adam's person and life, but also lists his works, including the *De Quadripartito exercitio cellae*:

DE MAGISTRO ADAM CARTVSIENSI

Si cui in uoto fuerit scire magister Adam cuius figure et habitudinis exstiterit, noverit eum fuisse statura mediocrem, iuxta mediocritatem stature satis corpulentem, facie hilarem, capite caluum, et tam pro uenustate morum quam pro etate et canicie ualde reuerendum.

Quia uero idem uenerabilis uir magister Adam, sacre scripture intelligencia non mediocriter effulsit, antequam Wytham aduenerit, plures tractatus diuine pagine edidit quos in duobus codicibus magnis compegit. Qui codices quia ea que in illis continentur in modum omeliarum digesta sunt, *sermonarii magistri Ade* appellantur. Plurima etiam opera in domo de Witham, ubi per uiginti pene quatuor annos monachus eiusdem ordinis uidelicet Cartusiensis sancte et humillime

[10]   3 (Montreuil-sur-Mer, 1887), p.129ff.
[11]   *Saint Bruno et l'Ordre des Chartreux* (Paris, 1883).
[12]   In his unpublished bibliographical collections and his influential articles in DTC II/2, col.2274-2318 (Chartreux) and VI/2, col.1966-1967 (Guigues II).
[13]   Dom Ganneron's study, edited by P. Laurent, was finally published in Paris in 1863. Cf. for the *De Quadripartito exercitio cellae* p.115.
[14]   RAM 5.
[15]   The text was first indicated by E. Margaret Thompson, *A History of the Somerset Carthusians* (London, 1895), pp.71, 73-74. It was again referred to by H. E. Allen, *Writings ascribed to Richard Rolle* (New York, 1927), p.237, but published in a defective transcript by E. Margaret Thompson, 'A Fragment of a Witham Chronicle and Adam of Dryburgh, Premonstratensian and Carthusian of Witham', *Bulletin of the John Rylands Library* 16 (Manchester, 1932). A more competent transcript appeared in Dom André Wilmart, 'Magister Adam Cartusiensis', *Mélanges Mandonnet* 2 (Paris, 1930), pp.145-161. Cf. also Dom André Wilmart, 'Maître Adam Chanoine Prémontré devenu Chartreux à Witham', *Analecta Premonstratensia* 9 (1932), 209-232.
[16]   Hugh Farmer proposed a new edition some years ago, but it does not seem to have been printed to date.

semper sub obediencia uixit, [opera] digne memoria commendanda elaborauit. Ex quibus est libellus *super canonem misse*. Iterum liber *de quatripertito exercicio celle*. Iterum *libellus super oracionem dominicam* ad Hucbertum archiepiscopum. Iterum libellus quem uocauit *speculum discipline*. Iterum libellus qui dicitur *dialogus magistri Ade*. Iterum libellus quem uocauit *Exameron*. <Iterum> libellus *de consanguinitate Anne matris beate Marie, et beate Elizabeth matris sancti Iohannis baptiste*. Iterum libellus qui dicitur *secretum meum michi*, et plura alia opera meritoria et scripta fecit et edidit que ad presens memorie mee minime occurrunt.

Sub priore de Wytham nomine Alberto uiri preclarissimi quatuor conuenerunt, quorum primus fuit magister Adam, qu(on)dam abbas ordinis Premonstrensis domus eiusdem ordinis nomine Driburge. Secundus fuit magister Robertus prior maioris monasterii et ecclesie cathedralis Wyntonie. Tercius extitit magister Walterus prior ecclesie cathedralis Batonie. Quartus autem iuuenis quidam nomine Theodericus secularis. Porro uiri isti et precipue tres illorum, preter honorem et reuerenciam prelacionis qua quondam preminebant, sciencia, doctrina et eloquencia tam clari extiterant, ut singulorum laudes stilo uenustiori explicari et dignius mererentur efferri quam paruitatis mee sermo possit explere.[17]

Of Adam's works listed for his Carthusian period[18] only the *De Quadripartito exercitio cellae* seems to have survived – a treatise which in style and presentation closely resembles his Premonstratensian writings,[19] though the latter have been judged more favourably by critics.[20]

We cannot date the priorate of Albert at Witham precisely. The early years of the charterhouse, founded by Henry II as part of his penance for the murder of Thomas à Becket, had been difficult, and it had only flourished after the arrival of Hugh of Lincoln, a former procurator of the Grande Chartreuse, who was elevated from the priorate of Witham to the bishopric of Lincoln on 21 September 1186.[21] Robert, prior of Saint

---

[17] Quoted from Dom André Wilmart, 'Magister Adm Cartusiensis', pp.146-147. The Cotton Vespasian MS. is a collection of disparate items – cf. *ibid.*, p.145, n.4.

[18] Several scholars have suggested that sermons survive from his Carthusian period, though it is difficult to accept that he preached often as a Carthusian. To date no such sermons have appeared in print. François Petit, *Ad Viros Religiosos*, p.52, maintains: 'Un recueil de lettres a certainement été copié.'

[19] Cf. particularly *De tripartito tabernaculo*, PL 198, 609-792; *De triplici genere contemplationis*, *ibid.*, 791-842; and *De instructione animae*, *ibid.*, 843-872.

[20] Cf. François Petit, *Ad Viros Religiosos*, p.52: 'Malgré toute sa science spirituelle, l'ancien prélat de Dryburgh n'avait pas une expérience de la vie cartusienne égale à celle qu'il possédait de la vie norbertine, et le traité nous semble bien inférieur de ce point de vue au *De triplici contemplatione* et au *De instructione animae*.' Cf. also Adam's treatise *De ordine et habitu atque professione canonicorum regularium*, PL 198, 439-610.

[21] For a fairly detailed account of Witham charterhouse cf. R.M.Woolley, *St Hugh of Lincoln* (London, 1927). Chapter 3 is devoted to 'The Founding of Witham'. Dom Charles le Couteulx, *Annales Ordinis Cartusiensis* 2, under 1170, p.323ff and under 1178, p.449-450, needs revising in the light of modern research. The

Swithun's (Winchester) and Walter, prior of Bath, have, however, both been identified[22] and in the *Magna Vita Sancti Hugonis*, written by the Benedictine Adam of Eynsham, who entered Hugh of Lincoln's service on 12 November 1197, there is a further portrait of Adam, drawn no doubt from the life, as Adam of Eynsham accompanied Hugh on his regular and lengthy visits to Witham charterhouse:

Erat uero apud Witham uir summe ac in rebus diuinis, pene dixerim, incomparandae eruditionis et doctrinae, qui, dimissa abbatia ordinis Praemonstratensis quam regebat, ad huius se conuersationis stadium mirabiliter sublimando deposuerat. Dicebatur magister Adam de Driburch. Qui, amore praeuentus uitae contemplatiuae, cuius a primaeuo iuuentutis flore felici desiderio aestuauerat, cuius et primitias diu iam felicius praelibauerat, datis sibi caelitus pennis columbae, ad hanc solitudinem conuolauerat, ubi, per quina circiter annorum lustra, sub felicissimo contemplationis somno requiescebat. Cum isto frequentissimum erat sancto pontifici colloquium. Hi, quasi geminae tubae argenteae ductiles, caelestis eloquii nitore splendentes ac regularis disciplinae exercitiis, subtilius mutuis sublimium exhortationum clangoribus fortia militiae spiritualis studia incitare non desistebant. Ingerebat eremita pontifici ex Scripturis exempla perfectorum et dicta praelatorum, incusans modernorum inertiam pastorum quorum adeo mores et studia ab eximiorum uestigiis exorbitarent suorum decessorum, adeo degenerarent a uirtutibus eorum. Interea et ad ipsum cui loquebatur reflectens sermonem, 'Te,' inquit, 'homines plurimi tamquam bonum ac magnum ecclesie Dei rectorem mirantur; set queso te, ubi saltem umbra digni pastoris in gestis tuis relucet? Nec de mediocritate uite ac conuersationis tue nunc michi sermo est. Sit modo cum imminentis iam illius aduersarii faciem generalis uirtutum precedit egestas; sit, inquam, modo cum ad ianuam iam assistit filius hominis nec inuenit fidem super terram; sit modo preconio dignus qui pessimus non fuerit, uocetur beneficus qui mala quaecumque potuerit proximo suo non intulerit. Et hec quidem perfectio potentibus magna uidetur, si aliquem iuuent et non uniuersos premant. Tales nunc sancti habentur et laude digni.

'Quid uero de commissorum tibi negotiatione talentorum sentiemus? Que lucra, quas usuras reportaturum te confidis inter illos egregios institores qui, omnia terre marisque pericula experti, non modo plantauerunt set etiam ornauerunt et munierunt ecclesiam sanguine suo? Hii ut fame pereuntes refocillarent, de longe portantes panem suum, in hiis ultimis oceani sinibus delitescentes nugas qui perierant requisierunt, quos ab ipsis portis mortis ad ciuitatem Domini uirtutum reduxerunt. Illi quidem laborauerunt, et uos in labores eorum, non ad laborandum set pene dixerim ad lasciuiendum, ut autem temperantius loquar, ad ludendum et feriandum introistis.

charterhouse was not fully constructed by the time of St Hugh's elevation to the bishopric.
[22] Cf. Dom André Wilmart, 'Magister Adam Cartusiensis', pp.149-151.

Vnde uinea Domini Sabaoth inculta iacet, sentibus operta squalet. Conculcant eam omnes qui pretergrediuntur uiam, maceria enim lapidum eius diruta est, et nemo est qui resarciat sepem eius.

Huiuscemodi satis innumera is prosequens, ut erat fons exuberatissimus celestis doctrine, reciprocam ab episcopo petebat et recipiebat sermonis uicem.[23]

Unfortunately, it is not possible to date the *De Quadripartito exercitio cellae* precisely, but in his prologue, after indicating that he is writing about Carthusian life from personal experience, he laments the brevity of that experience, which would scarcely justify venturing to write a treatise on it, if he were not under the vow of obedience. As Hugh was elevated to the bishopric of Lincoln in 1186, and Adam entered the charterhouse after his departure, the treatise, allowing for the novitiate, cannot be written before 1188 or 1189 – a date which would correspond with the prior B (= Bovon) addressed in the prologue. As Bovon died c.1201, this would appear to be the latest possible date, but a date around 1190 would correspond better with Adam's disclaimer that he was a beginner in the solitary life. The somewhat obscure Pauline reference based on 1 Cor. V, 3, referring to the prior as being present in spirit, even if absent in body, presumably indicates that Bovon was at the Grande Chartreuse for the General Chapter of the Order, though it is unlikely that the prior made the long and dangerous voyage every year even at this period – later the English priors only attended in leap years.

Ignoring the five Le Mans manuscripts reported by François Petit,[24] only three complete manuscripts appear to be extant: Grenoble Bibliothèque municipale MS. 397, presumably from the charterhouse of Portes, dating in my opinion from the thirteenth century (without attribution of authorship);[25] Charleville Bibliothèque municipale MS. 181, a fourteenth century manuscript from the charterhouse of Mont-Dieu, which significantly contains *Vita beati Hugonis Lincolniensis episcopi* – again there is no author indicated for the *De Quadripartito exercitio cellae*;[26] and Trier

---

[23] Cf. the edition by Decima L. Douie and Hugh Farmer in *Nelson Medieval Texts*, 2 vols. (London, 1962), vol. 2, pp. 52-54. The edition has since been reprinted by the Oxford University Press, but it does not entirely replace J. F. Dimock's ancient edition, *Rerum Britannicarum medii aeui S. Hugonis episcopi Lincolniensis*, Scriptores Rolls Series (1864), where funds permitted a more leisurely annotation. The *Vita* was written c.1212.

[24] Cf. above, n. 7.

[25] The MS. was probably transferred from the charterhouse of Portes to the Grande Chartreuse in the late seventeenth century, when Dom Innocent le Masson was collecting material for the history of the Order and seeking to replenish the library after a disastrous fire. It passed to the Bibliothèque municipale in the aftermath of the French Revolution. Written on parchment, in the original binding, it consists of 151 folios. Contents: ff. 1-69v De quadripertito exercitio cellae; ff. 69v-151 'Osculetur me osculo oris sui. Hec est vox synagoge que christum venturum in mundum didicerat ab angelis, cognoverat in patriarchis, audierat in prophetis ... The text of this commentary on the Canticle of Canticles breaks off abruptly at the end.

[26] A quarto MS., containing (1) Incipit liber qui dicitur bonum universale de

Stadtbibliothek MS. 755, formerly numbered 588, dating from the middle of the fifteenth century, from the charterhouse of Trier, again without any indication of authorship.[27] Additionally, there are two insignificant fragments in London British Library Harley MS. 103, dating from the fifteenth century, and Oxford Merton College MS. 19, dating from the fourteenth century.

The treatise was analysed superficially by Dom Sebastian Maccabe in the introduction to his abridged translation, and subsequently by E. Margaret Thompson[28] and Bulloch.[29] A more profound study by an anonymous Carthusian monk of Sélignac, who died as a recluse at Camaldoli, has unfortunately remained not only unpublished, but also virtually inaccessible. M.-M. Davy has also offered a detailed analysis in French.[30]

François Petit comments on its content:

> On y remarque une belle description des charmes et des avantages du chapitre général. Ceci est le fruit des chapitres de Prémontré, l'auteur qui n'a jamais été prieur, n'ayant pas eu l'occasion d'assister aux chapitres de la Chartreuse. La première partie met en valeur les caractères généraux et les avantages de la vie cartusienne: la pratique de l'humilité et de la mortification à la suite du Christ, la retraite dans la paix de la cellule, – la cellule était pour Adam la grande nouveauté de la chartreuse, puisque les Prémontrés, comme les cisterciens, vivaient en commun dans le cloître, – et enfin le parfait renoncement au monde.
>
> C'est pourquoi la chartreuse est un vrai paradis.
>
> La seconde partie est entièrement consacrée à recommander les quatre exercices du religieux: la lecture, la méditation, qui revêt huit formes différentes, la prière et avant tout la prière canoniale; enfin le travail des mains, qui consiste surtout dans la transcription des manuscrits. Adam avait toujours aimé cette sorte de travail. Jean de Kelso vantait son talent de miniaturiste. ...
>
> Ce qui est très remarquable dans cet ouvrage, c'est qu'Adam, qui jusqu'à son entrée à la chartreuse n'a compté que trois exercices religieux: lecture, prière, travail, en compte maintenant quatre, en distinguant la méditation de la lecture. Ceci est un pas considérable dans la systématisation de la vie spirituelle. Ce pas s'est fait sous

proprietatibus apum; (2) Incipit vita domine Marie de Oegnies, edita a magistro Jacobo de Vitriaco, episcopo Acconensi; (3) Incipit tractatus de instructione cuiuslibet religiosi; (4) Incipit vita beati Hugonis Lincolniensis episcopi; (5) Incipit quaedam utilis instructio religiosorum iuvenum; (6) Incipit liber de quadripertito exercitio cellae.

[27] The MS. arrived in the Stadtbibliothek from the charterhouse in 1803. The numbering of the folios is recent. It contains: ff.1-120 Liber de quadripertito exercitio cellae; ff.121-217 Tractatus de triplici via ad Deum; f.218 blank; f.219 carries merely the title of the following tractatus; ff.220-245 Spiritualis philosophia de necessaria et salutari.

[28] *The Carthusian Order in England* (London, 1930), chapter XI: 'The Quadripartite Exercise of the Cell', pp.354-367.

[29] *Adam of Dryburgh*, chapter 10: 'Adam on the Carthusian Ideal', pp.152-161.

[30] RAM 13 (1933), 124-145.

l'influence de Hugues de Saint-Victor.

Adam cite dans cet ouvrage le Pseudo-Denys, qu'il n'avait jamais cité antérieurement. Il est donc à penser que ce sont les Chartreux qui le lui ont révélé.[31]

After commencing: 'To the Reverend Lord and Father, much loved in the bowels of Christ, B., prior of the poor men of Christ dwelling at Witham, professed of the Carthusian Order, from an unworthy servant of God and of the servants of God', Adam is careful to retreat personally from public view, and frequently in the treatise he claims that he is ashamed to present himself as an authority, when it would be more fitting for him to learn rather than to teach. He insists: 'We cannot speak without a real confusion, without blushing for shame. Should we not blush to teach others without learning ourselves? One will only perceive our nakedness and thus our turpitude.'[32] Again and again he stresses in his highly repetitious style that he should be learning rather than teaching, and he concludes his work with the disclaimer: 'We have said nothing new in this treatise; we are merely confident that we have written nothing against truth. However, if we have written anything that may be misinterpreted, we pray that it may be ignored. We pray with a pious humility and a humble devotion that you, Reverend Father, present in spirit though absent in body, that if you find any spiritual sustenance in this work you

[31] *Ad Viros Religiosos*, p. 53. The reference to Pseudo-Denys is to be found in PL 153, 856 A-C. All further references to Adam's text will be taken from Migne's edition, giving the number of the column. The English translations are provisional. Petit offers a discussion of specific aspects of Adam's thought – Les exercices, La lecture, La méditation, La prière (pp. 89-92) – but most of his quotations are taken from Adam's Premonstratensian works. He devotes chapter IV to 'Le Mystique' (pp. 93-105). Under the heading 'Les sources de la théologie mystique' he comments: 'C'est ici surtout que la difficulté de synthétiser la pensée d'Adam se fera sentir. Il présente une telle richesse de doctrine et un tel enchevêtrement de synthèses partielles, qu'on a toujours peur d'omettre des éléments importants de sa pensée. Cela tient à ce qu'à une connaissance approfondie de S. Augustin, de S. Grégoire le Grand et de S. Bernard, il joint une connaissance d'experience extrêmement riche, bien qu'il s'en défende parfois. Or ses expériences ne cadrent pas toujours avec celles de ses devanciers.' (p. 93) He goes on to consider 'La continuité de la foi et de la contemplation', 'La contemplation est une connaissance', 'La contemplation est un repos', 'Les préparations mystiques', 'Les nuits', 'Les lieux', 'Les noces spirituelles', 'Le rôle de l'amour dans la contemplation', 'Le don de Sagesse', 'Analyse psychologique de la contemplation', 'L'objet de la contemplation', 'La place de la contemplation dans l'ordre de la grâce', 'Les fruits de la contemplation', and 'La propagande mystique', where he concludes: 'La seule chose importante c'est de ne chercher, de ne désirer que Dieu. S'il est permis de le désirer, il est permis de le prêcher. Adam n'a fait que cela toute sa vie. Ce fut son unique souci, le seul but de son labeur acharné.' (p. 105) Here again Petit cites almost exlusively texts from Adam's Premonstratensian period, and Dom André Wilmart has demonstrated in his 'Magister Adam Cartusiensis' that whole passages of the *De Quadripartito Exercitio Cellae* echo his earlier writings, and, in fact, a lengthy text of the *De triplici genere contemplationis* was merely incorporated into the Carthusian treatise. The details are given on pp. 158-159.
[32] 866B-C.

will intercede for this poor sinner, who has written down all his thoughts in a single book, not as he should, but as he could.'[33]

The treatise is written in a richly ornate style – so ornate and repetitious that it often gets on the nerves of the modern reader. Both philosophical and mystical in the atmosphere it creates, it constitutes a veritable panegyric of the solitary life, doubtless based on the doctrines of Guigo's *Consuetudines Cartusiae*. He urges that the life of the Carthusians is modelled on the life of Christ in the desert. Silence and solitude are the *sine qua non* of the Carthusian existence: 'Our life is a life of solitude; we must divorce ourselves in life and spirit from the world and all that is of the world, so that we are in our hearts and our habitations true solitaries. Our whole occupation should be to praise God, to pray to him, and to listen to him. The life of the cell is as essential to the interior life as water is to fish and the sheepfold to sheep.' Adam, claiming that he is only writing under obedience to his prior, maintains that he who lives in the cell, lives in heaven, playing on the words *cella* and *caelum* or *Caeli aula*. Guigo du Pont in his *De Contemplatione* was similarly to claim that the Carthusians would be exempted from a heavenly novitiate, because they had served their novitiate on earth. Some fifty years earlier William of St Thierry in his famous letter to the brethren of Mont-Dieu had praised the sublimity of the Carthusian vocation in comparable terms.

The *De Quadripartito exercitio cellae* deals in detail with reading, meditation, prayer, and manual work, but thirteen chapters, 18-30, or more than a third of the work, are devoted to meditation.

At the beginning of his work Adam indicates its main divisions and the titles of his chapters. From the Carthusian General Chapter, where the priors are assembled, a river flows out to water the paradise of the Order, so that all the members participate in its 'sweet sublimity and sublime sweetness'. The Carthusian was the beggar at the rich man's gate, and everything in the charterhouse was to be marked by simplicity and frugality. The earthly paradise which the order constituted was watered by its four rivers, which are charged with symbolic significance. The river Physon – the reading of the Holy Scriptures – waters the region of Evilath. In reading God's word we find that true wisdom which will not only hold us back from evil words but also even from wayward thoughts.[34] The river Gihon[35] descends abruptly and flows all around Ethiopia, indicating the value of meditation, whilst the Tigris denotes the power of prayer, which flies like an arrow directly to God.[36] Finally, the Euphrates symbolises the active part of the Carthusian life, that time devoted to manual labour,[37] which takes its place, if a comparatively minor one, between the study of the Scriptures, meditation and prayer, which are all based on Biblical sources.

[33]   884B-C.
[34]   827-830.
[35]   830.
[36]   864.
[37]   880.

The work abounds in analogical and allegorical interpretations of Holy Writ[38] and certain words or concepts occur repeatedly throughout the work, such as *asperitas*, *suavitas*, and *quietas*.

Adam claims that the essence of the Carthusian Order is to be found in the *probabilis externa exercitatio*, by which he signalises the practice of the virtues of humility and prudence; the *iugis cellae solitudo* – the peaceful dwelling in the cell; and the *perfecta saeculi abiectio* – the total renunciation of the world.[39] Among the cell's many advantages, its sublimity is derived from the perpetual solitude which it affords to its inhabitant. Without the solitude of the cell the whole round of the Carthusian observance would be barren and the separation from the world unfruitful. From the prescriptions of the *Consuetudines Cartusiae* he demonstrates how the Carthusian customs guarantee the maximum solitude for the individual monk. In winter the whole period between Prime and Terce and in summer between Lauds and Prime, and all the year between Vespers and Compline are devoted to spiritual exercises. From Terce to Sext in winter and Prime to Terce in summer, manual work – mainly the copying of manuscripts – was to be practised, and again from None to Vespers all the year round.

The monk's cell is a garden of delights, watered with consolations of the highest order. Perpetual solitude is true paradise, because it constitutes the *aula caeli*, the gate of heaven. The Lord is truly in the monk's cell, because it is the house of God. Here is the gracious visage of Rachel, the joyous and fruitful repose of the Blessed Virgin. The troubled activity of Martha is unknown to the dweller of the cell. The monk may devote himself to the calm, agreeable, luminous and delicious languor of Mary as she washed Christ's feet.[40]

Adam is sufficient of a realist to admit, however, that the cell has its problems and temptations. Though he loves his cell with passionate devotion, the solitary may nonetheless suffer temptation. Adam is, however, reassuring: 'You are not alone in your cell. Are you alone when you pray to your father in the spirit, having closed the door of your heart to all frivolous and useless thoughts? Are you alone when your luminous

---

[38] There are, however, also a number of patristic quotations and even a few from secular writers. Thus Saint Augustine is quoted in cols. 850, 853, 860, 861, 862, 874 and 875, the main references coming from *De Trinitate* and *Regula clericorum*. St Gregory the Great figures at cols. 849, 852, and 873, where the *Moralia* and *Hom. 8 in Ezechiel* are cited. St Benedict's authority is invoked in cols. 818, 830, 862, 863, and 882. Denys's *Celestial Hierarchy*, which must presumably have been in the Witham library even at this early stage, is quoted in col. 856, and Boethius's *De consolatione philosophiae* in cols. 808 and 850. St Hilary is cited in col. 863, Sulpicius Severus in col. 883, and Yvo Bishop of Chartres in col. 882. As might be expected, Guigo's *Consuetudines Cartusiae* are invoked several times: cols. 821, 822, 883-884. More surprising are the citations from Ovid's *Metamorphoses*, col. 849, and Aristotle's Physics, col. 854.

[39] 806ff.

[40] 810.

intelligence has brought you to meditate on the angels who see God's face without ceasing in heaven?'[41]

Adam underlines Guigo's assertions in the *Consuetudines Cartusiae* that it is dangerous for a monk to leave his solitude. The monk even risks eternal bliss if he lightly deserts his cell. Curiosity about what is going on outside the cell is no occupation for a Carthusian. He who dissipates his time outside the cell has not grasped the rewards to be found in the cell. He is living in total ignorance, for the Carthusian needs the cell as a fish needs water. The little fish allec, as soon as it is pulled out of the water, dies; but the same letters which form allec are to be found in cella!

Outside the cell the monk may feel a temporary consolation in the diminution of the austerity, but this illusion will not last, and it will be followed by bitterness and a terrible desolation – an anguish of spirit which may even approach agony. Total dissipation and a distaste for all things spiritual may invade the heart. Adam outlines the numerous afflictions to which the solitary is subject. The lion is ever alert to tempt him, and some of the temptations are indeed subtle. The siren will suggest that so much learning and brilliance is lost when it is buried in the cell. Such gifts must be used for the benefit of mankind in general – they might indeed assure the salvation of many. Is it not sheer egotism to think only of saving one's own soul? Adam thus warns the solitary to guard his cell not only in body, but also in spirit, as the spiritual desertion of the cell – giving one's imagination free run – is even more dangerous than physical absence.[42] The human heart is alas! inconstant, vagabond, always seeking new experiences. One must continually seek tranquillity through prayer. If all else fails, one must reflect on one's duties in the monastic estate. Recollecting that the Fathers of the Desert were afflicted by *tristitia*, he urges that monks should be joyful. The solitary should always examine carefully all means to extricate himself from temptations, but if a tempest really assails him, there is one supreme remedy. 'When you are troubled or in anger, pussilanimous, or afflicted by sadness, when a terrible storm arises in your heart, lift up your head, fly to Christ, throw yourself at his feet with a silent cry that penetrates and resounds. On the theatre of your soul cry out to Christ to aid you, because you are perishing.'[43]

Adam then cites numerous Biblical examples to prove the necessity and fruitfulness of dwelling in solitude. Like Naomi, the Carthusian who leaves his cell goes out full, but returns in total destitution. What was pleasing to him before is now bitter. Famine drove Naomi to wander through Moab, where she was a stranger, for her true home was Bethlehem, the township in which Christ was to be born. The monk should remain in his cell, for there he will find the spiritual food he needs. Bethlehem signifies the 'house of bread' and in Bethlehem his soul will be stilled. Yet if he gives way to discontent, he will wander forth as Naomi did, and quit Bethlehem, but after the famine that Naomi fled from, abundance came to

41   *Ibid.*
42   817-818.
43   844.

Bethlehem, and Naomi came back sad and disillusioned. The Carthusian should be warned by her fate.[44] Enoch also experienced the joys of solitude, and God manifested himself to Noah under the appearance of a dove, when Noah was dwelling in the arc, which was itself a form of cell. Jacob also perceived the famous ladder stretching up into heaven whilst he was meditating, even if he was asleep at the time![45] The inhabitant of the cell is a second Moses, for the monk too, under the guidance of divine grace, has been carried away from the flotsam and preoccupations of this world and borne to the sweet and peace-giving repose of the cell. Moses ascended a mountain and sat on a stone whilst he lifted up his arms to heaven to put to flight the enemies of Israel through the power of his prayers. Aaron and Hur sustained him, because his arms became weary and would have fallen, which would have allowed the enemies of Israel to vanquish them. Moses's ascent of the mountain demonstrates the sublimity of prayer. The solitary is counselled to sit on a rock, the rock of the firm stability of his thoughts. To sustain his arms reaching up to heaven, he must call on the aid of humility and charity.[46]

The monk is not where his body pins him down, but where his ardent spirit soars. He has renounced all terrestrial goods as transient and without significance, devoting all his attention to what is holy, superior and eternal.[47] Ceaselessly traversing the increasingly fertile pastures of his soul, he frequents the choirs of the patriarchs, the assemblies of the prophets, the senate of the apostles.[48] The Carthusian must be truly humble and surrender himself to the workings of God's spirit. Adam counsels: 'You who dwell in a cell, you will hear three voices – your own, that of the angels, and that of the Creator of all things. Certain conditions are prerequisite to praying properly – peace of heart, for instance. Forgive those who have offended you. If you yourself have committed evil, banish the evil from your mind, and think of it no more. Look with a loving eye on those who have injured you, speak to them with a perfect benevolence, not making any allusion to what has happened.'[49] For Adam, the solitary is indeed one of the elect. When he prays, God's ear is open for him; when he reads God's mouth speaks in his ear.[50]

Meditation produces various effects, Adam teaches his reader: knowledge, fear, love, piety, judgment, rebirth of the soul, admiration, loving regard of all things visible and invisible. Its aim is to arrive at a pure and simple regard of eternal truth – *mens sobria et sancta ... per visionem potius intellectualem ... ipsam veritatem beatis oculis concupiscit.*[51]

Meditating the Biblical texts, the Carthusian in his cell should in all tranquillity pass each age of human history before his eyes. He will then

[44] 816.
[45] 810.
[96] 867.
[47] 851.
[48] *Ibid.*
[49] 841.
[50] 825; 826; 813.
[51] 831.

perceive how miraculously God's providence has worked for man's benefit.[52] Among his eight modes of meditation, he particularly recommends meditating the incarnation of Christ with all its attendant circumstances – the virginal conception, the swaddling clothes, the nourishing of Christ at Our Lady's breast, the submission to the law of circumcision. The events of Christ's life, such as Christ saving St Peter when he tried to walk on the waters, are equally proposed to the solitary's attention.[53]

Adam then expounds the negative theology of Denys,[54] declaring what God is not, before proceeding to an Augustinian presentation of the mystery of the Trinity.[55] Meditation on such topics must become habitual for the solitary.

The Carthusian's activity is limited to manual work – *opus manuum* – which is intended to afford the spirit the relaxation it may need, but it should take the form of a prolongation of the monk's intellectual occupations, and for this the copying of manuscripts was, of course, the perfect solution, allowing the Carthusian to preach with his hands, if not with his mouth, again echoing a famous passage in the *Consuetudines Cartusiae*. He admits that not all are gifted enough to copy manuscripts, but others might work on the illuminations, or prepare the binding or parchment.[56]

In any event, the Carthusian, whether occupied in manual work, study or prayer, should never quit his solitude. Faithful to the round of Carthusian exercises, joyful in his seclusion, the monk is already one of the blessed.[57] Adam urges: 'If you understand all your advantages, you will perceive clearly what is the calm of the cell, its nature and quality, its greatness. You will enjoy its softness, its suavity, its charm, its serenity, its delights and its radiation. No one on this earth can otherwise estimate such a soft sweetness. No other human being can be compared to you. Some exceed you in the temporal sphere, but their capacity for joy and delight is less than yours. They are ignorant of the fullness of your riches.'[58] The Carthusian is sheltered from all that is vain and superficial. He is dedicated uniquely to the search for perfection. He is the intimate friend of God, no longer of this world, but of the world beyond.

[52] 865.
[53] 843.
[54] 856.
[55] 861.
[56] 880-881.
[57] 814.
[58] 818.

OPUS DEI, OPUS MUNDI:
PATTERNS OF CONFLICT IN A
TWELFTH-CENTURY MIRACLE COLLECTION

Gordon Whatley

In the course of the nineteenth century, European scholars laboriously edited and published many of the medieval *libri miraculorum*, the books containing accounts of the posthumous miracles of individual saints and their relics.[1] The English Rolls Series, for example, is quite heavily laden with *miracula*, such as those of St Edmund, king and martyr, St Dunstan, St John of Beverley, and the immense books of miracles associated with Thomas of Canterbury.[2] Among the major collections edited by French scholars are those of St Benedict at Fleury and St Faith at Conques,[3] and one could doubtless cite similar sets of examples for most of the other countries of Western Europe.[4]

The books of miracles edited by those nineteenth-century scholars have not gone unread, but it would be no exaggeration, I think, to say that they were read perhaps with something less than exhilaration and total absorption. To conscientious historians in quest of conventional historical information, reading the *libri miraculorum* must have been an excruciating

---

[1] The most complete list is that of the Bollandists, *Bibliotheca hagiographica latina*, 2 vols. (Brussels, 1898-1901), with the *Supplementum* (Brussels, 1911), arranged alphabetically by saint, and including *vitae* first, followed by *miracula*. An important introduction to the genre will be the study by Pierre Boglioni, *Les recueils de miracles*, forthcoming in the series, Typologie des sources du moyen âge occidental (Louvain). See also Benedicta Ward, *Miracles and the Medieval Mind* (London and Philadelphia, 1982). Regrettably, I have not yet seen the recent work by P.-A. Sigal, *L'homme et le miracle dans la France médiévale* (Paris, 1985).

[2] William Stubbs, ed., *Memorials of St Dunstan*, RS 63 (London, 1874), 69-324; Thomas Arnold, ed., *Memorials of St Edmund's Abbey*, RS 96, vol. 1 (London, 1890), 26-208; James Raine, ed., *Historians of the Church of York and its Archbishops*, RS 71, vol. 1 (London, 1879), 261-347; J. C. Robertson and J. B. Shepherd, eds., *Materials for the History of Thomas Becket, Archbishop of Canterbury*, RS 67, vol. 1 (London, 1875), 137-546, vol. 2 (1877), 21-281.

[3] E. de Certain, ed., *Les miracles de Saint Benoît*, Soc. de l'hist. de France, publications in octavo, 96 (Paris, 1858); A. Bouillet, ed., *Liber miraculorum S. Fidis* (Paris, 1897).

[4] The major modern collection of medieval miracle books remains that of the Bollandists in the *Acta Sanctorum* (ASS), begun in Antwerp in 1643 and published in the order of the calendar months, January-November. The last volume appeared in 1925. The series, for which as yet no December volumes are projected, is more thorough in its attention to the saints' *vitae* than to the *miracula*, and the nineteenth-century editions cited in the previous notes supplemented the work of the Bollandists in this respect.

disappointment, since they seem to consist of mainly implausible, stereotyped, repetitive episodes largely devoid of interesting factual or contextual material. Antonia Gransden's broad and valuable survey of English historical writing in the Middle Ages represents what has probably been the majority response of modern historians to the miracle collections. The only ones that interest her are those, like Hermann of Bury's *Miracles of St Edmund*, that can be read between the lines as the history of a community. To the hundreds of pages containing the shrine miracles of St Thomas of Canterbury, on the other hand, she devotes barely a couple of sentences. Even in Hermann's collection, which she values for its contributions to 'local history', Professor Gransden de-emphasises the miracles themselves, implying that Hermann used them merely for decoration.[5]

Other modern historians, however, have begun to exhibit a new and more positive interest in and appreciation for the *libri miraculorum*. Among those whose work I have come across are Ronald Finucane and Pierre-André Sigal, whose work seems to have influenced that of Finucane himself. To these two scholars, and several others like them, as Finucane puts it, 'there are miracles and there are miracles'. What he means by this is to draw a distinction between the type of miracles frequently found in saints' *vitae* and those in the posthumous miracle collections. To Sigal and Finucane, the posthumous miracles are more likely to be historically reliable than the *vitae* of the saints because, unlike many of the latter, they are a record of recent events in the life around the shrine, compiled in many cases from oral reports of the *miraculés* themselves or of other eye witnesses. If read in the right way, with the right questions asked of them, such collections can yield large amounts of information about medieval social classes, disease and medicine, and local customs, as well as about pilgrimages and other religious practices.[6]

Sigal admits that the *liber miraculorum* does constitute a literary genre, and is the result often of a certain amount of selectivity and screening by the author, with some distortion of the truth, 'déformation des faits'. But modern methods of investigation, such as 'content analysis', can distinguish usually between episodes that derive from legend and those that rest on

[5] Antonia Gransden, *Historical Writing in England c.550 to c.1307* (Ithaca, NY, 1974), 125-26, 307. Until quite recently, historians have tended to view the miracles in Bede's *Historia ecclesiastica* in a similarly unserious light. See, e.g., Bertram Colgrave, 'Bede's Miracle Stories', in A.H. Thompson, ed., *Bede, His Life, Times, and Writings* (Oxford, 1935), 202-29, esp. 224-29. Even the author of a more constructive approach cannot resist comparing Bede's miracle stories to amusing if pertinent anecdotes in an after-dinner speech: Henry Mayr-Harting, *The Coming of Christianity to England* (NY, 1972), 46-49.

[6] Ronald R. Finucane, 'The Use and Abuse of Medieval Miracles', *History* 60 (1975), 1-10. See also P.-A. Sigal, 'Maladie, pèlerinage et guérison au XIIe siècle. Les miracles de saint Gibrien à Reims', *Annales ESC* 24 (1969), 522-39. A recent work applying methods of quantitative analysis to large numbers of medieval miracle stories, on the assumption that the stories are historically reliable, is that of Donald Weinstein and Rudolf Bell, *Saints and Society* (Chicago, 1982).

fact.[7] Unfortunately, in the *Annales* article in question, Sigal does not do any 'content analysis' and it appears that he relies mainly on scholarly intuition as to which authors to trust for authenticity. Then he proceeds to analyse their miracle books for geographical and sociological data, using quantitative methodology with graphs, maps, and charts.

Some miracle collections more than others may well lend themselves to this quantitative approach, which certainly produces interesting results. I am thinking particularly of late-medieval collections in which the *number* of miracles at a shrine is impressive and strongly emphasised by the author, and in which the individual episodes are relatively brief and plainly told, providing plenty of names and places of origin, and various other ostensibly factual details.[8] Many collections, however, particularly those dating from the early-medieval period through the mid-twelfth century, are not of this sort, but contain instead episodes of varying length organised into structures of various kinds and purposes, and written by people who are recognisably and self-consciously authors, *literati*, rather than shrine-keepers. For these writers the genre of the *miraculum* is, like the liturgy in which it had its place alongside the saint's *vita*, a kind of *ars sacra*. In my opinion, literary modes of analysis are more appropriate than the quantitative for gaining insight into the meaning and purpose of such texts, although I am far from suggesting that historians in general should leave the *miracula* alone.[9] Nor am I proposing here to attempt to lay down a methodology for analysing miracle texts. One would have to have read and studied many more of them than I have, even to contemplate such a task. Instead I will simply offer a preliminary analysis of portions of a specific *liber miraculorum*, using such methods and intuitions as come naturally to one trained in literature. It seems to me that only after a fair number of such attempts have been made will it be possible to begin to formulate a reliable approach to this difficult but rich and copious body of medieval writing.

The collection with which this paper is concerned is the *Miracula sancti Erkenwaldi episcopi*,[10] the miracles of Saint Erkenwald, who was bishop of

[7] Sigal, 'Maladie', 1523.

[8] Finucane's book, *Miracles and Pilgrims. Popular Beliefs in Medieval England* (London, 1977), draws much of its material from dossiers of this sort, many of which were drawn up for use in canonisation proceedings. It is only fair to say that, while I have reservations about the treatment of miracle literature by Finucane and Sigal, I have benefited enormously from their work as a whole.

[9] A good example of a judicious historical reading of a miracle collection is the recent article by D. W. Rollason, 'The Miracles of Saint Benedict: a Window on Early Medieval France', in Henry Mayr-Harting and R. I. Moore, eds., *Studies in Medieval History Presented to R. H. C. Davis* (London, 1985), 73-90.

[10] The work is #2601 in *Bibliotheca hagiographica latina*. My edition and translation is forthcoming in *The Saint of London: the Life and Miracles of Saint Erkenwald*, Medieval & Renaissance Texts & Studies 58 (Binghamton, NY). Portions of the present paper, particularly towards the end, contain material treated in greater depth in the introduction to *The Saint of London*, ch. 3, pt 3. For permission to use such material here, I am grateful to the Center for Medieval & Early Renaissance Studies, State University of New York at Binghamton.

London early in the Anglo-Saxon era. The work was composed, probably in 1141 or 1142, by a nephew of Bishop Gilbert the Universal, and he is most likely the same person as a canon of St Paul's named Arcoidus, or Arcoid as I shall refer to him.[11] The only surviving MS copy that remotely resembles the original is in Corpus Christi College, Cambridge, MS 161, of about the year 1200. The *Miracula*, as I shall refer to the work from now on (and which is treated as if grammatically singular), occupies about twelve folios, containing a prologue and nineteen or twenty-one chapters, depending on how one divides them up. The *Miracula* is still unprinted, and not many people have read it, especially since there is a more accessible redaction, a rather drastic one which thoroughly obscures the character of the original, by John of Tynemouth in his *Sanctilogium Angliae*, printed most recently by Carl Horstmann.[12] Henry Wharton, in the latter part of the seventeenth century, read the original *Miracula* in manuscript and called it a 'splendid' work.[13] I heartily agree with him.

Anything like a full analysis of Arcoid's *Miracula* would be impossible and more than tedious here. The main focus of what follows will be on one aspect of the work and chiefly on one miracle episode. But first a word or two about the structure of the work as a whole.

Some work has been done, as Finucane has pointed out, on the classification of miracle types,[14] but only Sigal, as far as I know, has attempted to analyse the literary structure of individual collections. He concluded that miracle collections are usually organised internally either in chronological sequence, with a basically historical or annalistic intention, or thematically, according to miracle type, with more didactic thrust.[15] One does not have to read far in such works, however, before one discovers that these two basic formats are frequently combined and subdivided in interesting ways to suit the purposes of the individual hagiographer, purposes which are more complex than Sigal's straightforward schema allows. In Arcoid's *Miracula*, for example, there is a chronological section: chapters IV-XV. Mir. IV, which begins this sequence, is a dramatic, highly coloured account of the great fire of London of 1087, during which, Arcoid records, the old Anglo-Saxon minster of St Paul's was destroyed, but Erkenwald's shrine, and a flimsy linen cloth draped over it, were miraculously preserved. As a preamble to Mir. V, Arcoid briefly describes the ambitious rebuilding efforts of Bishops Maurice and Richard of Belmeis, spanning the years 1087-1128, and the virtues and learning of Arcoid's uncle, Bishop Gilbert, who died in 1134. The main subject of Mir. V proper, the healing

[11] Beryl Smalley, 'Gilbertus Universalis, Bishop of London, 1128-34, and the Problem of the "Glossa Ordinaria"', *Recherches de théologie ancienne et médiévale* 7 (1935), 238.

[12] *Nova Legenda Angliae*, 2 vols. (Oxford, 1901), 1: 393-405.

[13] *De episcopis et decanis Londinensibus* (London, 1695), 18.

[14] Useful reference works are Cobham Brewer, *A Dictionary of Miracles* (London, 1884) and C. Grant Loomis, *White Magic* (Cambridge, Mass., 1948). The most complete, however, is J. Bagatta, *Admiranda orbis christiana*, 2 vols. (Venice, 1700).

[15] 'Histoire et hagiographie. Les miracles aux XIe et XIIe siècles', *Annales de Bretagne et des Pays de l'Ouest*, 87:2 (1980), 237-57, esp. 249-54.

of the shrivelled and paralysed hand of Benedicta, a pilgrim from Tuscany, seems to have occurred on Erkenwald's feast day, 30 April, in 1138. The ensuing episodes, up to and including Mir. XV, cover the rather crowded period of 1138-1141, the climax of which is the temporary translation of the saint's coffin from the great Norman crypt, where it must have been since Maurice's time (i.e. c.1107) into a stone container in the new choir of the upper church. This is the only episode for which Arcoid supplies a full calendar date: 16 February, 1140.

The episodes that precede and follow the chronological set, however, are noticeably non chronological. The events in the last little group, Mir. XVI-XIX, appear to have taken place before the 1140 translation described in Mir. XIV, so that after Mir. XV we actually move back in time. Moreover, Mir. XV-XVIII seem to have been grouped together as in Sigal's 'plan ... thématique': in each of them St Erkenwald appears to the *miraculé* in a vision, speaking to or touching the person, and in one case beating him with his crozier. The purpose of this feature of the *Miracula*'s structure is not self-evident, but it appears that Arcoid wished to indicate some kind of alteration in the state of the saint after the translation of the body. The hagiographer Goscelin, in his account of the translation of the relics of St Augustine of Canterbury, speaks of the day of the saint's deposition as the feast of his entry into heaven, but the day of his translation, he says, is the day of his rebirth among his people on earth.[16] This may be what Arcoid is suggesting, though anachronistically, by the suddenly visible activity of Erkenwald after his translation in Mir. XIV. Clearly, we are not dealing with a work of straightforward reportage, but rather with one in which chronology, not to mention fidelity to fact, is subservient to theology and the religious imagination.

A similar impression is conveyed by the three episodes that comprise the first group, Mir. I-III, which are among the most elaborate and most carefully composed of the whole *Miracula*. They include lots of interesting details of the sort that would interest a historian (including, for example, teaching methods at old St Paul's school in Mir. I, episcopal jurisdiction over escaped prisoners in Mir. III, and, as we shall see, an instance of vehement lay anti-clericalism in Mir. II). But these miracle episodes lack any hint of a historical context in which to place their intriguing contents and they seem to me to be the most demonstrably fictional or 'legendary' of the whole work.

One feature of most miracle episodes, in any collection, is a tendency to conform to certain stereotypical narrative patterns and subjects, which some modern scholars call topoi. While this tendency does not necessarily or totally negate the historicity of the episode, it certainly renders the credibility of the author more suspect. In Arcoid's *Miracula* this is par-

[16] 'In priori festo [viz., of Augustine's deposition], de seculi agone & tenebris ad solem gloriae palmatus ascendit; in isto [viz., of the translation] de diuturno humi ergastulo suam lucem ostendit, & de aeterno honore ad vitalia busta nos revisit. Illic de mundano utero superis nascitur, hic de sepulchrali alvo nobis renascitur ... Tunc aeternae pacis somno quievit, nunc de tam longaevo sopore nostra manu motus evigilavit.' *Historia translationis*, c.1, ASS Maius, VI:413.

ticularly the case with Mir. I and II, each of which involves not one such topos, but two of them artfully synthesised into one complex episode. The same phenomenon occurs in other collections, and it occasionally results in a miracle story so long that the author apologises for exceeding what was apparently considered the normal length, thereby prompting the reader to recognise the *miraculum* in question as something of a *tour de force*.[17]

Arcoid's Mir. II is a good example of this long *miraculum* genre. The story may be summarised as follows:

> It is the feast of St Erkenwald, and all the people of London are on holiday in the saint's honour. The city is filled with joy and good will, but one man alone is pointedly ignoring the festival and morosely going about his daily business. In the course of his work (which is not specified) he carries a bundle of wood into the church-yard of St Paul's and throws it down against the minster wall, on the other side of which is the shrine of the saint. Just as he does so, a canon of the cathedral is leaving the church, and the workman adopts a belligerent posture. The canon rebukes him for disobeying the rules regarding servile work on the feast day, explains to him at some length the purpose of the feast and the great benefits, both spiritual and physical, that people derive from the saint's presence among them, urges him to repent and pray to Erkenwald for forgiveness, and finally warns him of the possible consequences of persisting in his disobedient irreverence. The layman in response ignores the priest's call to repentance and launches into a sarcastic and angry diatribe against the whole clerical order. He rails at the clerics for leading an idle, useless existence of ludicrous singing and moaning, which leaves them too much time to meddle in the business of people whom they both despise and envy. With the triviality of the clerical existence he contrasts the useful and necessary life of himself and his cronies, including even their own feast days, which occur when they have accumulated enough spare cash for some extra food and drink. The layman also belittles Erkenwald himself, jokingly asking if the saint would feed him if he were to quit his work to celebrate the holiday, an idea which he pronounces ridiculous. The canon tries to quieten the man down, warning him again of disaster if he does not cease his blasphemies. Whereupon, the workman angrily picks up his bundle, storms off across the church-yard, trips over a half-buried skull, falls and strikes his head on a tombstone, and dies instantly, *suimet ruina conquassatus et extinctus*, as Arcoid puts it with a certain relish.
>
> The news of the blasphemer's death travels quickly and soon a great crowd gathers around his body for a sort of impromptu *post mortem*.

---

[17] Cf. the remarks of Aimon of Fleury (fl. early eleventh century), in book 3, ch. 13, of the *Miracula sancti Benedicti*, ed. de Certain, *Les miracles de S. Benoît*, 158-59, and those of Osbern of Canterbury (fl. late eleventh century), *Miracula sancti Dunstani*, ed. Stubbs, *Memorials of St Dunstan*, 151.

While some actually question the fate inflicted on him as cruel and unforgiving, the majority recognise it as a just punishment of one who so gravely insulted God's priests and God's friend, St Erkenwald. Arcoid ends the episode by admonishing his audience to see the story in the same light, and to pray to St Erkenwald to intercede with God for the forgiveness of their sins and for the hope of eternal life.[18]

As I suggested earlier, Mir. II is a synthesis of two separate though related hagiographical topoi. The more obvious of the two is that of divine punishment for doing illegal servile work on a feast day or Sunday. Examples of this topos occur as early as Gregory of Tours and there are some in just about every collection of miracles. In most variants of this topos the offender is first rebuked, or warned of possible consequences, by a priest or some other devout person. On stubbornly refusing to desist from work, the offender is then physically stricken in some appropriate fashion. In Mir. XII of Arcoid's *Miracula*, for example, Vitalis the skinner laughs at his fellow artisans passing by on their way to church on the feast day, when they admonish him for working on his hides. Whereupon the blade of his knife flicks up and pierces one of his eyes, and Arcoid comments acidly that the pain left Vitalis with no choice but to lay aside his work.[19]

Closer analogues to Mir. II, however, occur in two early-twelfth-century miracles of St Benedict, in which in each case the offender, in refusing to cease work when warned to do so, replies that he must work in order to eat, a theme harped on by Arcoid's workman in Mir. II.[20] A close analogue to another aspect of Mir. II occurs in a slightly later work, the life and miracles of St Otto of Bamberg, in one chapter of which a Polish peasant is reprimanded by a priest out in the fields for harvesting corn on the feast of the Assumption. The farmer, whose wife is working with him also, replies by asking what sort of doctrine this is that forbids men to do good and necessary things, and he accuses the priest of envying him his involvement in useful work, *nostris utilitatibus*.[21] This theme, of the usefulness of secular tasks, and the clergy's envy of them, is paralleled in the layman's diatribe in Mir. II, though there it is much more developed. It is a species of anti-clericalism that I have so far failed to find represented in the anti-clerical literature of the twelfth century and later, or in the satirical portraits of the peasantry of the later Middle Ages.

The Polish farmer in the life of St Otto is punished with death by a paralytic stroke so severe that he has to be buried with his sickle and a sheaf of corn still gripped tightly in his hands. The quite different, though equally macabre death of the workman in Mir. II leads us to the second

---

[18]   CCC 161, f. 35.

[19]   CCC 161, ff. 42v-43r.

[20]   Both the episodes are in book 8 of the *Miracula S. Benedicti*, by Ralph Tortaire (late eleventh or early twelfth century), ed. de Certain, *Les miracles de S. Benoît*, 330, 331.

[21]   ASS Jul., I: 369. The same passage is quoted by Bagatta, *Admiranda orbis christiana*, II: 330.

hagiographical topos involved here: that of profaning the saint's shrine itself, the sacred *locus* of the cult. The miracles punishing illegal servile work, which comprise the first topos, invariably occur, predictably, out in the fields or in the offender's place of work, away from the saint's shrine, which is precisely where the culprit does not wish to be. Mir. II is unusual in that the layman chooses to flaunt his irreligious attitude within the churchyard itself and Arcoid manages to suggest in various subtle ways that there is physical as well as verbal violence in his assault on St Erkenwald and his priests. This also is a feature not associated with the first topos, of feast day violation, but it is common in stories about people who profane shrines.

A very early, but surprisingly close analogue to this aspect of Mir. II is an episode in Gregory of Tours' *Gloria Martyrum* (c.60), concerning the shrine of St Nazaire in the Loire region. A soldier named Britto, who is one of the henchmen of a certain Count Waroch of Brittany, comes one day into the abbey church and seizes, in the presence of the abbot, a golden belt that has been left on the altar, along with its elaborate trappings, as an offering to the saint. The abbot argues with Britto, warning him of the danger of offending the saint and also explaining to him, in a brief *predicatio*, that the purpose of the gold is to provide food for the poor people of St Nazaire's territory in time of famine. The abbot adds that Britto would do better to make an offering of his own instead of trying to take this one away. Britto is unmoved, threatens to kill the abbot if he doesn't stand aside, and calls for his horse to be brought to the church door. The abbot warns him again about possible divine vengeance on such acts, and also tells him that it is forbidden to mount a horse in the precincts of the church (a delightfully gratuitous touch). Britto takes the gold belt and its trappings, mounts his horse inside the porch and rides off, but as he does so he cracks his head against the lintel of the gateway, breaking his skull. He dies shortly afterwards.[22]

Although the immediate circumstances are obviously different, the basic narrative structures of Arcoid's and Gregory's stories are closely parallel. In each case a layman rudely invades the precincts of a saint's shrine and deliberately begins to effect an act of sacrilege; each intruder is confronted by a cleric of high rank who not only warns him of the probably grave consequences of his offence, but also preaches to him about the physical and spiritual benefits of the shrine and cult he is profaning; the cleric in each story also invites the layman to relent and participate in the saint's cult, but the profaner responds with violent, sacrilegious words, and the cleric in turn issues a second warning of dire consequences. Finally the intruder departs unrepentant, having accomplished the intended profanation, and promptly suffers a fatal concussion while still inside the sacred precincts.

I am not suggesting that Arcoid's Mir. II is directly modelled on

[22] *Monumenta Germaniae Historica* (MGH), *Scriptores Rerum Merovingicarum* (SRM) I: 529-30.

Gregory's story of Britto & St Nazaire (though this is quite possible[23]), but rather that they are both variants of a common type or topos that is widely represented throughout medieval miracle literature. A knowledge of the topoi behind Arcoid's story allows us to understand better what effects he has aimed at and achieved. What is interesting here is that he has chosen to use this profanation topos as the structural basis of a tale about the violation of Erkenwald's feast day. The resulting synthesis makes for a more than usually drastic case of secular sacrilege, since we now have two different kinds of sacrilege combined in one incident. Arcoid has enriched the effect by providing canon and layman with speeches of a length and scope that are unparalleled in these types of miracle stories (at least those I'm familiar with). The profanation topos gave Arcoid the precedent for a brief clerical discourse explaining the benefits of a saint's cult, and in the other topos the offending layman sometimes justifies his disobedience in a few words, as we have seen but Arcoid has expanded these verbal roles into substantial monologues uttered by representative spokesmen of irreconcilable philosophies: on the one side the sacramental life of the church presented as a means to salvation and also as a focus of duty and obedience; on the other side, a secular materialism that has no use for anything associated with religion and the divine. The layman's beligerent disregard for the rules governing servile work is seen to be rooted not only in irreverence for Erkenwald and the saints in general, but also in a basic hostility towards and contempt for the whole system of the *opus Dei* and the clerical life from which it is inseparable.

It is hardly conceivable that these speeches are 'authentic'. They are almost certainly Arcoid's work from beginning to end. He has admitted in the proem to the collection that records of past miracles at Erkenwald's shrine were not kept;[24] the story behind Mir. II survived, if that is the right word, only in the popular memory. But since Mir. II lacks any kind of time reference and the characters are anonymous, and since its basic moral is so clearly ecclesiastical, it does not seem very likely that it is a tale from local oral tradition at all. 'We must believe that this happened...,' Arcoid says in his preamble.[25] The story must be believed, in other words, not for

---

[23] The author of the anonymous *Vita sancti Erkenwaldi*, composed by my estimate around the turn of the eleventh century, uses *verbatim* phrases from another miracle story of Gregory of Tours, in his *Historia Francorum*. See Whatley, '*Vita Erkenwaldi*: an Anglo-Norman's life of an Anglo-Saxon Saint', *Manuscripta* 27 (1983), 77.

[24] 'Sed que audita et uisa dulciter memorie mandauerat [populus], litteris ligare ne aufugerent, proh dolor, neglexit. Irruens itaque mors et ipsos uirtutum diuinarum testes absorbuit et sanctitatis inditia ... ex magna parte deleuit.' *Miracula*, Proemium, CCC 161, f.33v.

[25] 'Illud quoque quis fidelium audiat et non expauescat, quod ... credendum est accidisse cuidam homini ... qui ... morte terribili omnibus beati presulis parrochianis innotuit.' *Miracula*, Mir. II, CCC 161, f.35r. Notice that even the verb 'innotuit' here is ambiguous and indefinite as to time: it could mean that the wretched man 'became famous' among the parishioners of that time, or that he 'has become famous' and is still remembered as such. Arcoid seems to want to suggest the latter, but he stops short of being fully explicit.

its historical authenticity but because its meaning and import are timelessly true and vital to the good of the Christian community around Erkenwald's church and shrine.

Appropriately, the story is placed at the outset not in historical time but in a liturgical continuum: the narrative begins by summarising a diocesan decree that on Erkenwald's approaching feast day the people of London should cease from secular pursuits, 'seculariis studiis intermissis', and work with their prayers instead: 'ad ecclesiam conuenirent, suisque precibus ac tanti patroni erkenwaldi tam corpori quam anime necessaria obtinere laborarent'. Arcoid then tells how the people look forward to the feast day, 'dies optatus', and when it arrives they vie with one another to show their devotion to the saint both with their fine clothes and good behaviour. The result of their happy efforts, he concludes, is an atmosphere of such exultation that a foreigner observing the religious zeal, 'studium religionis', in clergy and people alike, would think he was in the heavenly Jerusalem, 'ubi spiritus beati sempiterno gaudio fruuntur'.[26]

Arcoid's comparison between the Londoners and the souls in bliss may seem extravagant, but it is highly appropriate in a story about work and holidays. Daily work, particularly physical labour, was in the Christian view, starting from Genesis 3, 17-19, the punishment for and emblem of man's sin and fall from grace. To rest from it, as on the sabbath or a saint's feast day, was to anticipate salvation and the redeemed soul's return to paradisal bliss, not by doing nothing, but rather by doing work which was in itself, ideally, effortless and blissful: praising God. St Augustine himself likened to play or game the good works – almsgiving, fasting, vigils, liturgies, and reading the scriptures – that he recommended to widows as *delicias spiritales*, 'spiritual delights'. Thus to observe the sabbath, or other such holiday, religiously was a way of affirming one's devotion not simply to a particular saint or to God, but also to the whole idea of the bliss to come, as envisaged by the Church. The soul would find its joyful rest in the ceaseless tranquil activity of adoring God, an activity foreshadowed most visibly in the continuous round of the liturgy of office and mass, the *opus Dei*.[27]

For the blasphemous layman, on the other hand, there is only one kind of work: hard, physical work which only strong men can do, *opus virorum fortium*, and which produces the necessary things of earthly life such as food and money. Holiday, for him, is a day for no work of any kind, but for simple debauchery. In his ceaseless (and always unfulfilled) quest for money and physical satisfaction, he is a type of the carnal man, the unredeemed Adam whose fate (as imposed on him in Genesis 3) – to labour for one's bread and then to die – is recalled in Arcoid's first word

[26] Mir. II, CCC 161, f. 35r.
[27] For Augustine's thoughts on the sabbath and the character of eternal rest, see letter no. 55, c. ix, 17: PL 33.212-13; on *bona opera* as *ludus*, see Joseph Zycha, ed., *S. Aurelii Augustini de bono uiduitatis*, CSEL 41, sect. v, pars III (Prague/Vienna/Leipzig, 1900), 338-339, and Robert A. Markus, 'Work and Worker in Early Christianity', in John M. Todd, ed., *Work: Christian Thought and Practice* (London/ Baltimore, 1960), 22-23.

describing him, 'laboranti', and then in his own reiterated insistence on having to work in order to eat. Finally it is dramatised in the not-so-subtle symbolism of the half-buried skull that causes his fatal fall. Earthbound as he is, dedicated to the mundane and the mortal, absorbed in himself,[28] he cannot conceive of what the clergy do as necessary or useful work. In his carnality he cannot believe in or understand the delightful work of the holiday liturgy and devotion. The canon does not try to refute the labourer's arguments about clerical idleness and uselessness; they have been refuted in advance by Arcoid's elaborate description of the feast day itself as an image of heavenly life, and as a day for a special kind of holy labouring that layfolk may do on these special occasions, but that the clergy perform continuously.

Mir. II is a uniquely elaborate treatment of the topos of miraculous punishment for working on a holy day. It seems no accident that Arcoid located such a virtuoso piece in a place of prominence near the beginning of his collection. For it seems to function there as a sort of introduction to and summation of the later, comparable episodes of divine punishment for different forms of sacrilege: Mir. VI, X, XII, XVII. Mir. II, which is a more comprehensive, extreme, and detailed working out of the topos of punishment for sacrilege, serves to dramatise, discuss, and make explicit at the outset what is left largely implicit in these later episodes and in comparable episodes in other collections. What Arcoid wants his readers to grasp, apparently, is the connection between indifference to the saints and indifference to the Church's sacramental system as a whole. The layman's irreverence towards Erkenwald is rooted in a deep-seated irreverence towards the clergy and their priestly function, and towards the life of the Church in general.

It is tempting to see Mir. II and the later stories of conflict between the cult of St Erkenwald and recalcitrant London laymen as evidence for a historical conflict between the clergy and burgers of London during the first half of the twelfth century. In support of this view, following the methods of Sigal or Finucane, one could point out that most of the healing miracles benefit unmarried women or foreigners, while all the punitive miracles are aimed at male Londoners. But other evidence available to historians suggests a different picture. Relations between the cathedral chapter and the city during this period are generally believed to have been close.[29] The canons were neither monks nor recluses aloof from the urban world beyond the church yard. They had town houses and suburban manors, some were from London families, and the charters reveal them to have been continuously associated with their lay counterparts in matters

[28] St Augustine remarks, in the letter cited in the previous note, that the soul finds only temporary rest in physical pleasures, and that these weigh the soul down, impeding its capacity for transcendence, turning it in upon itself and inducing pride, 'quia se pro summo habet, cum superior sit Deus. Nec in tali peccato impunita relinquitur, quia *Deus superbis resistit*', etc. *Ep.* 55, c.ix, 18: PL 33.213.
[29] C. N. L. Brooke, 'The Composition of the Chapter of St Paul's, 1086-1163', *Cambridge Historical Journal* 10 (1951), 122-23, who cites also J. H. Round, *The Commune of London* (Westminster, 1899), 36-38.

of business and property. Occasional lay recalcitrance or irreverence is only to be expected, but the *Miracula*'s impression of a stand-off between churchmen and laymen does not seem very plausible from a historical point of view.

It *does* seem to me probable, however, that Arcoid and his fellow clerics would have been anxious to promote Erkenwald's cult at this time, and to persuade or frighten as many people as possible into participating in the feast days and contributing with their purses. The emphasis on punitive miracles in the *Miracula*, in other words, may well be looking to the future rather than reflecting the past. The St Paul's chapter had suffered a series of financial body blows during the late 1130s, losing not only the bishop's revenues and some prebends to the crown during a lengthy episcopal vacancy but also an enormous amount of cash that had been spent on the long wrangle over the episcopal election, including an expensive junket to Rome led by one of the candidates, Abbot Anselm of Bury.[30] The chapter's decision in 1138 to provide Erkenwald with a new and costly silver shrine (first mentioned in Mir. VI) looks very like it was intended to increase publicity and provide a focus for visitors and donations, so as to help defray the ongoing expenses of the great building program, expenses which in the past had been borne in part by the bishops. The church was only half-finished in Arcoid's time, and the financial burden could only have been aggravated by another bad fire in 1135/36, which Arcoid does not mention.[31]

I do not believe, however, that Arcoid's motives in composing the *Miracula* were solely of this pragmatic kind. There is enough evidence elsewhere in the work to indicate that he himself was deeply disturbed by some of the intellectual developments within clerical ranks in Western Europe in his lifetime. Attitudes towards saints' cults, relics, miracles, and hagiography were all affected, like everything else to do with the Church, by the increasing vogue of logic and theological inquiry, and by the new interest in nature and natural causes, that accompanied the growth of the schools. Heresies advocating, among other things, resistance to or disregard for saints' cults were in the news in the early 1140s when Arcoid was writing the *Miracula*.[32] There was a spirit of scepticism and criticism abroad that aroused the resentment of traditionalists who, like Arcoid,

[30] The vacancy and the election story are described by Ralph de Diceto, *Abbreviationes chronicorum*, entries for 1136-38, ed. Stubbs, *The Historical Works of Master Ralph de Diceto*, RS 68, 2 vols. (London, 1876), I: 248-52. On Anselm of Bury, see E. W. Williamson, ed., *The Letters of Osbert of Clare, Prior of Westminster* (Oxford, 1929), 192-200. For further discussion see Whatley, *The Saint of London*, ch. 3, pt 1.

[31] Mir. XIV provides evidence that the Romanesque choir at least was complete and in use by 1140, but work on the remainder of the huge cathedral continued for decades later. See Rose Graham, 'An Appeal about 1175 for the Building Fund of St Paul's Cathedral Church', *Journal of the British Archaeological Association*, 3rd ser., 10 (1945-47), 73-76. The fire of 1135/36 is mentioned by Matthew Paris, *Chronica Majora*, ed. Henry R. Luard, RS 57, 7 vols. (London, 1872-83), II: 163.

[32] On the heresies associated with Henry of Lausanne and Peter of Bruys, see R. I. Moore, *The Origins of European Dissent* (New York, 1975), 82-114.

had not only a vested interest but also, one must assume, a genuine faith in a sacramental and miraculous order of creation.[33] My hunch is that Arcoid's violently cautionary tales about defiantly irreverent laymen are addressed as much to his fellow clerics as to the laymen. The latter could not read them for themselves anyway, and the canon in Mir. II is hardly speaking directly to the illiterate artisan when he says, in the midst of his little sermon on Erkenwald's cult:

> Nor is it any man's place to press for an accounting (*enumerare*) of these miracles, or for an explanation of them; rather it is our duty to write out the history of them, nothing more.[34]

The workman himself does not mention Erkenwald's miracles: remarks such as these are more obviously aimed at learnedly sceptical critics of miracle tales (among whom was Arcoid's contemporary, Henry of Huntingdon[35]) who were attempting to apply more rigorous criteria to claims of sanctity and miracles.[36] At the end of the longest miracle episode, Mir. IV, in which Erkenwald's shrine and linen pall miraculously survive the great fire of 1087, Arcoid bursts into a tirade against 'Vigilantius', a fourth-century opponent of relics cults.[37] Like Archbishop Hildebert of Le Mans[38] a few years before, Arcoid here is doubtless using the name of the ancient heretic to signify the opinions of actual contemporaries. Guibert de Nogent, for example, argues in his *De pignoribus* that the saints should be commemorated for the quality of their lives, and their moral and spiritual examples followed, but that their mortal remains, like everyone else's, should be left in decent oblivion, below ground.[39]

Arcoid's *Miracula* is by no means a polemical tract on the order of Peter the Venerable's *Contra Petrobrusianos* (1148),[40] but in my view it may legitimately be read as a narrative expression of one of the controversial issues in clerical circles of the time. At the heart of the work is a deep sense of the sacramental aspect of Christianity, and a corresponding lack

---

[33] For more detailed discussion and bibliography, see Whatley, *The Saint of London*, ch. 3, pt 3.

[34] *Miracula* II, CCCC 161, f. 35v.

[35] Henry devotes a separate book of his *Historia Anglorum* to a collection of English miracles, but significantly the great majority are extracted verbatim from Bede, so uneasy is Henry about the reliability of miracle stories. His personal qualms about popular saints' cults and miracle tales are expressed in the prologue to *Historia*, IX, most of which was omitted in the Rolls Series edition. For text and translation of the prologue as it appears in Cambridge University Library MS Ii.2.3, see Whatley, *The Saint of London*, ch. 3, pt 3.

[36] For a survey of medieval criticism of saints' cults, see Klaus Schreiner, '*Discrimen Veri et Falsi*. Ansätze und Formen in der Heiligen- und Reliquienverehrung des Mittelalters', *Archiv für Kulturgeschichte* 48 (1966), 1-53.

[37] Mir. IV, CCCC 161, f. 39r. For St Jerome's epistolary tract attacking Vigilantius, which is the sole source of our knowledge of the latter's writings, see PL 23.353-68.

[38] *Venerabilis Hildeberti Cenomanensis episcopi epistolae*, II, 23, PL 171.237-38, 240.

[39] PL 156.626.

[40] James Fearns, ed., *Petris Venerabilis contra Petrobrusianos hereticos*, CCCM 10 (Turnhout, 1968).

of interest in relgious individualism, mysticism, asceticism, theological inquiry, nature and natural science, the *vita apostolica*, or any other manifestation of the intellectual *novitas* of the age, with the possible exception of 'eloquentie uirtus'.[41] The moral life is barely glanced at; Christian morality is represented mainly in terms of humble, unquestioning devotion to the saints and participation in the liturgy and sacraments of the Church. God's redeeming grace passes to sinful humanity through a variety of material channels such as water, oil, wine, bread, precious metals, fingers of priests, the hewn and painted stones and wood of churches, and the bones of the holy dead. Far from being an inner condition of every Christian soul, the Church is a physical place where the divine presence is felt and enjoyed through the material remains and gleaming reliquaries of the saints, and through the ministrations and liturgical labours of the priests. Contemporary scepticism about devotion to relics arouses Arcoid's anger because to him it seems like an attack on the sacramental character of the Church. The crass materialism of the workman in Mir. II is, to someone of Arcoid's way of thinking, not that far removed from the high-minded scepticism of 'Vigilantius', who, according to Arcoid, dismisses the relics of the saints as mere 'dry bones ... ashes ... vile cadaver(s) ...'.[42] The intellectual's repugnance at the adoration of bodily remains, and his corresponding insistence on the primacy of the moral and the spiritual, along with his increasing awareness of natural causes, might lead paradoxically to a more fundamental materialism, as he progressively denies the presence of the supernatural in the natural, to be left with nothing but the physical in the world around him. The eventual result of such thinking is a loss of faith in the amazing but crucial possibility of the 'humanorum corporum resurrectio', which Arcoid sees represented in, for example, the miraculous survival of Erkenwald's shrine and pall during the burning of the old Saxon minster.[43] Peter Brown has recently argued that it was this concern for the resurrection of the flesh that brought the aging Augustine of Hippo to lend his own support and credence to the relic cults of north Africa, overcoming his own enduring scepticism about modern miracles.[44]

Viewed from this perspective, Arcoid's ostensibly excessive emphasis on the dangers of failing to honour St Erkenwald's cult, and his periodic, violent outbursts against sceptics and detractors, are more intelligible. The tales of lay sacrilege in the pages of the *Miracula* should probably not be taken too literally or historically (although some of the shorter episodes may well be based, however loosely, on actual events that today would be reported as industrial accidents). In Mir. II, in particular, Arcoid has taken the hagiographer's stereotypically blasphemous peasant and made of him

[41] 'Eloquentie uirtus' is the opening phrase of the *Miracula*: CCCC 161, f. 33r.
[42] Arcoid, in the passage cited above, n. 37, attributes these phrases to Vigilantius, but they have no immediate parallel in Jerome's summaries of Vigilantius's actual writings, among which there were also attacks on clerical celibacy and the cult of the Virgin.
[43] Mir. IV, CCCC 161, f. 38r.
[44] Peter Brown, *The Cult of the Saints* (Chicago, 1981), 75-79.

an image of unregenerate man immersed in the physical and the utilitarian, oblivious to the redeeming presence of the saint or the promise of the afterlife. In the larger context of the *Miracula* the wretched man represents all those, learned and lewd, who, for whatever reason, criticise the saints' cults, look askance at miracle tales, and reject the pomp and ceremony of the great feast days. For the author of the *Miracula* such days express the essence of the Christian religion, and while his attitude may seem reductive and simplistic, events of later centuries have proved him something of a prophet and vindicated his paranoia. Not only did the saints' cults become one of the Lollards' and later the radical Protestants' favourite targets, but, in a more fundamental way, the sceptics and moralists who have sought to improve religious practices, by eradicating the more overtly magical and superstitious aspects of the life of the church, have helped reduce drastically its place in human society. The materialist layman of Mir. II, who boasts of the purely secular feast days on which he and his cronies celebrate food and drink *per se*, would have approved wholeheartedly of Thanksgiving Day.[45]

[45] This is not to deny that for some people, including, one assumes, its first celebrators, Thanksgiving was and still is a religious festival; but for the majority it has become a purely secular feast day, celebrating the harvest of material plenty in the New World.

'FOR THE COMMUN AT UNDERSTAND': *CURSOR MUNDI* AND ITS BACKGROUND

Sarah M. Horrall (†)

One important and sometimes neglected way in which knowledge of scripture and scriptural exegesis made its way from the cell to the world was through the medium of vernacular biblical paraphrases. Although widely read and influential in their own day, these works are not highly regarded nowadays except as raw material for dialect studies. Few have been properly edited, and even fewer have been discussed seriously for the content of their ideas. This paper will discuss the longest, the most widely copied, and indeed the most intellectually sophisticated of the Middle English biblical paraphrases, *Cursor Mundi*. I propose to discuss the way in which its author transmits ideas from the cell to the world by outlining the sources used by the poet, showing how he chose and shaped his material, and making some suggestions about the author, the audience he was addressing and the later fate of his poem.

Cursor Mundi is a long Middle English poem of about 25,000 lines, composed in the north of England at the beginning of the fourteenth century, which tells the history of the world from Creation until Doomsday.[1] Its author tells us that he is a cleric, and he emphasises that he wrote his poem for 'lewed' men, but this is all we definitely know about the circumstances of its composition.

Critics and bibliographers have had a hard time categorising it, usually classifying the *Cursor* among Comprehensive Works of Religious Instruction.[2] This grouping is really based mainly on length and the *Cursor* as it was originally written has little in common with other works so classified – *Handlyng Synne*, for instance, or the *Pricke of Conscience* – which are organised by topic. *Cursor Mundi* is rather a chronologically arranged narrative of world history of the sort which had been seen for centuries as the basic information a catechumen needed before reception into the Christian Church. St Augustine, in his enormously influential *De Catechizandis*

[1] The standard edition of *Cursor Mundi* (hereafter *CM*) is by Richard Morris (1874-93; rpt London, 1961-6). Four volumes of a new edition have also appeared: *The Southern Version of Cursor Mundi*, vol. I ed. Sarah M. Horrall, vol. III ed. Henry J. Stauffenberg, vol. IV ed. Peter H. J. Mons, and vol. II ed. Roger R. Fowler (Ottawa, 1978, 1986, 1987, 1988). Subsequent references will be made by line number to MS BL Cotton Vespasian A iii as printed in Morris' edition. The text in this manuscript is the most complete extant witness to the poet's original intention.

[2] See, e.g., John Edwin Wells, *A Manual of the Writings in Middle English* (New Haven, 1916), and George Watson, ed., *The New Cambridge Bibliography of English Literature*, vol. I (Cambridge, 1974).

Rudibus, had emphasised that such a *narratio* should be the first thing taught to new converts. He outlined a plan for teaching all of human history, from Gen. 1:1 through to the Last Judgement, the Resurrection of the body, the punishment of the wicked and the joys of heaven. In discussing this *narratio* he said:

> we ought to present all the matter in a general and comprehensive summary, choosing certain of the more remarkable facts that are heard with greater pleasure and constitute the cardinal points in history.[3]

The impulse to catechetical *narratio* was heightened in the twelfth century by the renewed emphasis on the literal sense of biblical exegesis. Beryl Smalley and M. D. Chenu particularly have drawn attention to the 'New Awareness of History', to what Hugh of St Victor called the *series narrationis*.[4] This new consciousness found its chief expression in Latin in Petrus Comestor's *Historia Scholastica*, but when the Paris schools moved on to construct *Sentence* commentaries and *Summae*, the interest in historical matters continued to develop in the vernacular literatures of western Europe.

The connection of *Cursor Mundi* with Petrus Comestor has long been made. The first edition of the poem, which began to appear in 1874, was accompanied by a section called 'Inquiry into the Sources of the *Cursor Mundi*' by Dr Haenisch. Of the nine sources which he noted, only one, the *Historia Scholastica* of Petrus Comestor, seemed to be used throughout the poem, as a source for both Old Testament and New Testament history. In the hundred years since Haenisch wrote, articles on the sources of the *Cursor* have appeared at a rate of one every thirty years or so. These have failed to change the impression that *Cursor Mundi* depends heavily on the *Historia Scholastica*.

The truth is that the *Cursor* has much more in common with Old French biblical paraphrases than it has with Comestor's school text. Besides various short translations and paraphrases of small sections of the Bible, the twelfth and thirteenth centuries in France witnessed the composition of a number of very long works dealing with biblical history.[5] The most popular of all these works was written toward the end of the twelfth century, the so-called *Bible* or *Bible de Sapience* of Herman of Valenciennes.[6] It is dedicated, like the

---

[3] Augustine, *De Catechizandis Rudibus*, translated as *The First Catechetical Instruction* by Joseph P. Christopher (1946); rpt New York, 1978), p. 18. See the discussion in Virginia Day, 'The Influence of the Catechetical *Narratio* on Old English and Some Other Medieval Literature', *Anglo-Saxon England* 3 (1974), 51-61.

[4] Beryl Smalley, *The Study of the Bible in the Middle Ages* 2nd edn (Oxford, 1952); M.-D. Chenu, *Nature, Man, and Society in the Twelfth Century*, ed. and trans. Jerome Taylor and Lester K. Little (Chicago, 1968), 162-201. The reference to Hugh is on p. 168.

[5] See Hans Robert Jauss, ed., *La Littérature didactique, allégorique et satirique* (Heidelberg, 1970), Grundriss der romanischen Literaturen des Mittelalters VI/1-2. The standard studies of the French paraphrases are still Jean Bonnard, *Les Traductions de la Bible en vers français au moyen âge* (Paris, 1884) and Samuel Berger, *La Bible française au moyen âge* (Paris, 1884).

[6] Herman of Valenciennes, *La Bible von Herman de Valenciennes*, vol. II ed. Otto

Cursor, to the Virgin, and tells the story of the world from the creation to the assumption of Christ and Mary. It survives, in whole or in part, in thirty-four manuscripts, at least seven of which were copied in England. In the thirteenth century, several similarly massive biblical histories were written in French: the *Bible des sept états du monde* of Geoffroi de Paris; the *Bible* of Jehan Malkaraume, which attempted to combine biblical history and classical legend and was never finished; the so-called *Traduction anonyme de la Bible entière*; the *Bible en françois* of Roger d'Argenteuil; and, at the very end of the century, the *Bible* of Macé de la Charité.[7] Three of these works survive only in one manuscript, but the *Traduction anonyme* is known in three manuscripts, and Roger d'Argenteuil's work from at least twelve French manuscripts and a Middle English translation.

These are clearly the works which the *Cursor*-poet has in mind when he states in his introduction:

> Þis ilk bok it es translate
> Into Inglis tong to rede
> For the loue of Inglis lede,
> Inglis lede of Ingland,
> For the commun at understand.
> Frankis rimes here I redd
> Communlik in ilka sted
> Mast es it uroght for frankis man:
> Quat is for him na frankis can?   (232-40)

In spite of what this passage has been taken to imply, the *Cursor*-poet does not simply translate a pre-existing Old French work. What he does do is to imitate the methods of the Old French authors, carefully compiling his poem from earlier works in French, Latin and Middle English.

The Old French work whose structure bears the closest resemblance to the structure of *Cursor Mundi* is the *Bible des sept états du monde* by Geoffroi de Paris. Both poets divide world history into ages, both poems begin with a versified table of contents, and an elaborate description of paradise. Both poets have interpolated the events of the history of the wood which became Christ's cross in their proper chronological places in the biblical narrative. Both poets carry their histories right down to the moment of the last judgement, with subsequent descriptions of the other world as well. However, in spite of structural similarities, there is absolutely no evidence to show that the *Cursor*-poet knew Geoffroi's work. Geoffroi's compilation, in fact, is essentially a cut-and-paste job, gluing together a number of pre-existing narratives to make as complete a work as possible. The *Cursor*-poet, while also concerned with completeness, is much more conscious of proportion and of the focus of his work.

Moldenhauer, vol. III ed. Hans Burkowitz, vol. IV ed. Eugen Kremers, vol. V ed. Ernst Martin (Griefswold, 1914); *Li Romanz de dieu et de sa mère*, ed. Ina Spiele (Leyden, 1975).

[7]   See Jauss 1836, 1848, 1924, 1492, 1852. For Roger d'Argenteuil see also Phyllis Moe, ed., *The ME Prose Translation of Roger d'Argenteuil's Bible en françois*, Middle English Texts 6 (Heidelberg, 1977).

The *Cursor Mundi* is organised around the concept of the six ages of the world. Old Testament and New Testament are given roughly the same amount of space, even though this entails a certain readjustment of the traditional arrangement. The first four ages begin, as usual, with Adam, Noah, Abraham and David. The fifth age is supposed in the Augustinian scheme to begin with the Babylonian captivity, and end with Christ's birth. However the *Cursor*-poet disposes of the Captivity briskly in three lines at the end of the fourth age (9197-9), and devotes the fifth to the debate of the four daughters of God and the miraculous childhoods of Mary and then of Christ. The sixth age, under this scheme, begins with Christ's baptism and continues until the poet begins to speak of the coming of anti-Christ and the Last Judgement (21847).

The pivotal event in the poem is, not surprisingly, the passion of Christ, and its clearly expressed devotional emphasis is on the Virgin, as the prologue announces. The events recounted under each age are kept remarkably relevant to these two central concerns. At the end of the fourth age and again at the end of the fifth the poet reminds us that all the Old Testament section has been, not a prefiguring of the New, but 'To reherse þat lady kynne', to give Mary's family background (9229-32, 12733-8). His criteria for including or excluding material are often dictated by his consciousness of his narrative structure. He includes the apocryphal stories of Moses, David and Solomon as they concern the history of the Cross Wood which culminates in the crucifixion, but he omits Petrus Comestor's popular account of the childhood of Moses because, although the stories are interesting in themselves, they do not bear on the main events.

The poet is also alert to certain themes and recurring motifs in his work. In an unusual account of Paradise (684-700) he describes a golden age in which the wolf lay down with the sheep, the deer with the lion and the hound with the hare. The ultimate source for the passage is Isaiah 11:6-8, but the *Cursor*-poet has produced his version by combining lists he found in the *Historia Scholastica* and the Old French *Traduction anonyme de la Bible entière*. He uses the same situation, this time ironically, in his unique description of Noah's Flood, when once again hostilities vanish and the wolf swims beside the ram, the lion with the hart and ladies with their servants. Somewhat similar scenes occur much later in the storms and chaos that accompany Doomsday.

A theme which recurs several times is that of the continued degeneration of the physical world after the Fall. The *Cursor*-poet translates remarks on this subject from several places in the *Historia Scholastica*, but adds to the evidence by quoting several lines from Grosseteste's *Chateau d'amour* about the loss of light in the sun and moon (701-10). The passage is inserted into the *Cursor* some nine thousand lines before the poet begins his main translation of Grosseteste's work.

The Marian material in *Cursor Mundi* provides an example of the poet's characteristic methods of working. Although Herman of Valenciennes had also dedicated his *Bible* to Mary, her presence was largely ignored throughout large stretches of his narrative. Rosemary Woolf, in her book on

the *English Mystery Plays*, points out that it is only in the mid fifteenth
century that the tradition became firmly established 'that the history of
salvation must begin, not with the Annunciation as had previously been
done, but with the story of Joachim and Anna'.[8] The story of Mary had
begun to be combined with salvation history in some thirteenth-century
Latin works,[9] but the *Cursor*-poet integrates all the episodes of Mary's life
with world history for the first time in Middle English, placing each one into
the narrative in chronological sequence. The result is so much material on
the early life of the Virgin and Christ that it forces the *Cursor*-poet into his
idiosyncratic interpretation of the ages of the world.

Another point to note is that he is aware of several different sources
available to him and he consciously either chooses one over another or
integrates two versions. For the story of Mary's childhood and marriage, he
uses Wace's Anglo-Norman poem *L'Etablissement de la fête de la
Conception Notre-Dame*, although the same material was available to him in
the Latin *Gospel of Pseudo-Matthew*, which he used for the incidents of the
Childhood of Christ.[10] The death and assumption of the Virgin is taken from a
Middle English source, the so-called *Southern Assumption*, a borrowing
which incidentally proves that the poem is not taken over wholly from an
Old French source, but was rather compiled by the *Cursor*-poet himself.[11]
The poet is aware that he is involved in a different kind of translation here,
for he says:

> In sotherin englis was it draun,
> And turnd it haue i till our aun
> Langage o northrin lede,
> Þat can nan oþer englis rede.   (20061-4)

Probably the most important point to be noticed about the *Cursor*-poet's
Marian stories, as about all his material, is that they function almost
exclusively on the literal rather than the allegorical level. Almost never does
the poet interpret events figurally. The only two exceptions which I have
noted in the entire poem are five lines on Moses' burning bush (5745-50) and
two lines on Aaron's rod (6909-10), both of which are said to be
'foresceuings' of the Virgin.

It is also an incident concerning Mary which shows the poet transcending
the chronological framework of his narrative and coming close to portraying
the history of his own time, that audience moment which Professor Kolve
notes that the cycle play writers invariably neglect.[12] After the account of the

[8]   Rosemary Woolf, *The English Mystery Plays* (Berkeley, 1972), p.161.
[9]   See the brief discussion in Sarah M. Horrall, ed., *The Lyf of Oure Lady*, Middle
English Texts 17 (Heidelberg, 1985), pp. 9-11.
[10]   *The Conception Notre Dame of Wace*, ed. William Ray Ashford (Menasha, 1933);
Pseudo-Matthaei Evangelica in Constantinus de Tischendorf, ed., *Evangelica
Apocrypha* (1876; rpt Hildesheim, 1966).
[11]   George H.McKnight, re-ed., *King Horn, Floriz and Blauncheflur, and the
Assumption of Our Lady*, ed. J.Rawson Lumby, EETS OS 14 (London, 1901).
[12]   V. A. Kolve, *The Play Called Corpus Christi* (Stanford, 1966), pp.101ff.

end of the world, the pains of Hell and joys of Heaven, the *Cursor*-poet appends the story, also from Wace's French narrative, of the institution of the Feast of the Immaculate Conception in England. The miracle occurs on English soil, and in the recent historical past, a fitting ending for a work by such an ardent nationalist.

Much of the rest of the work is produced in a similar way by interweaving various narratives. The *Cursor*-poet draws heavily on two of the Old French biblical histories mentioned previously, the *Bible* of Herman of Valenciennes and the *Traduction anonyme de la Bible entière*.[13] These he adapts and corrects at will. During the story of Joseph in Egypt, although he largely follows Herman's narrative, he refuses to use several traditional French features of the story. In *Cursor Mundi* it is Potifar's wife who attempts to seduce Joseph, not the queen of Egypt as in French tradition, and the *Cursor*-poet does not mention the ships in which the brothers had sailed from home.

The *Cursor*-poet begins the story of the Cross Wood in his Genesis section, beginning with Seth's journey to Paradise to procure the seeds for the tree which will provide the wood for Christ's cross (1237ff). The poet begins by using a Latin source, the *Vita Protoplausti Adae*, but when the story reaches Moses (6301ff) he abandons the Latin and relies on the French version in the *Traduction anonyme*, except for occasional details. The story of Moses is compiled from this poem, with additions from Herman's *Bible*, other stories apparently from the Vulgate, and a résumé of later events taken from Honorius of Autun's *De Imagine Mundi*.[14]

The poet is conscious of having to reconcile several versions of the same story. After describing the thirty silver circles which David put around the Cross tree, which later became the thirty pieces of silver paid to Judas, the poet adds cautiously:

> And þus sais sum opinion,
> Bot sua sais noght þe passion.   (8843-4)

Not all of the narratives in the work are quite so extensively interwoven, of course. Some works, especially well-known apocrypha dealing with a brief span of human history, are simply translated extensively in their proper chronological order. The Old French sources used mainly in this way are the *Chateau d'amour* of Robert Grosseteste, *L'Etablissement de la fête de la Conception Notre Dame* of Wace, and, toward the end, an anonymous Old French poem on the judgement, *Les Quinze signes du jugement dernier*.[15] Latin narratives used in the same way are the *Gospel of Pseudo-Matthew*,

[13] Lois Borland, 'Herman's *Bible* and the *Cursor Mundi*', *Studies in Philology* 30 (1933), 427-44; Philip Buehler, 'The *Cursor Mundi* and Herman's *Bible* – Some Additional Parallels', *Studies in Philology* 61 (1964), 485-99; Sarah M. Horrall, 'An Old French Source for the *Genesis* Section of *Cursor Mundi*', *Mediaeval Studies* 40 (1978), 361-73.
[14] See notes to these lines in Horrall, *Southern Version*.
[15] *Le Château d'amour de Robert Grosseteste Evêque de Lincoln*, ed. J. Murray (Paris, 1918); Erik von Kraemer, *Les Quinze signes du jugement dernier* (Helsinki, 1961).

telling of Christ's childhood; the *Gospel of Nicodemus*, telling of the harrowing of hell; the lives of the Apostles, apparently compiled from a work by Isidore and an Irish pseudo-Isidorean one; the *Vita Anti-Christi*, telling of the coming of Anti-Christ; a description of Christ's physical appearance from the apocryphal letter of Lentullus; and the lament of the Virgin known as the *Dialogue of St Bernard*.[16]

It must be admitted that the poet does use Petrus Comestor's *Historia Scholastica* throughout his work to provide details. For instance, the story of the nakedness of Noah, according to Comestor, confirms the fact that underwear had not yet been invented, and the *Cursor* translates this remark (2047-8). The poet even names Comestor at l.1921: 'piers mayner, þe god clerk', but when he comes to write a rapid summary of kings and judges, for instance, he ignores Comestor and turns instead to the very similar but slightly fuller account in *De Imagine Mundi* (6993ff).

Into his usually serious narrative, the poet occasionally inserts a bit of information of a different kind, often popular folklore. He ends the story of Abel's murder with a riddle: Abel was the man who was born before his parents, and who took his grandmother's maidenhead (1197-9). His story of Lot's wife, turned into a pillar of salt which was constantly licked by animals yet constantly renewed, is found in many early travellers' tales (2855-60). His comparison of Christ to a lion is in the bestiary tradition (18639-60). He gives an estimate of the distance the angels fell from heaven to hell (507-10). The ultimate origin of the measurement seems to be Moses Maimonides' *Guide of the Perplexed*, although it became widely known through its inclusion in the *Legenda Aurea*.[17] The *Cursor*-poet, perhaps in an attempt to make it more respectable and more English, attributes it to Bede, whose works on cosmology were already well known.

All of the sources so far discussed have been narrative ones, but the *Cursor*-poet also uses a number of what may be loosely termed theological or catechetical sources. Although Augustine had emphasised catechetical *narratio* for his converts, the emphasis of catechetical instruction shifted in the thirteenth century to more abstract discussions of the elements of the Faith. One popular handbook for the new mode of instruction was the *Elucidarium* of Honorius of Autun,[18] and it is interesting to observe that the *Cursor*-poet neatly combines the two approaches, the older historical one with the new. He uses the *Elucidarium* extensively, from the beginning of the poem, for his explanation of the nature of the Trinity and the process of

---

[16] H.C.Kim, ed., *The Gospel of Nicodemus* (Toronto, 1973); Isidore, *De Ortu et Obitu Patrum PL* LXXXIII; Pseudo-Isidore, *De Ortu et Obitu Patrum, PL* LXXXIII. Adso Dervensis, *De Ortu et Tempore Antichristi necnon et tractatus qui ad eo dependunt*, ed. D.Verhelst, Corpus Christianorum Continuatio Mediaevalis XLV (Turnhout, 1976). Ernst von Dobschütz, *Christusbilder: Untersuchungen zur christlichen Legende* (Leipzig, 1899); for bibliography on the Planctus Mariae tradition see Donald C.Baker, John L.Murphy and Louis B.Hall Jr, eds., *The Late Medieval Religious Plays of Bodleian MSS Digby 133 and E. Museo 160*, EETS OS 283 (London, 1982), pp.19-20.

[17] See Horrall, *Southern Version*, n. to ll.507-10.

[18] *L'Elucidarium et les lucidaires*, ed. Yves Lefèvre (Paris, 1954).

creation, to the description of the pains of hell and the joys of heaven at the end. Comments from this source crop up everywhere. During his version of the *Chateau d'amour*, for instance, the *Cursor*-poet inserts into Grosseteste's recapitulation of the fall of man a comment from the *Elucidarium* explaining why the angels could not ransom Adam (9771-82).

Theological and explanatory comments from other sources are briefer: an allegory of the four evangelists pulling Christ's cart comes from Petrus Riga's *Floridus Aspectus* (21263ff); the two 'fore-showings' of Mary come from Honorius of Autun's *Speculum Ecclesiae*; a few lines on the Fall echo Sedulius' *Carmen Paschale* (795-6). The *Cursor*-poet quotes Ambrose on baptism (19881ff), Innocent III on old age (3555ff), Isidore on geography (2091ff). Some of these comments clearly come to the poet at second hand, such as Gregory's answer to the question of whether a man eaten by a wolf which was in turn eaten by a lion could be resurrected whole (22895ff). The poet in fact takes this story from the *Elucidarium*.[19] However, like a conscientious graduate student, he has gone back to check the originals of at least some of his second-hand quotations. He is translating from the *Historia Scholastica* when he says 'as tellis us Metodi' (2004), but the *Cursor Mundi* goes on to quote more of the *Revelations* of Pseudo-Methodius than Comestor does. Similarly, the poet is translating Comestor when he says 'Iohn gilden-moth sais wit þis dome/ Þat he fand in a nald bok' (11380). But the poet then went back to John Chrysostom's homily and translated further material which Petrus Comestor omitted.

Like the narrative sources, the theological sources are compiled with great intelligence. In describing the creation of the world, for instance, the poet offers two alternative explanations (343-50). The first, which he takes from the *Elucidarium*, says that God first created a jumbled mixture of the elements which were then combined to form the world as we know it.[20] The second explanation begins with Augustinian terminology and describes the simultaneous creation of the physical world, the angelic world and time. The physical world begins as a *prima materia*, 'þe mater of þe four elements', which initially existed without form. As matter cannot exist without form, however, the *Cursor*-poet goes on to modify his statement, not in Augustine's terms, which were allegorical, but with the explanation given by Hugh of St Victor in his *Adnotationes Elucidatoriae in Pentateuchon*.[21] This is indeed a sophisticated poem.

In all, the *Cursor*-poet can be shown to have used at least twenty-four different texts as sources, nineteen of them Latin and five Old French. At this point, one may well ask what kind of audience he expected this translated erudition to appeal to. He himself says only that he is writing for 'lewed men' who can't read French, but the surviving manuscripts of his work help to identify the actual readers of the work somewhat more precisely.

[19] *Ibid.*, III, 45.
[20] *Ibid.*, I, 20.
[21] Sarah M. Horrall, 'The *Cursor Mundi* Creation Story and Hugh of St Victor', *Notes and Queries* n.s. 23 (1976), 99-100.

Nine manuscripts of *Cursor Mundi* are extant, one of them a fragment, another a partial text only. Of these, all but one were, as far as we know, in lay hands. Only Laud misc. 416 belonged to Anne Colville, a nun of Syon Abbey. It is possible to infer something about the social status of some of the other owners. MSS BL Cotton Vespasian A iii and BL Additional 36983 may have belonged to merchants, judging by indentures and accounts kept on their flyleaves.[22] On the other hand, BL Additional 31042 was copied and owned by the gentleman scribe Robert Thornton. Towards the end of the fourteenth century, a new 'edition' of the poem was made at Lichfield for the market in the south of England. Two manuscripts of this edition survive, Cambridge, Trinity College R.3.8 and London, College of Arms, Arundel LVII, and there is evidence of another in similar format, an ancestor of the extant Laud misc. 416 and BL Additional 36983.[23] These manuscripts are rather elegantly produced in large format on parchment, and the College of Arms manuscript had several quite nicely painted initials.

Moving up the social scale, the manuscript which is now Göttingen Universitätsbibliothek theol. 107r was written and very elaborately decorated for an armigerous patron, probably from either southern Lincolnshire or Yorkshire. This manuscript is one of the very few remaining Middle English manuscripts of the fourteenth century to contain scenes to illustrate its text. Their presence testifies both to the high regard in which the poem was held by at least one reader, and to the social standing of that reader.

Who, then, produced this poem? Although we may never be completely certain of the answer to that question, we can, I think, make some inferences about the circumstances of its composition.

We cannot know for certain how long the poet took to write *Cursor Mundi*. However, a translation of the *Dialogues* of St Gregory into 24,000 lines of Anglo-Norman took seven years, and even Lydgate, at his supposed rate of composition, would have taken at least five years to complete the work.[24] Line by line comparison of the poem with its sources everywhere shows that the poet translated these texts directly, and did not rely on memory. He has the habit of interpolating a quotation from another work into the one he is currently translating, suggesting that he worked with several volumes open before him.

Over a period of perhaps five to ten years, then, the poet must have had access to a fairly substantial library, including not only the standard Latin works, but a number of appropriate volumes in French as well.[25] Yet a long

[22] This has already been noted by Charles V. C. Ross, 'An Edition of Part of the Edinburgh Fragment of the Cursor Mundi', B.Litt. Diss. (Oxford, 1971), p. 13.
[23] Evidence for this will be presented in Horrall, *Southern Version*, vol. V, forthcoming.
[24] M. Dominica Legge, *Anglo-Norman in the Cloisters* (Edinburgh, 1950), pp. 61-2.
[25] R. M. Wilson, 'The Contents of the Mediaeval Library' in Francis Wormald and C. E. Wright, eds., *The English Library before 1700* (London, 1958) shows that the Latin sources used by the *Cursor*-poet were found in most medieval libraries of any size. Some scholars doubt that the *Cursor*-poet was himself responsible for compiling the sources. See, e.g., Bernhard Ten Brink, *Early English Literature*, trans.

period of work in a good library was surely a great luxury when the *Cursor* was being composed, early in the fourteenth century. It has been estimated that, of the sixty-one years from 1296-1357, thirty-nine or forty were spent in active warfare in the north of England, a warfare compounded from time to time by famine, cattle plague, epidemics, apparently of typhus, and, if the prose *Brut* is to be believed, outbreaks of cannibalism as well.[26] Surely given these circumstances, the *Cursor* could only have been produced in one of the large monasteries of the north.

Although the original text of *Cursor Mundi* left its author in the early fourteenth century, the history of the modifications made to the poem in the next 150 years is a mini-history of changing tastes in devotional literature. The fragmentary manuscript in the Royal College of Physicians in Edinburgh is the only surviving witness to what, judging by the author's versified table of contents, was the poem he originally intended. At an early stage, the *Cursor* had added to it a penitential handbook with an anti-fraternal bias, as well as an exposition of the Creed and Pater Noster and two prayers (25684-29547, 24971-25618). The Göttingen manuscript also has added a song on the five joys of Our Lady (25619-25683). The Lichfield version of the *Cursor*, however, chopped the penitential handbook, the inserted lyrics and all the material after Doomsday, to produce a streamlined poem containing only the events of human history in strictly chronological order. Interestingly enough, this version calls itself a book of stories rather than a treatise and its text has been divided into smaller sections convenient for an evening's reading.

As the fourteenth century drew to a close, the *Cursor Mundi* seems to have been considered rather old-fashioned. Later readers preferred more affective and emotionally charged texts. As he was copying the poem at the end of the fourteenth century, the scribe of BL Additional 36983 substituted a rhymed translation of the Pseudo-Bonaventuran *Meditationes de Passione Christi* for the *Cursor*'s Passion story, and a long passage from the *Pricke of Conscience* replaces the *Cursor*'s account of Doomsday. Even manuscripts of the *Cursor* which had been copied earlier were not immune from being tampered with. Part of the Passion narrative in BL Cotton Vespasian A iii

Horace M. Kennedy (New York, 1883), p. 288; George L. Hamilton, review of Gordon Hall Gerould, *Saints' Legends* in *Modern Language Notes* 36 (1921), p. 238. One surviving manuscript of Old French biblical paraphrases, MS Arsenal 3516, does combine Herman's *Bible* and the *Traduction anonyme*, but not in the same way in which the *Cursor*-poet combines them. Even allowing for the possibility that he found several works together in the same manuscript, the poet must still have had access to a substantial library.

[26] For discussions of the devastating effect of the war and famine in the north see especially Jean Scammell, 'Robert I and the North of England', *English Historical Review* 73 (1958), 385-403; Ian Kershaw, 'The Great Famine and Agrarian Crisis in England 1315-1322' in R. H. Hilton, ed., *Peasants, Knights and Heretics* (Cambridge, 1976), pp. 85-132; G. W. S. Barrow, 'The Aftermath of War: Scotland and England in the Late Thirteenth and Early Fourteenth Centuries', *Transactions of the Royal Historical Society*, 5th ser., 28 (1978), 103-125; J. A. Tuck, 'War and Society in the Medieval North', *Northern History* 21 (1985), 33-52. The reference to the prose *Brut* is in Friedrich W. D. Brie, ed., *The Brut* (London, 1906), ch. 189, pp. 209-10.

was later erased, and a new version, based on the *Southern Passion*, was inserted, even though the alteration required the insertion of several additional leaves.[27] Robert Thornton in the mid fifteenth century switched to the *Northern Passion* rather than continue copying the *Cursor*. The *Cursor*'s decline in popularity is emphasised by the fact that it was never printed, even though Caxton was aware of its existence.

Yet *Cursor Mundi* continued to exert an influence on other works. From time to time, it has been posited as a source for a great many medieval religious works, including the *Pricke of Conscience*, *Iacob and Ioseph*, the *Northern Passion*, the Middle English translation of the *Revelations* of Pseudo-Methodius, a short poem describing Christ's physical appearance and the cycle plays.[28] Most of these are, however, simply analogues to the *Cursor*, having used the same, usually Latin, sources, and the similarities prove no more than that the *Cursor*-poet usually had a sure instinct for what appealed to readers.

There are some exceptions to this, however. I believe that the poet of *Cleanness* knew the *Cursor*, because of his description of Noah's Flood, which is highly unusual and very like that in the *Cursor*.[29] It is also quite clear that William Caxton used the *Cursor* in preparing his account of Old Testament history for his *Golden Legend*.[30] Caxton speaks of the work, which he doesn't name, with some reservation, introducing quotations with such phrases as 'it is said, but of none auctoryte'. Whatever his reservations, though, he transfers a fair amount of extra-biblical material from that source.

It is with Caxton's back-handed compliment – borrowing from the book without really approving of it – that I will leave *Cursor Mundi*. It is not a great work of literature, but its author brought a high degree of intelligence to his task of transmitting, in serviceable verse, a great body of information and narrative from the cell to the world.

---

[27] Carleton Brown, 'The Cursor Mundi and the Southern Passion', *Modern Language Notes* 26 (1911), 15-18.

[28] Some of the following references merely imply a relationship with the *Cursor* by remarking on its great similarity to the work under discussion. See Richard Morris, ed., *The Pricke of Conscience* (Berlin, 1863), ix-xii; Arthur S. Napier, ed., *Iacob and Iosep* (Oxford, 1916), pp. xiii-xiv; Frances A. Foster, *The Northern Passion*, vol. II, EETS OS 147 (London, 1916), p. 80; Charlotte d'Evelyn, 'The Middle English Metrical Version of the *Revelations* of Methodius; with a Study of the Influence of Methodius in Middle-English Writings', *PMLA* 33 (1918), pp. 152-4; Thomas W. Ross, 'Five Fifteenth-Century "Emblem" Verses from Brit. Mus. Addit. 37049', *Speculum* 32 (1957), p. 277, n. 12; Baker, *Late Medieval Religious Plays*, p. lxxxix; Lucy Toulmin Smith, ed., *York Plays* (1885; rpt New York, 1963), pp. xliv-xlv.

[29] Sarah M. Horrall, '*Cleanness* and *Cursor Mundi*', *Modern Language Notes* 22 (1985), 6-11.

[30] Sarah M. Horrall, 'William Caxton's Biblical Translation', *Medium Aevum* 53 (1985), 91-8.

THE AUDIENCE FOR
THE MIDDLE ENGLISH MYSTICS

S. S. Hussey

I suppose the usual idea of a mystic is of someone who decides that he or she cannot live a good spiritual life whilst caught up in the pressures of civilisation. So he withdraws from the world in order to become more sensitive to the spirit of God who rewards him with glimpses of the heavenly mysteries, glimpses which, in the life to come, will eventually become full sight. Such experiences may be dramatic: *raptus*, *hid divinite*, feelings of warmth, light and celestial song. But such a person may, too, suffer the misunderstanding, if not the direct opposition of his fellow-men; mysticism, as the old joke has it, begins in *mist* but ends in *schism*. All this is no doubt partly true, but mysticism (or, as they themselves called it, contemplation) is unlikely to appeal to more than a small part of humanity, even in the later Middle Ages when, we are sometimes told, the communal religious life had begun to lose something of its attraction or when the individual's rapprochement to his creator may have offered a defence from a society whose values seemed to be changing if not actually declining. So who on earth were the mystics addressing? Each other, a few disciples, a mere coterie? It seems a simple exercise – at least initially it seemed simple – to see what the texts themselves can tell us of the kind of audience (or audiences) envisaged. It would be impossible, even if I had the ability, to deal in a short time with all those Western European writers who might lay claim to the title of mystic, so I shall concentrate on five, all English: Richard Rolle, who died in 1349, possibly of the plague; the mid-late-fourteenth-century author of the *Cloud of Unknowing*, the *Book of Privy Counselling* and various minor works (whom I shall henceforward refer to as the *Cloud* author); Walter Hilton (d.1396), especially his *Scale of Perfection* and *Mixed Life*; Julian of Norwich, born (like Chaucer) in the early 1340s and whose *Revelations of Divine Love* recounts experiences beginning in 1373, but who was apparently still alive, over 70, in 1416; and last (but I am sure she would not have thought least, for all her self-identification as 'this creature') Margery Kempe of Lynn who also spans the last part of the fourteenth century and the fifteenth.[1] It is worth remembering that, although the bulk of

---

[1] I quote from: H. E. Allen, *English Writings of Richard Rolle* (1931); P. Hodgson, *The Cloud of Unknowing and Related Treatises* (Salzburg, 1982); E. Underhill, *The Scale of Perfection* (1923, a modernised text, quoted here by book and chapter); S. J. Ogilvie-Thomson, *Walter Hilton's Mixed Life Edited from Lambeth Palace MS 472* (Salzburg, 1986); E. Colledge and J. Walsh, *A Book of Showings to the Anchoress Julian of Norwich* (Toronto, 1978, 2 vols.); S. B. Meech, *The Book of Margery*

this writing is in English, certain of Rolle's works are in Latin (the *Incendium Amoris* and the *Contra Amatores Mundi*, for instance). So are a few of the minor works, perhaps private letters, of Hilton. Other works, notably the *Scale* and the *Cloud*, were translated from English into Latin, presumably in order to achieve wider currency.

The obvious place to begin is with the dedications, since the person to whom a work of this kind was dedicated presumably read it. But there are not very many of these. Ms CUL Dd. v. 64 dedicates Rolle's *Ego Dormio* to a nun of Yedingham (north Yorkshire) and the same manuscript has colophons stating that his *Commandment* (so called from its opening words) was intended for a nun of Hampole and the *Form of Living* (?1348, and so one of his last compositions) for *Margaretam anachoritam, suam dilectam discipulam*. These latter two may in fact be one and the same person, since movement from a less strict (a nunnery) to a more strict (an anchorite's) way of life was allowed – but not *vice versa*. The later of the two, the *Form of Living*, envisages someone recently enclosed:

> For þat þou has forsakyn þe solace and þe joy of þis world, and taken þe to solitary lyf, for Gods luf to suffer tribulacion and anguys here, and sithen com to þat blys þat nevermare blynnes, I trowe treuly þat þe comforth of Jhesu Criste and þe swetnes of his love, with þe fire of þe Haly Gast, þat purges all syn, sall be in þe and with þe, ledand þe, and lerand þe how þou sall thynk, how þou sall pray, what þou sall wyrk; so þat in a few 3ers þou sall have mare delyte to be by þi nane, and speke till þi luf and to þi spows Jhesu Crist, þat hegh es in heven, þan if þou war lady here of a thowsand worldes. (89.1)

but it advises her not to mistake appearance for reality:

> For I will not þat þou wene þat all er hali þat hase þe abet of halynes, and er noght ocupyed with þe worlde. (93.5)

The *Commandment* gives a similar warning:

> Thyne abett says þat þou hase forsaken þe world, þat þou ert gyven till Goddes servys, þat þou delyte þe noght in erthly thyng. Lok þan, þat it be in þi hert, als it semes in men syght. For na thyng may make þe religious, bot vertues and clennes of sawle in charite. (79.199)

Other phrases suggest the activity of a recluse:

> Men þat comes til þe, þai luf þe for þai se þi grete abstinens, and for þai se þe enclosed. Bot I may not love þe so lyghtly, for oght þat I se þe do withowten; bot if þi wil be conformed enterely to Goddes will. (102.82)

Kempe, EETS o.s. 212 (1940). For general information on the English mystics see A. S. G. Edwards, *Middle English Prose, A Critical Guide to Major Authors and Genres* (New Brunswick, 1984) and P. Szarmarch, *An Introduction to the Medieval Mystics of Europe* (New York, 1984).

... some special poynt of þe luf of Jhesu Criste, and of contemplatyf lyfe, þe whilk þou hase taken þe till at mens syght. (103.216)

If þou be in prayers and meditacions al þe day, I wate wele þat þou mon wax gretely in þe lufe of Jhesu Cryste, and mikel fele of delyte, and within schort tyme. (104.48)

But perhaps these are activities relatively newly begun.

Yet already in these texts a wider audience sometimes seems to be envisaged:

In þis werk [the English *Psalter*] I seke no strange Inglis, bot lightest and comunest and swilke þat es mast like vnto þe Latyn, so þat þai þat knawes noght Latyn, be þe Inglis may cum tille many Latyn wordes. (7.91)

and in the *Ego Dormio*

Þi flesche sal þou overcome with haldyng of þi maydenhede, for Goddes lufe anely; or if þou be na mayden, thorow chaste lyvyng and resonabel in thoght and dede, and thorow discrete abstinence. (67.196)

The second version of Rolle's *Meditations on the Passion* has no dedication and in part at least seems to be a meditative exercise (e.g. 32.143-7). Hilton addressed his Latin epistles to individuals, most notably the *De Utilitate et Prerogativis Religionis* to a priest, Adam Horsley, a senior member of the Exchequer, who was considering becoming a Carthusian. He eventually entered the Beauvale Charterhouse in Nottinghamshire and died there in 1423/4. But, even so, the letter is really a general defence of the religious life.

My next category is of address to a *type* of person rather than to a named individual. Since I have mentioned Hilton, I might continue by naming one or two of his other Latin letters and their *incipits*: *Ad Quendam Solitarium* (*Dilicte in Christo frater, obsecro te in visceribus Jesu Christi ...*); *Ad Quemdam seculo renunciare volentem* (*Dilecto in Christo fratri spiritum concilij & fortitudinis ...*); *De Ymagine Peccati* (*Dilecte michi in Christo frater, inter cetera qua michi scripsisti ...*). The *quemdam* suggests a specific addressee, but Horsley is the only one we know by name and the advice would be applicable to other people in a similar state. Hilton's *Epistle on Mixed Life* (in English) clearly has in mind one particular person who sought to combine the responsibilities of the active *life* with the desire for the peace of the contemplative *state*:

Þou schalt not vttirli folwen þi desire for to leuen occupacioun and bisynesse of þe world, whiche aren nedefull to vsen in rulynge of þi silf and of alle oþere þat aren vndir þi kepynge, and ʒeue þee hooli to goostli occupaciouns of praiers and meditaciouns, as it were a frere or a monk or an oþir man þat were not bounden to þe world bi children and seruauntes as þou art, for it falleþ not to þee, and ʒif þou do soo, þou kepest not þe ordre of charite. Also, ʒif þou woldest leuen vttirli goostli occupacion, nameli now aftir þe grace þat

God haþ ʒeuen vnto þee, and sette þe hooli to þe bisynesse of þe world, to fulfillynge of werkes of actif liyf as fulli as an noþir man þat neuere feeled deuocion, þou leuest þe ordre of charite, for þi staat askeþ for to doo boþe, eche of hem in dyuers tyme. Þou schalt meedele þe werkes of actif liyf wiþ goostli werkes of lif contemplatif, and þanne doost þou weel.   (89-103)

This is a deliberate extension of the Augustinian and Gregorian figure of the good bishop, but my point here is that it is a book which, whilst addressed to an individual with a particular problem, might be used by others. Its teaching is an interesting advance on Rolle:

Those contemplatives who are most on fire with the love of eternity are like those higher beings whose eagerness for eternal love is most enjoyable and outstanding. They never, or scarcely ever, engage in outside activity, or accept the dignity of ecclesiastical preferment or rank. They tend to keep themselves to themselves, ever ready to reach up to Christ with joyful song.

So begins chapter 3 of the *Incendium Amoris* (Penguin translation). In chapter 21 Rolle recognises that the alternation of the two lives is theoretically allowable but he does not see it as a practical possibility:

If any man could achieve both lives at once, the contemplative and the active, and sustain and fulfil them, he would be great indeed. He would maintain a ministry with his body, and at the same time experience within himself the song of heaven, absorbed in melody and the joy of everlasting love. I do not know if anybody has ever done this: it seems to me impossible to do both at once.

The *Incendium Amoris* is designed (especially in the last third of the book) for would-be contemplatives and an audience apparently capable of reading Latin. Yet its Prologue says unambiguously:

I offer, therefore, this book for the attention, not of the philosophers and sages of this world, not of great theologians bogged down in their interminable questionings, but of the simple and unlearned, who are seeking rather to love God than to amass knowledge.

This category and that of contemplatives are not, of course, mutually exclusive, but the absolutes of the text itself are, in its Prologue, somewhat fuzzy around the edges.

Hilton's major work, the *Scale of Perfection*, begins its first book (of two) with an address to a 'ghostly sister' who is a recluse. Chapter 1 says the object of the book is to show her how she may be spiritually as well as physically enclosed. Yet I do not think, as has sometimes been suggested, that this ghostly sister is altogether a fiction. She may, for one thing, have been only recently enclosed: chapter 3 speaks of the contemplative life as a 'mark' to be aimed at and says that 'thy state asketh for to be contemplative, for that is the end and the entent of thine enclosing'. She 'may not well use' reading of holy writ (because she has no Latin?) and so should occupy herself in prayer and meditation (ch. 15). The next chapter, after stating her unworthiness to practise the contemplative life, adds 'This I say to thee, not that thou shouldest forethink thy purpose and be mis-paid with thine enclosing' – beginner's doubts, perhaps. Chapter 22 speaks of 'thy beginning' and chapter 27, unambiguously, of the kind of prayer suitable to someone 'in the beginning of his conversion'. But, as Book I proceeds, it is evident that classes other than anchoresses are being addressed:

> And from this original sin and all other, thou shalt be saved, yea, and thou shalt be saved as an anker enclosed, and not only thou, but all Christian souls which trust upon this passion and meek themselves, acknowledging their wretchedness, asking mercy and forgiveness, and the fruit of this precious passion only, lowing themselves to the sacraments of Holy Kirk. (ch. 44)

If the reader of chapter 55 and chapter 70 is enclosed in a cell, or in chapter 71 'hast forsaken riches and mickle having of this world, and art in a dungeon', or in chapter 81 'seest no worldly things nor hearest', there are other chapters of the first book which, if excerpted, could stand simply as fundamental Christian teaching for all classes of men and women.

Book II, in its opening chapter, addresses the *thou* of Book I, a *thou* who 'covetest . . . to hear more of an image the which I have before times in party discried to thee', but this *thou* is never so specific as in Book I and the image is that of God in man, obscured by original sin, which many men may reform 'in faith' and some few 'in faith and in feeling'. It is hard to resist the conclusion that Book II, even if its final chapters talk of the mysteries revealed to the advanced contemplative (the privities of Holy Writ, the diversity of degrees in Holy Church and the kind of angels, the discomfiture of the devil), was addressed to a much wider audience than was Book I. It is pretty clearly separated from Book I by a number of years and their manuscript traditions differ in several respects. The second half of *Mixed Life*, with its advice about contemplation, also rather wanders away from its ostensible addressee. 'In nyȝtes, after þi slep, ȝif þou wolt rise for to serue þi lord . . .' (594) scarcely sounds like the man 'bounden to þe world bi children and seruauntes as þou art' (93), but, with the end in sight, 'þee or to anoþer man þat haþ þis manere of wirchynge in custoom' (786) seems to wrench Hilton's mind back to the declared purpose of the work.

From the various works of the *Cloud* author (who makes cross-references from one text to another) it is possible to piece together a picture of their intended recipient. He is twenty-four years old, was once living in the world but is now 'led to that more special life, a servant among his [God's] own special servants'. He is clearly both loved and chastised by the author, presumably his spiritual director, who talks of *we* and *us* as members of a special class ('We are both called by God to be contemplatives', ch. 73) and of other disciples too ('some of my special friends in God', ch. 47). The teaching of the *Cloud* is predicated on the assumption that we cannot deduce the nature of God from any prior premise, since God founded everything. Nor can we circumscribe God in human, spatio-temporal terms. We can therefore only say what he is *not*, not what he is. Even the greatest virtues are inadmissible in the description because they are necessarily couched in human language. Even so, if we cannot comprehend him by our intellect, we may do so through our love. This *via negativa* I can see might be too uncompromising, even reductive, for several tastes. What saves it for many modern readers – and perhaps it did for some medieval readers too – is the considerable intelligence of its author. He will have no truck with sophistry for its own sake (*curious*, in its frequent Middle English pejorative sense, is just about the dirtiest word in his whole vocabulary), but there are all the literary marks of a mind bent on making distinctions: antithesis ('Now trewly I trowe þat who þat wil not goo þe streyte wey to heuen þat þei schul goo þe softe wey to helle', 58.13); paradox ('For whi noȝwhere bodely is euerywhere goostly', 67.38); and the ability, greater than that of any Middle English prose writer I can think of, to maintain complete control of a lengthy sentence full of parentheses and subordinate clauses. Yet its Prologue suggests a limited readership:

> I charge þee & I beseche þee, wiþ as moche power & vertewe as þe bonde of charite is sufficient to suffre, whatsoeuer þou be þat þis book schalt haue in possession, ouþer bi propirte ouþer by keping, by bering as messenger or elles bi borrowing, þat in as moche as in þee is by wille & auisement, neiþer þou rede it, ne write it, ne speke it, ne ȝit suffre it be red, wretyn, or spokyn, of any or to any, bot ȝif it be of soche one or to soche one þat haþ (bi þi supposing) in a trewe wille & by an hole entent, purposed him to be a parfite folower of Criste, not only in actyue leuyng, bot in þe souereinnest pointe of contemplatife leuing þe whiche is possible by grace for to be comen to in þis present liif of a parfite soule ȝit abiding in þis deedly body; & þerto þat doþ þat in him is, &, bi þi supposing, haþ do longe tyme before, for to able him to contemplatiue leuyng by þe vertuous menes of actiue leuyng. For elles it acordeþ noþing to him.

He continues in the same vein: the book requires time to peruse, it is a developing argument and any rapid and partial assessment of it may lead a man into error. A similarly stern warning closes the penultimate chapter:

> Fleschly iangelers, glosers & blamers, roukers and rouners, & alle maner of pynchers, kept I neuer þat þei sawe þis book; for myn entent was neuer to write soche þing to hem. & þerfore I wolde not þat þei herde it, neiþer þei ne none of þees curious lettrid ne lewid men, ȝe, alþof þei be ful good men in actyue leuyng; for it acordeþ not to hem.

It acordeþ not to hem. But this may be a pious wish, incapable of strict fulfilment, and the tone is somewhat desperate. There can be no doubt of what its author intended to be its audience, but the fact remains that cheerfulness is always breaking in and that in the *Cloud*, although not to the same extent in his other works, there are long passages that would qualify as unexceptionable spiritual advice to readers of all manners of life.

If the *you* of some of these texts is sometimes unfocussed, it is by no means pointless. In Rolle once or twice, in the *Cloud* author occasionally, in Hilton more often still, the addressee appears in the role of questioner, objector, someone whose viewpoint demands consideration:

> But almost certainly someone is going to ask ... (*Incendium*, ch. 8)
> But if someone should ask ... (*Ibid.*, ch. 30)
> But now you will ask me ... (*Cloud*, ch. 6)
> Now perhaps you are saying ... (*Ibid.*, ch. 60)
> Well, you will say ... (*Ibid.*, ch. 68)
> Somtyme when I here some men say ... þat my writyng ... is so harde and so heiȝ, & so curious & so queinte þat vnneþes it may be conceiuid ... (*PC* 76.20)
> But now you ask ... (*Scale* 1.55)
> You may say that ... I reply (*Ibid.*, 83)
> Perhaps you say that ... (*Ibid.*, 71)
> But if you object ... I reply (*Ibid.*, 57)
> But ȝit askest þou me ... As vnto þis I may seie as me þenkeþ. (*Mixed Life*, 537)

This may well be a trick learned from philosophical debate, but it is difficult to be sure. It could represent authorial second thoughts, the result of comments on the early reception of the work. At the very least it provides the illusion of an attentive audience with something of a mind of its own.

An extension of this approach is the real or pretended request for more detailed treatment of a topic touched on earlier. We have already seen that the opening lines of *Scale* II attempt to comply with the reader's request 'to hear more of an image' and that *Mixed Life* was composed in answer to a particular man's problem. Hilton's treatise *On Angels Song* begins:

> Þow ȝernys perauenter gretely for to haue more knowynge & wyssynge þan þou has of aungels sange and heuenly sown qwat it is.

In fact the recipient here may well have been disappointed, since there is very little about what angels' song actually consists of: it is not even mentioned until line 67 - out of 195 lines in Takamiya's edition. The *Cloud* author's *A Pistle of Preier* opens:

> Goostly frende in God, as touching þin askyng of me how þou schalt reule þin hert in tyme of þi preier, I answere vnto þee febely as I kan ...

and the second sentence of his *Pistil of Discrecioun of Stirings* runs:

> Þou askist me counsel of silence and of speking, of comoun dietyng & of singulere fastyng, of dwelling in companye & of only-wonyng by þiself. And þou seist þou arte in grete were what þou schalt do ...

It may seem strange that I have not dealt with Julian of Norwich and Margery Kempe until now. There are, however, good manuscript reasons for this, and here numbers may help us a little. Rolle's works were widely disseminated and sometimes adapted in the process: some texts of the *Psalter* contain Lollard interpolations. There are 17 English manuscripts of the *Cloud* and 10 of *Privy Counselling*. Hilton's *Scale of Perfection* weighs in with 41 complete or nearly complete manuscripts of Book I in English and 25 of Book II – to which add 12 of Book I in Latin and 13 of Book II, since the Latin translation was made before the end of the fourteenth century, possibly even within Hilton's lifetime, and therefore was capable of influencing the English of some English manuscripts. (The total count of *Piers Plowman* manuscripts, for all three texts is 51.) Now the *Book of Margery Kempe* exists in just one manuscript, from Mount Grace Charterhouse, and although Julian's *Revelations* exist in two versions, the so-called 'short' and 'long' texts, the short text is extant only in one mid-fifteenth-century manuscript and the long text (apart from some fragments in a Westminster Cathedral manuscript) owes its preservation to the devotion of seventeenth-century Benedictines exiled in the Low Countries. The earliest surviving manuscript of this version is dated c.1650 and this is the text that Colledge and Walsh had perforce to use for their edition. The only possible alternative was another seventeenth-century manuscript which shows signs of adaptation and modernisation. This marked discrepancy in numbers between Julian and Margery on the one hand and Rolle, the *Cloud* and the *Scale* on the other cannot be entirely coincidental and is relevant to what we may deduce about the original audiences.

What her editors call (p. 291n) the 'clinical exactness' of Julian's recollection should not suppose a clear aim in her writing with an established viewpoint. She gives specific biographical details about the illness which resulted in her first visions: it took place on 13 May 1373 when she was thirty years and six months old. Perhaps the short text was composed soon afterwards. She meditated on her visions for over fifteen years before producing the longer version which was therefore not begun before 1388. But in the long chapter 51 recounting the allegory of the lord and the servant – neither contained in the short version nor mentioned in the summary which forms chapter 1 of the longer text – she tells of almost *twenty* years of continuous teaching:

> For twenty yere after the tyme of the shewyng saue thre monthys I had techyng inwardly as I shall sey: It longyth to the to take hede to alle þe propertes and the condescions that were shewed in the example, though þe thyngke that it be mysty and indefferent to thy syght. I assentyd wylfully with grett desyer, seeing inwardly with avysement all the poyntes and the propertes that were shewed in the same time, as ferforth as my wytt and my vnderstandyng wylle serve, begynnyng my beholdyng at the lorde and at þe servannt . . . (520.86)

This would bring the date to 1393, and there is, furthermore, the puzzling reference at the opening of the final chapter:

> This boke is *begonne* by goddys gyfte and his grace, but it is nott yett *performyd,* as to my syght. (731.1)

It is difficult to resist the conclusion that, in this sense if in no other, Julian is a kind of Langland, never completely letting go of her work. She does seem (especially in the later version) to refer to *we* and *us* more than the other mystics and generally to be addressing her 'even-cristians':

> Alle that I say of me I mene in person of alle my evyn cristen   (319.33)
> ...god, that of hys curteyse, loue and endlesse goodnesse wolld shew it generally in comfort of vs alle.   (320.37)
> ... oure good lorde spekyth in loue to all mankynd that shall be savyd, as it were alle to one person.   (399.14)

She is careful to distinguish a more advanced stage of contemplation ('a suttell felyng and a prevy inwarde syghte of hye partys', 569.54) available not to all but to those who have received infused grace:

> But this marvelous homelynesse may no man know in this lyfe, but yf he haue it by specialle schewyng of oure lorde, or of gret plenty of grace inwardly yeven of the holy gost   (315.55)

but she would never claim that she received such revelations completely or understood them perfectly. She is puzzled by the nature and the purpose of sin, for which the church teaches we are blameworthy but from which God's mercy constantly excuses us (718.11-15). It is a learning process for her too.

Margery Kempe's *Book* is written, not by Margery herself, but by amanuenses who wrote down her reminiscences of up to twenty years before. But here there is little of the control of Julian who confidently refers both forwards and backwards, and even less of Julian's growing understanding of contemplation. Instead it reads like a despairing attempt to bring some order to a kaleidoscope of journeys, visions, accusations and sobbings. How do you describe Margery? Exhibitionist? Hysteric? Neurotic? Or, the latest term I have come across, Maverick?[2] Or maybe Contemplative? I am sure Susan Dickman is correct in locating her as much in the devotional as in the mystical tradition.[3] It may be not altogether fanciful that Mountgrace (the provenance of the one surviving manuscript) was also the house of Nicholas Love whose gentle imagination plays over the gospel harmony which forms the basis of his *Meditations*, another not-really-mystical book. Rolle was a free-lance hermit, the *Cloud* author presumably a spiritual director with several disciples, Julian a recluse, Hilton an Augustinian canon. Margery is from Lynn, the daughter of a former mayor and the wife of a substantial citizen, in and of the world. Indeed it is the reactions of her contemporaries, whose approval she seems anxious to gain, that trouble her constantly. They cannot accept her white clothes (which God had ordered her to wear) because they were symbolic of purity,

[2]   R. Keickhefer, *Unquiet Souls* (1984), p.189.
[3]   S. Dickman, 'Margery Kempe and the English Devotional Tradition' in *The Medieval Mystical Tradition in England*, ed. M. Glasscoe (Exeter, 1982), 156-72. The rehabilitation of Margery Kempe continues in C. Atkinson, *Mystic and Pilgrim: the Book and the World of Margery Kempe* (1983), and S. Dickman, 'Margery Kempe and the Continental Tradition of the Pious Woman', *The Medieval Mystical Tradition in England* (Cambridge, 1984), 150-68.

especially sexual purity, and here was she, a married woman with several children. St Bridget of Sweden, whom she admires, had married at thirteen and had borne eight children, but the last thirty years of her life had been spent as a widow and she had been canonised in 1391 – scarcely an exact model. And all those visits to bishops that Margery made seem at least partly for approbation, not simply to refute accusations of lollardy.

Initially Margery seems to have been accepted by the world, but things begin to go wrong when she starts reproving people:

> Than thys creatur þowt it was ful mery to be reprevyd for Goddys lofe; it was to hir gret solas & cowmfort whan sche was chedyn & fletyn for þe lofe of Ihesu for repreuyng of synne, for spekyng of vertu, for comownyng in Scriptur whech sche lernyd in sermownys & be comownyng with clerkys. (29.28-32)

She was perhaps one of the first to discover that the Englishman abroad can be peculiarly difficult:

> Also þe Saraȝines mad mych of hir & conueyd hir & leddyn hir abowtyn in þe cuntre wher sche wold gon. & sche fond alle pepyl good on-to hir & gentyl saf only hir owyn cuntremen. (75.17-18)

As things get tougher she relies more and more on her relationship with Christ, a relationship which is not (as it had been in the earlier monastic tradition) allegorical but direct and personal. Mysticism – if we can still call it that – had come out into the world, but its terminology still reflected its origins in the disciplines of monastic spirituality.[4] Julian's allegory of the lord and the servant would have been outside Margery's comprehension. For, above all, Margery wants to *participate*. Julian sees a vision of Mary at the time of the Annunciation and can appreciate Mary's grief at the death of her son; Margery becomes the Virgin's handmaiden in bringing up the infant Christ and tries to comfort her with a hot drink (a *cawdel*, 195.8) when she returns home after the burial. Her direct access to Christ – in which He often takes the initiative – becomes her way of transcending the world while still remaining in it, a world whose humiliation of her can be offered up as a sacrifice to Him:

> & so sche was euyrmor strengthyd in þe lofe of owyr Lord & þe mor bold to suffyr shamys & repreuys for hys sake in euery place þer sche cam for þe grace þat God wrowt in hir of wepyng, sobbyng, and crying, þe which grace sche myth not wythstonde whan God wold send it. (74.22-27)

It is easy to mock Margery. She herself had no doubt about what she did and a surprising number of people did believe her. Her *Book* does provide evidence of some of the more advanced stages of the mystical progress. She

---

[4] Dickman (1980), p.164. Cf. Keickhefer (p.15): 'Rather than developing new models of saintliness to exalt the sanctity of marriage and work in society, the lay saints as well as the mendicants imbibed a spirituality transferred from the monastery … monastic spirituality had defined what a saint was, and monastic conceptions could not readily be superseded.'

(like Rolle) experiences sweet smells, sweet sounds and melodies ('nearly every day for 25 years', 88.2); chapter 36 recounts her mystical marriage to God and in chapter 85 an angel shows her her own entry in the Book of Life; she is given knowledge of what is to happen to her friends in the future (Julian asked once, but was refused); she distinguishes knowledge of Christ's manhood (before her pilgrimages abroad) from knowledge of the Godhead (afterwards, 208.24); she has 'many holy meditacyons and many hy contemplacyonys' (107.9 and cf. 83.11). But these latter manifestations are never really specified, as they are, for example, in the concluding chapters of Book II of Hilton's *Scale of Perfection*. So what might be the moral for a fifteenth-century reader of the *Book of Margery Kempe*? She gives away such money as she has (sometimes borrowed); she falls sick on several occasions; people despise her, tell lies about her and call her a lollard – *but*, God always cares for her and brings her home, home to Lynn in Norfolk, out of all her tribulations.

What can be said about the second generation of readers of these books? Some of the seed fell on rocks, sprang up quickly, but, lacking moisture, withered away. Hilton and the *Cloud* author both speak of young, misguided disciples, probably enthusiastic followers of Rolle's infectious teaching. 'I make a difference,' says the author of *Privy Counselling*, 'betwix hem þat ben clepid to saluacion & hem þat ben clepid to perfeccion'. But there were others who looked for the hundredfold return. Prominent among these were the Carthusians who had always evidenced concern for the copying of spiritual texts and for the correctness of the texts they copied. MS British Library, Harley 6579, of the *Scale of Perfection*, is a case in point. It belonged to the London Charterhouse and was evidently something of a working copy. Additions and corrections are made in the margins, between the lines, and occasionally over erasures. These editorial procedures are designed not, as nowadays, to come as close as possible to what the author originally wrote but to bring out the complete meaning of the text, which might well result in a fuller version rather than an earlier. The actual changes incorporated may or may not have been authorial: some of them, such as the famous 'Holy Name' passage added to chapter 44 of Book I of the *Scale*, probably were. The chapter divisions in Book I of the *Scale* are a whole jigsaw in themselves. The 'normal' version is divided into ninety-two or ninety-three chapters (depending on whether chapter 87 is numbered or not), but three manuscripts, Harley 6579, All Souls 25, and the Chatsworth manuscript, have traces of a division into twenty-eight chapters, possibly an arrangement to facilitate following the argument or perhaps simply convenient sections for daily reading in a religious house (all three of these manuscripts have Carthusian affiliations). In her recent edition of *Mixed Life*, Sarah Ogilvie-Thomson dispenses with the plethora of chapter headings and simply numbers the lines consecutively throughout. But that is not a solution available to the editor of a text the length of the *Scale*.

Throughout this paper I have been begging the question of listeners or readers. For Chaucer the connection between speaking poet and listening audience may well have been real. Even so, there are sufficient references in

Chaucer to *reading*: 'Turne over the leef and chese another tale' (*Miller's Prologue*, A 3177) near the beginning of the *Canterbury Tales* and 'Now preye I to hem alle that herkne this litel tretys or rede' (*Retraction*, I 1081) at its end – it is irrelevant here whether the *tretys* is the whole work or the *Parson's Tale* only. Chaucerian narrators sometimes appeal to their audience to correct, from their superior knowledge, what is amiss: scarcely, perhaps, extempore and out loud. I imagine that, for the medieval mystics, we must accept both kinds of audience, with the likelihood of private reading becoming more common. The *Cloud* Prologue, which I quoted earlier, raises both possibilities: 'or elles bi borrowing suffre it to be red, wretyn or spokyn'. The translator of Catherine of Siena's *Dialogo*, in his Prologue to the Middle English *Orcherd of Syon*, divides the work into seven parts, each with five chapters:

> This orcherd by Goddis grace my wil is to deuyde into seuene parties, and ech party into fyue chapitres, as ʒe mowe se and rede in þe kalender folowynge. ... ʒe mowe chese if ʒe wole of xxxv aleyes where ʒe wolen walke, þat is to seye, of xxxv chapitres, o tyme in oon, anoþir tyme in anoþir.[5]

Se and *rede* is clear, but the final phrase raises the possibility of a communal audience.

Several manuscripts of the *Scale* show Carthusian or Bridgettine provenance (the nunnery of Syon was just across the Thames from the Charterhouse of Sheen). But the greatest Carthusian corrector of them all was a certain James Grenehalgh, about whom we now know much more than we did, thanks to the recent monograph by Professor Michael Sargent.[6] In 1499 Grenehalgh was a professed monk of Sheen, but by May 1508 he had been – literally – sent to Coventry as a guest in the Charterhouse there:

> to remain there at the Order's discretion [as the community at Sheen asks, *added margin*], nor is he to be returned to the house of his profession by any visitors whatsoever. And if it pleases the prior and community, let him make a profession there, or anywhere he may be able to find someone willing to harbour him.

But he did not, and died in 1530, still a *hospes*, in the Charterhouse of Kingston-upon-Hull. Why he was sent from Sheen is a matter of interest in its own right and may have involved the attachment he formed for Joanna Sewell of Syon. I doubt if we should imagine Grenehalgh-Leander swimming from Sheen across the Thames to his Hero in Syon, but his superiors were evidently worried. More to our purpose here, though, is his work on (as far as can be determined) twelve manuscripts and two early printed books. He seems to have been especially interested in the *Scale of Perfection*, both in English and in Latin, the *Cloud of Unknowing*, and some at least of Rolle. Some figures of Dr Sargent's are instructive: roughly 1800 textual emendations in all, almost 1000 of them in three copies of the *Scale*,

---

[5]   P. Hodgson and G. M. Liegey, *The Orcherd of Syon*, EETS o.s. 258 (1966).
[6]   M. G. Sargent, *James Grenehalgh as Textual Critic* (Salzburg, 1984, 2 vols.)

about 650 of these occurring in the Rosenbach copy of the Wynkyn de Worde printed text of 1494, his prized copy which he presented to Joanna Sewell, perhaps on her profession in 1500. Bodley, Douce 262 has nearly 250 non-critical and over 300 critical annotations to the text of the *Cloud*. Into the Rosenbach *Scale* he enters corrections from (a) an unidentified manuscript, possibly one close to Lambeth Palace 472, (b) a manuscript rather like Cambridge University Library Ee. iv. 30, (c) Cambridge Trinity College B. 15. 18 (no. 354) into which he had previously copied corrections and (d) the Latin text of British Library, Harley 6576 (one third of the annotations in the Rosenbach copy are in Latin).

But your Grenehalghs come singly rather than in battalions. In the case of readers not quite so obsessive, copies are handed on (remember the concern of the *Cloud* author that they should not get into the wrong hands), compilations are made which include extracts from the mystics (the pilgrimage to Jerusalem from *Scale* II became something of a fifteenth-century classic). Lambeth Palace 472 is what is generally called one of the 'common profit' books,[7] following the formula on f. 260:

> This booke was maad of þe goodis of Jon Killum for a comyne profite. That þat persoone þat haþ þis booke committed to him haue þe vse þerof þe teerme of his lijf, preiyng for þe soule of þe same ion. And þat he þat haþ þe forseid vse of commissioun whanne he occupieþ it not, leene it for a tyme to sum oþer persoone. Also þat persoone to whom it was committid for þe teerme of lijf, vndir þe forseid condiciouns delyuere it to a noþer persoone þe teerme of his lijf. And so be it delyuered & committid fro persoone to persoone, man or womman, *as longe as þe booke enduriþ*.

and, later on:

> Memorandum þat þis boke be deliuered to Richard Colop Parchemanere of Londonn after my discesse. And in caas he die or I, þen I wol it be take to som deuowte persone to haue it vnder þe forme and condicioun wretyn in þe ende of þis boke heere tofore.
>
> Mordon.

Lower down still there is inscribed, in another hand, *Per me dominum Johannem Graunt* and the date 1493. The manuscript contains the *Scale* (both books), *Mixed Life, Eight Chapters on Perfection, Qui Habitat, Bonum Est* and the *Benedictus*: a fair selection from what was believed to be the Hilton canon.

And so texts often composed originally for recluses, perhaps recently enclosed, or for others professing the contemplative life, pass on, by way of florilegia and common profit manuscripts (of which there are others besides Lambeth 472), into the hands of devout, moderately well-off London tradesmen and merchants: Killum was a grocer, Colop a stationer, and Mordon either an attorney or else the Thomas Morden (d. 1458) who in 1433

---

[7] M. G. Sargent, 'Walter Hilton's *Scale of Perfection*: The London Manuscript Group Reconsidered', *Medium Ævum* 52 (1983), 189-216.

was treasurer of St Paul's and in the following year steward to the Bishop of London. A John Graunt of St Mary Magdalene, Bermondsey, died in 1495, almost exactly a hundred years after Hilton's own death. Or else into the possession of rich and devout women, like Lady Margaret Beaufort, mother of Henry VII, who commissioned the first printing of the *Scale*. The book Wynkyn de Worde produced for her also contained *Mixed Life*, designated as a 'third book'. I doubt whether these people saw themselves as mystics; rather, they found in such books a map to Jerusalem:

> Then if thou covet for to come to this blessed sight of very peace and be a true pilgrim to Jerusalem-ward, though it be so that I were never there, nevertheless as farforth as I can I shall set thee in the way thitherward. The beginning of the high way in which thou shalt go is reforming in faith, grounded meekly in the faith and in the laws of Holy Kirk.   (*Scale*, II, ch. 21, p. 305)

RICHARD ROLLE
AS ELITIST AND AS POPULARIST:
THE CASE OF *JUDICA ME*[1]

Nicholas Watson

I

There have been two periods during which the English eremitic writer
Richard Rolle has been taken seriously as an expounder of spiritual truths.
The first lasted from some time after 1349 (the year of his death) until the
English Reformation around 1530. If we can regard the vagaries of manuscript survival as at all an accurate indicator, few eremitic writers can have
had so large a readership as he did at this time. Hope Emily Allen's great
study of *Writings Ascribed to Richard Rolle, Hermit of Hampole, with
Materials for his Biography* lists nearly four hundred manuscripts now in
British or American libraries, and a further sixty from Continental Europe,
containing writings attributed to him.[2] The manuscripts leave the impression
that affection and respect for Rolle as an individual and as a writer was at
least as important a reason for the wide circulation he achieved as was the
practical usefulness of what he wrote.[3] Many of them include several of his
works, while a number attempt to amass all of them, as though preserving
his *ipsissima verba* in a collected version was deemed a matter of major
importance; a high proportion of their copies of his works (and large

[1] This paper is closely related to a book-length study entitled *Richard Rolle and
the Invention of Authority*, which I hope to publish shortly. I have not been able
to avoid referring to this unpublished work on a few occasions where I state a
position which is not part of the current scholarly consensus, insofar as one exists.
The paper was designed to be given at the conference, but through my own fault
was not in the event read. I am extremely grateful to Dr Michael Sargent for
inviting me to contribute the paper to the conference proceedings nonetheless.
[2] The work was published in London in 1927, and is henceforth referred to as
'Allen'. See pp. 563ff for Allen's tables of manuscripts containing works by or
purporting to be by Rolle. Several manuscripts discovered since 1927 are listed by
Nicole Marzac in her *Richard Rolle de Hampole: Vie et Oeuvres suivies du
Tractatus super Apocalypsim* (Paris, 1968), *passim*.
[3] Malcolm Moyes, in his 'The Manuscripts and Early Printed Editions of Richard
Rolle's *Expositio super Novem Lectiones Mortuorum*', *The Medieval Mystical
Tradition in England* III, ed. Marion Glasscoe (Cambridge, 1984), pp. 81-103,
examines the annotations and rubrics in several manuscripts of Rolle's works in
which passages concerned with the Holy Name occur, and concludes that 'in the
eyes of some medieval readers, the mere repetition of the word "Ihesu" in the
context of a Rolle work evoked a response denied to the same words in another
writer's work' (p. 91). Affection for Rolle as an individual is also evident in the
way manuscripts of *Incendium Amoris* contain small drawings of the hermit
(e.g. in MS Cambridge Mm.5.37), and annotate his accounts of his own experience
(as in MS Cambridge Dd.5.64, the marginalia in which refer to the hermit several
times by name).

numbers of works by other people) are attributed to him by name.[4] Some were especially widely-read; *Expositio super novem Lectiones Mortuorum* and *Incendium Amoris* survive in nearly fifty manuscripts, while *Emendatio Vitae* is in over a hundred, among which are copies of no less than seven independent English translations.[5] The parts of *Expositio super aliquos versus Cantici Canticorum* which are borrowed by a compilation from Rolle's works known as *Oleum Effusum*, as well as the whole of *Incendium Amoris*, were also translated into English, while his three English epistles were translated into Latin.[6] In the fifteenth century, a great many people must have dedicated their time to copying, translating and disseminating much of Rolle's output. Presumably many more spent at least as much time reading him.

Since the study of the early histories of the manuscripts of Rolle's works and of his reputation is still in its first stages, we are not yet in a position to say who all these readers were, or indeed why they responded so positively to him. They must have included men and women in many kinds of secular life as well as solitary and coenobitic contemplatives, priests and academics.[7] However, one paradoxical feature of the fifteenth-century response to Rolle of direct relevance to the theme of this conference seems to be discernible. While on the one hand he was evidently read widely by Christians in many different walks of life, with the kind of affection bestowed on a St Francis, on the other his works were perceived as full of lofty spiritual matter which was potentially dangerous and which was certainly not for everyone. There seems in fact to have been a tension between one perception of him as what we might call a 'popular' writer and another of him as a 'specialist' or 'difficult' one.[8] Manifestations of

[4]   See Allen *passim* for *incipits* and *explicits* which attribute works to Rolle (usually in practice to 'Richard, Hermit of Hampole'). Manuscripts which attempt to gather most or all of Rolle's works together include MS Bodley 861, Corpus Christi Oxford 193, Hereford Cathedral O.viii.I and Emmanuel 35.

[5]   See Marzac, *op. cit.*, pp. 46, 56, 57 for convenient references to MSS in which these works appear. For the English translations of *Emendatio Vitae*, see Margaret G. Amassian, 'The Rolle Material in Bradfer-Lawrence MS. 10 and its Relationships to Other Rolle Manuscripts', *Manuscripta* 23 (1979), pp. 67-78.

[6]   See Allen, pp. 68, 223-24, 262 etc. The English *Oleum Effusum* is printed in Carl Horstmann's *Yorkshire Writers: Richard Rolle, An English Father of the Church, and his Followers*, 2 vols. (London, 1895-96), II, pp. 186ff. (This great collection is also a splendid quarry for other translations, versions and adaptations of Rolle's works, such as the verse *Form of Living* (II, pp. 283ff). Richard Misyn's English translation of *Incendium Amoris* was published as EETS o.s. 106 (1896), edited by Ralph Harvey.

[7]   An academic interest in Rolle is evidenced by the 1483 Oxford edition of *Expositio super Novem Lectiones Mortuorum* (Allen, p. 9). For the scope of this work's readership in particular, see Moyes, *art. cit.*

[8]   In the context of this general introduction, the term 'popular' is not used of Rolle in any precise way; any interest in him as a writer or as an individual from outside the circle of professional contemplatives is treated as evidence of 'popular' interest. The term can be used with no more precision once it is being applied directly to Rolle's writing, in this case because, as we shall see, his own desire to

this tension are many and various. Walter Hilton's attempts to explain and
sometimes to reinterpret Rolle's pronouncements on the Holy Name and
on the experiences of spiritual *fervor* and *canor*, express something of the
complexities of his feelings towards Rolle, and show us one spiritual
instructor trying to repair the damage done by the dissemination at a too-
popular level of the writings of another. The hermit Thomas Bassett's
Defensorium, written in response to the assertions of an unnamed
Carthusian that Rolle's teaching led men astray, reflects divisions in the
ranks of England's principal disseminators of contemplative writing over
the suitability of his work as spiritual instruction.[9] While the Carthusians
did copy Rolle's works extensively,[10] and while many of those works were
to be found in the libraries of Sheen and its Bridgetine sister-house,
Syon,[11] it has nonetheless been suggested that a Carthusian compilation
named *De Excellencia Contemplationis* might represent an attempt by
members of the order to gather together and to separate from the rest the
more acceptable elements of his writing.[12] The many signs of Rolle's fame
outside the cloister include the *Officium et Miracula* written in the 1380s
which seems to indicate a popular cult of the hermit,[13] the medieval tendency
to ascribe to Rolle unspecialised contemplative works such as *The Prick of*

---

popularise is so general and abstract. I hope it will become clear that the concept is
nonetheless a useful one.

[9] For Hilton's reservations about Rolle, and for Bassett's *Defensorium*, see Michael
Sargent, 'Contemporary Criticism of Richard Rolle', *Analecta Carthusiana* 55:1
(1981), pp. 160-205; pp. 178-82 deal with Hilton's attitude to Rolle, while pp. 188ff
contain a diplomatic transcription of the *Defensorium*.

[10] See Michael Sargent, 'The Transmission by the English Carthusians of some
Late Medieval Spiritual Writings', *The Journal of Ecclesiastical History* 27 (1976),
pp. 225-40.

[11] See e.g. Margaret Deanesley's introduction to her edition of *Incendium Amoris*
(Manchester, 1915), and her 'Vernacular Books in England in the Fourteenth and
Fifteenth Centuries', *Modern Language Review* 15 (1920), pp. 345-58.

[12] See Michael Sargent, *James Grenehalgh as Textual Critic*, Analecta Carthusiana
85, 2 vols., 1984), pp. 37-38. This account of *De Excellentia Contemplationis* remains
a conjecture until someone looks carefully at the compilation. Medieval editions of
Rolle's works do on occasion seem to reflect a measure of dissatisfaction with
them. The 'short version' of *Incendium Amoris*, for example, omits all that work's
autobiographical writing (see Deanesley's edition of *Incendium Amoris*, which
brackets passages omitted in the short version), as though the editor felt such
material to be inappropriate to a treatise on the contemplative life. On the other
hand, the same short version usually appears in manuscripts with the compilation
Oleum Effusum, which includes major autobiographical passages from *Incendium
Amoris* and which is an important sign of the medieval personality cult of Rolle:
another instance of the complexity of medieval responses to Rolle. In general,
perhaps our familiarity with and respect for Walter Hilton and the author of
The Cloud of Unknowing leads us to exaggerate the extent of fifteenth-century
suspicion of Rolle.

[13] See *The Officium and Miracula of Richard Rolle of Hampole*, ed. Reginald
Woolley (London, 1919). The *Miracula* mostly consists of minor healing miracles
performed near Rolle's shrine on local people and pilgrims, suggesting that a
popular cult of the hermit had grown up.

Conscience or *The Mirror of St Edmund*,[14] and the early appearance in print of a number of works attributed to Rolle.[15] Yet the only time Rolle even came close to writing a genuinely 'popular' work was with *Emendatio Vitae*, and it is noteworthy that Wynkyn de Worde should have published the *Contemplacyons on the drede and loue of god*, the *Remedy ayenst the troubles of temptacyons* and *Hore beate Marie virginis* all under the name of Rolle without printing a single genuine Rolle work. Perhaps he agreed with the author of the *Contemplacyons* that even material like the 'three degrees of love' outlined in Rolle's most straightforward works (the English Epistles and *Emendatio Vitae*) was too complex, or too controversial, for his readers.[16] In the fifteenth century a desire to treat Rolle as in various senses a 'popular' writer seems to have coexisted with unease over regarding most of his genuine works in that light, and with a contrary perception of him as a writer for specialists.

A similar desire to treat Rolle as a popular writer was manifested in the second period of his fame, which began with the publication in 1895-6 of Horstmann's monumental *Richard Rolle, an English Father of the Church* and extended until perhaps the early 1930s. During this period his readership was of course much smaller than in the fifteenth century. Nonetheless, a few English readers, whose appetite for mysticism was being sharpened by the writings of Baron von Hügel, Evelyn Underhill and others,[17] was captivated not only by the material Horstmann included, but also by the brilliant and often fantastic biography that makes up the introduction to his second volume.[18] In this account the blessed Richard Hermit is at once a latter-day St Francis and a Protestant evangelist before his time, an anti-intellectual and a social reformer out to convert the world. He is also utterly charming, tramping around the countryside like a character out of G. K. Chesterton, preaching love to the masses, and warming the hearts of those who had grown cold by pondering too long on the hair-splitting subtleties of Churchmen (etc.). Here, once he could be suitably modernised and made more widely accessible, was the English holy man and mystical activist that contemporary High Church Anglicanism needed. Within thirty years of the publication of Horstmann's biography, numerous books, articles and modernised anthologies proclaimed the teaching, the charm and the virtues of the man who made mysticism relevant. Among these were R. H. Benson's sadly dreary novel about Rolle, *Richard Raynal, Solitary* (1906), and his anthology from Horstmann, *The Book of the Love of Jesus* (1909);[19] Geraldine Hodgson's *The Sanity of Mysticism*

[14]   See Allen, pp. 345-68 for a summary of Latin and English works incorrectly attributed to Rolle.

[15]   See Allen, pp. 9-13.

[16]   See Horstmann, *op. cit.*, II, pp. 74-75 for this passage in the *Contemplations*.

[17]   Baron von Hügel's *The Mystical Element of Religion* was published in 1908, while Evelyn Underhill's *Mysticism* was published in 1911, both in London.

[18]   See Horstmann, *op. cit.*, II, pp. v-xliii, a highly entertaining and often illuminating performance.

[19]   The novel places the hermit's life in the fifteenth century, and its events bear little resemblance to what is known of Rolle's biography, but is nonetheless

(1926), along with two slimmer volumes, *The Form of Living and other Prose Treatises of Richard Rolle of Hampole* (1910), and *The Privity of the Passion* (1923); E.M.M. Comper's modernisation of Misyn's fifteenth-century translation of *Incendium Amoris* and *Emendatio Vitae*, which has an introduction by Evelyn Underhill (1914), her modernisation of *Contemplations of the Dread and Love of God*, which she ascribes to a 'wandering hermit' disciple of Rolle's (1916), and her biography, *The Life of Richard Rolle* (1928); Verier Elwyn's evangelising *Richard Rolle, A Christian Sannyasi* (1930),[20] and George Heseltine's *Selected Works of Richard Rolle* (1930).[21] To a contemporary aware of all these works, Rolle must have seemed destined to regain his reputation as a major English devotional writer.

However in 1927 the picture of Rolle as a joyous populist was decisively challenged by Hope Emily Allen's great work on the hermit. Allen presents him in quite different terms from Horstmann and his successors: essentially as a writer of difficult Latin works largely concerned with the solitary life, who was responsible for few of the innumerable vernacular treatises printed by Horstmann, and who appears assertive, narrow-minded and little interested in the world outside the cell except when it criticised him. The psychoanalytic assumptions underlying this new portrait were at least as crude as anything in Horstmann's account of the hermit, but Allen's scholarship and the length, difficulty and repetitiveness of Rolle's newly highlighted Latin works proved overwhelming. In spite of a desperate rearguard action by Geraldine Hodgson, whose 1929 study *Rolle and 'Our Daily Work'* attempts to salvage one short treatise for laypeople as a genuine Rolle work,[22] his reputation as a popular writer – as a mediator between the difficult world of mysticism and the everyday world – was largely ruined. It is presumably partly because of this change in how Rolle has been perceived that scholarly and general interest in him has been so moribund for the last fifty years. He has been downgraded to the rank of first and least of the 'Five English Mystics', the proper subject

clearly a fantasia on Horstmann's life of Rolle. Benson published both his works concerned with Rolle shortly after his reception into the Roman Catholic church.
[20] Published in Madras by the Christian Literature Society for India, as no.3 in their series *Bhaktas of the World*. (This version of Horstmann's Rolle seems to make a more convincing *sannyasi* than he does a medieval English hermit.)
[21] All the aforementioned works were published in London, unless stated otherwise, mostly by Anglo-Catholics. George Heseltine was the first English Roman Catholic to write widely on Rolle, apart from the wayward convert Benson, and significantly drew as extensively on the work of the French Catholic scholar, Noetinger, as on any of his English predecessors.
[22] Hodgson writes that 'four of the Writings which Miss Hope [*sic*] has excluded, at any rate tentatively if not positively ... Rolle's lovers will decline to give up save on incontrovertible evidence that he cannot have written them' (p.104). One of these four is 'Our Daily Work'. Mary L. Arntz's study, *Richard Rolle and 'The Holy Boke Gratia Dei'*, Elizabethan and Renaissance Studies 92:2, ed. James Hogg (Salzburg, 1981), pp.lxxiiiff reassesses the evidence, and like Allen finds decisively that Rolle did not write either the 'Holy Boke' itself, or the section of it Hodgson called 'Our Daily Work'.

for brief 'profiles' and the academic limberings-up of graduate students.[23] Taking both Allen and her predecessors into account, the modern appraisal of Rolle has in many ways been quite different from the medieval enthusiasm for him, but has been similarly and interestingly self-divided.

Rolle's reputation as a popular writer in the fifteenth and the early twentieth centuries was partly dependent on false ascriptions, and in the latter period on a degree of wishful thinking and sentimentality. It remains true, nonetheless, that the division perceptible in both periods between this view of him and one of him as a difficult and specialised writer reflects an important thematic and structural division within many of his own works. There is a crucial if paradoxical sense in which Rolle actually tried to be the popular writer he was perceived as being by readers of Horstmann. In this paper I wish to confront the paradoxical relationship in Rolle's writings between elitist and popularist or evangelistic impulses. After outlining very briefly the way in which his thought as a whole seems at once to exclude and to include the common reader, I shall examine a short work, *Judica Me*, in which both impulses counterpoint one another particularly clearly. Although this work has never been much read and is far from being central to Rolle's literary career, it provides insights into the pressures and urges under which that career developed, and is thus a useful, if indirect, witness to some of the aspects of his thought that have caused medieval and modern reception of his works to be so mixed.

II

The structure of Rolle's thought is intimately connected with the idiosyncratic nature of his religious life. Piecing together the biographical information found in his works and in the *Officium*, it seems that he became a hermit without ecclesiastical sanction and followed his vocation somewhat independently of its usual constraints;[24] for example, he changed his place of abode and his patron more than once,[25] while the tone of his

---

[23] For both 'profiles' and the considerable body of thesis material on Rolle (among which several editions of works by Rolle are extremely useful), see variously in *The 14th-Century English Mystics: A Comprehensive Annotated Bibliography*, by V. M. Lagorio and R. M. Bradley (New York, 1981).

[24] The *Officium*, composed in anticipation of Rolle's canonisation, is anxious to present him in as conventional a light as possible, for example by stressing the consistency of some of his actions with canon law (lectio viii). If Rolle had received the ecclesiastical sanction that hermits were supposed to have, it seems highly probable that it would have said so. (For regulations governing hermits see the eremitic rules published as 'Regulae Tres Reclusorum et Eremitarum Angliae saec. xiii-xiv' by P. L. Oliger (in *Antonianum* 3, 1928, pp. 151-190 and 299-320), p. 305, and pp. 85-90 of R. M. Clay's *The Hermits and Anchorites of England*, London, 1914.)

[25] For Rolle's eremitic wanderings and criticisms thereof see e.g. the *Officium* lectio viii, pp. 1-3 of *Judica Me Deus*, ed. J. P. Daly, Elizabethan and Renaissance Studies 92:14, ed. James Hogg (Salzburg, 1984), and *Incendium Amoris*, ed.

whole *oeuvre* indicates that he was more outspoken than was politic in the circumstances. Although it seems unlikely that he was ever in any kind of official difficulty with the ecclesiastical authorities, he frequently alludes to his critics and enemies in a way that suggests that he was a controversial figure, at least locally and in his own mind. One can see why he might have been so; as an educated man not in orders who lived as a hermit while writing numerous works of spiritual instruction, he must have been extremely unusual and a natural object of suspicion.

Partly as a product of the criticism to which he tells us he was subjected, and no doubt partly out of the convictions that originally led him to adopt his singular way of life, much of his writing career was devoted to defining, defending and glorifying eremiticism, with a vehemence that suggests the strength of his own identification with his subject. Not since Peter Damian had the solitary life had so eloquent or at least so pugilistic an apologist. However, Rolle's literary version of eremiticism was at least as idiosyncratic as his lived version. In his writing the solitary life is not merely an ascetic life of prayer and meditation lived out in isolation from the world. Rather, it is intimately tied to a set of progressive spiritual and mystical experiences, which his works recapitulate over and over again, the model for which is the course of Rolle's own eremitic career. Beginning with the hermit's conversion from the world, this model culminates – after a period of spiritual exercises which eventually enable the hermit to 'see into heaven'[26] – with the famous triad of spiritual sensations *fervor*, *dulcor* and *canor*. These experiences, particularly *canor*, represent the summit of the spiritual life; in a famous passage (cap. 15 of *Incendium Amoris*), he describes how he received them all at a young age. For Rolle, the genuine solitary is always specifically one who has achieved the gift of *canor* or who is on the way to doing so. It is these links between his own experience, the eremitic life in general and a highly particular mysticism that gives Rolle's writing its individuality, its exclusiveness and its periodic arrogance. Oddly enough, it is also this mysticism which impels those writings in a quite opposite direction, evoking their air of charm, evangelistic zeal and popularism. Both sides of Rolle's reputation are products of different aspects of the same experiences and literary themes.

This fact can best be demonstrated by looking briefly at the group of writings that embody Rolle's central creative effort. At some time during the 1330s and 1340s, he composed a great series of works extolling the solitary life and his own spiritual experiences, and placing them in an ambitious metaphysical framework. From a stylistic point of view these works – *Incendium Amoris*, *Tractatus super Psalmum Vicesimum*, *Expositio super aliquos versus Cantici Canticorum*, *Liber de Amore Dei contra Amatores Mundi* and *Melos Amoris* – are among the rococo glories of medieval Latin, but their content is disappointingly simple and repetitive.

Margaret Deanesley (Manchester, 1915), pp. 175.25-9.

[26] This is the experience which Allen (*passim*) calls 'The Opening of the Heavenly Door', borrowing Rolle's own habitual image, which is in turn derived from Revelations 4.1.

Insofar as they are concerned with theological assertions at all, the works are all for the most part engaged in enlarging on the following propositions: that man must choose between love of the world and love of God; that the mature lover of God is one who has experienced *fervor*, *dulcor* and *canor*; that *canor* is a participation in the spiritual songs sung by the angels and the blessed in heaven; that whoever receives *canor* is thus in effect already a member of the Church Triumphant, and is one of the *perfecti* who will assist Christ at the Last Judgement; that *canor* can only be received and experienced in isolation, since earthly tumult of any kind renders it inaudible; that the solitary life is thus ideally suited to receiving the gift of *canor*; and that since it makes accessible the supreme spiritual experience that man can attain on this earth, the solitary life is superior to all other forms of the religious life, and ought to command the respect of the rest of the Church Militant.[27] In defining the solitary life in this way, Rolle also of course accords himself an extraordinarily high status in the Church: an effective, or at least a very daring, response to criticism. Few can reach the highest levels of the contemplative life, and in order to make clear his own special status, Rolle is often inclined to stress this rarity; he acknowledges that of all the *auctores* of the past 'few or no writers even refer to this gift of *canor*',[28] and in cap. 34 of *Incendium Amoris* he laments the absence of others who share his mystical life. Those who do reach that level – who will presumably usually be solitaries – can be seen as fundamentally different from all other members of the Church, having in a certain sense already completed their earthly *via* and attained the goal of their heavenly *patria*.[29] It is thus not surprising that their numbers will be limited.

It would be difficult to imagine a more elitist way of defining the solitary life than that I have just outlined. However, diverse features of the same group of works produce a puzzlingly different impression. While on the one hand Rolle's purpose in writing the whole group seems to have been to extol 'the glory and the perfection of the saints', as he puts it in *Melos Amoris*,[30] and thereby to demarcate their ecstatic holiness from the more mundane virtues of the rest of the Church, these works on the solitary life

[27] These propositions remain unchanged throughout Rolle's career, although different works emphasise them in different ways, and they are not always stated categorically. Probably the work in which they are stated most lucidly is *Contra Amatores Mundi*, ed. Paul Theiner (Berkeley, 1968), especially in caps. 1 and 4.
[28] 'Pauci ergo sunt, vel nulli qui illud referunt ...' etc. (*Contra Amatores Mundi*, cap. 4.120.)
[29] Rolle is careful to state this idea in as orthodox a way as possible, by insisting that the *electi* or *perfecti* (as he calls these supremely elevated contemplatives) are still capable of mortal sin. See e.g. cap. 19 of *Incendium Amoris*. His belief that certain Christians have a special status above that of all others is of course not uncommon in the Middle Ages. Aquinas himself writes of the *pauperes* – those who have lived the apostolic life – as assisting Christ at the Judgement, and thus as evading Purgatorial fires (*Summa Theologica* III, q. 89, arts. 1-2).
[30] E.g. 'De gloria et perfeccione sanctorum precellencium postillas proferam', *Melos Amoris*, ed. E. J. F. Arnould (Oxford, 1957), p. 15.6-7; the phrase is a recurrent one in the work.

also betray a strong evangelistic impulse: a desire to convert, or at least to impress, as many people as possible. In spite of the esoteric content of *Incendium Amoris*, that work's prologue states Rolle's intention of writing for the unlearned as well as the learned, and concludes that in the work, 'I excite everyone to love, and try to demonstrate to all the super-fervent and supernatural effect of love'.[31] *Contra Amatores Mundi* does not state its intended audience explicitly, but is clearly also written for mankind as a whole; it contains frequent invocations to 'homo', and particular ones to young men and women.[32] A pretence that one is writing for everyone can of course act as a cover for writing for no one, for oneself or for a small sectarian group, but the genuineness of Rolle's determination to appeal to all is born out by the highly self-conscious charm of much of what he writes. The famous opening of *Incendium Amoris* is a sustained attempt to woo the reader by presenting Rolle and his startling initial experience of *fervor* in as attractive as possible a light. Both *Contra Amatores Mundi* and *Expositio super aliquos versus Cantici Canticorum* contain autobiographical anecdotes and many passages of ecstatic devotion which seem calculated to appeal to a wide audience of Latin readers.[33] Rolle had worked hard for the affectionate respect that was accorded him in the fifteenth century. Only *Melos Amoris*, with its enormous vocabulary, its tortuous structure, its consistent eccentricity of expression and its sheer length, is as impermeably esoteric as Rolle's teaching might have made everything he wrote.

A number of different explanations can be given for the coexistence of elitist and popular impulses in Rolle's writing. One is that as a result of his insecurities he is always aware of the audacity of his own thinking, and tries to compensate for it by wooing the reader lest he turn into an

[31] *Incendium Amoris*, p.147.29-31: 'Universos excito ad amorem, amorisque superfervidum ac supernaturalem affectum utrumque ostendere conabor'. The passage was famous both in the Middle Ages and earlier in this century, when it was sometimes used as proof of Rolle's anti-intellectual leanings. In fact the 'rudibus et indoctis' to whom he dedicates the work (p.147.11) may be synonymous with the *pauperes* whom he often speaks of and who are specialised and saintly contemplatives rather than uneducated people in any ordinary sense, while his dismissal of theologians and philosophers is promptly followed by a discussion of their aptitude for love (p.147.9ff). Rolle seems to be deliberately confusing the issue of whom he is writing for in order to aspire to a universal audience.

[32] See e.g. cap.6.256, 'O homo ... qui amare intendis'; cap.7.1, 'O pudice virgines'; cap.7.24, 'O mulieres impie', etc. The work as a whole imitates a spoken address to a shifting group of auditors, including abstractions such as 'amor' (cap.7.274) and 'visio beata' (cap.7.183).

[33] See the opening of cap.6 of *Contra Amatores Mundi* for an anecdote of diabolical temptation, and the whole of the last chapter for a compelling demonstration of the warmth and spiritual ecstasy possible to the lover of God. In *Expositio super aliquos versus Cantici Canticorum*, the whole of the commentary on the phrase 'oleum effusum' (pp.37.8-48.20 in Sister E.M.Murray's Fordham thesis edition of 1958) exemplifies Rolle's ability to work what are essentially quite conventional devotional *motifs* (familiar from the poems of John Hoveden and Walter of Wimborne) into his idiosyncratic vision of the spiritual life, and hence to popularise it.

opponent. He tends to insist that his subject is not the particular one of the solitary's experience of *canor* but the general one of the need for all to love God; the title of the *Liber de Amore Dei contra Amatores Mundi* in itself makes that claim, which implies the relevance of his writing for all. Since in practice he often does write so particularly about *canor*, the inference we are bound to draw is that that experience itself has universal relevance; and with remarkable self-contradictoriness, Rolle holds that this is so, while in most of his works continuing to assert that only solitaries have the capacity to be true contemplatives. To read a work like *Contra Amatores Mundi* in a logical way is to conclude that Rolle thought that everyone should be hermits and attain the highest state; indeed, his evangelistic zeal and the extent of his abstraction from the contingencies of the earthly Church's existence are such that there is a real sense in which this does represent his opinion. As a *perfectus* himself, he has a duty to teach the rest of the Church, to exercise his verbal gift of *canor* for the benefit of those *in via* as well as singing with those *in patria*. What else is he to teach but the primacy of divine love, and the importance of *fervor*, *dulcor* and *canor* as the principal products and means of attaining divine love?

This account of the contrary impulses in Rolle's works is of course sketchy, ignoring a good deal of detail and stating baldly what are sometimes no more than the underlying assumptions, or the conclusions which a work allows the reader to reach for himself. Nonetheless it is between these poles of elitism and popularism, and within the ground marked out by the few and extraordinarily simple positions I have outlined, that Rolle's thought moves. These impulses in the mutually exclusive directions of esoteric and universal appeal can indeed be seen in isolation in two late works which display diametrically opposing attitudes to their audiences while retaining a remarkable theological similarity. One is *Melos Amoris*, which is notorious for its involutedness not so much of thought as of language, and which suggests a writer indifferent to the needs of contemplatives less advanced than himself.[34] It is an abstract, highly emotional and for the most part self-absorbed ecstasy, which evidently attracted a small and sophisticated readership in the fifteenth century.[35] Its technical brilliance and difficulty render it as hermetic as

[34] Unlike H. E. Allen and others, but like several recent scholars, I regard *Melos Amoris* as one of Rolle's late works, and give what I hope are compelling reasons for this in chapter 3 of *The Invention of Authority* (see n.1); I see no reason why it should not be closely contemporaneous with, or even later than, *Emendatio Vitae*. For already-published opinions that the work was composed late in Rolle's career, see Sara de Ford, 'Mystical Union in the *Melos Amoris* of Richard Rolle', in *The Medieval Mystical Tradition in England*, ed. Marion Glasscoe (Exeter, 1980), pp.173-202, and J. P. H. Clark, 'Richard Rolle as a Biblical Commentator', *Downside Review* 104 (1986), pp.165-213, especially pp.192-97.
[35] Sara de Ford properly argues that we should regard most of *Melos Amoris* as an 'ecstasy', not as a ratiocinative discourse; see her 'The Use and Function of Alliteration in the *Melos Amoris* of Richard Rolle', *Mystics Quarterly* 12 (1986), pp.59-66.

Finnegan's Wake. The work which best displays the opposing tendency is *Emendatio Vitae*, which was understandably by far the most frequently copied of Rolle's works during the medieval period. In *Emendatio Vitae*, the whole system of overt links between the eremitic life, Rolle's way of living it and his model of spiritual ascent has been suspended, so that the work can concentrate exclusively on the clear and generalised exposition of the 'nine steps' of spiritual ascent and of the mystical experiences to which they lead.[36] The work does not state for what occasion or purpose it was written. Some of its manuscripts dedicate it to a 'William', perhaps a certain Magister William Stopes, and probably a member of the secular clergy;[37] in any case, it is clear that Rolle did not primarily have an audience of solitaries or contemplatives in mind when he wrote it.[38] If *Melos Amoris* is self-consciously his most esoteric work, *Emendatio Vitae* is Rolle's most complete attempt to adapt his teaching to the general reader, to make *canor* and the path of interiorisation and world-denial that leads to it widely accessible.

III

The existence of *Emendatio Vitae* is a sign that at least towards the end of his career Rolle was conscious not only of wanting to convert the world

---

[36] 'Per hos novem gradus praetactos ad puritatem mentis ascenditur ...': the opening of cap. 10 of *Emendatio Vitae* (f. cxxxix.v of F. Faber's edition of some works of *D. Richardi Pampolitani Anglosaxonis Eremitae*, Cologne, 1536).

[37] Allen, pp. 518-20. That the recipient was a priest I deduce from the praise accorded the Mixed Life in cap. 12 (f. cxli.v-cxlii.r): 'Cum enim constet vitam contemplativam digniorem esse ac magis meritoriam quam activam vitam, et omnes contemplativos instinctu dei amantes solitudinem et propter contemplationis dulcedinem in amore sunt praecipue ferventes, liquet utique quod solitarii dono contemplationis summis sunt ad perfectionem maximi: *et si forte aliqui sint in eo statu quod et contemplativae vitae culmen arripiunt, et tamen praedicationis officium implere non desistunt: isti solitarios licet in contemplatione summos et solis divinis intentos non necessitati proximorum in hoc superant, quod caeteris operibus aureolam propter suam praedicationem merentur.*' (Italics mine.) The italicised words are so extraordinary a reversal of Rolle's normal insistence that the contemplative life is the higher the more it consists of solitude and the less concern it shows for the world (including other Christians), that either Rolle had changed his mind, which I think unlikely, or he was adapting his stance for a priest who was also a contemplative. (Compare the argument put forward with respect to *Judica Me* below, which sees Rolle failing so to adapt himself earlier in his career.)

[38] The work can be described as a collection of brilliant generalisations about the spiritual life, which does not draw the literalistic conclusions about how it should be lived that are evident in many of Rolle's other works. For example, cap. 2, entitled 'De Contemptu Mundi' (Faber, *ed. cit.*, f. cxxxv.v) is not a plea that the reader should become a hermit, but essentially a moral exposition, as is cap. 3 (f. cxxxvi.r), 'De Paupertate', which focusses on poverty of spirit. Cap. 4 (f. cxxxvi.v), 'De Institutione Vitae', is not about how a contemplative should spend his or her day, but is an exposition of the sins that are to be avoided – and so the list goes on.

in the abstract, but also of how his mysticism and characteristic manner of writing might be adapted to that end. *Judica Me* shows that a desire to be of practical assistance and to exercise his role as a teacher of the Church was with him at a much earlier stage. It is generally agreed that *Judica Me* is among Rolle's first works, written before he had articulated his mystical experience in the definitive way he records in *Incendium Amoris*, and before he had developed much of the stylistic and tonal sophistication he exhibits elsewhere.[39] He wrote it at the request of a priest who seems to have been an intimate of his, and who presumably asked for a manual of instruction that would be of professional use to him.[40] What he received was both less and more than that. Rolle took and slightly adapted three short sections of a lengthy tripartite manual, the *Oculus Sacerdotis*, which its author, William of Pagula, had recently completed,[41] and added apologetic and didactic material of his own to form a strange hybrid work in four parts: a sermon concerning the Judgement, which begins with a defence of the writer's recent decision to change his place of abode, and ends with a discussion of how the reader should mend his life and ascend to the love of God (*Judica A*); a short exposition of the duty of a priest to practice what he preaches and avoid ignorance, prefaced by a defensive prologue (*Judica B1*); an abbreviated confession manual (*Judica B2*); and a model sermon, which takes the form of another exposition of the Judgement (*Judica B3*). The work as a whole thus attempts three things at once: to defend its writer from his detractors; to instruct the priestly reader to shun evil and to convert his own soul; and to help him to instruct his parishioners through preaching and the confessional to live their lives worthily as active Christians. The combination of intentions is unusual in mingling the indirect mode of instruction typical of the pastoral manual (which teaches its reader how to teach others) with the direct mode typical of the homily, in which the reader is the ultimate object of the writer's concern.

[39] Both Allen (pp. 94ff) and the work's editor Daly (pp. li-liii) agree that the work is an early one. Clark (*art. cit.*) implies the same conclusion, since his major criterion for placing Rolle's commentaries in chronological order is that the more derivative ones can be expected to be earlier than the more independent ones – a position I find generally convincing. Since *Judica Me* is directly dependent on a source, it may well have been written at the same stage of Rolle's career as the commentaries most evidently based on the *Glossa Ordinaria* (e.g. *Super Threnos*, *Super Apocalypsim*).

[40] Rolle indicates that the work has been commissioned at p. 18.1-2: 'Cupienti mihi peticione vestre satisfacere ...' That the person who commissioned it was a priest is clear from the things Rolle regards as useful for him ('ad utilitatem legencium', p. 18.18); that he was an intimate of Rolle's is shown by the appeals made to his knowledge of the purity of Rolle's intentions (p. 2.8-11), and by references to events and people which the work does not need to explain (pp. 2.19-3.5).

[41] For an account of the *Oculus Sacerdotis*, see Leonard Boyle, 'The *Oculus Sacerdotis* and some Other Works of William of Pagula', *Transactions of the Royal Historical Society* V (1955), pp. 81-110. *Pars Oculi*, the first part of the manual but the last to be written, seems to have been completed c.1327-29, *Dextera Pars* five or six years earlier (pp. 105-06).

Unlike *Emendatio Vitae*, *Judica Me* has not been among Rolle's more popular successes. Although eighteen surviving manuscripts contain parts of the work, medieval copiers evidently did not find all of it equally helpful; only five manuscripts contain the whole work, while the others omit from one to three of its parts in a great variety of ways.[42] Partly as a result of this heterogeneity in the manuscript presentation of the work, modern writers on Rolle have almost all denied it integrity as a single, consciously-structured entity. Allen describes it as 'a collection of four loosely connected tracts', an opinion in which Marzac and Daly (the latter somewhat reluctantly) concur.[43] This view of *Judica Me* is not surprising, for there is much about its structure that is unusual and unsatisfactory. However, there is no doubt that it is a single work, planned carefully with specific ends in view.[44] Rolle's problem, as we shall see, is that his intentions are not wholly integrated with one another, and on occasion conflict in a manner that undermines the work's unity and clarity. The short investigation of the work which follows highlights the points of tension between its different purposes in a way that helps to account for *Judica Me*'s partial failure to achieve its goals. More important, it focusses us on the nature of the popularist and the elitist impulses evident in Rolle's career from its beginning, and provides a shadowy clue as to how they can coexist with such intimacy in most of his major works.

As Father Leonard Boyle explains, 'in purpose ... the *Oculus Sacerdotis* was meant to embrace all aspects of the *cura animarum* to which a parish priest was committed'.[45] Its first part, *Pars Oculi*, is a penitential manual whose treatment of confession practice is supplemented by a long section on the prescribing of penance that indicates which sins a parish priest may

[42]   See Daly, pp. xxviff for charts and analyses of the various manuscripts. Daly believes that all are descended from a single archetype, which must have contained the complete work.

[43]   Allen p. 93, N. Marzac, *op. cit.*, pp. 41-43 (where she treats the parts of the work as four separate works), Daly, pp. lii-liii. However, Allen calls the four parts of the work *Judica A* and *Judica B1 B2* and *B3* (terms I also use), indicating her belief that the last three parts are more closely related to one another than they are to the first. At one point (p. 105) she implies that she thinks of *Judica Me* not as four but as two works, *A* and *B*.

[44]   I hope this will become obvious. There is no evidence that the work was written as two or four separate 'tracts' and good literary evidence that it was not. Daly points out the unity of the work's theme very usefully: 'The *Judica A* is an earnest plea not to judge others ... *Judica B1* is a plea that Rolle's priest friend will judge his own life ... In the *Judica B2* Rolle offers a handbook to confessors for their important duty of judging sins ... the *Judica B3* is a sermon on the Last Judgement ...' (p. xi). *Judica B1* introduces the last two parts of the work by stating that Rolle has compiled things which 'vestro statui profutura iam video' (p. 18.15); *Judica B2* acknowledges a change in the tone and subject of discourse by beginning 'istis iam dictis ad utilitatem vestris' (p. 27.1). A number of references to the priest's office in *Judica A* (e.g. p. 13.12-18) make it clear that part of the work was, like the rest, written for a priest. All in all, a stronger case could be made for the disunity of almost any of Rolle's other works than it can for *Judica Me*.

[45]   Boyle, *art. cit.*, p. 84. The work and its subsequent revisions were 'widely appreciated' throughout the fourteenth and fifteenth centuries (p. 94).

and may not absolve. The *Dextera Pars* 'is concerned with the parish priest ... as pastor',[46] and mainly consists of preaching material and matters relating to pastoral care, while the *Pars Sinistra* is a long treatment of the theology of the sacraments. Rolle abridged parts of *Pars Oculi* for *Judica B2*, and borrowed from different sections of *Dextera Pars* for half of *Judica B1* and most of *B3*; the first part of *Judica Me* seems not to have been derived from any source. The structure that results can only be called a pastoral manual in the loosest sense. Rolle omits all discussion of the practicalities of the Christian life; all mention of sacramental theology (dealing as briefly as possible with absolution in his treatment of confession); all reference to the canons of the Church and to the liturgy; almost all issues of Church discipline; in short, virtually all the particularities which make up the bulk of William of Pagula's manual. Where in *Pars Oculi* the exposition of a model confession is preceded by advice as to how to confess individuals from different walks of active life, and is followed by a discussion of the penitential canons which determine how the process of their absolution is to be organised, *Judica B2* is concerned only with the model confession itself – with the most generalised part of the work.

Why did Rolle make these kinds of omissions? It seems that in this work as so often elsewhere he was actively aware of his own status as a hermit while he wrote, and wanted to focus only on the area in which he regarded himself as a specialist: that of the inner life. He draws our attention to his eremitic life at the beginning both of *Judica A* and *Judica B1*,[47] and throughout his works associates the solitary life with the interior life of the spirit; in his model, the hermit's conversion from the world is a turning from flesh to spirit, and from outer to inner.[48] He thus has nothing to do with the mundanities of the regulations by which the earthly Church governs itself, or with the particular treatment which different kinds of active Christians require when they come to confess. In other words, only to a limited extent does he overcome his own specialisation and engross himself in the niceties of the secular priest's job. In *Judica B2* he shows the priest how to identify and reprove sin, and in *Judica B3* he demonstrates one way for a preacher to move the hearts of a congregation, because both these tasks touch on the inner life, and both are primarily affective. Almost everywhere in the work, he actively avoids theological discussion, the imparting of mere knowledge and the treatment of what might be considered the more formal aspects of the priestly office.

These omissions should not be regarded merely in a negative light, for they represent an early statement of Rolle's invariable and exclusive stress on the inner life. Moreover, *Judica Me* itself positively asserts the same priority, by beginning with a homily (*Judica A*) that does not form a part

---

[46]   *Idem*, p. 88.

[47]   'Si heremita dicerer cuius nomine indigne vocor ...' (p. 2.2-3); 'Nonnulli nempe cum heremeticam vitam considerant, me etiam heremitam non esse inpudenter affirmare non formidant' (p. 18.7-9).

[48]   In cap. 13 of *Incendium Amoris*, an important discussion of the eremitic life, Rolle quotes Hosea 2.14, as proof of its interior nature: 'Ducam eam in solitudinem et loquar ad cor eius' (p. 180.12-13).

of the 'manual' structure of the rest of the work. Before being instructed in his pastoral duties, Rolle's priestly reader is obliged to think about his own inner life: about the necessity of avoiding hell, the importance of good living in achieving that object, and about the manner in which he can ascend to a greater awareness of and response to the love of God. Elsewhere he and his parishioners are on several occasions adjured to avoid formalism (the disparity between an outward act and its inward significance). If the priest is to preach virtue, he must himself perform the same virtuous deeds as he extols, and even try to do better.[49] If the parishioner is to confess his or her sins, they must be 'poured out like water', none being held back and no mental reservation being made.[50] *Judica Me* ends with three *exempla* in which the dead return to tell their former associates that they have been damned or are being seriously punished in purgatory for just the category of sins which the work as a whole condemns: the failure to be truly contrite in confession, to make adequate restitution and to perform good deeds with good intentions rather than out of vainglory.[51] Such an ending sums up Rolle's overarching didactic purpose in writing *Judica Me*, which can be stated as having been to point those in active life, who might be inclined to over-emphasise the im-

---

[49] 'Sed et cogitare ut bona que communi populo predicare intenditis, vosmetipsi secundum quod status vester exigit eadem immo digniora instanter agatis, ut cum alios de suis culpis iuste reprehenditis de vosmetipsis easdem culpas extirpetis' (p. 18.20-24).

[50] Rolle is here borrowing from *Pars Oculi*, but dramatises William of Pagula's dry exposition highly successfully. The whole passage (pp. 32.7-33.16) is worth quoting: 'Postmodum brevem superaddat exhorticionem dicens, "*Effunde tamquam aquam cor tuam coram Domine*" (Lamentations 2.19). Nam ceteri liquores velut vinum, oleum et lac, quando effunduntur, adhuc saporem in vasis retinent, et difficile exeunt; aqua vero cum effunditur, de facili tota simul egreditur. Sunt enim quidam qui effundunt se sicut vinum, qui moram faciendo et seipsos excusando, adhuc tamen voluntatem peccandi secum retinent. Alii sunt qui se effundunt sicut oleum, de quo cum effunditur adhuc in vase retinetur pars eius, qui in confitendo celant aliqua peccata mortalia vel timore penitencie preterite vel pudore impediti. Talibus dicendum est: Curari non desiderat qui vulnera occultat; non est medicina apponenda dum ferrum est in vulnere. Alii sunt qui ad modum lactis se effundunt, qui licet peccata sua confiteantur et aliquo modo penitentes videntur, tamen aliquam dulcedinem et delectacionem in peccatis sibi reservant. Contra quod dicit psalmista: *Iocundum sit ei eloquium meum; ego vero delectabator in Domino* (Psalm 103.34). Tunc quippe eloquium hominis Deo iocundum dicitur cum integra confessione et devota oracione se effundens omnem mundi vanitatem a se abicere conatur. Effunde igitur sicut aqua cor tuum, non excusando sed fortiter accusando, nec aliquod peccatum nec aliquam delectacionem peccati in te morari permittendo, quia non sequitur veniam qui vult unam retinere culpam.'

[51] See pp. 77.20-79.6. Daly prints in parentheses two more *exempla* which seem unlikely to have been in Rolle's original, since they are not carefully related to the work as a whole, unlike the three that all the manuscripts of *Judica B3* have in common. His paragraphing at this point also obscures the coherence of Rolle's conclusion; in reading the passage as containing three *exempla* followed by three *moralitates* (rather than *vice versa*), he links each *exemplum* up with the wrong *moralitas*, and so makes the whole look more like random didacticism than it truly is.

portance of the outward deed, towards the supreme importance of the spiritual disposition that underlies and is the inner truth of action.

The urgency of this purpose touches all parts of the work. Rolle greatly desires direct didactic contact with his reader, and selects his pastoral material to allow himself as much such contact as possible, as well as to stress its importance for the priest. Thus *Judica B3* is not only a model sermon on the Judgement; like *Judica A* it is also intended to be responded to directly by the reader.[52] *Judica B2* is the most abstracted part of the work, but even here Rolle is focussing on the essentially dramatic situation of the priest confessing the penitent. *Judica B1* is concerned with the inner purity needed for the priest to exercise his office properly (as well as with the other qualifications, including a knowledge of the Scriptures, that he requires),[53] and thus addresses him directly. Indeed, at several points in this part of the work, Rolle's sense of urgency causes him to undermine his own structural divisions, and to address the priest more evangelistically than his immediate purpose warrants. *Judica A* and *Judica B1* are divided not only by the new prologue that opens the latter but by the different perspective each adopts towards the reader's moral life; the first part is intended to address the priest as an individual soul, the second as a religious functionary with an *ex officio* duty to live virtuously. Rolle is evidently unhappy about the possibility of creating the impression that virtue is merely a professional adjunct, and in effect interrupts his exposition of the qualifications a good priest needs to extol (once again) the merits of 'caritate non ficta' – of charity for its own sake.[54] The tone and subject of *Judica A* temporarily reemerges in a digressive passage of impassioned affective prose.[55] Only once Rolle has stressed the need to

---

[52] At the opening of *Judica B1*, Rolle explains that he is not allowed to preach in public: '... quod ego nondum in publico predicando cogor dicere ...' (p. 18.18-19). There is perhaps a sense in which *Judica Me*, and a number of his other works, compensate for this fact by giving him opportunities to preach on paper. *Judica B3* is not described as a model sermon in *Judica Me*, although it is derived from one in the source and may be presumed to have had that purpose as well as being intended to touch the reader directly.

[53] See pp. 23.6-26.3, and note the emphasis Rolle places on Bible study, quoting a number of verses that William of Pagula had not included, and adding his own exhortations.

[54] P. 19.14.

[55] The passage reads as follows: 'Quicumque enim es qui accedis ad iudicandum alios, prius discucias teipsum et iudica ut tu recte in teipso iudicatus etiam alios recte iudicare possis. Quoniam igitur necesse est ut unusquisque ad celestia regna tendens caritate non ficta informaretur, illam vobis, scilicet, caritatem Dei et proximam, pre omnibus et in omnibus habendam commendo, sine qua, utique, nec quisque salvari poterit et cum qua nec aliquis peribit. Unde et scire debetis quod qui Deum non diligit, proximum amare nescit; nam in amore Dei, proximum addiscit diligere, et in dileccione proximi amorem Dei nutrire. Sed si amoris divini dulcedinem sentire cupitis, oportet profecto ut totum cor vestrum ad querendum Christum prebeatis. Ipse enim dicit: *qui diligit me sermonem meum servabit* (John 14.15). Hoc est ergo Deum diligere: omnia eius precepta ex amore iusticie incessanter custodire. Unde et sciendum est quod amor Christi cum magno labore, magnaque spirituali exercitacione, videlicet, per iuges oraciones et devotas

love God regardless of office can he return to his subject with the bridging statement that someone thus marked by a firm faith, a certain hope and by true charity can at last be trusted with the instruction of others.[56] Similarly, *Judica B1* ends by digressing from its exposition of the need for a pastor to be learned, in order to extol the essential help provided by the Scriptures in the soul's ascent to Divine love.[57] It is as if, at these points, the indirect nature of the pastoral manual's engagement with its reader's soul is itself identified with formalism, and so is swept aside.

In *Judica Me*, Rolle's 'specialist' emphasis on the inner life is thus far from being at odds with a form of popularism. It precludes him from writing a conventional manual for his priest friend, but actively encourages the work's intimacy of engagement with and fervent evangelising of the reader. In the 'digressions' just noted, Rolle evinces frustration at the distance imposed upon his discourse by the manual form he has adopted. However minor its manifestations here, much is latent in such frustration: the fact that all his subsequent works (with the exception of his biblical commentaries) engage the reader directly and affectively; that the other work in which he comes close to a pastoral mode of writing, *Emendatio Vitae*, deals only with the reader's inner life, generally avoiding discussion of the physical conditions and active works which surround that life; perhaps even that the mystical experience that he perceived as of pre-eminent importance, the experience of *canor*, he interpreted as one of unbounded and spontaneous communication. Indeed Rolle's reworking of a pastoral manual into the evangelistic instrument that *Judica Me* largely is seems to suggest that his subsequent career as an eremitic writer will be wholly occupied with appealing to as wide an audience as possible. This apparently bodes well for a harmonious relationship in the rest of Rolle's writing career between his sense of himself as *ex officio* a specialist of the inner life and his impulse towards popularism – for the two themes are tied closely together.

Yet, as I have suggested, this harmony is not in practice consistently in evidence in any of the works in which Rolle attempts to appeal to a wide audience, except for *Emendatio Vitae*. Indeed, my exposition has treated

meditaciones, menti fideli acquiritur – et in magno gaudio cum quis amorem eius habuerit possidetur. Distat ergo inter amorem Dei et amorem mundi. Nam in principio amor mundi ad modum suum dulcescit, sed in fine amarissimus est. Amor vero Christi in inicio pro penitencia nos cogit amarescere, sed paulatim in nobis crescens mirabili leticia nos facit habundare. Vos igitur firma fide, certa spe, vera caritate insigniti, secure ad curam animarum accedite, ut recte instructi etiam alios recte instruere valeatis. Ista namque tria sacerdoti pertinent, scilicet, bona vita, scientia recta, predicacio discreta. Nihil tam periculosum est apud Deum, nec tam turpe apud homines, quod quis senciat veritatem et non libere pronunciat illam.' (pp.19.9-20.11) Rolle is here concerned to stress the impossibility of separating the proper exercise of the priestly office from a priest's own spiritual life.
[56] 'Vos igitur firma fide, certa spe, vera caritate insigniti, secure ad curam animarum accedite ...' (p.20.6-7).
[57] 'Diligenter ergo stude et perscrutare libros in quibus quod ad salutem anime tue et aliorum pertinent poteris invenire. Nam procul dubio, si delectacionem in sacra scriptura niteris querere, etiam in divino amore rapieris iubilare.' (pp.25.11-26.3)

the popularist and specialist sides of Rolle's works as antithetical, by dubbing the latter 'elitist'. What prevents the two themes from enjoying the harmonious relationship they seem to have in *Judica Me*? A hasty summary of parts of *Judica A* indicates that the harmony is not always present here either, and helps to show why this is so.[58]

One of Rolle's intentions in writing the work, as I said, was to defend himself against charges that he behaved in a way inappropriate for solitaries by changing his place of abode. Evidently he was worried by these charges, for he gives over the opening of the work to self-vindication. They probably aggravated his sense of the incongruity that might be perceived in his writing of a pastoral work for a secular priest, by pointing up the vulnerability of his own status as a hermit. He deals with them skilfully, in such a way as to introduce a version of the main theme of *Judica Me* (the importance of judging not by appearance but by reality) from the start. He asserts that he will be judged by God who sees his heart, not by man who can see only his external features, and stresses that his bodily movement has had only the purpose of bringing him to a place where he can enjoy greater spiritual stability.[59] The defence at least appears satisfactory, for after this opening he seems able to embark on the homiletic treatment of the damnation of the sinner with assured authority.

However, the defensive motif continues to be present in *Judica A*, and at the end of the homily reemerges in a disruptive and unexpected way. The moral that is drawn from the section's long inspection of the progress of the sinner towards hell is twofold: negatively, abstain from sin; positively, if you wish to be perfect, turn from the love of the world to the love of God.[60] The final pages of *Judica A* focus on this positive moral as they build a description of the spiritual height that the priestly reader will attain if he persists in his good works and his spiritual exercises. At this stage of his career, Rolle's ideas as to the nature of spiritual ascent have not been fully articulated, but it seems as though he is attempting something like the generous inclusiveness of *Emendatio Vitae*, in helping the priest scale the spiritual heights that are the particular preserve of the contemplative.

It may well have been his intention to assist his friend in this way. But the text does something quite different, and manages to emphasise instead the *gulf* between the solitary life and what is obtainable by the priest. The

---

[58] The subject-matter of the following paragraphs is discussed in much more detail in part II of chapter 4 of *The Invention of Authority*.

[59] 'A Deo qui scrutatur cor et renes volo iudicari, non ab homine qui solummodo vident ea que exterius apparent, quoniam qui de alienis cordibus iudicare presumit, indubitanter sciat quod in errorem cadit; et qui motum corporis de loco ad locum instabilitatem mentis pronunciat absque dubio grave pondus super se posuisse cognoscat ...' etc. (p.1.2-7).

[60] 'Hec scribo vobis ut non peccetis, ut motibus illicitis viriliter resistatis ...' etc. (p.10.11-12); 'si vis etiam perfectus esse, audi Dominum dicentem: Nisi quis renunciaverit, inquit, *omnibus que possidet, non potest meus esse discipulus* (Luke 14.33)' (pp.11.26-12.2).

following passage builds towards the climax of the moral section of the homily:

> With the fervour of charity, prayer and tears, smother the children of Babylon, that is, wicked thoughts and depraved desires. May the poisonous desires of the world and the flesh not grow, but be sternly thrown down and almost destroyed by an abundance of spiritual joy. Turn from worldly comfort so that you may come to pleasure and comfort in the love of Christ. For he who desires earthly things will not experience divine consolation, nor is the sweetness of eternal love imbued in that soul who delights in the changes and the chances of this present life. Wonderful is the heavenly sweetness, and it is not granted to clingers to earthly things. Remember then that *narrow is the way that leads men to heaven*, so that few go by it, and *wide is the road which leads to hell and many go by it*. It would seem hard and all too bitter to you to be punished eternally with the devil. So may it seem sweet to you to toil a little in the service of Christ, so that afterwards you may rejoice with Christ for ever.[61]

At this point, Rolle is clearly addressing the priest, as he has been throughout *Judica A*. Yet at the climax of this passage, a remarkable change of address occurs, and the text quite suddenly appears to assume an audience not of a single secular clergyman but of potential solitaries, now addressed in the plural:

> If the desert delights you so that you live in solitude, or at least if you wish to keep continually to your solitary intention, know that initially you will have hard labour. But as you grow gradually in the love of Christ, you will come to ineffable joy. Yet because of the bitterness of the entrance, no wise man will leave the spacious and pleasant road. At the entrance we are badly stung, but in the middle and at the end we rejoice in celestial sweetness. O happy sadness which is at once followed by divine consolation! For the desert rejoices to be visited by Christ's poor.[62]

[61] 'Ardore caritatis et oracionis et lacrimarum, suffoca parvulos Babilonis, id est, iniquas cogitaciones et pravos motus. Mundi et carnis desideria nociva non crescant, sed potius habundancia spiritualium gaudiorum subtus quasi interfecta iaceant. Abhorreas solacium mundi ut invenias delectacionem et solacium in amore Christi. Consolacionem namque divinam non sentit qui terrenam cupit, nec dulcor eterni amoris in illa anima infunditur que in fluxibilibus et instabilibus huius vite presentis delectatur. Mirabilis est dulcedo celestis que non conceditur inherenti rebus terrenis. Recordare itaque quia *arta est via que ducit hominem ad celum* et ideo pauci vadunt per eam, et *lata* est *via que ducit ad infernum* et *multi* transeunt *per illam* (Matthew 7.14, 13). Durum et nimis amarum tibi videtur perhenniter cruciari cum diabolo. Ergo dulce tibi videtur modicum in servicio Christi laborare, ut postea sine fine cum Christo possis gaudere.' (p.15.8-10)

[62] 'Si vos delectat heremus ut in solitudine habitetis, vel saltem si singulare propositum teneatis iugiter, scitote quod in principio durum laborem habetis. Sed paulatim in amore Christi crescentes, ineffabile gaudium invenietis. Verumptamen propter asperum introitum nullus sapiens spaciosam et delectabilem derelinquet viam. In inicio graviter pungimur, sed in medio et in fine celesti suavitate

The promises made here recall the last remarks addressed to the priest, but with important differences. Where the priest is offered joy 'now', in heaven, the hermit will attain it 'gradually' on earth; where *narrow is the way* applies to the whole of the priest's earthly journey, that of the hermit is only difficult at the beginning ('the bitterness of the entrance'). Rolle boldly states that solitaries can reach the sweetness of heavenly joy in this life ('in the middle'); he has been more cautious in relation to the priest. What has been smuggled into the exposition under cover of these imprecise parallels – and in the context of increasingly explicit autobiographical statements – is an expression of the superiority of the solitary life to that of the secular clergy, and implicitly to all others:

> For I feel such joy in my desire for the habitation of a hermit that I cannot, nor do I wish to, express it. Let me never, then, go so rudely astray that I speak anything evil or offensive about those who seek to be hermits. Under that name I do not fear the devil, I despise worldly things, I subdue the flesh to the spirit. Blessed be the name of hermit and the singular plan of life in which I learn to love, I become assustomed to sing, I wait securely for salvation. I do not despise any order in the church, but I praise and love the solitary one most greatly.[63]

The concessive 'I do not despise any order in the church' in fact points up the gulf between other states of life and Rolle's own 'intention to be alone'. Where the priest was warned to fear a fall from grace, Rolle awaits his salvation securely and has begun his heavenly rejoicing already.

Thus at a crucial point in an exposition of the inner life that has apparently been adapted for a priest, Rolle breaks the thread of his own discourse and appropriates the discussion for the purpose of praising the solitary life. The harmony between Rolle's sense of himself and of other hermits as specialists of the inner life and his evangelistic desire to share his knowledge breaks down in the insistence that the spiritual life at its highest is practised only by hermits. Since he reminds us so insistently that he is one of those hermits, and since *Judica A* has begun with self-defence, it seems clear that the motive force behind this strange manoeuvre is apologetic. Rolle is concerned to stress the distinctive and important nature of the solitary life as a way of dealing with his detractors, and perhaps of justifying his composition, as a self-proclaimed hermit without ecclesiastical office, of *Judica Me*.

The way a didactic passage of *Judica A* is disrupted by the intrusion of

delectamur. O felix tristicia quam statim sequitur consolatio divina! ... Letatur enim heremus a pauperibus Christi visitari.' (pp.15.22-16.8)
[63] 'Tantum namque gaudium sencio sub heremitice habitacionis voluntate ut nec volo nec possum illud inerrare. Absit igitur ut tam crudeliter deviarem quod aliud sinistrum sive demeritum de appetentibus heremum loquerer. Sub cuius nomine diabolum non timeo, terrena contempno, carnem spiritui subiugo. Benedictum sit illud nomen heremeticum et illud singulare propositum in quo amare disco, iubilare consuesco, salvacionem securus expecto. Nullum in ecclesia ordinem reprehendo, sed solitudinem maxime diligo ac laudo.' (p.16.9-16)

apologetic material is interestingly parallel to the manner in which the measured exposition of the priest's duties in *Judica B1* is disrupted by intimate appeals to him to catch fire with the ardour of charity. As with the 'digressions' in *Judica B1*, the implications of this passage in *Judica A* are large, for in the wake of *Judica Me* Rolle was to write a whole series of works the principal purpose of which was to extol the solitary life. Although it appears that Rolle's concern for the status of the solitary life was even more urgent than his desire to reach out to all with his message of the vital importance of charity, it is clear on the other hand that the impulses that lie behind what I have called the 'elitist' and the 'popularist' sides of Rolle's writing are not altogether divergent.

'NOGHT HOW LANG MAN LIFS; BOT HOW WELE': THE LAITY AND THE LADDER OF PERFECTION

George R. Keiser

In 1488(?) William Caxton printed the *Royal Book* (STC 21429), a translation of the *Somme le roi* of Frère Lorens of Orleans that he had made 'atte requeste of a worshipful marchaunt & mercer of london' (sig. u9ʳ). Caxton's translation of this immensely popular, late-thirteenth-century compilation contains a general discussion of reasons for keeping the commandments, in which appear the following lines, underscored by an early owner of the British Library copy (C.10.b.22):

> Secondly, longe lyf which ought not to be nombred in the nombre of yeres/ but in the nombre of good vertues. And in lyf which is wythoute synne.   (sig. b5ᵛ)

The worshipful London mercer who brought the *Somme le roi* to Caxton for translation and printing must have recognised that many pious laymen and -women among his contemporaries felt a strong desire for vernacular writings that offered guidance and direction for living a life numbered in the number of good virtues. The soundness of his judgment, and that of Caxton in printing it, is borne out by the fact that the translation, with its reminder that 'holy scrypture calleth euery man a king which wysely and parfytly can gouerne and dyrecte hymself after vertu' (sig. u9ʳ), was in sufficient demand for Wynkyn de Worde to issue an edition for himself and for Richard Pynson in 1507 (STC 21430, 21430a).

The desire for English vernacular books of moral and spiritual guidance seems to have begun in earnest among the laity in the mid-fourteenth century. Dan Michel of Northgate was probably responding to that desire when in 1340 he prepared the *Ayenbite of Inwyt*, his prose translation of the *Somme le roi*, 'uor lewede men/ vor uader/ and uor moder and uor oþer ken/ ham uor to berȝe uram alle manyer zen.'[1] About three decades later another writer, perhaps William of Nassington, made still another of the many Middle English translations of the *Somme*, this one in verse, under the title *Speculum Vite*, 'al for lewed men namely/ That can no manner of clergy' (BL MS Additional 33995, f. 1ᵛ).[2] Not long afterwards, in the third quarter of the century, the author of *The Abbey of the Holy Ghost* addressed 'all those that ne may not be bodily in religion, that they may be ghostly'.[3] Late in the

[1]   Ed. R. Morris, EETS, os 23 (London: Trübner, 1866), 262.
[2]   This and subsequent passages taken from the text of *Speculum Vite* preserved in BL MS Additional 33995 are quoted with gracious permission of the British Library.
[3]   *Religious Pieces in Prose and Verse*, ed. G. G. Perry, rvsd edn (1867, 1914; rpt New

first decade of the next century the author of *Dives and Pauper* clearly
directed his comprehensive work to an audience, as defined by its recent
editor, of the 'newly literate, worldly, somewhat credulous yet pious
laymen',[4] whom he seems to have reached in some number, to judge from an
extensive manuscript tradition and, subsequently, three printed editions.

By the second decade of the fifteenth century vernacular writings of moral
and spiritual guidance for both laity and clergy were available in sufficient
abundance to cause a translator of Suso's *Horologium Sapientiae* some doubt
about the need for his efforts:

> But there-with considerynge the multitude of bookes and tretees
> drawen in-to englysshe þat now ben generally communed, my wyll
> hath ben wyth-drawen dredynge that werke somewhat as in
> waste.   (STC 3305, f. A3ʳ⁻ᵛ).

Among that abundance are two devotional treatises that I shall discuss in this
paper: *A Ladder of Foure Ronges* and the closely related *Holy Boke Gratia
Dei*. These two works illustrate very well the theme *De Cella in Seculum*, for
they represent attempts to make the fruits of monastic piety accessible to
their devout contemporaries. In still another respect these works are fit
subjects for this occasion because *Ladder* is a translation of a monastic
treatise composed by a close associate of St Hugh of Lincoln and one of the
four manuscripts preserving portions of *Gratia Dei* is in the library of
St Hugh's cathedral, the well-known Lincoln Cathedral Library MS 91.

In this paper I shall explore how the English writers of these two works –
themselves members of monastic houses, I believe – transformed materials
from their monastic heritage to make it more accessible and how wide an
audience they reached. The author of *Ladder of Foure Ronges* seems to have
had in mind an audience consisting primarily of clerics, both within and
outside the cloister, but also including the very pious among the laity, and he
reshaped his material accordingly, at the same time continuing to hold to the
original purpose of encouraging and instructing the reader in the exercise of
contemplation. After we have considered this exceptionally artful work, we
shall turn to the more complicated and problematic *Gratia Dei*. In looking at
that treatise we shall see how the author worked a very thorough
transformation of *Ladder* and his other sources in order to reach a still wider
audience, bringing to it a message very much like that expressed in the earlier
quotation from Caxton's *Royal Book*.

> ffor-þi is noght to tell bi how lang man lifs: bot how wele. ... Thou sal
> noght deme þe man has lang lifid þof he gang with a stafe stoupand &

York: Greenwood, n.d.), 51. The text from which this edition was made is preserved
in Lincoln Cathedral Library MS 91, one of two volumes copied c.1430-50 by Robert
Thornton, the Yorkshire gentryman whose devotional interests I have explored in
'"To Knawe God Almyghtyn": Robert Thornton's Devotional Book',
Spätmittelalterliche Geistliche Literatur in der Nationalsprache, bd 2, *Analecta
Cartusiana* 106:2 (Salzburg: Universität Salzburg, 1984), 103-129.
[4]   Ed. P. H. Barnum, vol. 1, pt 1, EETS, os 225 (London: Oxford UP, 1976), x.

be grai-harid: bot deme him so halde as he has wele lifid.   (A 54^v, 55^v; YW 137, 139)[5]

How the author of *Gratia Dei* transformed *Ladder* and other devotional writings to address this concern and how well he succeeded in doing so will be the principle areas of investigation in the second portion of the paper.

Turning first to *Ladder* we must note that it is a translation of *Scala Claustralium*, an influential twelfth-century treatise on contemplation, composed by Guigo II, ninth prior of the Grande Chartreuse, who lost the associate he hoped would be the support of his later years when St Hugh was sent to serve as prior at Witham, the first English Carthusian foundation. *Scala Claustralium*, or *The Ladder of Monks*, is, in the words of a modern student and admirer, a monastic theologian's account of 'his theory of the spiritual life as arising out of his experience of that life'.[6] Specifically, *Scala Claustralium* describes a four-stage spiritual exercise by which the monk may taste 'the joys of everlasting sweetness' (p. 82; 'eternae dulcedinis gaudia degustans', p. 84).[7] Put simply, the exercise consists of a reading of scripture, reasoned meditation upon its hidden truth, a turning to god in fervent prayer, and a lifting of the mind to God through contemplation. The special significance of the *Scala* has been described as follows: 'Guigo's contribution lies first in his understanding and insistence on the causal relationship of the four steps, their necessary inter-relatedness, and then in Guigo's concept of the ladder and its steps as symbolic in the neo-platonic sense' (Egan, p. 108).

In time *Scala Claustralium* was revised and rearranged to produce what the recent editors of Guigo's writings observe is a version 'less schematic and less obviously didactic, and thus more suitable for devotional reading'.[8] The work enjoyed wide circulation in this version, which is extant in at least a dozen English manuscripts. Late in the fourteenth century this revised version came to the attention of a very skilful writer, perhaps another Carthusian, who turned it into the English prose work, *A Ladder of Foure Ronges by the Which Men Mowe Wele Clyme to Heven*. As I have already suggested, the English translator made serious modifications to his source in order to create a work accessible to a wider audience than the exclusively monastic one intended by Guigo.

---

[5]   In parenthetical citations following quotations from *Gratia Dei*, A refers to BL MS Arundel 507, L to Lincoln MS 91, H to Huntington Library MS HM 148, YW to *Yorkshire Writers*, vol. 1 (London: Swan Sonnenschein, 1894). Following each sigil is a folio or page number.

[6]   Keith J. Egan, 'Guigo II: The Theology of the Contemplative Life', in *The Spirituality of Western Christendom*, ed. E. R. Elder (Kalamazoo: Cistercian Publications, 1976), 111.

[7]   Quotations from the Latin are taken from the text edited by E. Colledge and Walsh, Guiges II le Chartreux, *Lettre sur la vie contemplative, Douze méditations*, Sources Chrétiennes 163 (Paris: Les éditions du cerf, 1970). The English translation is that of Colledge and Walsh in *The Ladder of Monks and Twelve Meditations* (Garden City: Doubleday, 1978).

[8]   Colledge and Walsh, Introduction to *The Ladder of Monks and Twelve Meditations*, p. 40.

That he succeeded in this attempt and created a treatise of enduring interest, especially to nuns and pious laywomen, is attested by the three surviving manuscripts. The earliest of these, MS Douce 322 at the Bodleian Library, contains a notation indicating that it had been given to the Dominican house at Dartford in Kent by William Baron, who was active in both London and Westminster, during the period 1430 to 1470, as an officer of the Royal Exchequer and a participant in London affairs. Presumably the volume was made for Baron in the metropolitan area in the third quarter of the century, for it was given to Dartford for the special use of his granddaughter, when she was a member of the house. A second miscellany preserving *Ladder*, British Library MS Harley 1706, was probably copied from Douce 322, 'for a devout woman reader, or readers and listeners, in a convent or piously-inclined lay household, somehow in touch, perhaps by intermediaries, with the context of Douce 322',[9] according to Ian Doyle. From at least 1507 until the time of her death in 1537, it was in the possession of Elizabeth de Vere, Countess of Oxford. The final copy was made by William Darker, a member of the Carthusian house at Sheen, whose hand appears in several manuscripts from about 1500, and who may have made the volume containing *Ladder*, Cambridge University Library MS Ff.6.33, for the Brigittine nuns at Syon.[10]

Without manuscript evidence for the period between the time of its creation in the late fourteenth century and its copying into Douce 322, a period of perhaps seventy-five years, we must proceed cautiously. However, we can say that if *Ladder* had been circulating among similar readers in that period, then it was reaching an audience very like that which the author intended to reach. Guigo had specified, in a prologue not found in the revised Latin version, that he was writing his 'thoughts on the spiritual exercises proper to cloistered monks' (p. 81; 'quae de spiritali exercitio claustralium excogitaveram', p. 82), and in the work itself he described the exercises as 'a ladder for monks by which they are lifted from earth to heaven' (p. 82; 'scala claustralium qua de terra in coelum sublevantur', p. 84). In what seems a significant modification, the English author described his work as 'the ladder of cloysterers, & of oþere Goddis lovers' (100/6-7),[11] implying with that ambiguous addition an inclusive attitude very much in contrast to Guigo's exclusivity. While circulation among clerics both within and outside the cloister may have been his principal intention, the translator must have been aware of the possibility that his treatise would reach those pious and newly literate members of the laity who were eager for vernacular devotional writings.

[9] A. I. Doyle, 'Books Connected with the Vere Family and Barking Abbey', *Transactions of the Essex Archaeological Society*, n.s. 25, pt 2 (1958), 229-230. All the information in this paragraph is drawn from Doyle's study.
[10] A. I. Doyle, 'A Survey of the Origins and Circulation of Theological Writings in English in the 14th, 15th and early 16th Century', Cambridge Univ. Ph.D. Dissertation 2301-2302 (1953), 2.227.
[11] Numbers following quotations from *Ladder* indicate page/line references to the edition by Phyllis Hodgson, which appears in *Deonise Hid Diuinite*, EETS, os 231 (1955; rvsd rpt London: Oxford UP, 1958).

More forceful and explicit evidence may be found in some of the English author's four lengthy interpolations into his source, especially his detailed excursus on grace. Guigo had made the point that while meditation is the seeking 'with the help of one's own reason for knowledge of hidden truth' (p. 82; 'occultae veritatis notitiam ductu propriae rationis investigans', p. 84) in scriptural reading, he also firmly cautioned that reason alone is not sufficient. The meditator must also have pondered upon the purity of heart, the desire for which leads him to prayer and makes him receptive to divine grace. Whereas the original treatise by Guigo reaches this point more slowly and deliberately, the reviser of Guigo's text brought forward, from the ending to very near the beginning, a passage recapitulating the main points of the treatise and stressing the causal relationship among the four stages of the exercise and the importance of grace.[12] Finding the subject readily prominent in the revised version of *Scala* before him, the English writer chose to develop more fully, in a lengthy and detailed excursus on the nature and kinds of grace, a topic of significant interest among his contemporaries.

The author's development of this difficult subject in the excursus is admirably deft and clear. He begins with an explanation of two kinds of grace, the first being common grace that informs all creatures and permits movement and feeling, the second reserved to mankind, making man worthy to receive the gift of the Holy Ghost – that is, the third kind of grace. Before taking up that third kind, however, the author gives a careful exposition of the relation between grace and free will, emphasising that the cooperation and assent of the will is necessary for receipt of the third and very special kind of grace, the gift of the Holy Ghost that moves men to good works. The remarkable ease and clarity with which the author develops the subject has led Colledge and Walsh to suggest that the English translator was 'a cleric accustomed to addressing unlearned audiences, and one with a high degree of catechetical expertise, who knows how to explain difficult points of doctrine without confusing his hearers with the terminology and tortuous arguments of the Schools'.[13] That the style of the excursus permits relatively easy access to a difficult subject probably explains why the *Ladder of Foure Ronges* seems to have circulated in books belonging to nuns, and it adds support for the possibility that the author thought his work would reach pious laymen and -women.

A second interpolation, thematically related to the preceding, may tell us still more about the author's intended audience. In this instance the author takes up the theme of the insufficiency of reason alone, which Guigo had illustrated by recalling that the pagan philosophers 'had not the grace to understand what they had the ability to see' (p. 85; 'non meruerunt percipere quod poterant videre', p. 92). After using this example, the English author

[12] For a fuller explanation of the nature of the revision, see Colledge and Walsh, *The Ladder of Monks*, pp. 39-40.

[13] *The Ladder of Monks*, p. 45. If this description seems to conflict with my earlier suggestion that the author was a member of a monastic house, we must not overlook the possibility that his entrance into the cloister could have followed some years as a secular cleric familiar with the demands of pastoral care and hence familiar with techniques for reaching such an audience.

goes further, perhaps beyond anything that Guigo might have conceived, by using two rhetorically powerful, if hypothetical examples. The first is 'a symple olde pore woman' – a 'man or woman' in the Harley 1706 text (f. 51ʳ) – 'that neyther sothely can sey the Pater Noster ne the Crede' (110/7-9), but who through the gift of God learns to pray. The second example is 'a pore sely man þat so dul of witt is, ... thouȝe he shulde lese his hedde he cowde not bryng to an eende a reson', but who by the gift of God, 'may wele be callid a maistyr ouere alle other that this name beryth, that vnwytty so kan teche wysdom withoute wittys to fele & vndirstonde that thurwe no witte of this worlde men may reche to, so þat man doo that therto fallyth, and bowe the ere of his herte to lysten that lore' (110/12-21).

These examples – hypothetical, but still so concretely realised – lend strong rhetorical support to the author's argument for meekness, as they were intended to do. Yet they may have a double purpose. While undercutting the intellectual arrogance, real or potential, of a more learned reader, they would also encourage the unlearned into whose hands the treatise might have come – parish priests without a full university education, nuns, or pious laity – to continue with the spiritual exercises set forth in the treatise. They assure such readers that any uncertainties they feel are appropriate in the face of God's might and not cause for failing to persist in these exercises.

The artful use of concreteness for rhetorical effect is everywhere evident in the *Ladder*, and as Phyllis Hodgson has shown, the clarity and simplicity resulting from it contribute to the 'intimate, ... warmly devotional' tone that characterises the treatise.[14] Perhaps the most effective, certainly the boldest instance of this concreteness is an extended tavern-metaphor illustrating the contemplative union with God. The scene is so remarkable and so revealing of the author's skill, temperament, and purpose that I shall not resist the temptation to reproduce a large portion of it here.

> So doth God Almyȝty to his loveris in contemplacion as a tauerner that good wyne hathe to selle dooth to good drynkeris þat wolle drynke wele of his wyne & largely spende. Wele he knowith what they be there he seeth hem in the strete. Pryvely he wendyth and rowndith hem in the eere & seyth to them that he hath a clarete, and þat alle fyne for ther owyn mouth. He tollyth hem to howse & ȝevyth hem a taast. Sone whanne they haue tastyd therof and that they thynke the drynke good & gretly to ther plesauns, than they drynke dayly & nyȝtly, and the more they drynke, the more the[y] may. Suche lykyng they haue of that drynke that of none other wyne they thynke, but oonly for to drynke þeir fylle and to haue of this drynke all their wylle. And so they spende that they haue, and syth they spende or lene to wedde surcotte or hode & alle that they may, for to drynke with lykyng whiles that them it good thynkith. Thus it faryth sumtyme by Goddis loveris that from þe tyme that they hadde tastyd of this pyment, that is of the swettnesse of God, such lykyng þei founde theryn that as

14 '"A Ladder of Foure Ronges by the Whiche Men Mowe Wele Clyme to Heven." A Study of the Prose Style of a Middle English Translation', *MLR* 44 (1949), 470.

drunkyn men they did spende that they hadde and ȝafe themself to
fastyng and to wakyng & to other penauns doyng. And whan they
hadde no more to spende they leyde their weddys, as apostelys,
martyrys, & maydenys ȝounge of ȝeris dyd in their tyme. Summe
ȝafe their bodyes to brenne in fyre, summe lete her hedys of to be
smytte, summe ȝafe her pappys corvyn from ther breestys, summe
ȝaf ther skyn drawn from the flessh, and somme their bodyes wyth
wylde horsys to be drawe. And alle that they dyd they sette it at
nouȝt for the desyre of that lastyng wele that they desired fully to
haue in the lyfe that is withouten eende. but this likyng is here ȝeven
but for to taste, but all tho that desyre fully to haue it, them behovith
to folowe Crist fote by fote, and evyn lyke steryn hym wyth their
lovys, as these drynkeris the tavernarys doon. Therfor whan God eny
gostly lykyng to thy sowle sendyth, thynke that God spekyth to the,
& rownyth in thyn eere, & sayth: 'Haue nowe this litelle, and taste
how swete I am'.   (113/20-114/16)

If this imagery brings Chaucer to mind for students of English medieval
literature, it does so for two reasons. First, the extended development of the
image, as well as the subject, recall the extended development of the tappe-
and-tonne image in the *Reeve's Prologue*, and we see why the Host should
accuse a creator of such an extended image of practising the art of preaching.
Second, we recall the opening of the *Pardoner's Tale*, with its conventional
treatment of the tavern vices, and our memory of the convention (in *Piers
the Plowman*'s portrait of the Glutton, for example) causes us to wonder
about the source and purpose of this witty and unconventional use of the
tavern image.

Guigo offers some precedent, though only a general one. Employing
sensual imagery to describe spiritual experience – not an unprecedented
technique in monastic and mystical writings – Guigo compares the text,
'Blessed are the pure in the heart, for they shall see God' (p. 83; 'Beati
mundo corde, quoniam ipsi Deum videbunt', p. 86) to 'a grape that is put
into the mouth filled with many senses to feed the soul' (p. 83; 'Ecce breve
verbum sed suavi et multiplici sensu refertum ad pastum animae, quasi uvam
ministravit', p. 86). To develop his meaning, he expands the image, 'So,
wishing to have a fuller understanding of this, the soul begins to bite and
chew upon this grape, as though putting it in a wine press' (p. 83; 'Hoc ergo
sibi plenius explicare desiderans, incipit hanc uvam masticare et frangere,
eamque quasi in torculari ponit', p. 86). A little later, having explored some
of the significance in the scriptural text, Guigo observes, 'Do you see how
much juice has come from one little grape?' (p. 84; 'Vides quantum liquoris
emanavit ex minima uva', p. 90).

While Guigo's images of the grape and the wine press may have
encouraged the author of *Ladder* to use the tavern imagery, he probably
borrowed it directly from a French or English version of the *Somme le roi*,
where it appears in the treatment of sapience. Though I cannot offer
conclusive proof, my suspicion is that the author relied on a particular verse
translation of the *Somme*, that is, the work known as *Speculum Vite* and

often attributed to William of Nassington, and I shall give my reasons for
that suspicion presently. For the moment, though, I shall use the text of the
Speculum Vite found in British Library MS Additional 33995 to illustrate the
relation between the *Somme*, of which it is a reasonably faithful translation
in this part, and the *Ladder*.

Both the *Somme* and the Middle English *Ladder* use the same image of the
ladder of perfection, and they describe it in similar ways. In *Ladder* we hear
that 'This is the ladder that Jacob sawe ... þat stode vpon the erthe and
raw3t into heuyn, by the which he sawe angellis of heuyn goyng vpward &
downward' (101/4-6). The corresponding description in the *Somme* is very
close, as we can see from these lines of the *Speculum Vite*:

> Þe laste degree and þe heghest þis es
> Of þe steghe of parfytnes
> Þat jacob sawe with ghastely eghe
> Þat whilk reched to heuen so heghe
> Þat aungels vppe and doun went
> Als godde almyghty had þam sent.   (f. 87ᵛ)

Coming upon the image in the text of Guigo from which he was working,
the author of *Ladder* may have had the corresponding image from the
Somme brought to his mind, and with it might have come the discussion of
contemplation that follows it in the *Somme*.

In that treatment of contemplation, Frère Lorens compares the fleeting
experience of God in contemplation to a taste of wine. In the version found
in *Speculum Vite*,

> ... bot a lytell tast
> Thurgh whilk men feles þe sauour mast
> Of godde þat es so swete and soft
> Als men does þat tastes oft
> Þe gode wyne.   (f. 88ʳ)

These small tastes, according to Frère Lorens, increase the appetite, which
cannot be fulfilled in this life.

> Bot when men comes in þe gret tauerne
> Þat men heres þis haly men yherne
> Þar þe tunnes er ful of blissed drynk
> Þat es mare swete þan herte may thynk
> Þat es þe blisse with-outen ende
> To whilk we hope þat we sal wende.   (f. 88ʳ⁻ᵛ)

Working his way toward the image of God as the fountain or well of everlasting life, Frère Lorens reaches it by way of another, which may have
pricked the imagination of the author of *Ladder*:

> Of þis blissefull drunkennes
> Þat ful of peese and of ioy es
> Spekes dauid on þis wyse
> Of þe blisse of paradyse

And says/ Lorde/ alle sal þai be
Drunken of þe grete plente
Þat in þi hous es so gode
And þa þat filled er of þe flode
Of þi delyte þat swete bihoues be
ffor þe welle of lyf es with þe. (f. 88ᵛ)

If Frère Lorens's imagery is the source of his tavern scene, the English author of *Ladder* need have known it only from a French or Anglo-Norman text. My own inclination to believe that he used *Speculum Vite*, perhaps as a pony for a French text, stems from one intriguing piece of evidence – specifically, these lines from the tavern-scene:

Suche lykynge they haue of that drynke
that of none other wyne they thynke
bot oonly for to drynke þeir fylle
and to haue of this drynke all their wylle.

(113/28-32)[15]

The author of *Ladder* had recently been reading tetrameter couplets, such as those in *Speculum Vite*, and their rhythms remained in his mind.

In any case, it is significant that the *Somme le roi*, a work remarkable for its effective use of concrete imagery, should have appealed to the author of *Ladder*. Perhaps like its early translators, Dan Michel of Northgate and William of Nassington, he understood that the techniques employed by Frère Lorens were very effective means for reaching 'lewed men'. In his desire to reach them through simplicity and concreteness, he shared a taste not only with Dan Michel and William, but also with the author of *Gratia Dei*, to whose work we shall now turn.

In an examination of *Gratia Dei* we are at a particular disadvantage, for no complete text of the original is extant. Still, it is possible, as Sr Mary Luke Arntz demonstrated in her edition,[16] to achieve a substantial reconstruction from the fragmentary and abbreviated forms found in four fourteenth- and fifteenth-century manuscripts. The introductory section of *Gratia Dei*, really a reworking of the excursus on grace from *Ladder of Foure Ronges*, is fully preserved in two manuscripts, Lincoln Cathedral 91 and Huntington Library HM 148. Two leaves in National Library of Scotland MS 6126 contain a part of this introduction, and British Library MS Arundel 507 contains an abbreviated version.[17] Immediately following this introduction

---

[15] These lines are printed in prose in Phyllis Hodgson's edition and presumably appear as prose in the manuscript. In the approximately 560 lines describing the tavern vices in the treatment of *Gula* in the Additional 33995 text of *Speculum Vite* (ff. 78ʳ-81ʳ), the *think-drink* rhyme occurs three times. Nowhere in these lines is there an instance of *fill-will* rhyme; however, there are five instances of *will-skill*, one of *ill-will*, and one of *spill-fill*. This cluster might well suggest use of *fill-will*.

[16] *Richard Rolle and þe Holy Boke Gratia Dei: An Edition with Commentary* (Salzburg: University of Salzburg Press, 1981). This edition is a reprint of a 1961 Fordham dissertation, completed before the discovery of the fragmentary manuscript at the National Library of Scotland.

[17] For further details concerning the contents and relations of the manuscripts see the

in the Lincoln, Huntington, and Arundel MSS is a statement of the overall design of the work: a three-part structure, with exposition of the profitable use of time in honest work, the proper and prayerful spirit with which to perform that work, and instructions to present an outer bearing that will express a love of God and stir others to the good.

For an understanding of the overall design and development we have only the Arundel text, made by a monk at Durham in the late fourteenth century and severely abridged in the copying. The Lincoln manuscript, copied by Robert Thornton of East Newton, in the North Riding of Yorkshire, apparently in the second quarter of the next century, and the Huntington manuscript, perhaps a little later but still close in time to the Lincoln manuscript, offer more complete texts of all the first part and portions of the second.

It is significant that Arundel 507 is the work of a monastic scribe and that the other two manuscripts may derive from monastic exemplars. The fact that the Huntington manuscript, before its acquisition by the California Library earlier in this century, had been in the possession of the Ingilby family of Yorkshire and that ancestral members of this family were among the founders of Mount Grace is one of several pieces of circumstantial evidence suggesting a possible connection between the volume and that Charterhouse. Equally tentative, but equally tempting to believe is that Robert Thornton might have acquired his exemplar from the same house, perhaps directly or through his association with lay benefactors of Mount Grace. Alternately, he may have obtained it from Joan Pickering, a nun at Nun Monkton and a sister of Thornton's neighbour and associate, Sir Richard Pickering of Oswaldkirk, for Joan seems the likely source of other devotional texts he copied.[18]

The possibility that all three manuscripts may have direct or indirect monastic associations is fitting, for it seems likely that *Gratia Dei* is a compilation made in a monastic setting. As his borrowings reveal, the author had access to a large body of Latin and vernacular texts such as we might expect to find in that setting, including some of distinctly monastic origins – *Ladder of Foure Ronges*, *Vitas Patrum*, and *The Sayings of the Fathers*. The writings that he knew best were probably those of Richard Rolle, whose style deeply influenced his own prose. Not only as a stylist, but in a still larger sense, as a writer continuing the vernacular tradition of contemplative literature, the author is a worthy descendant of Rolle.[19] His purpose, it seems clear, was to broaden the tradition that extended from *Ancren Riwle* to Rolle to *Ladder of Foure Ronges* by making it possible for his contemporaries in the active life to share in its spirit. Specifically, the author of *Gratia Dei* was attempting to create a work, corresponding to *Ancrene Riwle* or Rolle's

introduction to Arntz's edition, pp. vi-xliii, and 'Þe Holy Boke Gratia Dei', *Viator* 12 (1981), 289-317.
[18] For further details concerning the information in this paragraph, see Keiser, 'Þe Holy Boke Gratia Dei', 304-14, and 'More Light on the Life and Milieu of Robert Thornton', *SB* 36 (1983), 111-119.
[19] On the author's sources and indebtedness to Richard Rolle, see Arntz's edition, pp. xliv-cix.

Form of Living, which was of interest to a monastic audience, as the Arundel manuscript indicates, but which would also permit uncloistered clergy and pious laity to partake in some way of what C. A. J. Armstrong decribes as 'the spiritual treasure won in monastic solitude'.[20]

That the author of *Gratia Dei* hoped to bring his reinterpretation of the monastic and contemplative ideal to a wide audience is not in doubt. Whereas conclusions about the intended audience of *Ladder of Foure Fonges* were entirely speculative and inferential, we have more compelling evidence in the case of *Gratia Dei*. In an allegorical passage late in the second part of the work and preserved only in the abbreviated version of the Arundel manuscript, the author has Dread give this account of the inhabitants of hell:

> glotones, licheours, robbeours, theues; Riche men with þaire seruantʒ, þat þe pouer harmed; domesmen þat wold noght deme, bot it ware for mede; countours þat þe wrange bi þaire sotilte mayntiend; demesters þat leal men dampnid and delyuerid starke theues; werkmen þat falsli swynkis & takis ful hire; tilmen þat falsli tendis; prelates þat has cure of mannes saulis, þat noiþer chastis ne techis þaim; Of all lede of men þat wrangli has wroght; þare I sagh þat ilkan bitterli it boght. (A 64ʳ; YW 1.153)

Having this catalog begin with blatantly damnable sinners – gluttons, lechers, robbers, thieves – and then move rapidly to specific members of the middle classes would have little rhetorical justification, unless the author intended his work to reach the newly literate members of those classes and to remind them that their seemingly unremarkable moral failures would lead them to eternal damnation.

If the proposition that his treatise would come into the hands of workmen and tillmen seems to be stretching a point, the optimism is the author's, not mine. In his directions for daily prayer he seems to have in mind an audience more removed from the 'abbey orlogge' than Chaucer's 'povre wydwe' and more dependent on Chauntecleer's crowing.

> Quykli rise of þi bed at þe bel ryngynge, & if na bel be þare, cok be þi bel; if þare be noiþer cok ne bel, goddis luf wakyn þe. (A 58ᵛ; YW 144)

> Wende to þe kirk or oratori; & if þou mai wyn to nane, þi chambre make þi kirk. (A 59ʳ; YW 145)

Unquestionably, his audience includes the pious of the rural North:

> When þou comes to þe toune til ese þi bodi, seke þider þare þou mai mast honestli duell for þine state, & in mast pece. ... Seke noght where þou mai best be fed, for þare per-auenture are mani sterings to

[20] C. A. J. Armstrong, 'The Piety of Cicely, Duchess of York: A Study in Late Medieval Culture', in *For Hilaire Belloc*, ed. D. Woodruff (New York: Sheed & Ward, 1942), 83. This very fine essay has recently been reprinted in C. A. J. Armstrong, *England, France and Burgundy in the Fifteenth Century* (London: Hambledon Press, 1983).

syn. Herbery þe with na woman, bot if þou knowe þaim for gode of
lang tyme. (A 65ʳ; YW 155)

Remarkable though it seems, the author of *Gratia Dei* may have believed in
the possibility that his work might even reach those distant parishioners to
whom Chaucer's Parson trudged on foot to visit, those brothers of
Chaucer's pious Plowman. Such optimism was perhaps more common than
we think reasonable to imagine. In British Library MS Harley 2398, along
with the *Memoriale Credencium*, a book of instruction for lay readers, and
in several other manuscripts,[21] there is preserved 'A schort reule of lyf for
euerych man in general and for prestes & lordes & laboreres in special, how
ech schal be saued in his degre' (f. 188ᵛ).

To instruct this audience, the author of *Gratia Dei* modified the excursus
on grace from *Ladder of Foure Ronges* to intensify its hortatory tone, to
introduce the rule that follows. The clear explanation that he gives of how
man is strong with God's grace and helpless without it and of how man must
prepare to receive that grace in order to perform the acts of daily life is the
theoretical foundation on which the rule is built. Turning to the subject of
honest work, the author delivers a vigorous exposition of the theme, *vita
fugit, mors sequitur*, and then explains at length how man loses time through
idleness, vain occupation, and an improper spirit for performing good
works. With wordplay on *profit*, *pay*, and *meed*, he presses the point that
truly profitable work is that which pays God and deserves heavenly meed.

In the second part, devoted to spiritual exercises, the author first explains
what is necessary for prayer and what hinders it. In the remainder of this
part he sets forth in abundant detail a rigorous regimen of prayer, to be
performed in the spirit of affective devotionalism. In the course of doing so,
he describes the spiritual union with God and its after-effects, borrowing
extensively from *Ladder of Foure Ronges* in this exposition, though omitting
the tavern-image, and he strongly urges meditation on the life and passion of
Christ, incorporating into his rule Richard Rolle's 'Meditation on the
Passion and of Three Arrows of Doomsday'. This part of the work
culminates with an exposition of the penitential spirit, but it does conclude
on a hopeful note, insisting that thoughts of heavenly bliss inspire men to
love virtue and flee sin. The third and final part of *Gratia Dei*, extant only in
the abbreviated Arundel form, treats the need for exemplary conduct in all
dealings with one's fellows.

From beginning to end *Gratia Dei* is infused with intense energy, which is
apparent even in the abbreviated Arundel text. If this energy is overbearing
at times, it is also the source of much that is admirable in the treatise,
especially the fluent, colloquial, and sometimes very graceful style of *Gratia
Dei*. Compiling his treatise from numerous vernacular devotional writings,
the author modified the style of all his borrowings, except those from
Richard Rolle, to achieve the consistently intense and hortatory tone with
which he presses home his points. Elsewhere I have demonstrated in detail

---

[21]   See R. E. Lewis, N. F. Blake, A. S. G. Edwards, *Index of Printed Middle English
Prose* (New York: Garland, 1985), 71, no. 203.

his ability to transform poorly developed exemplary material into a sharply focused illustration, all the more effective for his skilful use of rhetorical ornament. Here I will simply call attention to his reworking of a small part of an exemplary narrative, in which a man foolishly takes a fiend disguised as a pilgrim into his house. In his source the author found this passage:

> When þei of dyuerse þingis hadden told togider, þis cursyd spirit stert ouer þe fijr to a cradil þat þe mannys child lay inne & strangled þe child & vanyschid awey sone anoon.[22]

To this compare the revised version by the author of *Gratia Dei*:

> When þe man had spoken with þe pilgrym as he wende he had bene, and he had spyrred hym of ferre tyȝynges as men does pilgrymes, þe fend styrte to þe childe in þe credill and wrathe þe neke in twa & keste it in þe fyre, and vanyste awaye sodanly, & thus at his partynge he qwytt þe man his gud dede.   (L 249ᵛ; YW 319)

The additional detail in the subordinate clauses, suggesting an atmosphere of camaraderie, makes the action that follows more sudden and more horrifying, as does his giving the fire a more functional purpose. Much like his predecessor, the author of *Ladder of Foure Ronges*, this writer had an almost instinctive grasp of how to put concrete detail to its best rhetorical use.

Still, it must be conceded that such an intense and hortatory tone allows little opportunity for subtleties and fine distinctions. The problem is obvious when we compare *Gratia Dei* and *Ladder of Foure Ronges* and notice the loss not only of some fine psychological insights, but also of the careful distinctions among meditation, prayer, and contemplation, made by Guigo and preserved by the English translator.

Especially surprising is the author's omission of any treatment of the distinction between the active and contemplative lives and of what this distinction might mean for those outside the cloister. Two works with purposes similar to *Gratia Dei* and close to it in time – Walter Hilton's *Mixed Life* and *Dives and Pauper* – attest that both pious laymen and secular clerics were troubled by their inability to carry out worldly responsibilities and undertake a demanding spiritual regimen at the same time. Perhaps their careful attentiveness to such concerns is an indication why *Mixed Life* and *Dives and Pauper* seem to have enjoyed wider and more enduring interest than *Gratia Dei*.

How a contemporary audience might have responded to the strengths and weaknesses of *Gratia Dei* and whether they were satisfied by its ambitious attempt to address their spiritual needs are questions to which there can be no certain answers. Nevertheless, it is tempting to find evidence for tentative answers in the manuscript forms in which *Gratia Dei* is extant. *Ladder of Foure Ronges*, as we have seen, is preserved in three important devotional

---

[22] F. G. A. M. Aarts, ed., *Þe Pater Noster of Richard Ermyte* (The Hague: M. Nijhoff, 1967), 17/26-28. For other illustrations of how the author of *Gratia Dei* reshaped his borrowings from this treatise, see Keiser, 'Þe Holy Boke Gratia Dei', 296-98.

miscellanies copied in or near the metropolitan area, which were in use by nuns and laypersons from the mid- and late fifteenth century, probably up to the time of the Henrician reformation. A much shorter piece, and hence easier to copy, *Ladder* was written in a more readily accessible dialect than the Northern dialect of *Gratia Dei*. Further, *Ladder* found some favour among the Carthusians at Sheen, who were active in the dissemination of vernacular devotional literature in the metropolitan area. In view of these advantages enjoyed by *Ladder* and of the likelihood that a larger proportion of metropolitan manuscripts survive than do provincial manuscripts, the preservation of *Gratia Dei* in four, admittedly incomplete versions is very impressive. Indeed, it seems even more so when we consider that, unlike the case with *Ladder*, none of these was copied from another in the surviving group, that the geographical area of their circulation extends from the North Riding of Yorkshire to Durham, and that of the two manuscripts whose early provenance is known, one belonged to a member of the Yorkshire gentry and another to a Durham monk.

Admittedly, the nagging questions raised by the forms of preservation persist. Putting aside chance survival of the National Library of Scotland fragment, we have, first, the puzzling, ineptly-copied Huntington text, which breaks off near the end of the last leaf of a quire. Was there to have been another quire of nearly equal length, to the copying of which a scribe with failing eyesight never returned? Or, did a monastic superior who had assigned its copying, perhaps 'in remissionem peccatorum nostrum', look at its quality and decide that further expenditure of vellum might itself be a peccant act requiring remission on his part?

With the Arundel and Lincoln manuscripts we have a slightly better basis for speculating as to why the scribes copied only portions of *Gratia Dei* and whether their doing so constitutes a response, particularly an unfavourable one to it. The Arundel manuscript, copied by a Durham monk, is a more or less conventional monastic commonplace book. Though I know of few others in English, Latin volumes of this kind are, I believe, common enough. The scribe of BL MS Harley 485, for example, which contains a text of the revised *Scala Claustralium* and which is very close in time to Arundel 507, shares many interests with the Arundel scribe – Victorine writings, Anselm, Augustine, proverbs and sayings, passion literature, and confessional and penitential writings. And he also shares the inclination to compile excerpts, abstracts, and selections. Thus, the state of the text in *Gratia Dei* in the Arundel manuscript is a manifestation of the monastic mentality, not an unfavourable reflection upon the treatise. If anything, the fact that the scribe copied so much of *Gratia Dei* is a comment on his interest in it and admiration for it.

Robert Thornton, the scribe who copied the Lincoln manuscript, seems to have derived many of the devotional writings in the volume from monastic sources, directly or indirectly. Very likely, familiarity with monastic attitudes and customs, such as we see in Arundel 507 and Harley 485, shaped his own attitude and his readiness to abridge and take excerpts from his examplars. Yet the particularly curious way in which he copied portions of

Gratia Dei does invite thought, all the more so because his is the one text we have that is clearly produced by and for a lay reader.

In a paper printed in an earlier number of *Analecta Cartusiana* (see n. 3 above), I have argued that the contents of Thornton's devotional book and their arrangement reveal the scribe to be a man of particular tastes and preferences. Of significance to us is an apparent preference for shorter, more compendious works than *Gratia Dei* was. It is understandable then that his first impulse was to extract from it a portion of its treatment of prayer and to use it in conjunction with another treatise on prayer. Having done so, he then began to copy *Gratia Dei* from the beginning. Though we will never know his reasons, we may wonder whether he was so impressed by the treatment of prayer that he reconsidered his original impulse and determined to copy all of the treatise. Yet after transcribing all the first part and a portion of the second, he broke off, well before he had reached the treatment of prayer he had previously copied. Perhaps, as I suggested in my earlier study, Thornton found the copying of this lengthy treatise overwhelmingly tedious at the very time that he acquired a text of the more succinct *Abbey of the Holy Ghost.*

The length, the difficult dialect, and sometimes overbearing energy, the unqualified insistence on a severe regimen of prayer, the lack of any exposition of the doctrines specified in the Lambeth Constitutions, mere chance – all or any of these factors may explain why we find no complete text of *Gratia Dei* and why it seems not to have had the extensive circulation of treatises of similar nature: Walter Hilton's *Mixed Life, Abbey of the Holy Ghost* Edmund's *Mirror*, Gaytrige's *Sermon*. We cannot know for certain, and we are well advised not to press too hard for conclusions based on the enigmas of the Thornton manuscript. What we can conclude, though, is that like its predecessor, *Ladder of Foure Ronges, Gratia Dei* had an impressive, if limited circulation, reaching both a lay and clerical audience. For at least a few men and women of northern England, it provided valuable moral and spiritual direction, teaching them to live a life numbered in the number of virtues, and it continued to do so more than a half-century after its compilation. For that it deserves our attention and admiration. Looking at it in relation to *Ladder of Foure Ronges*, we can see that it represents a bold attempt to extend the efforts of that treatise in bringing monastic piety outside the cloister and into the world.

CURA PASTORALIS IN DESERTO

Vincent Gillespie

In 1433, William de Anthorp, rector of Dighton, bequeathed to the Prior and Convent of Mountgrace charterhouse a silver cup gilt, twelve spoons and a book called *Pupilla Oculi*.[1] In 1343, Hinton charterhouse lent a copy of Robert Grosseteste's *Templum Dei* to another house of the order.[2] At the end of the fifteenth century, or perhaps very early in the sixteenth, William Darker, a professed monk of Sheen charterhouse, copied a text called *Speculum Christiani* 'in remissionem peccatorum suorum'.[3] The *Pupilla Oculi* was composed by John de Burgh, Chancellor of the University of Cambridge, around 1385 as a reordering and updating of William of Pagula's *Oculus Sacerdotis*, an influential handbook for priests with the cure of souls, dating from early in the fourteenth century.[4] The *Templum Dei* is a pastoral guide to the *cura animarum* by a reforming bishop of the thirteenth century.[5] The *Speculum Christiani* is an early fifteenth-century pastoral miscellany consisting of eight *tabulae* covering the catechetic syllabus and other areas of priestly responsibility.[6] All three books, along with others of an overtly catechetic or pastoral nature were written in, circulated between, or passed into the ownership of English charterhouses in the later medieval period. They illustrate not only the somewhat random nature of acquisition by bequest, but also the specific production of books within the house, apparently for the use of the house, and the circulation of materials between houses to facilitate the development of library resources. Why were books of pastoral care owned

---

[1] E. M. Thompson, *The Carthusian Order in England* (London, 1930), pp. 236, 330. Hereafter cited as *COE*.
[2] *COE*, pp. 322-3.
[3] London, British Library MS Additional 22121, fol. 84r. For a list of other manuscripts copied by Darker, see M. B. Parkes, *English Cursive Book Hands 1250-1500*, revised reprint (London, 1979), p. 8. His death is recorded in the obit lists in 1513.
[4] L. E. Boyle, 'The *Oculus Sacerdotis* and some other works of William of Pagula', *Transactions of the Royal Historical Society*, 5th ser., 5 (1955), 81-110, reprinted in *Pastoral Care, Clerical Education and Canon Law, 1200-1400* (London, 1981).
[5] *Robert Grosseteste: Templum Dei*, ed. J. Goering and F. A. C. Mantello, Toronto Medieval Latin Texts (Toronto, 1984), which includes an up-to-date bibliography.
[6] *Speculum Christiani*, ed. G. Holmstedt, EETS, o.s. 182 (1933 for 1929); V. Gillespie, '*Doctrina* and *Predicacio*: The Design and Function of Some Pastoral Manuals', *Leeds Studies in English*, new ser., 11 (1980 for 1979), 36-50.

and produced by an order whose way of life was minimally coenobitic and whose members were rigorously separated from the ways of the world?

I

From early in its history, the Carthusian order recognised that withdrawal from the temptations of the world did not eliminate the need for pastoral care of those in its communities. In the *Statuta Antiqua*, it is made clear that the general chapter of the order 'quod habet curam animarum nostrarum', exercised its pastoral function over the order in a variety of ways, some of which closely paralleled the care exercised by an episcopal synod over the pastoral welfare of the diocesan family.[7]

For most purposes the chapter's pastoral function was devolved to the Prior of the individual house. In Guigo's *Consuetudines*, the Prior is required to take especial care of the sick, the weak, and those afflicted by temptation, neatly combining the spiritual and physical leechcraft so beloved of theorists of the *cura animarum* from Gregory onwards.[8] In the *Statuta Antiqua* his responsibilities to the community are more explicitly developed from the *Consuetudines* outline. Like the secular priest in a parochial context, much store is placed on the example he offers his fellow monks:

> Prior quanvis omnibus verbo et vita prodesse debeat et cunctorum sollicite gerere curam, monachis tamen a quibus sumptus est quietis et stabilitatis et ceterorum quae ad eorum vitam pertinent exercitiorum: exemplum maxime probere debet.

But his duties are also specified. He must take recordation (that is, assign the readings for the following week), hear confessions, housel and comfort the sick and bury the dead. He also has the responsibility of preaching in chapter 'vel cui placuerit iniungere, beneficia insinuare et salutationes'.[9]

Thus the statutes lay on him the *cura animarum* of his monks (and indeed of the lay brethren, of whom more will be said later) without offering any advice or indication as to how these duties should be executed. This is hardly surprising. Little monastic legislation and few *regulae* devote much space to the implementation of the pastoral charge. Furthermore the

---

[7] Part 2, cap. 7, section 9, in *Statuta Ordinis Cartusiensis a domino Guigone priore Cartusie edita* (Basel, 1510), which contains the *Consuetudines* of Guigo, the *Statuta Antiqua*, the *Statuta Nova* (1368) and the *Tertia Compilatio* (1509). The edition is unfoliated. For an account of the development of Carthusian legislation, see *COE*, pp. 103-30; J. Hogg, 'Everyday Life in the Charterhouse in the Fourteenth and Fifteenth Centuries', in *Klösterliche Sachkultur des Spät-mittelalters* (Vienna, 1980), 113-146; Sr B. Barrier, *Les activités du solitaire en chartreuse d'après les plus anciens témoins*, Analecta Cartusiana 87 (1981).
[8] *Guigues Ier, Coutumes de Chartreuse*, Sources Chrétiennes 313 (Paris, 1984), cap. xxxviii, p. 240.
[9] Part 2, cap. 6, sections 1, 5 and 9; cf. *Coutumes*, cap. xv, p. 198; *Statuta Nova*, part 2, cap. 5, section 10.

legislation which shaped and defined the nature of the pastoral responsibilities of the Carthusian prior was promulgated for the most part before the developments in pastoral theology which were recognised and given new impetus by the Lateran Council of 1215.

In provincial and diocesan legislation throughout the thirteenth century, English bishops can be seen grappling with the need to provide advice and support for their parochial clergy.[10] Developments in pastoral theory showed a move away from the older emphasis on forensic confessional practice to a broader definition of spiritual care. This was reflected in the course of the thirteenth century in new kinds of handbooks and manuals, distinct from canonical penitentials.[11] Given the little guidance provided by the legislation (even in the *Statuta Antiqua* of 1259), it was natural that pastoral practice in charterhouses should evolve in line with developing pastoral theory in the world and, indeed, that charterhouses should themselves make use of new aids and techniques of *cura animarum* as they were disseminated into diocesan and parochial practice. It was equally natural, however, that the order's legislation should appear conservative in its injunctions, though subsequent modifications and decrees by the General Chapter show the assimilation and codification of the best custom and practice, and occasionally the outright condemnation of unacceptable pastoral procedures.[12]

Thus, reflecting the pre-Lateran council pastoral emphasis on penitential matters, the early legislation stresses that one of the Prior's main responsibilities was hearing the confessions of the monks and the brethren. A weekly general confession in chapter could be supplemented by private confession in the cell of a particular monk. The two confessions were slightly different in character:

[10] The literature is substantial, but see, for example, M. Gibbs and J. Lang, *Bishops and Reform 1215-1272* (Oxford, 1934); C. R. Cheney, *English Synodalia of the Thirteenth Century* (Oxford, 1941, repr. with new intro., 1968); 'Some Aspects of Diocesan Legislation in England during the Thirteenth Century', in *Medieval Texts and Studies* (Oxford, 1973), pp. 185-202; D. L. Douie, *Archbishop Pecham* (Oxford, 1952); J. H. Srawley, 'Grosseteste's Administration of the Diocese of Lincoln', in *Robert Grosseteste, Scholar and Bishop*, ed. D. A. Callus (Oxford, 1958), pp. 146-77; L. E. Boyle, 'Robert Grosseteste and the Pastoral Care', in *Pastoral Care* (1981), pp. 3-39; W. A. Pantin, *The English Church in the Fourteenth Century* (Oxford, 1955).

[11] P. Michaud-Quantin, 'Les méthodes de la pastorale du XIIIe au XVe siècles', *Miscellanea Medievalia* 7 (1970), 76-91; *Sommes de casuistique et manuels de confession au moyen âge (XII-XVI siècles)*, Analecta Medievalia Namurcensia 13 (Louvain, 1962).

[12] In 1443, the custom of some houses (possibly English) in reading the 'recommendaciones' of Anselm to dying monks is forbidden, and the reason given is 'si dicta recommendacio diligenter pensetur pocius ad statum laicalem quam monasticum dinoscitur pertinere'. Printed in *The Chartae of the Carthusian General Chapter*, ed. M. G. Sargent and J. Hogg, Analecta Cartusiana 100:2 (1983), p. 171. This volume prints the text of Rawlinson D.318, which belonged to London charterhouse and contains materials of particular relevance to the English province.

Quandocumque in capitulo confitemur, prolixitatem caveamus. In cella autem diffusius possumus confiteri.

Even so, private confession did not absolve the monk from the obligation to confess publicly, and while the general confession was taking place, the *Statuta Antiqua* order that 'per totum spacium confessionis nullus debet in ecclesia residere vel libros revolvere'. Priors, like their secular counterparts, are ordered to be 'solliciti' and 'discreti', and they also have the responsibility to instruct novices in how to confess.[13]

The Prior was initially at liberty and later under an obligation to depute his confessional function to other priests in the house, but certain reserved cases had to be referred to him for absolution, and in the cases of serious sin absolution was reserved either to the Visitor of the Province or to the General Chapter. The *Statuta Nova* (1368) emphasise that 'Prior cartusie habet potestatem absoluendi omnes personas ordinis in foro penitentie a peccatis, quam habet quilibet prior in personis sibi subiectis.'[14]

Of course many of the monks would have been priests themselves, and in the English province there is a steady stream of secular priests wishing to enter the order after exercising the cure of souls in the world or following an academic career. Such entrants could choose whether to become monks or to join the curious hybrid group of *clerici-redditi*.[15] It is likely, therefore, that most houses would have had some reservoir of experience in pastoral matters which could be drawn on when the need arose. Such recruits could add their experience to the corporate wisdom of the house and, perhaps more significantly, might be a source of books explicitly addressing problems of a pastoral kind.[16] One area where such expertise might be valuable was in the induction and training of novices. The legislation recommends that such training be put in the hands of a senior and reliable monk. There is no evidence of a novice master as found in many other orders.[17] Equally, perhaps because of the relatively small size of most foundations, there is no evidence of the existence of 'cloister schools' or of

[13] Part 2, cap. 11; cf. *Statuta Nova*, part 2, cap. 4, section 12; *Tertia Compilatio*, cap. 6.

[14] Part 2, cap. 3, section 1; cf. *Statuta Antiqua*, part 2, cap. 10, sections 1 and 15; cap. 6, section 55; cap. 11, section 1; *Chartae*, p. 189.

[15] There is no prosopography of the English Carthusian province, and the following examples are not the result of systematic enquiry. James Grenehalgh was *magister scholarum* before his ordination and later reception into the order; see M. G. Sargent, *James Grenehalgh as Textual Critic*, 2 vols., Analecta Cartusiana 85 (1984), I, 75-116. Walter Wyller, a monk of Hinton, is described in 1408 as having been a rector of a parish, and his Prior, Peter, had also been a secular priest; *COE*, p. 276. William Ireby, a monk of Mountgrace, was 'canonicus' (*BRUC*). Nicholas Hereford, the Oxford apologist for Wyclif, entered Coventry charterhouse in 1417 (*BRUO*). John Blacman may have been a *clericus-redditus* of Witham, see A. Gray, 'A Carthusian *Carta Visitationis* of the Fifteenth Century', *Bulletin of the Institute of Historical Research* 40 (1967), 91-107, p. 92.

[16] E.g. the gifts of Blacman (*COE*, pp. 317-22), discussed below.

[17] *Tractatus Statutorum Ordinis Cartusiensis*: 'Commendat prior nouicium vni ex senioribus quem ydoneum ad hoc cognouerit, qui eum horis competentibus visitans instruit eundem ad horas dicendas et ad ceteras obseruancias quas ignorare

the group training of novices which would, in any case, have been alien to the spirit of silence and solitude which characterised the Carthusian desert. Guigo's words suggest that the assignment of a mentor may have been *ad hoc*:

> Cui in cellam introducto seniorum aliquis deputatur, qui eum per unam vel si amplius opus fuerit ebdomadam, horis competentibus visitans, de necessariis instruat.

Guigo counsels that the full rigour of the regime should not be imposed at once, but that the novice should at first be treated 'blande leniterque maxime'.[18] The *Consuetudines* of 1499 give more detailed instructions on the preparation of novices and emphasise the role of the advisor in training the will of the novice away from worldly things:

> Sollicitudo eius cui nouicius committitur hec sit, vt doceat eum suas vincere voluntates et mores deserere seculares.[19]

All monks, including novices, were allowed two books from the library for their private use.[20] In addition to these, the *Statuta Antiqua* appear to allow monks to have in their possession a copy of the Articles of the Creed and to be able to recite them at will:

> Symbolum quod incipit firmiter credimus possunt habere et dicere quicumque volunt.[21]

It is not clear whether this was a commentary on the Creed or some other kind of catechetical compilation or exercise.

II

But if pastoral care in the upper house placed the Prior in the role of first among equals in the exercise of his pastoral ministry, his function in the lower house is more comparable to that of a priest in a secular environment. The lower house consisted of the *conversi*, the *redditi*, and, in the later houses, varying numbers of hired servants employed by the monastery to fulfil its domestic and agricultural needs.[22] In early foundations the lower house had its own church and the Prior or Procurator (a monk charged with special responsibility for the lower house) was enjoined to ensure that mass was celebrated at least three times weekly. Later foundations had only one church and divided it into two choirs with a substantial partition separating them, so that the converses could participate in the

---

nouicium non oportet', ed. J. Hogg, *Mittelalterliche Caerimonialia der Kartäuser*, Analecta Cartusiana 2 (1971), p. 324.

[18] *Coutumes*, cap. xxiii, p. 214; cf. *Statuta Antiqua*, part 2, cap. 23.

[19] Ed. Hogg, *Caerimonialia*, p. 294.

[20] E.g. *Coutumes*, cap. xxviii, pp. 222-3; *Statuta Antiqua*, part 2, cap. 16, section 9.

[21] Part 2, cap. 32, section 30.

[22] *COE*, pp. 123-5.

conventual masses. The Prior was to spend four weeks with the monks and the fifth with the converses.[23]

From the earliest legislation of the order it was assumed that the instruction and private prayer of the members of the lower house would be in the vernacular. Guigo's *Consuetudines* record that:

> Post matutinas, ad orationem constitutam festinant. Quam ideo scribere nolumus quia vulgaribus verbis, aliis ab aliis insinuatur.[24]

In the *Statuta Antiqua* it is the responsibility of the Prior to 'laicos instrui faciat in oratione materna et pater noster et credo et salutatione beate marie'.[25] As with the illiterate members of other orders, the office of the lay brethren was largely made up of repetitions of the *Pater Noster* and *Gloria Patri*.[26] Indeed Prior Basil in his *Consuetudines* of 1156 explicitly forbade the lay brethren to have any books in church, and this prohibition was repeated in 1432.[27] Their role was to labour for the good of the community – 'cum conversi et redditi recipiantur post salutem animarum praecipue pro labore' – but their spiritual wellbeing depended upon the catechetic and pastoral activities of the monks from the upper house deputed to their care.[28] The significance of this is that the Carthusian order had direct experience of vernacular instruction of a pastoral and catechetic nature which predated by some years the concern for similar vernacular instruction for the laity as a whole. Moreover, while later developments in lay catechetics and devotion clearly nourished themselves on monastic experiences in the instruction of lay brethren and especially of sisters, from 1230 onwards there is no need to assume that this was a one way traffic.[29]

A primary means of instruction and exhortation for the lay brethren seems to have been the capitular sermon. The Procurator is encouraged by Guigo to preserve some time in his cell for meditation and reflection:

> et in archanis sui pectoris aliquid salubre quod fratribus commissis in capitulo suaviter et sapienter eructuet possit recondere. Tanto enim frequentioribus predicationibus indigent, quanto minus litteras norunt.[30]

---

[23] *Statuta Antiqua*, part 2, cap. 6, section 23.
[24] *Coutumes*, caps. xlii-iii, p. 250.   [25] Part 2, cap. 6, section 18.
[26] *Coutumes*, caps. xlii-iii, p. 250; part three of the *Statuta Antiqua* details the office.
[27] Cap. 48, ed. J. Hogg, *Die Ältesten Consuetudines der Kartäuser*, Analecta Cartusiana 1 (1970), p. 218; cf. *Chartae*, p. 151 (1432); *Statuta Antiqua*, part 3, cap. 28, section 3, where an exception is made for kalendars; *Tertia Compilatio*, cap. 11, section 10.
[28] *Statuta 1261, PL* 153, col. 1141. The *Magna Vita Sancti Hugonis* stresses that, despite their illiteracy, the lay brethren drew 'fiery sparks of spiritual intelligence' from what was read to them, ed. D. L. Douie and H. Farmer, Nelson Medieval Texts (London, 1961), p. 32.
[29] E.g. the catechetical and pastoral handbooks in the possession of monks of St Alban's, R. W. Hunt, 'The Library of the Abbey of St Alban's', in *Medieval Scribes, Manuscripts and Libraries: Essays presented to N. R. Ker*, ed. M. B. Parkes and A. G. Watson (London, 1978), pp. 251-77, pp. 273, 274, 275, 276. See also n. 83 below.
[30] *Coutumes*, cap. xvi, p. 200.

The illiteracy of the lay brethren placed particular obligations for their spiritual well being on the Prior and the Procurator.[31] When visiting the sick, the *Statuta Antiqua* stipulate:

> Tunc dicit infirmus confiteor si scit, si non, materna lingua generaliter confitetur facta antequam conventus congregatur privata confessione.[32]

On certain solemn feastdays, sermons could be composed either in Latin or the vernacular 'vel mixtim', depending presumably upon the intended audience. The converses could expect regular sermons from the Procurator and also sermons from the Prior or those deputed by him at times of major feasts.[33] Capitular instruction took place in the vernacular, and examples have survived in several European vernaculars of the range and style of the teaching.[34] The Visitor in his inspection of the house was to read certain sections of the statutes 'morose et distincte', and was to expound them 'propter laicos ... in vulgari'.[35] Given the demonstrable range and scope of the instruction provided, it is reasonable to suppose that some of the interest shown by the order in pastoral handbooks and guides to the cure of souls may be related to the functions of catechesis and sacramental ministration necessary because of the lay brethren.

But as the foundations began to grow in size, hired servants were added to the *familia* of many houses and these laymen, still in secular estate and in some cases married, posed further pastoral problems and created new sacramental and catechetic responsibilities for the Prior and Procurator. Their presence within the limits of the desert seems to have led to a blurring of the traditionally sharp distinction between members of the community and outsiders and, in the longer term, to have prepared the way for the difficulties encountered by the large metropolitan houses like London in distinguishing between the two kinds of laymen who could legitimately look to the order for pastoral guidance and spiritual direction.

The legal position is clearly stated in the *Antiqua Statuta Ordinis Carthusiensis de Sacris Ritibus*:

> Declaramus quod secundum privilegia nostra et statuta, et secundum decretalem positam in titulo de privilegiis in secundo libro in fine

---

[31] Cf. Adam's praise for the assiduity of Hugh's instruction of the lay brethren, *Magna Vita*, pp.43-4.

[32] Part 1, cap. 46, section 2.

[33] *Statuta Antiqua*, part 1, cap. 32, section 5; part 2, cap. 12, section 6; *Statuta Nova*, part 1, cap. 3, section 2. These sermons could be written out in advance: 'Quibus iniunctus est sermo, vel collatio in capitulo generali, possunt si volunt, illum et illam in scriptis recitare', *Tertia Compilatio*, cap. 9, section 12. On the responsibility of the Prior and Procurator, see *Statuta Antiqua*, part 2, caps. 6 and 8.

[34] *COE*, p.333 cites London, British Library MS Additional 11303, containing statutes for the lay brothers in English; London, British Library MS Cotton Nero A.III contains vernacular forms of confession and other catechetic materials; Hogg, *Caerimonialia* prints vernacular texts under a rubric *de capitulo laycorum* (pp.62-9). For related matters in the German province, see W.D. Sexauer, *Frühneuhochdeutsche Schriften in Kartäuserbibliotheken* (Frankfurt, 1978).

[35] *Statuta Nova*, part 2, cap. 1, section 19.

dictae decretalis, possumus ministrare ecclesiastica sacramenta servitoribus nostris domesticis.[36]

But although the promulgation was clear enough, the matter continued to give concern. In 1478, John Walsyngham, Prior of London charterhouse, asked the General Chapter if the Prior or a confessor deputed by him had power 'quantum ad forum conscientiae' over the 'mercenarios et alios famulos nostros ac etiam hospitantes seculares inter nos'. The Chapter's response referred him back to the privileges of the order.[37] The *Statuta Antiqua* encourages houses to avoid confessing 'those not committed to us', but allows them to be given counsel and to be persuaded to go to their own priest or bishop.[38] The *Tertia Compilatio* of 1509 clarifies the position concerning the hearing of confessions, illustrating how far the severity of the original decree limiting confession to those of the order had been weakened by the passage of time and the increasing contact between the order and the world:

> Confessiones secularium et aliorum qui de ordine nostro non sunt, mercenariis exceptis qui nobis domestice famulantur, sine suorum superiorum licentia audire non possumus nec debemus.[39]

Similar modifications can be observed with regard to preaching. The *Statuta Nova* of 1368 state categorically:

> Nullus de ordine publice predicare presumat, nisi in claustro vel capitulo monachorum et conversorum, nec ibidem aliquis secularis nisi quantum statuta volunt admittatur.

The *Statuta Antiqua* allow that 'familia et alia seculares interesse poterunt sermonibus in capitulo conversorum quandocumque prior domus viderit expedire'.[40] The *Ceremonial* recently printed by James Hogg shows that such laymen did attend chapters of the *conversi*. After the feasts of the coming week have been expounded in the vernacular, the text instructs: 'tunc exeunt seculares et nouicii, si qui ibi fuerint, et fratres dicunt culpas suas'.[41]

The order was privileged to offer *all* the sacraments to its domestics. Confession, anointing, burial and the eucharist all lay within the usual priestly range of activity envisaged and experienced by the order's early legislators.[42] The presence of married servants and, it appears, of some women servants also brought the likelihood of other sacraments being in demand. In 1448, the Charterhouse of Witham which, as the original

---

[36] *PL* 153, col. 1130.
[37] *Chartae*, p. 99.
[38] Part 2, cap. 11, section 14. Section 15 adds, concerning those sent to the order by bishops or priests, 'recipere vel non recipere erit in optione nostra'.
[39] Cap. 6, section 2; the prohibition against confessing women remained in force. Cf. the 1499 *Consuetudines*, ed. Hogg, *Caerimonialia*, pp. 260-1.
[40] Part 2, cap. 10, section 4; cf. cap. 32, section 31.
[41] *Caerimonialia*, p. 65.
[42] See the duties of the Prior in *Statuta Antiqua*, part 2, cap. 6.

English foundation, preserved the physical separation of the churches of the monks and lay brothers, petitioned the bishop to be allowed to put a baptismal font into the chapel of the Blessed Virgin in the Friary church (that is, the church of the converses), for the convenience of the lay servants now employed on the estate. Part of the glebe of the chapel was to be set aside for a cemetery for their use.[43] Yet in 1442, the *Acta* of the General Chapter records the stern injunction 'item prohibemus quod nulla persona Ordinis baptizet', and repeats the earlier prohibitions about hearing the confessions of women.[44]

Similarly, although the order was allowed to confess its lay servants, problems of relative jurisdiction keep obtruding and complicating the relationship. Confessors were allowed to absolve from mortal sin, but not from excommunication or irregularity, according to the 1499 *Consuetudines*.[45] Yet in 1502 the Prior of London asked the General Chapter if it was possible to absolve 'mercennarios nostros' (that is, the hired servants) from a great sentence of excommunication imposed by canon or provincial statute or synod. The answer was 'Possumus absolvere in casibus curatorum sed in reseruatis episcopis non possumus nisi commitantur nobis.'[46] This blurring of the edges of relative jurisdiction was a potential canonical headache, and led the English province to a broadening of its pastoral role beyond the already quite considerable responsibilities accruing to the order by virtue of the constitution of its houses and the evolution of their administration.

Changing circumstances led the English province to look for guidance about customary teaching. The fourteenth-century *Statuta Nova* decreed that 'conuersi et redditi habitantes infra parrochias seculares in festis colendis et non colendis illis per omnia se conforment'.[47] But at some point in the fifteenth century, an English house questioned the General Chapter about whether the converses working in the parish church within the boundaries of the charterhouse ought to follow the secular mode of attending festivals. If they expected movement from the order in the light of extraordinary circumstances, they were to be disappointed. The answer is blunt: keep to what is written in everything and you will not have to ask so many questions.[48]

Similar problems landed London charterhouse in very hot water. An unusual feature of the site of the plantation was an existing church built in a public cemetery which was adapted and extended by the community.[49] Because of its metropolitan position – unique in the English province – London had particular problems about preserving the isolation of the desert. As the chronicle of the house puts it: 'from the beginning of the

[43] *COE*, p.144.
[44] *Chartae*, p.132.
[45] Ed. Hogg, *Caerimonialia*, pp.261-2.
[46] *Chartae*, pp.220-1.
[47] Part 3, cap. 2, section 8.
[48] *COE*, p.265.
[49] W. St J. Hope, *The History of London Charterhouse* (London, 1925), pp.1-52; *COE*, pp.167-98.

first foundation women were always wont to enter the church, and the brethren for fear of the common folk did not dare to forbid them'. In 1405 two altars were hallowed 'and this was done with the intent that women might be able to hear masses there, and so by degrees be shut out from the church'.[50] The same year the Visitors of the Province reported on this practice to the General Chapter and ordered the Prior and Procurator to have a wall built to exclude women from the body of the church. They insisted that a start should be made on the work within fifteen days.[51]

As part of the same report the Visitors called the Prior to order concerning his public preaching which had always been considered unacceptable. Although the statutes allowed laymen to be present at capitular sermons in the lower house at the discretion of the Prior, what had been going on at London could hardly be described as discreet:

> Priori districtissime inhibemus ne amplius procuret sermonem fieri in cimitorio exteriori domus, nec faciat campanam pulsari pro populo congregande.

The enclosure was reapplied with strictness and the London chronicler, perhaps with an eye to the General Chapter, records that 'after this ordinance the monks, saving the Prior and the Proctor, have not gone outside the gate made in the aforesaid wall to this day for any cause whatever'.[52] In 1470 London was ordered to stop 'seculares ... cum canibus et tumultu' from hunting 'in ortu magno conventuali'. Equally eccentric is the evidence that Coventry ran a school inside the desert.[53]

Women had always been forbidden to enter the Charterhouse and the legislation repeatedly emphasises that dispensations concerning the confessing of laymen did not apply to women.[54] The *chartae* for 1423 show the order grappling with the problem:

> Mulieres amodo in domibus Ordinis, prebendarie et donate non fiant sine magna et matura deliberacione Visitatorum prouinciarum et approbacione Capituli Generalis alias huiusmodi prebende irrite sunt et inanes.[55]

Visits and benefactions substantially increased the order's contact with the laity.[56] Particular difficulties were experienced when benefactors wished

---

[50] Hope, p. 42 (Latin text, p. 49).
[51] *Chartae*, p. 114.
[52] Hope, pp. 43-4.
[53] *Chartae*, p. 206; *COE*, pp. 213-14.
[54] *Coutumes*, cap. xxi: 'mulieres terminos intrare nostros nequaquam sinimus', p. 210; *Statuta Antiqua*, part 2, cap. 26, section 3; cap. 28, section 10; *Statuta Nova*, part 2, cap. 6, section 22; *Tertia Compilatio*, cap. 6, section 2; *Consuetudines Basilii*, cap. 48, section 24, ed. Hogg, *Consuetudines*, p. 217. The 1470 *chartae* forbid familiarity and speech with women 'propter pericula et scandala' in terms which imply that such contact may not have been infrequent (p. 204); James Grenehalgh may have fallen foul of such prohibitions in his spiritual relationship with Joanna Sewell, see Sargent, *Grenehalgh*, I, 90-2.
[55] P. 133.
[56] Cf. the *chartae* injunction for 1455 (p. 182) about the admission of seculars

to visit the recipients of their endowment, especially if those benefactors were women. In 1422 monks are strictly forbidden to eat with seculars 'nec ipsos admittant ad mensam suam in cellis suis', and in 1416 the English province is particularly chastised for allowing eating and drinking in cells with 'others'.[57] Bequests and benefactions carried obligations to pray for souls and to celebrate masses and although they formed a useful addition to income they also led to the dilution of original ordinations about burial within the limits of the house. (Even women were allowed in when safely defunct.)[58]

There were problems about individual monks receiving sums of money. The Vicar of London wrote to the General Chapter reporting that the Visitor had vested such monies in the hands of the Prior and that they were used for buying books, for repairing the fabric and for other approved expenses.[59] In 1494 London sent a series of questions about gifts to individual monks. Can the Prior accept money for the use of a particular monk? No. Can the Prior accept a book on condition that a certain monk has particular and singular use of it in his lifetime? No. Even if it is useless to anyone else? No. The answers uphold earlier statutory prohibitions, but such bequests clearly happened.[60] In 1440 Robert Alne, examiner of the ecclesiastical court of York and a chantry priest, bequeathed to 'Dompno Johanni Alne, monacho ordinis Cartusiensis London., cognato meo, Orologium Divinæ Sapienciæ cum coopertura de pargameno'.[61]

As part of their endowments, some houses had the advowsons of parishes and became *de jure* responsible for the pastoral care of those parishes. Mountgrace, for example, acquired a substantial part of its recorded income from spiritualities in Lincolnshire. Hull established a special chantry, and Axholme's endowment included the papal grant of

'extra statum donati vel prebendarii', repeating an earlier ruling in the *Statuta Antiqua*, part 2, cap. 26, section 5.

[57] *Chartae*, p.132; p.118. Cf. Gray, '*Carta Visitationis*', 99, for similar admonitions to the Prior and Procurator of Hull in 1440.
[58] The cells of London charterhouse, for example, were largely endowed by laymen, see Hope, pp.55-104. Similar benefactions played a part in the building of Hull, another urban charterhouse. Thompson's accounts in *COE* give ample evidence of the obligations occurring from gifts and benefactions. On burial see, e.g., *COE*, pp.186, 204, 213. William Heghfeld de Swyn (ob.1403) asked to be buried in front of the sanctuary at Hull and awarded the community a pittance on the day of the burial of his will which was written in the Hull charterhouse, *Testamenta Eboracensia*, I, Surtees Society 4 (1836), 325.
[59] *Chartae*, pp.216-17 (1496). The *Chronicle* of the London House records the care with which Dan John Homersley passed on gifts of money to the Prior (Hope, pp.60-1).
[60] *Chartae*, p.215; cf. the 1261 *Statuta*, cap. 52, section 52, *PL* 153, col.1137.
[61] *Testamenta Eboracensia*, II, Surtees Society 30 (1855), 79; Margaret Norton of Bilburgh (ob.1506) left the residue of her estate to her sons William and 'Dan John Norton of Mountgrace', *Testamenta Eboracensia*, IV, Surtees Society 53 (1869), 92; Dame Jane Strangeways (ob.1500) left 10 marks to Mountgrace for prayers for the souls of her and her husband (buried at Mountgrace) and 'To dane Thurston at Mountgrace [probably Thurston Watson (ob.1505)] Xs. To dane Richard Methley Xs.', p.189.

the indulgence of St Mary of the Angels, which gave a plenary indulgence to penitents who visited the house on the feast of the Visitation and contributed to the fabric.[62]

These kinds of contacts with the laity, and indeed with the secular clergy and clergy of other orders, must have increased the order's awareness of pastoral needs and of developments in pastoral techniques, in addition to their internal exercise of most aspects of the *cura animarum*.[63]

III

In his *Consuetudines*, Guigo envisaged the making of books as the Carthusian order's distinctive contribution to the external *cura animarum*. In his well-known dictum, repeated by Adam in the *Quadripartite Exercise of the Cell* and reflected and refracted in many legislative texts and commentaries throughout the medieval period, Guigo wrote:

> Libros quippe tanquam sempiternum animarum nostrarum cibum cautissime custodiri et studiosissime volumus fieri, ut quia ore non possumus, dei verbum manibus predicemus.

By copying books we make 'heralds of the faith'. We hope for recompense from the lord for those who are corrected from error by our books, who progress 'in catholica veritate', who repent of their sins, and who burn with desire for the heavenly homeland.[64] What these remarks suggest is that the copying undertaken by the Carthusians will encompass a number of different kinds of books, from those refuting heresy, through books teaching the faith and encouraging patience, to the mystical and devotional treatises for which the English province was particularly noted in the later middle ages. Although Love's *Mirror of the Blessed Life of Jesus Christ* explicitly sets out to refute the errors of the Lollards, and therefore might be assigned to the first category of books, the English province has not been noted for any book-making contribution to penitential or pastoral catechetic practice.[65]

However, surviving Carthusian booklists and other evidence of book

[62] Victoria County History of Yorkshire, 3 (1974), 190-3; Victoria County History of Lincolnshire, 2 (1906), 158-60; *COE*, pp.150, 159, 205-6, 214, 215, 223, etc.

[63] *Statuta Antiqua*, part 2, cap. 9, sections 18-22 allow bishops and priests to preach (except in chapter) and religious and secular priests to celebrate mass at the order's private altars.

[64] *Coutumes*, cap. xxviii, pp.223-4; cf. *Statuta Antiqua*, part 2, cap. 16, section 10. The London *Chronicle* applauds Dan John Homersley's assiduous bookmaking, recording that he was kept supplied with parchment by a priest not of the order, and recounting a vision of the Virgin and this clerical benefactor who 'pointed out to him his mistake, where he made default in writing, and kindly warned him to amend the book' (Hope, p.62).

[65] The most recent survey is in Sargent, *Grenehalgh*, I, 15-55, with addenda II, 578-91. On Love see also A. I. Doyle, 'Reflections on Some Manuscripts of Nicholas Love's *Myrrour of the Blessed Lyf of Jesu Christ*', *Leeds Studies in English*, new ser., 14 (1982-3), 82-93.

ownership reveal a number of books related to the pastoral care to have been known to or owned by houses of the English province.[66] Reflecting the emphasis of the legislation, quite a few of these are related to confessional and penitential practice. John Blacman's gift to Witham Charterhouse included *Bartholomeus de Casibus Consciencie* and a *forma audiendi confessionem* in one volume, while another, now Oxford, Bodleian Library MS 801, contained the *Lucerna Consciencie, interrogaciones fori penitencialis* and a *tractatus de virtutibus et viciis*. Another of his gifts contained the *tractatus de penitencia Roberti Grostest* and the *tractatus inquirendi peccata in foro penitentiali*. Blacman also gave a copy of Augustine's *De falsa et vera penitencia*. Andrew Holes, Archdeacon of Wells, bequeathed another copy of Bartholomeo de San Concordio's *Summa de Casibus Conscientiae* to Witham in 1477.[67] William Anthorp bequeathed a *Pupilla Oculi* to Mountgrace in 1433, and this text covered penitential and catechetic matters.[68] More broadly catechetic books include Blacman's gift of an exposition of the Lord's Prayer, which was likely to be valued in an order where the lay brethren built their office around that prayer, and which reflected the popularity of the *Pater Noster* as a focus for basic catechetical teaching. He also gave *sermones dominicales*.

Books received through bequest may not, of course, reflect the needs or interests of the beneficiary house. Lists of books travelling between houses (as copies, to be copied, or after being copied) may, however, indicate more accurately texts that were in current demand or were considered to be relevant to the needs of the community.[69] In 1343, for example, Hinton lent a number of books to another house which included two specifically designed for priests with the cure of souls. Grosseteste's *Templum Dei* 'specialiter ... sacerdotibus conuenit quorum corpora "templum sunt spiritus sancti"'. With much use of schematic tables and diagnostic penitential charts, Grosseteste's work provides an excellent popular guide to the rudiments of the faith, using the petitions of the *Pater Noster* to bind together the other catechetic elements. His comment on the *Pater Noster* table accurately characterises the whole work: 'in hoc tabula est tota cura officii pastoralis'. The 'Liber qui sic incipit *Qui bene presunt presbyterii*' also lent by Hinton was a copy of a thirteenth-century

---

[66] The evidence is presented in *COE*, pp.313-34.

[67] *COE*, pp.316-22. Holes bequest is now Oxford, Magdalen College MS 191.

[68] *COE*, p.330; bequests of books to charterhouses were made by William Loryng (1415), canon of Salisbury and King's Clerk (three books of meditations); John Gregory (1429), a layman of Bruton, Somerset ('Syding' de gallic'); John Shirforde (1417), canon of Wells (all his books at Barnewalle under the same conditions as his previous gift of books); William Walleworth (1385), olim Lord Mayor of London, whose brother Thomas was a canon and vicar-general of York (a lives of the saints, a glossed psalter, a Hugucio and a 'librum vocatum veritas theologie'), see S. Cavanaugh, 'A Study of Books Privately Owned in England 1300-1450', unpublished Ph.D. thesis (University of Pennsylvania, 1980), pp.542, 389, 786, 905.

[69] The *Statuta Nova* decreed that the clothes of a dead monk should remain in the house of his death, but 'libri vero et alia que non debentur ex ordine ad domos proprias remittantur', part 2, cap. 3, section 9.

manual by Richard of Wetheringsett concerned not primarily with penitential matters but with the nature of the priestly life of those who labour 'in verbo et doctrina'. William of Pagula, whose *Oculus Sacerdotis* set new standards for the tradition of Latin pastoral aids to the parish clergy, cited *Qui bene presunt* as a good example of the type of broadly conceived pastoral manual available in the early fourteenth century for simple priests exercising the cure of souls. Wetheringsett had an active view of the priesthood. Faith and morals are more important to him than the detection, punishment and absolution of sins: 'in fide enim et moribus consistit summa christiane religionis'. Like the later *Speculum Christiani* he uses mnemonic verses at the beginning of his expositions and like the *Templum Domini* he uses the seven petitions of the *Pater Noster* as a catechetic holding pattern, describing the prayer as 'brevitate sermonis ... que continet utriusque vite necessaria'. By the standard of later works neither of these texts is particularly sophisticated, but both show a pragmatic awareness of pastoral problems that marked a significant step forward from earlier penitentials. Through these two works, Hinton had contact with the best of the new English techniques of presentation of pastoral material. The same Hinton list also contains a copy of the *Manipulus Florum* of Thomas of Ireland, an influential *florilegium* of *auctoritates* arranged topically, the only book in this category explicitly designed for the use of preachers.[70]

When Dom John Spalding (ob.1528) returned to Hull from London, he took with him a 'parvus liber de diversis materiis cuius iid folium incipit *Decem sunt precepta*', either a commentary on the Decalogue or, more likely, a collection of expositions of the catechetic syllabus ('de diversis materiis'). In 1519, a monk of London's journey to Mountgrace permitted the transfer of 'a lytell penaunce book wryttyn' – so described to distinguish it from similar printed books.[71] Thus although the bulk of the material moving around the order seems to have been mystical and devotional in nature, there was a small but significant interest in catechetic and pastoral texts.

Manuscripts known to have been in Carthusian hands, but whose provenance is uncertain, show similar interests.[72] London, Lambeth Palace Library MS 410, from Hinton, contains a copy of the popular pseudo-Bernardine/pseudo-Augustine *Speculum Peccatoris*; London, British Library MS Harley 237, from Mountgrace, is a theological miscellany

---

[70] COE, pp.322-3; *Templum Dei*, ed. Goering and Mantello, pp.29, 38. An account of this and the *Qui bene praesunt* is found in F. Kemmler, *'Exempla' in Context*, Studies and Texts in English 6 (Tübingen, 1984), pp.39-59. Quotations from *Qui bene* are from Oxford, New College MS 94, fols.28r, 33v. M. A. and R. H. Rouse, *Preachers, Florilegia and Sermons: Studies on the Manipulus Florum of Thomas of Ireland*, Studies and Texts 47 (Toronto, 1979), who do not mention this copy.

[71] COE, pp.324-6, 328.

[72] Thompson says that no remains have been found of the library of Hull, but Dr Rod Thompson informs me that Lincoln Cathedral Library MS 209, a collection of Rolle's Latin works, was owned by the house c.1400.

containing the *Cibus Anime*, covering the Creed, Commandments and Deadly Sins; a short listing of catechetical elements supported by Latin authorities; the Latin pastoral manual *Quoniam circa deum*; the *Elucidarium Sancti Anselmi*; a vernacular exhortation to dying men; and a sermon on the text 'Ego sum pastor bonus'. London, British Library MS Additional 37049, the famous Carthusian miscellany probably from Mountgrace, included the English verses on the Decalogue from the *Speculum Christiani* supported by Latin authorities. William Darker, a professed monk of Sheen, included among his scribal activity a copy of the *Speculum Christiani* (now London, British Library MS Additional 22121) and Cambridge, University Library MS Ff.6.43, containing two vernacular expositions of the Lord's prayer, vernacular patristic authorities on prayer and, as in the *Speculum Christiani* he copied, several exhortations and short meditations, apparently his own work.

IV

So works bequeathed to the order, books circulating within the order and books apparently made within the order all reveal some interest in catechetic and pastoral material. It has already been noted that Guigo conceived the making of books as the order's contribution to the *cura animarum*. Adam's *Quadripartite Exercise* emphasises the importance and utility of the work:

> Hoc quodammodo opus, opus immortale est; opus (si dicere licet) non transiens sed manens: opus utique, ut si dicamus, et non opus, opus denique quod inter omnia alia opera magis decet viros religiosos litteratos.[73]

The views of Guigo and Adam were given strong support by Jean Gerson in his *De Laude Scriptorum*, perhaps written for the Carthusian Oswald da Corda, author of the *Opus Pacis*, a treatise on textual emendation within the order. As Chancellor of Paris, Gerson was ideally placed to reflect the changing emphasis in pastoral theology and to refract the concerns of secular diocesans for the benefit of the Carthusians. The premise of his defence of the making of books is unequivocal:

> Scriptor idoneus et frequens librorum doctrinae salutis agit opus bonum de genere; et opus hoc, si proveniat ex caritate, meritorium est vitae aeternae, nec servile dicendum est.[74]

Like Guigo, he sees the role of the scribe and the maker of books as

[73]   *PL* 153, col. 881; see Sargent, *Grenehalgh*, I, 15-16.
[74]   J. Gerson, *Oeuvres Complètes*, ed. P. Glorieux, ix (Paris, 1973), 423-34, p. 423. Gerson makes it clear that he is referring to the copying of books rather than their composition, distinguishing between biblical Scribes (= *conquisitor*, *scrutator*, or *dictator*) 'quales apud christianos dicuntur theologi seu theologiae professores' and copyists. His text will concern 'scriptoribus quasi mechanicis et manualibus librorum' (p. 424).

fulfilling a range of different functions, depending on the kind of material being promulgated. He summarises these in a verse:

> Praedicat atque studet scriptor, largitur et orat
> Affligitur, sal dat, fontem lucemque futuris
> Ecclesiam ditat, armat, custodit, honorat.

Picking up Guigo's notion of silent preaching and Adam's references to the 'opus immortale', Gerson writes: 'Certe si lingua silet, manus praedicat, et fructuosius aliquando quanto scriptura venit ad plures uberior quam transiens sermo.'[75] The writer is worthy of the preacher's crown because he writes 'ut supponitur, non impar animarum salvificans zelus, scribendo sicut alteri loquendo'. *Zelus animarum* can be exercised as well by writing as by speaking – indeed some people need writing because 'vox intrans per unam aurem exit per alteram, nec revocatur ut scripta'.[76] The *scriptor* can exercise spiritual almsgiving by being a liberal giver of his written words 'ad opitulationem animarum', and Gerson again recalls Guigo by emphasising that the writer (be he composer or scribe) writes 'nunc adversus errores et scrupulos per eruditionem doctrinalem atque consilii, nunc ad consolationem salutarem'.[77]

A significant part of the writer's role, according to Gerson, is his support for the Church and its institutions and ministers. The Church is enriched by books and they contribute to improving the *cura animarum*. 'Dicitur in proverbio vulgari: les bons livres font les bon clercs: boni libri bonos clericos efficiunt.'[78] Books arm the church for the fight against heresy and preserve it from error. For this reason Gerson advocates the availability of books for the laity 'ut docerentur per se legendo eos', translated into their vernacular if they are not otherwise able to understand.[79] In discussing catechetic instruction and the need for an adequate provision of materials, he argues that problems arise because instruction is not properly given and because the instructors are not properly trained:

> apud quos nec brevissimus tenor unus habetur divinorum praeceptorum nec sacramentorum nominatio, nec numerus articulorum, compelluntur habere synodalia quaedam instituta: bene quidem, sed illud oportuit facere non tamen aliud omittere.[80]

Guigo and Gerson both emphasise the need for pastoral and penitential material to be made available if the *zelus animarum* is to be realised through adequate *cura animarum*. Did the English Carthusian province share an understanding of this need? The order's distinguished role in the production and dissemination of mystical and devotional materials is now well documented. A glimpse of how texts circulating inside the order

[75] *Ibid.*
[76] *Op. cit.*, 425.
[77] *Op. cit.*, 426.
[78] *Op. cit.*, 430.
[79] *Op. cit.*, 432. He excludes Scripture, but specifies works of morality, devotion, lives and legends of saints and holy meditations.
[80] *Op. cit.*, 433.

achieved a wider popularity is found in the Lansdowne manuscript's account of the transmission of *The Revelation of the Hundred Pater Nosters*, a devotion which was, for reasons already discussed, particularly suitable for the order. The manuscript reports that:

> A Monke of the Chartre hous of london sent in wryting the Rule and Reuelacion of the forsaid prayer to A brother of the same ordre atte Mountgras in the northe countre.[81]

The monk of Mountgrace, delighted with his new acquisition, replied to the monk of London, sending him a prayer to be added to his devotions:

> And more ouere he said in his letter this wyse: In this last yere I sent to a devoute preest of my knowlegge a copy of the Reuelacion ... which ye sende me. And the same preste sent dyuers copies to certeyn of hys Frendes, of whom ther was a good husbond man harde of the grete vartu and grace of the forsaid prayers he vsed it dayly as deuoutly as he coude.[82]

The chain of transmission is telling (Carthusian to secular priest; priest to laymen), and is characteristic of the perceived spread of devotional texts from religious to secular use in the course of the fourteenth century.[83]

A similar pattern may be noted in the transmission of the life of Jerome by Simon Wynter of the Bridgettine House of Syon, whose links with Sheen and London charterhouses, particularly concerning the production and circulation of books, are well known. Wynter urges his patron, the Duchess of Clarence, 'that hit sholde lyke your ladyship first to rede hit and to do copye hit for yourself & syth to lete oþer rede hit & copye hit, who so wyll'.[84]

It is in the nature of the circulation pattern described in these two examples that texts originally produced in an enclosed milieu would, if they proved popular, soon proliferate to the extent that copies circulating outside the order would soon outnumber those within.

[81] F. Wormald, 'The Revelation of the Hundred Pater Nosters', *Laudate* 14 (1936), 165-82, p. 180.

[82] *Op. cit.*, 181.

[83] See the account and bibliography in V. Gillespie, 'Vernacular Books of Religion', in *Book Production and Publishing 1375-1475*, ed. D. A. Pearsall and J. J. Griffiths (Cambridge, forthcoming 1989). The *Speculum Inclusorum* is an interesting example of this movement. The Latin version circulated inside the Carthusian order: London, British Library MS Royal 5 A. V was given to Coventry 'ex providentia et dono domni Roberti Odyham'. Odyham (ob. 1480) was a professed monk of London and became Prior of Coventry and a copy was carried from London to Hull by Spalding (*COE*, p. 324). The unique Middle English version (London, British Library MS Harley 2372) was given to almshouses in Stamford, Lincs. 'by the gyfte of Sir John Trus chapleyn ... and prest in the seyd beyd house', see *Speculum Inclusarum auctore anonymo anglico saeculi XIV*, ed. P. L. Oliger, Lateranum, new ser., 14 (1938).

[84] Quoted by G. Keiser, 'Patronage and Piety in Fifteenth-Century England: Margaret, Duchess of Clarence, Simon Wynter, and Beinecke MS 317', *Yale University Library Gazette* (1985), 32-46, p. 41.

This pattern may be discernible in the circulation of two catechetic and pastoral works already mentioned: the *Cibus Anime* and the *Speculum Christiani*. These two works are intimately related, the *Cibus Anime* being the source for the Latin authorities in the *Speculum Christiani*. Some vernacular sections and other material in the *Speculum Christiani* are also found appended to some copies of the *Cibus Anime*. Both works were popular. Fourteen copies survive of the *Cibus Anime* in its two recensions, and well over fifty of the *Speculum Christiani*, which was first printed c.1484.[85] The first recension of the *Cibus Anime* covers the catechetic syllabus in two books. The second recension adds a third book of exhortations to the contemplative life, which may also have circulated independently, and which bears all the hallmarks of Carthusian spirituality.[86]

The copies of the *Cibus Anime* suggest that the apparatus of chapter headings and numbers may have been developed after the text was first written, and it is possible, therefore, that it was not originally compiled as a work of easy reference.[87] One model of its growth which fits the available evidence well is that it was originally compiled in a non-practical context, for example a monastic house (and the *Cibus Anime* has a tone of fraternal exhortation even in its catechetic sections), achieved a certain, perhaps local, popularity and, as copies and users proliferated away from the home environment, an apparatus was developed to equip it more fully for a practical role as a pastoral work of reference, circulating perhaps among the secular clergy. It is also possible that the apparatus evolved through use in one centre, either a monastic house or a large institutional foundation (for example a secular cathedral). The *Speculum Christiani*, compiled by someone who was intimately acquainted with the *Cibus Anime*, and using other works also found in copies of the *Cibus Anime*, may well have been compiled in the same centre that first produced the *Cibus Anime*, but could be the product of adaptation elsewhere to fit the needs of secular priests with the cure of souls.[88] One of a sequence of related texts which use Latin authorities from the *Cibus Anime* to support vernacular materials is a moralisation of the Lady Altar at York Minster, which may be an indication of where, or for whom, the adaptation of the resources of the *Cibus Anime* took place. (The Lady chapel was founded by the important pastoral figure Archbishop Thoresby.) The decalogue verses in the *Speculum Christiani* are also found in the didactic play of the Doctors in the Towneley revision of the York cycle, indicating local interest in the text.[89]

[85] See Gillespie, '*Doctrina* and *Predicacio*'; for a detailed account of both texts, see V. Gillespie, 'The Literary Form of the Middle English Pastoral Manual, with particular reference to the *Speculum Christiani* and some related texts', unpublished D.Phil. thesis (Oxford, 1981).

[86] V. Gillespie, 'The *Cibus Anime* Book 3: A Guide for Contemplatives?' in *Spiritualität Heute und Gestern*, Analecta Cartusiana 35:3 (1983), 90-119.

[87] Gillespie, 'Literary Form', pp. 193-9.

[88] *Op. cit.*, pp. 228-43.

[89] Oxford, Corpus Christi College MS 132, fols. 60r-71v. The Lady Altar Moralisation does not appear to use material from *Cibus Anime*, but the other

The limited knowledge of early owners of the *Cibus Anime* points to some Carthusian interest and involvement. London, British Library MS Harley 237 was at Mountgrace, although it may not have been written there. London, British Library MS Harley 3820, containing extracts from book 3 of the *Cibus Anime*, was given to a recluse of Sheen charterhouse. In a memorandum of 1500 listing books lent by the London house to a monk leaving for St Anne's charterhouse in Coventry there is a work which may well be the *Cibus Anime* in a thin disguise:

> Item Esca anime cujus 2m folium incipit *daua*.[90]

Moreover one of the books listed in the library of the Bridgettine brethren of Syon (MS M.37) has contents all of which can be related to the *Cibus/ Speculum* tradition, with the exception of a 'Tractatus qui intitulatur Speculum salvacionis humane continens duas partes cum utriusque capitulacione premissa', which at sixty-three folios is the right size for a copy of the two-book recension of the *Cibus Anime*, characteristically listing the chapters at the beginning. Many of Syon's books passed through Sheen or were copied there.[91]

The *Cibus Amine* may have been composed in a Carthusian milieu with the intention of aiding the pastoral care through the provision of better tools for its execution, perhaps initially only for the benefit of those exercising the *cura pastoralis* within the community. There is an echo of Prior Guigo's description of books as 'tanquam sempiternum animarum nostrarum cibum' in the usual title of the *Cibus Anime*. The association of the work with the Carthusians provides a philosophy for its composition, an intellectual environment and library resources for its composition, and the expertise with which it could be initially copied and subsequently disseminated.[92]

As for the *Speculum Christiani*, Darker copied it in London charterhouse. One of the continental copies, which seem to ramify from a copy in Bruges, was copied by a J. Raphorst, who was a professed Carthusian of Bruges, and the order may well have provided the channel through which the text passed into continental circulation.[93]

texts (a couplet moralisation of the dream of Nebuchadnezzar and extracts from the *Scale of Perfection* on conscience) do so extensively; A. C. Cawley, 'Middle English Metrical Versions of the Decalogue with reference to the English Corpus Christi Cycles', *Leeds Studies in English*, new ser., 8 (1975), 129-45.

[90]   *COE*, p. 326.

[91]   V. Gillespie, 'A Syon Manuscript Reconsidered', *Notes and Queries*, new ser., 30 (1983), 203-5. On the Sheen/Syon link, see the summary in Sargent, *Grenehalgh*, I, 31-55 and notes.

[92]   The metaphor is a devotional commonplace, but it has wide currency in the writings of the Carthusians.

[93]   University of Utrecht MS 173, part of which is dated 1458. Raphorst returned to Utrecht in 1478 and apparently died there in 1493; A. I. Doyle, 'A Text attributed to Ruusbroec circulating in England', in *Dr L. Reypens – Album*, Studien on Tekstuitgaven von Ons Geestelijk Erf 16 (1964), pp. 153-71, p. 157 n. 23. On the links between English and Continental charterhouses, see M. Sargent, 'The Transmission by the English Carthusians of some Late Medieval Spiritual

The Carthusian interest in both works is shared by priests connected to York Minster. Thomas Garton, mentioned in a colophon requesting prayers for three members of the Garton family in Cambridge, Trinity Hall MS 16 (an important early copy of the two-book recension of the *Cibus Anime*), might be identified as the chantry priest who served as Sub-Treasurer of the Cathedral from 1404 to 1418, whose superior until his death in 1414 was John Newton the bibliophile and an important figure in the dissemination in the works of Rolle in conjunction with the Carthusians.[94] Three other chantry priests left copies of the *Speculum Christiani*: Robert Est left his copy to his native church of Briggesley in 1474-5 and at the same time ordered the return of his letters of confraternity to the charterhouses of Mountgrace and Hull; Robert Lythe left a copy in 1479 to a priest who would pray for him; and Thomas Symson left his 'librum vocatum *Speculum Christianorum*' (possibly a copy of one of the printed texts) to 'Domino Johanni Couper, cappellano' in 1491.[95] Parish priests, clerks and laymen in the province of York also seem to have had an interest in the work: Thomas Prowet, vicar of Pinchbeck in Lincolnshire, left a copy in 1476 to a dominus T. Kele; John Corve, a married clerk, left a copy to be chained in the choir of Wenlock parish church in 1437; Arthur Ormsby, of Ormesby in Lincolnshire, a notable layman, left a copy (bound with meditative material) to the Archbishop of York in 1476.[96] The chaplain of a chapel in Walsingham (either in Durham or the famous Marian shrine in Norfolk) seems to have owned a copy early in the fifteenth century, and a 'domino Gylbarto barton' owned another copy, though the dialect is of Derbyshire.[97] The dialect of most copies, however, points to a north-east Midlands, probably Lincolnshire, provenance for the vernacular sections of the text.[98]

Writings', *Journal of Ecclesiastical History* 27 (1976), 225-40; R. Lovatt, '*The Imitation of Christ* in Late Medieval England', *Transactions of the Royal Historical Society*, 5th ser., 18 (1968), 97-121; cf. the cautions of A. I. Doyle, 'Carthusian participation in the Movement of Works of Richard Rolle between England and other parts of Europe in the 14th and 15th Centuries', in *Kartäusermystik und Mystiker*, Analecta Cartusiana 55:2 (1981), 109-20, partly answered by Sargent, *Grenehalgh*, II, 580. All continental copies of the *Speculum Christiani* omit the vernacular verses.

[94] Gillespie, 'Literary Form', pp. 234-9. On Garton's career, see *Testamenta Eboracensia*, III, 52.

[95] *Testamenta Eboracensia*, III, 159, 199n., 160n.

[96] Prowet: ex inf. A. I. Doyle; Corve: Prerog. Ct. Canterbury 21 Luffenham, *Prerogative Court of Canterbury Wills 1383-1558*, Index Library 10, British Record Society, 1893, p. 143; Ormsby: M. Deanesly, 'Vernacular Books in England in the Fourteenth and Fifteenth Centuries', *Modern Language Review* 15 (1920), 349-58, p. 357; H. R. Plomer, 'Books Mentioned in Wills', *Transactions of the Bibliographical Society* 7 (1902-4), 99-121, p. 116.

[97] Cambridge University Library MS Additional 6150, front flyleaf; Oxford, Bodleian Library MS Additional A.268, fol. 36v.

[98] M. Laing, 'Studies in the Dialect Material of Medieval Lincolnshire', unpublished Ph.D. thesis (Edinburgh, 1978). Although a Lincolnshire dialectal provenance might appear to argue against York as a centre of dissemination, there were strong ecclesiastical links between the county and city, which was, in any case, a sig-

Was the composition of both or either works perhaps the result of some collaboration between the Carthusians and the secular diocesan authorities? Both the dioceses of York and Lincoln have demonstrable interests in improving the standard of pastoral care in their parishes in the century following 1350.[99]

Are these works evidence of the Carthusian order's interest in preaching with the hands? Both share a Carthusian emphasis on the *cibus animarum*: 'Cibus mentibus est sermo dei' as the *Speculum Christiani* puts it. And the peroration of the *Speculum Christiani* echoes the exhortations of Guigo and Adam:

> Magnum enim meritum est illi & multum premium habebit in futuro, qui scribit uel scribere facit doctrinam sanam ea intencione, ut ipse querat in ea, quomodo sancte uiuat, & ut alii eam habeant, ut per eam edificentur.

According to the final authority of the *Speculum Christiani*,'Nullum sacrificium ita placet deo sicut zelus animarum.' The Carthusian order's experiences of *cura pastoralis in deserto* may offer an explanation for the composition and dissemination of these two pragmatic and influential works concerned with the *cura animarum*.[100]

nificant regional centre of book production: B. Dobson, 'The Residentiary Canons of York in the Fifteenth Century', *Journal of Ecclesiastical History* 30 (1979), 145-74, pp. 154-5. Robert Est's birthplace was in Lincolnshire; Henry Bowet, Archbishop of York from 1407 to 1423, had been archdeacon of Lincoln from 1386 to 1401. On book production, see J. B. Friedman, 'John Siferwas and the Mythological Illustrations in the *Liber cosmographiae* of John de Foxton', *Speculum* 58 (1983), 391-418; 'Richard de Thorpe's Astronomical Calendar and the Luxury Book Trade at York', *Studies in the Age of Chaucer* 7 (1985), 137-60.
[99] On the diocese of York, see J. Hughes, 'Religion in the Diocese of York 1350-1450', unpublished D.Phil. thesis (Oxford, 1985); J. H. Moran, 'Education and Learning in the City of York 1300-1560', *Borthwick Papers* 55 (1979); Gillespie, 'Doctrina and Predicacio'; on the diocese of Lincoln, see D. M. Owen, *Church and Society in Medieval Lincolnshire*, History of Lincolnshire 5 (1971); Gillespie, 'Literary Form', pp. 241-3.
[100] Holmstedt, p. 241.

LOLLARD INTERPOLATIONS AND OMISSIONS
IN MANUSCRIPTS OF *THE PORE CAITIF*

Sr M. Teresa Brady

On two counts, the late-fourteenth-century collection of religious tracts known as *The Pore Caitif* stands as an appropriate example of what can happen on the journey from the cell to the world: works originally written for recluses can gain a wider audience among clerics, religious orders of women, and lay people, and orthodox tracts can be infiltrated with Lollard opinions. The first instance is illustrated by the fact that the compiler of *The Pore Caitif* extracted from Richard Rolle's *Emendatio Vitae*, *The Form of Living* and the *Commentary on the Canticles* carefully-gradated excerpts that would lead his audience of 'symple men and wymmen of good will' through the preparatory stages of self-denial, temptation and patience to a glimpse of the joys of infused love in contemplation.[1] It is the second phenomenon, however, that I wish to examine in this paper.

The compiler of the *Pore Caitif*, assembling his fourteen tracts probably in the final decade of the fourteenth century, would inevitably have been aware of Wycliffite currents of thought circulating in England. No theological writer of the time could have been untouched by the more than twenty years of debate over such vital religious issues as came under attack. In fact, the anthology was long thought to be the work of Wycliffe himself. Biographers and editors who examined the text based their judgments on three or four manuscripts available to them, and if they found what seemed to be Lollard opinions, they concluded the treatise had been written by the Reformer or one of his followers.[2] They noticed that the full text or parts sometimes

I wish to express gratitude to the Deans' Council of Pace University for a grant awarded in 1984 that enabled me to do the preliminary research for this paper and to the American Philosophical Society for an award in 1986 which combined with an additional grant from Pace University gave me opportunity for the research in British libraries necessary to complete the study.

[1] Cf. my articles 'Rolle's *Form of Living* and *The Pore Caitif*', *Traditio* XXXVI (1980), 426-435; 'The Seynt and His Boke: Rolle's *Emendatio Vitae* and *The Pore Caitif*', *14th Century English Mystics Quarterly* 7 (1981), 20-31; and 'Rolle and the Pattern of Tracts in *The Pore Caitif*', *Traditio* XXXIX (1983), 456-465.

[2] Available to John Lewis, for example, were two Lollard-infiltrated texts in Trinity College Cambridge MS 336 and CUL MS Ff.vi.55: *The History of the Life and Sufferings of the Reverend and Learned John Wyclif, D.D.* (Oxford, 1820), 202. Waterland was familiar with these and with two orthodox manuscripts, CUL MS Ff.vi.34 and St John's College Cambridge MS 49: Letter to Lewis in *The Collected Papers of Reverend John Lewis*, BL MS Rawlinson D 376, f.108. The St John's manuscript was suspect, however, because satirical poems on friars covered the

circulated in Lollard anthologies, and that the pseudonym 'pore caitif' resembled the Lollard 'coward synful caitif', 'þis pore scribeler', and 'symple creature' used in the *Glossed Gospels*.[3] Early cataloguers perpetuated the wholesale ascription of innumerable English treatises to Wycliffe which, fortunately, modern scholarship has largely cleared away. The underlying problem in the case of the *Pore Caitif* was that no one had examined all fifty-four manuscripts of full or partial texts, and conclusions were drawn based on piecemeal evidence.

The completion of the collation of thirty surviving manuscripts of the full text of *The Pore Caitif* and twenty-four manuscripts containing partial texts or fragments makes it possible here to offer some definitive statements on the Lollard interpolations and omissions that occurred as the text was copied by scribes in the late fourteenth and fifteenth centuries. A study of the manuscript descent and of the collations indicates that in all likelihood, the original *Pore Caitif* text that came from the hands of the compiler was orthodox. Quite soon, however, that same evidence suggests that the Lollard infiltration began. The majority of extant *Pore Caitif* manuscripts contain the orthodox text, but twelve manuscripts have significant insertions and/or deletions of materials usually linked with the Lollards. This phenomenon is not at all unusual. A number of Middle English religious works that enjoyed wide circulation suffered tampering by scribes with Lollard views and so survive in both orthodox and heterodox versions, as we shall see later in the paper. In *The Pore Caitif*, these topics relate to doctrine, worship and discipline and include images, confession, oaths, the legend of the composition of the Apostles' Creed, preaching, and persecution. The medievalist will recognise the topics verifiable as of Lollard interest from the writings of Wycliffe and his followers, from documents identifying various propositions they held, from matters examined at the trials of suspected heretics and mentioned in abjurations, or from defences undertaken by orthodox respondents to the errors. Several additional topics which the Lollard-infiltrated manuscripts expanded seem to reflect particular interests rather than opposition to doctrine or ecclesial practice, and so are presented separately. In the comparative citations given below, the term 'Group I' refers to manuscripts containing the orthodox text. Representative

flyleaves. These were edited by Francis Lee Utley: 'The Layman's Complaint and the Friar's Answer', *The Harvard Theological Review* XXXVIII (1945), 141-7, who noted 'there is neither Lollard nor Franciscan bias in the treatise to make it a springboard for the two poems', 142. Vaughan had seen the contaminated texts of Lambeth Palace Library MS 484, but also the orthodox version in Lambeth Palace Library MS 541 and Trinity College Dublin MS 520: *Tracts and Treatises of John de Wycliffe, D.D.* (London, 1845), 92. Margaret Deanesly's references to the *Pore Caitif* are drawn from the orthodox CUL MS Ff.vi.34, but her list of fourteen manuscripts does contain three, MSS Bodley 3, Bodley 938, and CUL Ff.vi.55 which do have Lollard materials: *The Lollard Bible and Other Medieval Biblical Versions* (Cambridge, 1920), 347. It is impossible to know, of course, if she had fully examined these, for she pronounced the *Pore Caitif* 'without Wycliffite bias', 347. For a fuller history of the early ascription of the *Pore Caitif* to Wycliffe or to the Lollards see my article '*The Pore Caitif*: An Introductory Study', *Traditio* X (1954), 542ff.

[3] Deanesly, 276.

quotations are drawn from British Library MS Harley 2336. The term
'Group II' refers to manuscripts that evidence Lollard infiltration; here, the
sources of the quotations vary, depending on the passage under
consideration.[4] These manuscripts, together with the sigla used to identify
them, include the following:

A.   MSS with full text of *PC*:

1. (A[1]) British Library MS Add. 30897
2. (B) Bodley MS 3
3. (C) Trinity College Cambridge MS 336
4. (K) Lambeth Palace Library MS 484
5. (M) University of Glasgow Hunterian MS 496
6. (N[1]) University of Glasgow Hunterian MS 520
7. (W[1]) New York Public Library MS 68
8. (Y) British Library MS Harley 2322

B.   MSS with partial texts of *PC*:[5]

1. (A[2]) Bodley MS Add. B66 (# 3,1,2)
2. (N[2]) Cambridge University Library MS Ff.vi.55 (# 1,2,3)
3. (W[2]) Westminster School MS 3 (# 7, 14)
4. (X[2]) Colchester and Essex Museum MS (# 4 imp., 5,6,7,8,9 imp.)

IMAGES

The exposition of the first commandment in the *Pore Caitif* tract, 'þe Ten
Heestis' defines the role of images in Christian worship. The passage in the
Group I manuscripts reads:

Fferþermor, God forfendiþ in þis comaundc:nent to make ony graue
ymage eþir oþir symylitude in entent to truste on hem eiþer to do
Goddis worschip to hem. And þis was vttirli forfendid to þe Iewis to
whom þese comaundementis weren ʒouun first, for vnstidfastnesse
of her feiþ. For þei weren so false in bileeue þat summe of hem
worshipiden þing made of God for her God, summe worshipiden þe
sunne & summe þe moone, & summe oþir licnessis of creaturis for
her God, and so þe worship þat was oonli due to God þei ʒauen to
oþir creaturis maad of God & to symilitudis & licnessis þat þei
hadden maad hem silf aʒens Goddis will. And þerfore it was vttirli
forfendid to hem to make ony symilitude eþir licnesse for þe greet

---

[4]   The spelling of the manuscripts is reproduced. Standard abbreviations are silently
expanded. Punctuation and capitalisation conform to modern practice, but are kept
at a minimum.
[5]   The numbers in parentheses refer to the *Pore Caitif* tracts the manuscripts contain,
as follows: 1. Þe Bileeue; 2. Þe Ten Heestis; 3. Þe Pater Noster; 4. Þe Counceil of
Crist; 5. Of Vertuous Pacience; 6. Of Temptacioun; 7. Þe Chartir of Heuene; 8. Þe
Hors eþir Armer of Heuene; 9. Þe Name of Ihesu; 10. Desier of Ihesu; 11. Of
Mekenes; 12. The Effect of Wille; 13. Actif Liif and Contemplatif Liif; 14. Þe
Mirrour of Chastite.

mawmetrie þat þei diden in hem, as it is foundun in many placis in þe
oold lawe.   (ff. 20ʳ-20ᵛ)

Implicit here is the position that *latria* (the worship reserved to God alone) is
not to be accorded images; yet images may be lawfully venerated. A
deviation from this version, however, occurs in Group II MSS C, K, M, N¹
and N² where the clause 'in entent to truste on hem eiþer to do Goddis
worschip to hem' (ll. 2-3) is omitted. The omission thus renders absolute the
prohibition against images: 'Forþermore in þis comaundement God
forfendiþ to make ony grauen ymage eþir oþir similitude eiþer liknes.'
(MS K, f. 18ʳ)

The text in the Group I manuscripts continues with a view of the
instructional and devotional role of images drawn from the letter of Pope
Gregory I to Bishop Serenus of Marseilles.[6] Incorporated into canon law,[7] this
view of images called attention to their educative role, but cautioned against
offering 'Goddis worship' to them:

> Alle suche symylitudis & ymagis shulden be kalendris to lewid folc,
> þat riȝt as clerkis seen bi her bookis what þei shulden do, so lewid
> folc whanne hem lackiþ teching shulden lerne bi ymagis whom þei
> shulden worshipe & folowe in lyuynge. To do Goddis worship to
> ymagis, ech man is forfendid, but to lerne bi þe siȝt of hem to folowe
> seyntis lyuyng, good it is to ech man. Þis sentence seiþ Seynt Gregory
> to Sirene þe bishop, as þe lawe witnessiþ.   (f. 20ᵛ)

Group II MSS C, K, M, N¹, Y and A² omit the passage and for the second
time apparently reject a legitimate use of images. MSS N¹, N² and A¹ (in the
margin) further observe that the use of images has good or bad effects, and
associate 'couetise of prestis' with the encouragement to venerate images.
This is one of the few anti-clerical references that occurs in the Group II
manuscripts. MSS N¹, N² and A¹ read:

> And þe same God þat was þanne is now wiþ þe same
> comaundementis. But here, as a greet doctour seiþ, ymagis doon boþe
> good and harm. Good þei doon to siche men to whom þei ben bookis
> to more loue God þanne þei schulden ellis; harm þei doon to siche
> men whom þei mowen þus to sette her hope endely in such ymagis or
> ellis scaterit her loue folily in ymagis. And in þese sinnes traueilen
> many folk boþe lewid and lerid, and couetise of prestis is moche cause
> of þese errour.   (MS N¹, ff. 43ʳ-43ᵛ)

With the exception of MSS Y and A² of Group II, all *Pore Caitif* manuscripts

[6]   *PL* 77, 1128. The quotation is found in orthodox works including *Dives and
Pauper*, ed. Priscilla Heath Barnum, EETS 275 (Oxford, 1976), I, 91; and 'A Sawley
Monk's Version of Grosteste's *Castle of Love*' in *The Minor Poems of the Vernon
MS*, ed. Carl Horstman, EETS os 98 (London, 1892), I, 410; and also in Lollard
works including the *Floretum* in MS Bodley 448, f. 272ᵛ; and *The Lanterne of
Liȝt*, ed. Lillian M. Swinburn, EETS os 151 (London, 1901), 85. I owe thanks to
Dr Christina von Nolcken for use of her microfilm copy of MS Bodley 448.
[7]   Gratian, *Decreti*, III d.3 c.27 in *Corpus Juris Canonici*, ed. A. Richter and
A. Friedberg (Leipzig, 1879-1881, 1928), I, 1360.

of both groups now have a section on appropriate attitudes in church before the Eucharist, the crucifix, and statues of saints.[8]

> Þerfore whanne men comen to þe chirche, first biholde þei vp to þe
> hiȝ auter, for þere is Goddis bodi in foorme of breed in box eþir in
> cuppe; and þanne heue þei vp to heuene þe iȝe of her soule þat is
> entent eþir þouȝt of herte, & with al þe miȝt & deuocioun of her
> 5 soule, þanke þei Almyȝti God þat he wole vouche saaf ech dai to
> come fro hiȝ heuene for helþe of her soule. & if þei seen ony licnesse
> of Crist don on þe cros, haue þei þanne mynde vpon þe bittir peynes
> & passioun þat he suffride for saluacioun of mannes soule & herteli
> þanke þei him þerfore. And aftir þat if þei seen ony licnesse eþir
> 10 ymage maad in mynde of ony oþir seynt, rere þei vp þe mynde of her
> soule to heuene, praiynge alle þe seintis þat ben þere to be meenes &
> preiers to God for hem, not bileeuynge eþir tristenynge þat þilke
> ymage eþir licnesse mai brynge ony man out of goostli eþir bodili
> meschif eþir ȝyue help eþir richesse eþir take awei. Ffor it is writun
> 15 in Goddis lawe þat þei moun neþir ȝilde to ony man neþir yuel
> neþir good; neþir þei moun ȝyue richesse neþir take awei. And
> þouȝ ony man make a vow to hem & ȝilde it not, þei shulen not
> seke it. Þei shulen not delyuere ony man fro deeþ, neþir restore a
> blynd man to his siȝt, þus seiþ hooly writ, but oonli to teche men bi
> 20 þe siȝt of hem to haue þe better mynde of hem þat ben in heuene,
> and to seche bisili what liif þei lyueden in erþe, þoruȝ þe which bi
> þe mercy of God þei ben now seyntis, & to folowe þilk liif in al þat
> man mai. (ff. 20ᵛ-21ᵛ)

Although seven manuscripts in Group II omitted the teaching of Pope Gregory (B and W[1] have it), all seven retain the teaching just quoted and presumably agree that images are what Pecock would later call 'rememoratyf or mynding signes'.[9] Behind the allusion to the crucifix, of course, is a body of varying opinions on the veneration due to it.[10] The position expressed in the Group I manuscripts is: the crucifix reminds of Christ's sufferings and death and man's duty of gratitude for this instrument of salvation. Devotion is 'before' or in the presence of the image, but not 'to' the image. The excerpt certainly affirms that images have no power to grant favours or work miracles, nor will they demand fulfilment of promises or vows made to them. MSS Y and A[2] omit the entire passage until l. 12 and then substitute: 'And þerfore no man bileue þat grauen ymagis moun bringe hem out of myscheef neiþir bodili ne goostly for þei moun not.' (MS Y, f. 43ᵛ) At l. 16,

---

[8] Similar instructions on behaviour in church are found in *The English Text of The Ancrene Riwle*, ed. Mabel Day, EETS os 225 (London, 1952), 7; in *Dives and Pauper*, I, 83; in *The Lay Folks' Mass Book*, ed. Thomas Frederick Simmons, EETS os 63 (London, 1879), *passim*; and in some of the courtesy books, e.g. *Early English Meals and Manners*, ed. Frederick J. Furnivall, EETS os 32 (London, 1868, 1931), 182.

[9] Reginald Pecock, *The Repressor of Over Much Blaming of the Clergy*, ed. Churchill Babington (London, 1860), I, 137.

[10] Aquinas, for example, approved adoration (worship or *latria*) of the cross: *Summa Theologica*, ed. Dominican Fathers (New York, 1947), II, Part III, q. xxv a. 3 2155.

they continue with the usual version. MS Rawlinson C69 of Group I omits the sentence on vows made to images and substitutes: 'nor þei may not make sek folk heyl nor make krokid men rith' (f. 20ᵛ).

A brief but more significant insertion occurs in l. 19 after 'hooly writ' where MSS C, K, N¹ and N² add the comment: 'but þese ymagis ben suffrid bisidis auctorite of bileeue ...' (MS K, f. 19ʳ). This grudging approval of a role images can fulfil erupts into open opposition when MSS C, K, M, N¹, N² and A¹ (in the margin) add two points: people are 'ouer lewde & to beestly' who cannot be mindful of the Lord and his passion and the lives and deaths of the saints without 'grauen eiþer peintid ymagis'; and images are often 'grauen ʒoten & peintide amys', contrary to faith and belief. The insertion reads in full:

> But certis þo folk ben ouer lewde & to beestly þat kunnen not haue in her mynde eiþer bringe in to her mynde þe goodnes of her Lord God & þe passioun þat he suffride for her saluacioun of her soule eþer symple & meke lyuynge & pacient suffringe of hise saintis wiþouten sich grauen eiþer peintid ymagis, þe whiche ben ful ofte grauen ʒoten & peintide amys & contrarie to oure feiþ eiþer bileeue. Of þe whiche þe holy profete Ieremye seiþ, þo ben veyn and a werk worþi scorn. & þerfore siþen, as Seint Poul seiþ, þat we ben þe kynde of God & eiris of Ihesu Crist, seche we þerfore moore bisily to knowe him by þe diueris & wondirful worchingis & creaturis þat he haþ maad him silf, þan bi þe werk of ony oþer man þat is ofte tyme reprouable. But as a greet doctour seiþ: for we knowen God litil, þerfore we louen him þe lasse. (MS K, ff. 19ʳ-19ᵛ)

One further omission from a passage on images occurs in the seventh tract of the *Pore Caitif*, 'Þe Chartre of Oure Heuenli Eritage'. This allegorical piece based on the form of a medieval land grant enumerates in detail the materials of which the charter is made. In the Group I manuscripts, the section on the seal reads:

> Þe printe of þis seel is þe shap of oure Lord Ihesu hanginge for oure synne on þe cros, as we moun se bi þe ymage of þe crucifix. (f. 88ʳ)

Group II MSS C, K, N¹, B, W¹, X² and Y omit 'as we moun se bi þe ymage of þe crucifix'. MS Stowe 38 of Group I also omits the line and substitutes 'as our bileeue techiþ us' (f. 107ᵛ). MS Y substitutes 'as þe gospel þat is our bileue techiþ us' (f. 99ʳ).

The attitudes toward images expressed in the insertions in the Group II manuscripts may be summarised: images are to be tolerated reluctantly rather than justified; they ought not to be necessary for devotion; it is clerical covetousness that encourages their use. Similar sentiments were expressed by Wycliffe and his followers.[11] Set against the background of the

---

[11] Wycliffe himself was tolerant of images in *De Mandatis Divinis*, 155-6. References to Wycliffe's Latin works are to the editions of the Wyclif Society (1883-1921); tract and page are given. In later works he cites the superstition, avarice or misguided extravagance they occasioned, for example: 'Sermo XIII', *Sermones*, I, 90-2. The Lollards claimed that the first commandment, which prohibited images, was still

more violent objections to images of the later Lollards, the opinions contained in the interpolated passages of the Group II manuscripts of the *Pore Caitif* are very mild. Two quotations, however, are of special interest. The first is attributed to a 'greet doctour' in the insertion of MSS N[1], N[2], and A[2] (p. 186 above) and may be a reference to Wycliffe's comment in *De Mandatis Divinis* which it resembles quite closely:[12]

> Et patet quod ymagines tam bene quam male possunt fieri: bene ad excitandum, facilitandum et accendendum mentes fidelium, ut colant devocius Deum suum; et male ut occasione ymaginum a veritate fidei aberretur, ut ymago illa vel latria vel dulia adoretur, vel ut in pulcritudine, preciositate aut affeccione impertinentis circumstancie minus debite delectur.

The second quotation, found at the conclusion of the inserted passage in MSS C, K, M, N[1], N[2] and A[1] (p. 188 above), is also in a tract on the ten commandments printed by Arnold. Although it has no significant Lollard materials, it circulated among the Wycliffites. The passage occurs at the end of the exposition of the first commandment in language almost identical with that in the *Pore Caitif* insertion: 'But for we knowyn him litil, we loven him þe lesse.'[13] In the *Pore Caitif*, 'a greet doctour' is credited with the statement; no reference to an author is made in the tract printed by Arnold. It is interesting that through the two quotations, both insertions of the Lollard-interpolated texts can be linked to Wycliffite materials.

Of all the topics to be examined, the veneration of images generated the

applicable in the New Law; the uneducated made the image itself the object of worship and so were guilty of idolatry; painted and sculpted representations were often inaccurate, and the rich cloth and jewels that adorned them were an ironic contrast to the poverty and suffering of Christ and the saints; profit-seeking clergymen encouraged cults of particular shrines and images, fabricating stories of miracles performed, thus diverting monies from the relief of the poor, the true images of God. Cf. 'Images and Pilgrimages' in *Selections from English Wycliffite Writings*, ed. Anne Hudson (Cambridge, 1978), 83, 85, 87; 'Of the Leaven of the Pharisees', 'How Satan and His Children', and 'Of Poor Preaching Priests' in *The English Works of Wyclif Hitherto Unprinted*, ed. F. D. Matthew, EETS os 74 (London, 1880, 1902), 7, 210, and 279 respectively; and *The Lanterne of Liȝt*, ed. Lillian Swinburne, EETS os 151 (London, 1917), 84-5. Opinions on images surfaced in the listings and condemnations of Lollard tenets; cf. 'Sixteen Points on which the Bishops accuse the Lollards' in *Selections from English Wycliffite Writings*, 19, 13; 'The Twenty-five Articles' in *Select English Works of John Wyclif*, ed. Thomas Arnold (Oxford, 1869-1871), III, 462-4; 'Twelve Conclusions of the Lollards', in *Selections from English Wycliffite Writings*, 27. They were a focal point of examination in the trials of those charged with heresy: *Fasciculi Zizaniorum Magistri Johannis Wyclif cum Tritico*, ed. Walter W. Shirley, Rolls Series (London, 1858), 370, 408-9, 429-30 and 444; J. A. F. Thomson, *The Later Lollards, 1414-1520* (Oxford, 1965), 24-8, 140 and *passim*; and Anne Hudson, 'The Examination of Lollards', *Bulletin of the Institute of Historical Research, University of London* 46 (1973), 154, 155. Images constituted one of the specified matters to be acknowledged in the various forms of recantation: 'The Examination of Lollards', 156.

[12]   p. 156.
[13]   III, 84.

largest number of variations in the Group II manuscripts. The materials on confession, now to be considered, were more briefly and subtly altered.

CONFESSION

There is no extensive treatment of the sacraments in the *Pore Caitif*; they are merely listed in the tract on the Creed, in the exposition of the ninth article: 'I bileeue in hooli chirche':

> Also it is to bileeue þat þe sacramentis of hooli chirche ben souereyn medicyns to recouncile to God soulis forsakinge synne & sorwinge þerfore. And þese ben þe seuene sacramentis ... (ff. 14ʳ-14ᵛ)

Brief remarks, rather than definitions, are attached to two sacraments in the list, the Eucharist[14] and Penance. The tag linked to Penance reads: 'Þe fferþe is penaunce, þat is as Seynt Gregory seiþ, to wepe for synnes don & eschewe to do þingis to be wept.' (f. 14ᵛ) Curiously enough, the materials of the tenth article 'I bileeue forȝifnesse of synnes' also have no reference to sacramental confession:

> Here we schulen bileeue þat þei þat amended her liif doinge veri penaunce & with leuyng of synne & kepen Goddis comaundementis & eenden in charite shulen haue forȝifnesse of alle her synnes. And also Crist þoruȝ his passioun & deeþ gatt us of his Fadir forȝifnesse of oure synnes. And he him silf vp þe Godhead euene with þe Fadir forȝyueþ al origynal synne & actuel also in taking of filouȝt.
>
> (f. 15ʳ)

It is only in a passing comment on the fifth article of the creed that the traditionally-phrased listing of the elements necessary for forgiveness of sin is cited:

> ... we shulde rise fro goostly deeþ bi þre maner medicyn, bi contricioun eþir sorwe of herte, bi confessioun, & satisfaccioun.
>
> (f. 7ʳ)

Presumably, the second item refers to sacramental absolution in confession.

---

[14]   The statement on the Eucharist reads: 'þe sacrament of þe auter, þat is Goddis fleish & his blood in fourme of breed & wyn' (f. 14ᵛ). If 'in fourme of breed & wyn' means the accidents of bread and wine, it accurately expresses the church's teaching that after the consecration the accidents remain, but the substance of the bread and wine become the body and blood of Christ. If, however, 'fourme of breed & wyn' means the substance of bread and wine remains, the statement is heretical. The formula frequently appears in Lollard tracts. Here, presumably, it refers to Wycliffe's belief that after the consecration the substance and accidents of bread and wine remained. In the absence of more detailed treatment on the sacrament in the *Pore Caitif*, no firm conclusions can be drawn. For works using the phrase, cf. Wyclif's 'Confessions on the Eucharist' in *Selections from English Wycliffite Writings*, 17; 'De Sacramento Altaris' in Matthew, 357; 'On the Twenty-five Articles' in Arnold, III, 484; and Oldcastle's statement at his trial in *Fasciculi Zizaniorum*, 438.

Group II MSS B, C, K, N[1] and N[2] alter this to read, 'confescioun to God cheefli', and state more precisely to whom satisfaction is to be made:

> ... we schulden rise fro goostly deeþ bi þre maner medicyns, þat is bi contricioun eþir sorewe of herte, bi confescioun to God cheefli, & bi satisfaccioun eiþer amendis makinge boþe to God & to man bi al oure kunnynge & oure power.   (MS K, f. 6ʳ)

MS B replaces the phrase 'al oure kunnynge & oure power' with 'feiþful werkis'. MSS Y and A[2] replace 'confescioun to God cheefli' with 'trewe knowlechinge to God' and rework the remainder of the statement on satisfaction:

> ... we schulden rise fro goostly deeþ þat is bi sorowe of herte for synne and trewe knowlechinge to God and so to make amendis & leeue oure synne for euermore and þus to haue mercy of God and to dwelle wiþ hym wiþouten ende. Amen.   (MS Y, f. 28ᵛ)

The situation here, then, is that seven manuscripts omit a reference to sacramental confession and substitute the opinion that acknowledgment of sin to God, along with sorrow and amendment, is sufficient for pardon. These revisions in the Group II manuscripts reflect both Wycliffe's and the Lollard position on auricular confession: the essential disposition for forgiveness was penitence of heart; if a person were contrite, oral confession was superfluous.[15]

[15] Wycliffe seems to have moved from an early position where he considered confession necessary, although to be made only to a 'predestined' priest not living in sin, to a later stance where he cited penance as necessary, but confession optional at the discretion of the penitent. He maintained God alone knew the nature and extent of man's sin and repentance, and therefore he alone forgave sin (*Sermones*, III, 27; IV, 100, 101; *De blasphemia*, 130). The confessor, on the other hand, did not know a man's sin or his disposition of sorrow, and could not be sure the sin was forgiven (*Sermones*, IV, 103; *Trialogus*, 328; *De blasphemia*, 121, 136, 145, 148, 151, 159). He frequently voiced his opposition to the law of Pope Innocent III requiring confession once a year (*Sermones*, IV, 101; *De blasphemia*, 115). He seems to have preferred public confession to private (*De blasphemia*, 120-1) and strongly objected to reserved absolution for certain sins (*De potestate papa*, 311). In *De blasphemia*, he says onfession is not a sacrament, the words 'I absolve thee' are not in Scripture, and the form of confession was neither used by the apostles nor is it found in Holy Writ (113, 124, 127, 130). His conclusion in the matter seems to be: God alone frees man from sin and, therefore, confession should be made to God. His teachings on confession were among the 'Twenty-four Conclusions' condemned at the Synod of Blackfriars in 1382 (*Fasciculi Zizaniorum*, 277-82, 493-7). Wycliffe's key ideas on confession were picked up by his followers and occur frequently in later Lollard writings: for example, the English Sermons (Arnold, I, 18, 35, 48, 136, 196) and in a tract on confession based on his *De eucharistia et poenitentia*, 'Of Confession' in Matthew, 328, 333, 335, 337, 338, 339, 340, 341, 345. Cf. also Point 2 of 'The Sixteen Points' in *Selections from English Wycliffite Writings*, 19, 20, 21, 150, 154; Conclusion 9 of 'The Twelve Conclusions', *ibid.*, 27-8, 145, 146; and Article 4 of 'The Twenty-five Articles' in Arnold, III, 455, 461-2. They frequently surfaced, as well, at the trials of various Lollard suspects (*Selections from English Wycliffite Writings*, 142n.); Questions on confessions to be asked of suspected Lollard heretics appear in Bishop Polton's *Register* ('The Examination of Lollards', 153, 155).

Two final alterations of passages on remission of sin should also be mentioned. In the allegorical tract 'Þe Hors and Armer of Heuene' there is a statement attributed to St Augustine that in the Group I manuscripts reads:

> Þerfore with mournyng & ofte forþenking of herte, with fasting, deuout preier & almesse dedis, such venyal synnes shulden be clensid & cast out of soulis, as Seynt Austyn techiþ.   (f. 99ᵛ)

MSS C, K, M and N¹ omit from this quotation 'clensid &'. Similarly, in a section 'Of Vertuous Pacience' where the Group I manuscripts have 'with sorowe, forsoþe, þilke þingis bihouen to be clensid, which þingis we han don with lust & likyng', MSS C, K, M and N¹ make a change: 'with sorowis, forsoþe, þilke þingis bihoueþ to be clensid with sorowe & penaunce, whiche þingis we haue doon wiþ lust & likinge' (MS C, f. 83ʳ). Were the words 'clensid &', in the first instance, too suggestive of confession? Are the specific means for cleansing inserted into the second passage meant to divert attention from confession as the usual means for forgiveness of sin? The awkward alteration with its repetition of 'with sorowis' and 'with sorowe & penaunce' obviously betrays the tampering with the passage.

OATHS

A third place where variant readings occur in the *Pore Caitif* is in the exposition of the eighth commandment, where reference is made to the form for administering oaths in court. The ceremony required the defendant to lay his hand on the 'hooli booke', take the oath, and kiss the book. It carries a strong warning to those who will forswear themselves, and in the Group I manuscripts is as follows:

> And vndirstonde what peril he haþ þat witingli beriþ fals witnesse & forsweriþ him silf on þe hooli book. Ffirst, if he sweriþ fals witingli, he forsakiþ þe help of alle þe wordis þat ben writun in þilk book & in alle oþir. And whanne he leiþ his hond on þe book forto bere fals witnesse witingli, he forsakiþ þe help of alle goode werkis þat euere he wrouȝte with hise hondis. And whanne he kissiþ þe book witingli sweringe fals, he forsakiþ þe help of alle goode preiers & of alle goode wordis þat euere he bede eþir seide with his mouþ. And þus he reneieþ God & his cristendom & þe sacramentis of hooli chirche & bitakiþ him to þe feend til he come to amendement.   (ff. 47ʳ-47ᵛ)

Group II MSS C, K, M, N¹ and N² omit the passage and have only a brief statement on false witness that retains the last clause of the excerpt above:

> Also he þat beriþ fals witnes witingli eþir wilfulli aȝens ony man forsakiþ God & his cristindom & þe sacrementis of holi chirche & bitakiþ him to þe feend unto þe tyme þat he come to amendement.
>
> (MS C, f. 49ʳ)

MSS B and W¹ also omit the passage of the Group I manuscripts but do not contain the substitution just cited. Thus seven of the Group II manuscripts register protest against the materials on oaths.

While statements on oaths appear only infrequently in Wycliffe's writings,[16] the later Lollard tracts, as H. G. Russell noted, indicate the Lollards were not opposed to oaths as such, but only to the form in which they were customarily put. They were willing to swear by God, but refused to swear by creatures including relics, the saints, and the Bible.[17] The evidence of the alterations made in the *Pore Caitif* indicates that the scribes responsible for the Group II manuscripts found the materials on forswearing on the Bible offensive and excised them.

COMPOSITION OF THE APOSTLES' CREED

Since this material has been noted more fully elsewhere,[18] I will just briefly record here the passage in the Group I manuscripts which was rejected, and the adjustments made in the manuscripts of Group II. The point of contention was the legend that each of the twelve apostles contributed a specific article to the Creed. Almost universally accepted in the Middle Ages, it was a favourite subject in stained glass, sculpture, and illumination, each apostle carrying an emblem with his particular clause.[19] The first tract of the *Pore Caitif*, 'The Bileeue', opens with an introductory consideration of the virtue of faith. The Group I manuscripts then describe the circumstances

[16]   In *Officio regis*, 218, he noted briefly that oaths are lawful. In *De mandatis divinis*, 192, he treated swearing under the second commandment and labelled thoughtless swearing one of the ways God's name is taken in vain. In the same place he cited conditions under which swearing was lawful (195-6), the three false excuses usually made to justify swearing (203-4) and affirmed that the commandment forbids swearing by any created thing unless such is demanded by truth and expedience (202). Many of these same points appear in the *Pore Caitif* and other tracts on the commandments, nor were they original with Wycliffe; they had become theological commonplaces. Wycliffe's Sermon LIII repeats many of these distinctions (*Sermones*, IV, 415, 417). In his later treatise, *Opus evangelium*, Wycliffe shifted his position somewhat, saying it was difficult to follow St Augustine in allowing oaths, for they are sometimes required for the sake of truth or expediency (180). His citing of James 5:12 and Mt 5:33-7, and of John Chrysostom on swearing as idolatry expresses again his hesitancy in permitting the taking of oaths (185-7).

[17]   'Lollard Opposition to Oaths by Creatures', *American Historical Review* 51 (1946), 668. This distinction is clearly stated in 'The Twenty-five Articles', Arnold, III, 483, and *The Lanterne of Liʒt*, 89. Another passage in the latter work outlines alternatives should the oath be refused, 88. The jurist's list of questions in Bishop Polton's *Register* specifically asks the defendant if swearing on a book is licit ('The Examination of Lollards', 154). The account of William Thorpe's trial records his refusal to swear on the Bible, and the consequences: *Fifteenth Century Prose and Verse*, ed. Alfred W. Pollard (New York, n.d.), 112, 121. In the topic 'Iuramentum' in the *Floretum* there are statements on the instances in which swearing is lawful or unlawful, the same Scripture quotations, and the same citations of canon law on blasphemy, and the false excuses for swearing (MS Bodley 448, ff. 113^r-113^v).

[18]   Cf. my article 'The Apostles and the Creed in Manuscripts of *The Pore Caitif*', *Speculum* 32 (1957), 323-5 and also Curt. F. Bühler's study, 'The Apostles and the Creed', *Speculum* 28 (1953), 335-339.

[19]   J. N. Kelly, *Early Christian Creeds* (New York, 1972), 4.

of composition of the Creed and assign the formulation of the first article to
St Peter:

> Aftir þe Assencioun of Ihesu Crist, þe Hooli Goost tauȝte þe
> apostlis al truþe needful to soule, & bi þe teching of him þei twelue
> settiden togidir twelue articlis, þe whiche alle þat wolen be saued
> moten stidfastli bileeue. Þe ffirst article of þe bileeue Seynt Petir
> puttide into þe crede bi teching of þe Hooli Goost, seiynge in þis
> wise: I bileeue in God Fadir almyȝti, maker of heuene & of erþe.
>
> (f. 4ʳ)

Each apostle is, in turn, credited with the contribution of an article, in the
following order: Andrew, James son of Zebedee, John, Thomas, James son
of Alpheus, Philip, Bartholomew, Matthew, Simon, Jude, and Matthias.
MSS C, K, M, N[1], N[2] and B of Group II protest the ascription of the articles
to particular apostles:

> Aftir þe Ascencioun of Ihesu Crist, þe Hooli Goost tauȝte þe
> apostlis al truþe needful to soule, & bi þe techinge of him þei XII
> settiden togidere XII articlis, þe whiche alle þat wolen be saued
> moten stidfastly bileeuen. But muse we not what apostil made which
> partie eiþer article of þis holi crede, but bileeue we stidfastli þat þe
> Holy Goost tauȝte it in hem alle.   (MS K, f. 3ᵛ)

A rubric 'ffirst article' introduces the Creed and the Latin text with English
translation of the article follows. Both the clause 'muse we not' and the
format of Latin text with English translation are characteristic of Lollard
practice in written exposition.[20]

Group II MSS Y and A[2] also omit the legend. The sentence 'But muse we
not ...' is absent; here, the equivalent introductory passage reads:

> Þerfore aftir þe Assencioun of Ihesu Crist, þe Holy Goost tauȝte þe
> apostlis al treuþe þat was needful to hem, & so bi techinge of þe
> Holy Goost þe twelue settiden togidere twelue articlis of þe crede, þe
> which alle þo þat wolen be saued moten stidfastely bileue. Þe first
> article is seid þus: (MS Y, f. 25ᵛ)

The remaining articles are cited by number and only in English.

The truth of the legend was questioned by Laurentius Valla at the Council
of Florence in 1438[21] and shortly after by Reginald Pecock,[22] but even before
them, objections were stirring in Lollard circles. Lambeth Palace MS 408 and
York Minster MS XVI.L.12 both contain a Lollard tract on the Creed which
also omits the identification of a particular article of faith with a specific
apostle. The text of this Creed is part of the Lollard version of Thoresby's

---

[20]   I am indebted to Dr Anne Hudson for her observation that 'muse we not' was a
clause characteristically used by the Lollards.
[21]   Kelly, 4-5.
[22]   R. H. Bower mentions a 'growing spiritual awareness' in men like Wycliffe and
Pecock toward the acceptance of the apostolic authorship of the Creed in 'Three
Middle English Poems on the Apostles' Creed', *PMLA* LXX (1955), 210.

Catechism[23] and is that printed by Arnold.[24] The rejection of the legend is worded almost identically as in MSS C, K, M, N[1], N[2] and B:

> Ne bysy we vs what þe apostyl made, ne what party of þis holy
> Crede, and whan þe apostelys gaderyd yt. For oure beleue techis vs
> þat God ordeynyd hyt al, and bad þat men schuld cun hyt and teche
> yt to oþer and ʒif prelatys faylyn in þis Crist seyde þat stonys
> schulde crye and secler lordys schuld in defawte of prelatys lerne and
> preche þe law of God in here modyr tonge. Ne study we nat how
> many partyes be in þis holy crede. For soþ it is þat alle þese partyes
> ben contenyd in thre.[25]

The full introduction here is of particular interest, because in addition to omitting the legend of apostolic authorship, it also rejects the time of composition and insists that if prelates fail to teach the Creed to the people, secular lords must do so and in the vernacular. In hindsight, we may observe that the Lollards were ahead of their time in rejecting the legend.

PREACHING

The materials just examined concerned issues long associated with the Lollards and their methodology in dealing with them was omission and insertion. Alterations in topics to be looked at now are less controversial and take the form of added *catenae* of quotations from Scripture, the Church Fathers, and later writers. This, too, was a characteristic technique they employed.

While preaching was one of the central issues of the Lollards with ecclesiastical authorities, there is nothing in the materials added to the *Pore Caitif* that reflects this controversy. The duty of priests to instruct and admonish the people by frequent preaching is treated in the *Pore Caitif* under the topic of 'goostly manslauʒtir' in the exposition of the fifth commandment. A subdivision, 'goostly manslauʒtir of mouþ', is defined as false flattery of others or praise of their sin and wickedness, together with the failure to warn them of danger or reprove their faults 'eþir for dreed eþir for couetise'. And the terse observation is added: 'in þis maner manslauʒtir ben summe prechours gilti' (f. 37[r]). In another subdivision, 'manslauʒtir of necligence eþir richelished', Ezechiel 3:17 is quoted to 'ech curat eþir prest': 'If þou spekist not to þe peple þat a wickid man kepe him fro his yuel weie, he shal die in hise wickidnessis; forsoþe, I shal seke his blood of þin hond.' (f. 39[v]) Here, the Group I manuscripts conclude the subject, but MSS C, K, N[1] and N[2] add a *catena* of quotations that reinforces the priest's duty to preach to the people:

---

[23]   *The Lay Folks Catechism*, 14-18.
[24]   III, 114-16.
[25]   *The Lay Folks Catechism*, 14-15. The article, 'Fides', in the *Floretum* does have a reference to particular apostles contributing specific articles, but the order is not the same as that in the *Pore Caitif* (MS Bodley 448, f. 81rb).

Þerfore seiþ Seint Ysidre: prestis schulen ben dampnyd for wickednes of þe peple if þei techen noȝt hem þat ben vnkonnyng eiþer blamen not hem þat ben synners. And þerfore seiþ Seint Grigori in þe comoun lawe þat euery man þat neiȝeþ to presthode takiþ upon him þe office of prechyng; for as he seiþ, þat prest terriþ God to grete wraþþe of whos mouth is not herd þe vois of prechyng. Ffor bi witnesse of Crist him self and also of his blessid apostlis & oþere seintis and docturus it is þe cheef dette and charge of euery prest in as muche as in hym is for to make þe lawe of God knowen to þe peple boþe bi holy lyuynge and trewe prechyng ffor as þe grete doctour Odo seiþ, as muche as a prest profiteþ with his good lyuynge, as muche he harmeþ wiþ his scilence. And þerfore God seiþ bi his prophete Isaye: crie and ceesse not, as a trumpe enhaunce þou þi vois and schewe to my peple her synnes. And eft God witnessiþ bi his prophete Ezechiel seiynge þus, for soþe, ȝif þou hast schewede eiþer spoken to a wicked man þat he kepe hym fro his wickednes and he wil not be turned fro his synne & fro his wicked weye, he schal deie in his wickednes, but þou forsoþe hast delyuered þin owne soule. (MS N, pp. 85-87)

A second interpolated passage on preaching occurs in the exposition of the seventh article of the Creed, 'He shal come to iuge þe liuyng and þe deed.' Various groups called to give an account at the last judgment will include churchmen who failed to preach the gospel by word and example. In the Group I manuscripts the section is as follows: 'Also þe prelat eþir curat shal acoumpte for hise sugetis, hou he haþ tauȝt hem bi lyuyng & bi word, as God seiþ bi his prophete.' (f. 10ʳ) Ezechiel is not named in the text, nor is the quotation supplied. MSS C, K, M, N¹ and N², however, cite Ezechiel as the author of the quotation, give the text, and add the gloss:

Also þe prelat eþir curat schal acounte for hise sugettis, how he haþ tauȝt hem bi lyuynge & bi word, as God witnessiþ bi his profete Ezechiel seiynge þus: If þou spekist not to a wickid man þat he kepe him from his yuel wey, he schal die in his wickidnes, forsoþe I schal seke his blood of þin hond, þat is as þe glose seiþ, þat prest þat prechiþ not truly & bisili to þe peple þe word of God schal be partiner of her dampnacioun which perischen in his defaute.

(MS K, f. 9ʳ)

There are no characteristically Lollard positions defended in the passages on preaching: no demand that laymen be permitted to preach, no plea for plain style, no objection to the required licensing of preachers. Later Lollard tracts would again quote Ezechiel, Isaiah and Gregory when dealing more strongly with the failure of prelates, curates and friars to fulfil the duty of preaching. They would voice objection to the required oath to refrain from attacking clerical offences, and argue that friars were licensed to preach fables but true men were barred from preaching the gospel as Christ commanded.[26] But the

[26] Wycliffe considered preaching the most important duty of the priest, to be preferred to Mass and the Divine Office (*Sermones*, II, 115; III, 74-5; *Polemical Works*, II, 405-607; *Opus Evangelium*, I, 42). Preaching was to be in English

only passages infiltrated here are the piled-up citations from Isidore, Gregory, Odo, Isaiah and Ezechiel. Recent studies of Margaret Aston and Anne Hudson on the political and social implications of Lollard literacy and use of the vernacular have provided new insights on their 'sedition' and 'heresy' and have done much to explain the fear and animosity they encountered.[27] The Lollards' strong commitment to preaching was obviously a major contributing factor to the opposition they met.

SUFFERING PERSECUTION

In two places in the Group I manuscripts, there are brief references to suffering persecution, and in both of these, several Group II manuscripts insert additional materials. The first instance occurs in 'Þe Hors and Armer of Heuene' where the reader is invited to reflect on the pains of hell and purgatory, that through fear of punishment he be dissuaded from sin. Toward the end of the section on purgatory, a statement in the Group I manuscripts notes that some have their purgatory on earth:

> Summe soulis ben clensid here & han her purgatorie with fier of tribulacioun & persecucioun, mekeli suffringe for þe truþe of God, and moche disese han for þei wolden lyue wel... (f. 100[r])

MSS C, K, M, N[1], W[1] and X[2] reinforce the passage with three quotations from Scripture on suffering persecution:

> & þerfore Seint Poul seiþ, alle þo men þat wolen lyue meekly eþir feiþfulli in Crist Ihesu schulen suffren persecucioun. Wherfore Crist seiþ him silf, Blessid ben þei þat suffren persecucioun for riȝtwisnes, for þe kingdom of heuenes is hern. & in anoþir place it is writen þat bi manye tribulaciouns it bihoueþ us to entre into þe kingdom of God. (MS K, f. 84[v])

Likewise, in the *Pore Caitif* tract 'Of Vertuous Pacience', the importance of patient suffering of tribulation that can 'enforgen to us a coroun' is stressed, 'for which þing hooli men louen tribulaciouns, for bi meke suffryng of hem þei knowe to come to euerlastyng ioie' (f. 83[r]). To this passage, MSS C, K,

(*Sermones*, II, 230; III, 115, 257, 270; *De Virtute Sacrae Scripturae*, II, 243); and in a plain style (*Sermones*, IV, 268-270). His declaration that laymen should be permitted to preach without licensing was condemned as erroneous at the Synod at Blackfriars (Thomas Walsingham, *Historia Anglicana*, ed. Henry T. Riley (London, 1863-4), II, 59). The later Lollard positions cited can be found in 'Of Prelates' in Matthew 105; nos. 7 and 10 of the 'Sixteen Points' in *Selections from English Wycliffite Writings*, 19, 22-3; and no. 6 of 'The Twenty-five Articles' in Arnold, III, 464; in 'Of Prelates', 65, 58; 'Of Feigned Contemplative Life', 188; 'How Satan and His Priests', 271 all in Matthew; Gregory, Isidore and Ezechiel are quoted in the *Floretum* under the topic 'Praedicare' in MS Bodley 448, f. 194[ra].
[27] Margaret Aston, 'Literacy and Sedition', *Past and Present* 17 (1960), 1-44; and *Lollards and Reformers: Images and Literacy in Late Medieval Religion* (London, 1984), especially chapter 6; Anne Hudson, 'Lollardy: the English Heresy?', *Studies in Church History* 18 (1982), 261-283.

M and N[1] add another quotation on suffering: 'for holi writ seiþ þat bi manie tribulaciouns it bihoueþ us to entre into þe kyngdom of God' (MS K, f. 71ᵛ)

Again, no controversial position is expressed, but the additional materials are interesting in light of the ecclesiastical and civil condemnation of Wycliffe and the Lollards.[28] The content of the interpolations resembles more the references in the English sermons than it does the later Lollard tracts; both the interpolations in the *Pore Caitif* and the sermons use the same scriptural quotations in a context of encouraging and strengthening those who were suffering persecution.[29]

MISCELLANEOUS TOPICS

The materials to be looked at now would hardly be labelled Lollard insertions if they had not surfaced in the collating of the manuscripts. While they certainly reflect the sect's propensity to supply *catenae* of quotations for given topics, they also seem to indicate particular interest in the obligation of parents to discipline their children, the duties of the married state, the just treatment of the working man, and the precept to observe the commandments.

1. Disciplining Children

In the exposition of the seventh article of the Creed, 'He shal come to iuge þe livyng & þe deed', space is allocated to a detailed account of the final judgment. Categories of people are identified who must account for their stewardship. The Group I manuscripts state that 'Þe fadir & þe modir shulen acoumpte for her child þat is unchastisid, as it is expresid in hooli writt, how Heli was poneshid for his sones bi cause þat he chastisid hem not as he shulde haue do.' (f. 10ʳ) MSS C, K and N[1] expand this slightly: '... how Heli þe prest was ponishid bi sodein & foul deeþ. ȝhe, and as clerkis seien

---

[28] For full accounts of the persecution of Wycliffe and the Lollards see: Thomas Walsingham, *Historia Anglicana*; *Fasciculi Zizaniorum*; Joseph Dahmus, *The Prosecution of John Wyclif* (New Haven, 1952); 'Lollardy and Sedition'; Gordon Leff, 'John Wyclif: The Path to Dissent', *Proceedings of the British Academy* 52 (1966), 143-180; Michael Wilks, 'Reformatio Regni: Wyclif and Hus as Leaders of Religious Protest Movements', *Studies in Church History* 9 (1972), 109-130; *The Later Lollards*, especially chapter 11.

[29] Sermon LII of the English Sermons, for example, quotes Christ's warning to his faithful followers of persecutions to come, making application to the situation 'þus now among Cristene men'. They are to study God's law, remember this prophecy, and know they are true disciples, although 'of þer ende þei ben uncerteyn' (Arnold, I, 154). Sermon LXVI assembles quotations from the Gospels that warn of persecutions to come (Arnold, I, 208-9). The later Lollard writings make frequent complaints that 'pore prestis' are being slandered, imprisoned as heretics, and hindered from preaching the truth of Christ's gospel. Cf. 'Of Clerks Possessioners', 119, 130, 134; 'The Order of Priesthood', 177; 'Of Servants and Lords', 237; 'Of Poor Preaching Priests', 279; 'Of Prelates', 87, 88, 94 in Matthew.

þat he is dampned for þat he chastiside not hise sones as he schulde haue doon.' (MS C, f. 10ʳ) MSS M and N² also have the insertion, but they omit 'and as clerkis ... dampned'. MS B, however, has a unique addition on the duties of parents to chastise their children:[30]

> Also þe fadir & þe modir schulen acounte for her child þat is unchastisid as it is expresly schewid in hooly writ hou Heli þe preest þoru necligence þat he chastiside not his sones as he schulde haue doon; þerfore, as þe storie telliþ, he fel doun bakward & brak his necke & þerfore as þe wiseman seiþ, bettre is to haue o child dredinge God þan a þousand wickide. And eft he seiþ, bettre it were to a man to die withoute children þan to leue wickid children bihynde hym & untauȝt, for þe folie of þe child schal be into sorowe to þe fadir & modir. And þerfore he techiþ men & wymmen to chastice her children seiynge he þat loueþ his child wol bisili chastise hym; for þouȝ þou smyte hym with a ȝerd, he schal not die. Chastise þou hym wiþ a ȝerd & þou schalt delyuere his soule fro helle. Þerfore medful is resonable chastisynge þe which is don wiþ loue & drede of God & for saluacioun of soule.
> (MS B, ff. 12ᵛ-13ʳ)

2. Chastity in the Married State

Another example of an inserted passage apparently of interest to the Lollards, concerns the married state. It occurs in the section of the sixth commandment at the conclusion of a biblical *exemplum* on Sara and Tobias which stressed the lust of Sara's previous husbands and the chastity of Tobias. The manuscripts of Group I pass from this story to a citation of Peter and Paul's teaching 'þat weddid men & wymen shulden in hooli tyme & in tyme of her preier, absteynen hem fro such lustis lest her preier be not graciousli herd of God bi cause of her fleshly delite' (f. 42ʳ). MSS C, K, M, N¹ and N² have at the conclusion of the passage on Sara and Tobias, however, the following insertion:

> And þerfore as a grete doctour seiþ, þe sacrament of wedlok stondiþ in þre principal þingis, þat is feiþ, children & chastite. For as Seint Bede seiþ, it is a foul abhomynacoun a man for to loue eiþer neiȝe his wyf eiþer a womman to hir housbonde for vnfrutful fleischli lust, for þus doon horlyngis & strumpetis. And þerfore weddide men & wymmen & also þei þat purposen to be weddide schulden take ensaumple of þat holy man Tobie how þei schulden use her wedlok in loue & drede of God and not for her fleischli lustis, ffor he seiþ: Lord God, þou wost eiþer knowest þat not bi cause of lecherie eiþer for fleischly lust I take my suster, but oonly þoru loue and drede to brynge forþ fruyt þat þi name, Lord, be blesside herbi in to worldis of worldis. And þerfore it sueþ here of þat who euer in matrimonie

---

[30] Similar materials can be found in 'Of Weddid Men and Wemmen and of her Children', MS Bodley 938, ff. 68ʳ-70ʳ; and in the *Floretum* under 'Filium', MS Bodley 448, ff. 83ʳ-83ᵛ.

suen oþer wyse in ony tyme her fleischly lustis synnen in lecherie, brekynge þe holy relygious chastite of wedlok. Also alle weddide folkis owen as seyntis seien, to kepe hem chast in solempne halidayes & ny3tis, as Sondaies & Cristmasse day and suche oþere hei3e festis. And also þei scholden absteyne hem in tyme of penaunce doynge for whanne men halowen & fasten, þei schulden be ful deuout in preiers absteynynge hem þanne fro alle suche fleischely werkis. (MS N¹, pp. 91-92)

All five manuscripts then pick up the citation of the apostles' teaching, smoothly making reference to the fact they have just alluded to it. The later Lollard tract 'Of Weddid Men and Wymmen and her Children' which occurs in the midst of the *Pore Caitif* tracts in MS Bodley 938 (X¹), has a few points similar to the quoted passage. The article 'Matrimonium' in the *Floretum* distinguishes three goods of matrimony as faith, sacrament, and children (MS Bodley 448, f.137vb). Although the addition is only an expansion of a theme from Scripture and two supporting theologians, it indicates a strong interest in 'states of life' materials and in speaking to the practical instructional needs of the laity that can be documented in other Lollard tracts.

3. Workmen's Wages

A brief passage toward the end of the exposition of the seventh commandment warns against withholding the workman's wages. In the Group I manuscripts it reads:

And no man with wrong withholde þe werkmannes hire, for þat is oon of þe foure synnes þat euere crieþ veniaunce bifore God, as Seynt Iame seiþ. (f. 46^r)

Here, MSS C, K, M, N¹, N², B and W¹ reinforce the teaching with two biblical references cited also in the *Floretum* f. 116^r, under 'Labor'.

And þerfore, God seiþ in þe þridde book of Holi Writ: Lat not þe hire of þin hired man dwelle wiþ þee ouer ni3t unto þe moorun. Also, þe holy man Tobie tau3te his son seynge: Mi sone, whanne ony man haþ wrou3te oughte to þee, anoon 3ilde þou hym his mede eiþer his hire. (MS N¹, p. 99)

Both this insertion and the one following merely expand the topic by additional scriptural quotations.

4. Obedience to the Commandments

Some observations on the necessity of keeping the commandments occur at the conclusion of the tract on the *Pater Noster*, reinforcing a quotation from John 14:15. The Group I manuscripts repeat the verse, supporting it further with two additional passages:

... who so loueþ him shal kepe his word. And þe wise man seiþ þat

he þat turneþ awei his eere þat he heere not goddis word, his preier
shal be cursid. And Seynt Poul seiþ, he is cursid þat loueþ not Ihesu
Crist.   (ff. 78ʳ-78ᵛ)

MSS C, K, M, N¹ and N² after 'his word' in l. 1 above, insert four supportive
quotations:

And eft he seiþ he þat bileueþ in me schal do þe werkis þat I do.

And efte Crist seiþ ʒif ʒe louen me, kepe ʒe myn comaundementis.

And eft he seiþ, he þat haþ my comaundementis and kepiþ hem, he
it is þat loueþ me.

And þerfore seiþ Seint Ioon, In þis þing we wityn þat we knowen
God, if we kepen his comaundementis; for he þat seiþ þat he
knoweþ God and kepiþ not hise comaundementis, he is a lier and
truþe is not in him.   (MS N¹, pp. 160-1)

They then resume with the quotations from Proverbs 28:9 and 1 Corinthians
16:22 in the Group I manuscripts, and insert a final addition which MSS B
and W¹ also have: 'And þe profete Dauiþ seiþ, Cursid ben þei þat bowen
awei fro þin heestes.' (MS C, ff. 78ʳ-78ᵛ)

5. Anti-Prelatical Satire

A final case of Lollard influence on a text will be mentioned. Westminster
School MS 3 (W²), dating from the mid-fifteenth century, is a large anthology
with a number of orthodox religious selections and several tracts with
Lollard connections. It contains one full tract from the *Pore Caitif* and
portions of two others. The complete 'Mirrour of Chastite' occupies folios
153ʳ-162ᵛ. Three almost jocular emendations occur in the fifth chapter of
this work, each employing the same refrain. The *Pore Caitif* compiler draws
passages from the Breviary to praise five virgin martyrs. In his account of
St Lucy he used a section from the first lesson of Matins, a portion of which
reads: 'She vndirstood þe gospel of Crist whanne she herde it rad.' (f. 133ʳ)
MS W² adds: 'wiþouten leue of onie prelatis' (f. 161ʳ). The second instance
occurs in his quotation from the first nocturne for the feast of St Cecilia who
'euere bar in hir herte hid Cristis gospel; neþir daies neþir nyʒtis ceesside
she fro Goddis spechis' (f. 134ʳ). MS W² adds again: 'wiþouten leeue of ony
prelatis' (f. 161ᵛ). The third occurrence, also in an excerpt from the breviary,
praises her for her good deeds, mentioning: '& bi hir weren baptisid in hir
hous mo þan foure hundrid men & wymmen' (f. 134ᵛ). Once more, the
scribe of MS W² added: 'wiþouten leue of ony prelatis' (f. 161ᵛ). The scribe's
insertions are undoubtedly linked to the mid-fifteenth-century ecclesiastical
climate; obviously provoking the remarks were the English church's
opposition to vernacular scripture and to preaching and administering the
sacraments without licence, and the prelates' efforts to stamp out Lollard
abuses.

A second small instance of infiltration may be the curious slip in the
opening section of 'Þe Chartir of Heuene'. Each man is here urged to study

'þe witt of þis bulle, for þe pardoun þerof shal dure withoute eende' (f. 86ʳ). The W² scribe added, 'And þerfore leuynge fals chartirs of stynkyng parchemyn wiþ roten selis' (f. 112ʳ). A series of dots underlines the phrase signifying it is to be deleted. Either the scribe thought better of what he wrote, or a corrector marked it for omission. What is of particular interest here in MS W², is that the presence of Lollard works in the manuscript and the brief comments made within the *Pore Caitif* tracts indicate the type of climate in which the *Pore Caitif* was circulating in the mid-fifteenth century.

The collations indicate that the manuscripts with Lollard insertions and omissions fall into several groups. To the largest of these, A¹, C, K, M, N¹ and N² must be added a manuscript from which only two folia survive. A single leaf, Bodley eng. th. C. 50, and another single leaf, Bodley eng. th. E 1, are catalogued separately, but script, ink, rubrics, running titles and paraphs, and identical format (twenty-six lines per folio in a written space of 143mm by 96mm) indicate that both derive from the same manuscript. The first-named contains an excerpt from the *Pore Caitif* 'Chartir of Heuene'; the second has the conclusion of the 'Chartir' and the beginning of 'Þe Hors eþir Armer of Heuene'. Although no directly Lollard opinions are expressed in the surviving fragments, collations show they match the Lollard group cited above in twelve small deviations. It is interesting, though fruitless, to speculate how many other manuscripts may have had similar Lollard passages and did not survive.

The Pore Caitif is in illustrious company in numbering manuscripts that suffered tampering at the hands of scribes with Lollard opinions. Other popular treatises with wide circulation that shared the same fate included *The Pricke of Conscience*, Rolle's *Psalter* and *Canticles*, Archbishop Thoresby's *Catechism*, and a version of the *Ancrene Riwle*.[31] Reflecting on this type of Lollard interpolation, Margaret Aston commented recently that it probably served to undermine their opponents' positions and to disseminate their own sectarian views under cover of orthodox titles. In that way they reached unsuspecting readers who would have avoided contact with openly heretical works.[32] Obviously, to write or even possess a Lollard manuscript in the fifteenth century was dangerous. Infiltration of popular

---

[31] For comments on *The Pricke of Conscience*, cf. Hope Emily Allen, *Writings Ascribed to Richard Rolle, Hermit of Hampole, and Materials for His Biography* (New York, 1927), 191-2. For Rolle's *Psalter* and *Canticles* see Allen, 190, and Dorothy Everett, 'The Middle English Prose *Psalter* of Richard Rolle of Hampole', *MLR* 17 (1922), 217-227, 337-350; and *MLR* 18 (1923), 381-393. The collaborative edition of Rolle's *Psalter* in a series of Fordham University doctoral dissertations is restricted to manuscripts of the orthodox text. Two, however, include a sampling of interpolated comments in appendices: Jerry D. Cavallerano, *Richard Rolle's English Psalter, Psalms 31-45* (Fordham University, 1976), appendix II; and Sandra S. Newton, *An Edition of Richard Rolle's English Psalter, the Prologue through Psalm XV with Introductory Notes and Glossary* (Fordham University, 1976), appendix II. The Lollard interpolations in Thoresby's *Catechism* are in *The Lay Folks Catechism*, ed. Thomas F. Simmons and Henry E. Nolloth, EETS os 118 (London, 1901). For insertions in *Ancrene Riwle* see Edmund Colledge, '*The Recluse*: A Lollard Interpolated Version of the *Ancrene Riwle*', *RES* 15 (1979), 1-15, 129-145.

[32] *Lollards and Reformers*, 211-12.

orthodox treatises was preferable.

But the question arises, was the Lollard infiltration of the *Pore Caitif* an organised effort? Dr A. I. Doyle thinks not, from indications of ownership of extant manuscripts. While the copyists 'included some of Lollard associations', he believes it 'would be mistaken to conceive of any clear division of such literature and the public on partisan lines'. The manuscripts with the Lollard intrusions were not the 'property of a distinct sect'.[33] Peryn Clanvowe, wife of the 'Lollard sympathiser' Sir Thomas Clanvowe, bequeathed a copy in her will in 1422, but the basic 'proof' of Clanvowe's Lollardy was the ownership of *The Pore Caitif*.[34] Other owners of copies seem to have been clergy, convents of religious women and a literate laity. Two studies on some additional aspects of the Lollard associations of *The Pore Caitif* on which I am currently engaged, may possibly shed some further light on this question, and provide a scenario that can help to account for the dynamics of the interpolations.

The identity of the compiler also remains a mystery. He was probably a cleric, a man of learning particularly interested in the instruction of the people in the basic elements of their faith and in prayer, and with a strong interest in the writings of Richard Rolle. He must have had available a well-stocked theological library and was concerned that a wider audience have access to such materials. He was orthodox on points being challenged in Lollard circles, and, based on selections he incorporated into his treatise, must have had a good ear for English prose. Most likely he never knew the full extent of the peregrinations destined for his text when he launched it into the world in the late fourteenth century with some such directive as 'Go, litel bok.'

---

[33] A. I. Doyle, 'A Survey of the Origins and Circulation of Theological Writings in English in the 14th, 15th and Early 16th Centuries with Special Consideration of the Part of the Clergy Therein' (Ph.D. Dissertation, University of Cambridge, 1953), 50.
[34] *The Fifty Earliest English Wills in the Court of Probate, London, A.D.1387-1439*, ed. Frederick J. Furnivall, EETS os 78 (London, 1882), 50. Cf. also Herbert B. Workman, *John Wyclif: A Study of the English Medieval Church* (Oxford, 1926), II, 392.

I am grateful to my colleagues Dr Martha Driver and Dr Lawrence Hundersmarck for reading the manuscript of this paper and offering suggestions.

THE POMANDER OF PRAYER:
ASPECTS OF LATE MEDIEVAL
ENGLISH CARTHUSIAN SPIRITUALITY
AND ITS LAY AUDIENCE

Rev. Robert A. Horsfield

The treatise *The Pomander of Prayer*, published on the eve of English Reformation, has survived as a complete work on the subject of private prayer. It was written in English by an author who has so far remained anonymous and, as far as is known, exists only in printed form. The four extant editions were published in 1528, 1530, 1531, and 1532, dates which suggest that the book enjoyed some popularity in its day.[1]

Its striking title was to cause confusion in identifying the author since it was later adopted by the Protestant writer Thomas Becon (c.1513-67), who published his work, *The Pomander of Prayer*, in 1558.[2] By the year 1578 his treatise had run through at least five editions and the title had changed to *The Pomander of Prayers*.[3] Becon's work differed greatly from the earlier *Pomander* both in content and tone. Becon's was a small pocket-size printed collection of some sixty prayers which were suitable for almost every conceivable occasion and could be used by different orders of society. Becon was both a renowned preacher who had studied under Latimer, and a prolific writer with some forty books to his name, whose works enjoyed a wide popularity on religious subjects promoting the Protestant cause. By contrast this *Pomander* is a treatise on prayer and is described in its own exhortation as 'good devoute fruytfull and catholicall thinkyng'. In spite of these obvious differences and the fact that Becon would have had to have written this *Pomander* at the age of fifteen, the work has mistakenly been attributed to him. One must not overlook the point, though, that in the post Reformation years Thomas Becon's name would be quite acceptable on the flyleaf should the book fall into the hands of questioning authorities.[4] It is possible therefore that it was inserted by catholics and designed to be deliberately misleading. Perhaps this prudent concern to escape condemnation is also the explanation of the

---

[1] *The Pomander of Prayer* was printed by R. Coplande in 1528 and 1530, R. Redman in 1531 and W. de Worde in 1532. The chapters are numbered but not the pages. I have used a copy of the Redman edition deposited at the John Rylands Library, Manchester, reference 12403.

[2] For a description of T. Becon's writings see H. C. White, *The Tudor Books of Private Devotion* (Wisconsin, 1951); also D. S. Bailey, *Thomas Becon and the Reformation of the Church in England* (Edinburgh, 1952).

[3] There are copies of the editions of 1563 and 1578 in the Bodleian Library, Oxford.

[4] A copy printed by de Worde in 1532 at the John Rylands Library, Manchester, R 16430 has Thomas Becon's name written on the inside cover.

fact that in some copies the words 'pope' and 'purgatory' are crossed out in the text.

The Protestant author Becon is not the only writer to have the work attributed to him. *The Short Title Catalogue* currently lists its authorship under the name of Richard Whitford, a brother of the Bridgettine House of Syon.[5] Whitford was an author of the 1530s with a reputation for addressing his works to the specific needs and difficulties of lay people. He was a man with a varied experience of life, a friend of More and Erasmus, who before joining Syon had studied at Cambridge and Paris; and had served as chaplain to the fourth Lord Mountjoy and afterwards to Bishop Fox of Winchester, Lord Privy Seal.[6] Whitford's best known book is *A Werke for Housholders* published in 1530, a treatise which makes the house rather than the cloister or the cell of the recluse the setting for its devotional teaching.[7]

There is no mention of Whitford's name in the text of the *Pomander*. However, the treatise begins with an exhortation to the readers, the author of which is described as a brother of Syon but not named. H. C. White comments, 'the brother of Syon is not identified, but in view of the date and undertaking it is tempting to think that he was Richard Whitford. The "exhortacion" certainly sounds like him.'[8] In my view, one should resist this temptation. We know from Whitford's preface to his *Martilogue in English after the Use of the Church of Salisbury*[9] that he made it a fetish to publish under his own name. He does so not for reasons of ambition but rather 'to offer myself unto correction'. He further complains that anonymity means that authors can write heresy and not be identified. In the light of such strongly held views we must exercise restraint in attributing the anonymous exhortation to Whitford, let alone the text.

A cursory reading of the *Pomander* might suggest that the use of the word 'wretche' in the text points to Whitford since he was fond of referring to himself as 'the wretche of Syon', a phrase which occurs frequently in his writings. But one should note that he usually accompanied the word 'wretche' with one or two additional words to make such expressions as 'the same wretche', 'the poor wretche', 'the same old wretche'. These phrases are not found in the *Pomander* and the use of the word 'wretche' was too commonplace in spiritual literature for us to suspect that Whitford might be the author wherever it occurs. However,

[5] A. W. Pollard and G. R. Redgrave, *A Short Title Catalogue* (revised by W. A. Jackson, F. S. Ferguson and K. Pantzer), vol. 2 (1976) ref. 25421.2.
[6] For a discussion of his writings see H. C. White, *Tudor Books* and G. Williams, 'Two Neglected London-Welsh Clerics; Richard Whitford and Richard Gwent', *Trans. of the Honourable Society of Cymmrodorion* (1961).
[7] The early translation of Thomas à Kempis' *Imitation of Christ* is often attributed to him, though Roger Lovatt suggests that may be a mistake. See Roger Lovatt, 'Imitation of Christ in Late Medieval England', *TRHS* (June 1967), p. 98 and G. Williams, 'Two Neglected London-Welsh Clerics', p. 23-32.
[8] H. C. White, *Tudor Books*, p. 153.
[9] A copy is deposited at Bodleian Library, Oxford (printed 1526/7).

we do know from his *Werke for Housholders* that he had a sympathy and understanding of family problems and that he made definite efforts in his writings to meet some of the difficulties encountered by lay and secular Christians. The *Pomander* would fit into this category of writing and it is the kind of literature which Whitford would wish to promulgate; but although this shows why Whitford's name is connected with it, there is no firm evidence that he wrote either the exhortation or the text.

The strongest evidence for claiming Carthusian authorship is the clear statement by the author of the 'exhortacion' that 'the drawer and auctoure of it [the *Pomander*] is one of the devoute fathers of the Charterhous of Shene whose virtue and lernyng is well approved'.[10] Two further references point to an association with the Order. Whilst these cannot be claimed as definitive in establishing Carthusian authorship on their own, in conjunction with the explicit statement just mentioned they have some weight. First, in the earliest copy of the *Pomander* owned by Lord Kenyon, there is on the title page a woodcut of a Carthusian kneeling at the foot of the Cross.[11] It should also be noticed that on the verso of the title page there is a woodcut of St Bridget of Sweden, a drawing which appears in several books by Whitford, having a special meaning for him since Syon was a Bridgettine House. The second reference is to a holy contemplative father who in his contemplation sees the soul of a Carthusian lifted up to heaven in the presence of glorious angels and saints where it was magnificently glorified for its past deeds. He was especially rewarded for remembering one of the blessed wounds of Our Saviour Jesus Christ 'at the time of saying his service'.[12] Knowles quotes Richard Methley's practice at Mount Grace of 'thanking God each morning, as he put on his habit, for the gift of his Carthusian vocation, and bearing witness to the esteem in which the order was held by all'.[13] This reference in the *Pomander* could be a similar attitude of a Carthusian expressing the same kind of pride in his Order as that felt by Methley.

It seems to me that this treatise was associated with both Sheen Charterhouse and the Bridgettine House of Syon. F.C.Francis concludes: 'it may well be that Whitford was the "brother of Syon" who wrote the exhortacion and that he was the first to recognise its worth and get it printed. We can believe that there was frequent communication between the neighbouring religious houses of Syon and Sheen.'[14] It is some fifty years since Francis wrote those words; it is now well established that there were strong links between Sheen and Syon. They were situated directly across the Thames from each other and as Dr Sargent writes 'their histories are intertwined and they seem to have borrowed each other's

[10] *Pomander*, Exhortacion.
[11] I am grateful to Lord Kenyon for his kind permission to inspect this copy. See also reference in E.Hodnett, *English Woodcuts 1480-1535* (Oxford, 1973), Additions and Corrections, p.34, and F.C.Francis, 'Three Unrecorded English Books of the Sixteenth Century', *Library* xvii, fig.3 p.190.
[12] *Pomander*, ch.10.
[13] D.Knowles, *The Religious Orders in England*, vol.2 (Cambridge, 1957), p.226.
[14] F.C.Francis, 'Three Unrecorded English Books', p.194.

books for shared textual transmission is common'.[15]

Sheen, founded by Henry V in 1415, was the last and wealthiest Charterhouse to be built in medieval England. There is evidence to suggest that it possessed a good library[16] and also a school, although little is known of it. It was noted as the home of such scribes and annotators as Grenehalgh, Mede, Dygoun, Doddesham and Darker. From this house came the fifteenth-century work *Speculum Devotorum*[17] and the early-sixteenth-century printed compendium *Speculum Spiritualium*.[18] It was a house associated with a literary circle which included Lady Margaret Beaufort, Fisher, More and of course the neighbouring house of Syon. I suggest that it was from this charterhouse that *The Pomander of Prayer* came.

In its contemporary setting the *Pomander* stands alongside a range of literature written by a religious for lay audiences. The increased literacy, prosperity and self-consciousness of the middle classes created an ever increasing public for whom books were made available. Professor Keiser points out that the possession of a collection of devotional writings by a layman of no particular social distinction was not unusual in the fifteenth century.[19] The *Pomander*'s subject matter dealing with aspects of prayer within the framework of ordinary domestic life lived in the contemporary world was not a unique topic for instruction. However, examples of works which were written in the vernacular by English Carthusians and addressed to a lay audience are rare. The *Pomander* is an example of the late medieval practice of adapting monastic practices and traditions to meet the needs of a newly literate laity who were striving to achieve a piety outside the walls of the cloister. This 'outreach' by the English Carthusians had been developing throughout the fifteenth century. There is sufficient evidence by the time of the *Pomander* to support a threefold claim. First, some members of the Order had entered the field of theological controversy. One can cite Nicholas Love's work, *The Myrrour of the Blessed Lyf of Jesu Christ*, published in 1410, which contained passages which were critical of the Lollards. It may well be that there is something of an afterthought about these passages, as Dr Doyle suggests,[20] but the fact remains that they were by the same author and show theological concern in their warnings against Lollardy. Secondly, members of the Order had composed devotional treatises for an audience beyond the cloister.

[15] M. G. Sargent, 'The Transmission by the English Carthusians of Some Late Medieval Spiritual Writings', *JEH* 27 (1976), p. 228.
[16] E. M. Thompson, *The Carthusian Order in England* (London, 1930), p. 331ff; N. Ker, *Medieval Libraries of Great Britain*, 2nd edn (London, 1964).
[17] *Speculum Devotorum*, Cambridge UL Gg. 1. 6; ed. J. Hogg, *The Speculum Devotorum of an Anonymous Carthusian of Sheen*, Analecta Cartusiana 11-13 (1973-85).
[18] *Speculum Spiritualium* (published 1510, Paris).
[19] G. R. Keiser, 'Lincoln Cathedral Library Manuscript 91. The Life and Milieu of a Scribe', *Studies in Bibliography* 32 (1979), 169-172.
[20] A. I. Doyle, 'Reflections of some manuscripts of Nicholas Love's *Myrrour of the Blessed Lyf of Jesu Christ*', *Essays in Memory of Elizabeth Salter*, Leeds Studies in English XIV (1983), p. 82ff.

Dr J. Hogg tells us that Richard Methley's *To Hew Heremyte* is clearly a reply to a request for spiritual guidance from a hermit, not a Carthusian. Dr J. Hogg also suggests that Methley's reputation as a spiritual director extended beyond the confines of the cloister.[21] Thirdly, as Dr Sargent and Dr Doyle have shown, the Order had distributed manuscripts and literature beyond the confines of the monastery.[22] The effect of this activity was to break down their isolation and give some credibility to the monastic ideal at a time when the standing of many other orders in England was low. The fact that the *Pomander* ran into four editions within a space of five years supports the claim that the Carthusians had an audience enthusiastic for their work.

From its content it is clear that the author of the *Pomander* has in mind prayer for the ordinary person in the world. However cloistered himself, his audience was not monastic: for instance, in explaining his reasons for writing the *Pomander* the author says, 'of late tyme I have bene instauntly desyred of certayne spirituall frendes to write some treatyse that might be inductyve and also demonstratyve to such devoute persones as lack lernyng and knowledge of holy scripture how and under what maner they might ordre them selfe in prayer'.[23] He aims to write 'for the unlerned that lack knowledge of holy scripture to instructe them in the ordre of prayer'. Later in the text he again refers to his audience ... 'and this I thynke doth fortune most ofte in good devoute people of the worlde for whom I specially wryte this treatise the which have a good mynde to serve God. But yet they have not experience of the delectable spirituall lyfe nor dyde never taste the swete delicious wynes of the lyfe contemplatife ...'[24] The author has in mind two levels of lay society. First, 'that man that is come of noble blode and ryall progency may be at lyberte to frequentate the churche and other secrete places at his pleasure for his devocion'.[25] Secondly, 'other men that be of inferiour degrees whether they be merchantes yeomen or craftesmen or of what condicion so ever they be they can not be excused but they may use moche prayer if they wyll'.[26] For both groups the author recommends such prayers as 'Jesu make me to love the with all my herte and al my soule' and 'Jesu have mercy upon me and forgyve me all my synnes'[27] – prayers which can be said at any time and in any place. He explains of the second group, 'For if they be rydyng or goying in journey they may have space ynough therto if they be at home at theyr occupacions or sellynge of theyr ware yet may they use suche shorte

---

[21]   R. Methley, *To Hew Heremyte*, ed. J. Hogg, Analecta Cartusiana 31 (1977), p. 101, and J. Hogg, *Mount Grace Charterhouse and Late Medieval English Spirituality*, Analecta Cartusiana (1980), p. 31.

[22]   M. G. Sargent, 'Transmission'; A. I. Doyle, 'A Survey of the Origins and Circulation of Theological Writings in English in the 14th, 15th, and early 16th Century', D. Phil. dissertation (Cambridge, 1953).

[23]   *Pomander*, The Prologue.

[24]   *Pomander*, ch. 5, p. 3.

[25]   *Pomander*, ch. 3, p. 7.

[26]   *Pomander*, ch. 3.

[27]   *Ibid.*

praiers as I have before sayd: in theyr shoppes or other places where they be.'[28] I note that a feature of the *Pomander* which is illustrated in these and other passages, is the author's use of the third person pronoun. It usually occurs in descriptive passages which relate to the main theme and illustrates a general point about prayer. Could this indicate that the first audience of the book is those who would instruct the laity?

The author explains his choice of the title *The Pomander of Prayer* by saying that just as a pomander when warmed gives off a fragrant smell, so he hopes for a 'fragrant smell of spiritual conversation and lyving to the devoute readers of it'. He hopes that readers will not be content with one reading of it but will keep it by them and read it time and time again. He explains his reasons for writing in English and not Latin because he was 'desyred both of lerned and unlerned to write this treatise'.[29] He apologises for his use of Latin quotations, promises to abandon them for English, but continues to quote in Latin with translation.[30]

Although the *Pomander* is, in the words of H. C. White, 'a combination of the academic with the homely and practical',[31] it is intended as an elementary text on prayer and not a work for the spiritually advanced. For that reason the author is at pains to avoid controversial theological debate. When he raises the subject of prayer for souls in purgatory he advances traditional teaching in favour of such prayers. He says that he does not wish to confute heretics, and his advice to readers, should they hear such false and erroneous doctrines, is not to argue but rather 'withdrawe your presence fro theyr company'.[32] A glance at the table of contents strengthens the view that he is writing an elementary treatise for the beginner. For example, the table of contents begins:

- The dyffynycyon of prayer
- That we shulde oft tymes use prayer
- Of the profyte that cometh by prayer
- Of iii thynges necessary to be consydered afore the begynnynge of prayer
- How there is two maners of prayers: of the whych one is called vocal, and the other mentall
- Of two thynges necessarily required to prayer

The *Pomander*'s main chapter is commonplace enough – the distinction between 'vocall and mentall prayer'.[33] Since he is a religious, he favours spoken prayers for lay folk and stresses that mental prayer is only to be used 'soberly and discretely' as it demands total concentration: 'for it is so laborous and so vyolente that within shorte space it wyll bryng a man unto such debilitacion and weykenes of brayne that it wyll cast hym in

---

[28] *Ibid.*
[29] *Ibid.*, The Prologue.
[30] *Ibid.*, The Prologue and ch. 3.
[31] H. C. White, *Tudor Books*, p. 154.
[32] *Pomander*, ch. 4, p. 4.
[33] *Ibid.*, ch. 5.

great danger of seckness or some other inconveyence'.[34] He reserves contemplative prayer for the cloister, making it clear that he considers this form of prayer to be the best: 'this prayer is of great excellency and dignity and is the very true and faithfull ambassadour between god and manes soule'.

I suggest that these passages underline his own status as a contemplative. He concludes this particular dissertation on prayer with some words of compromise: 'it is expedient for every person to exercise and use the maner of prayer whether it be mental or vocal in which they find most sweetness and increasion of devotion'.

The *Pomander* attributes its definition of prayer to Augustine: 'prayer is nothing else but an ascension of the soule from erthly thyngs to heavenly thynges that be above and a desire of thynges invysible'.[35] Heaven is 'the celestiall palys where as the kyng of all kinges and lorde of all lordes doth contynnually tarye'.[36] Prayer is a 'faithfull ambassadoure' to this 'celestiall palys' and requires the raising of the mind and desires towards heaven. Although the *Pomander* stresses that prayer is a mental activity it also quotes 'a certayne holy doctoure' (Bede) as saying 'As long as a man is doing any good deeds so long he is praying. And except he cease from doing good deeds – he ceaseth not to pray.'[37] It should all be done 'to the laude and prayse of God', a part of which is the giving of alms: and that, according to Augustine as quoted by the *Pomander*, is 'to give meat to the hungry, drink to the thirsty, and clothes to the naked'.[38]

The *Pomander* makes extensive use of quotations from biblical sources and spiritual authorities to support its teaching. These quotations appear throughout the treatise, drawing upon a variety of spiritual authors including, according to the author, Bernard, Augustine, Bonaventure, John Damascene, Bede, John Crysostom and Ludolphus of Saxony. Prayer is made to appear attractive and its profits rewarding.[39] The teaching is simple, direct and uncomplicated. For example, the *Pomander* assures the reader that whatever is asked for in faith, will be granted. Thus Elijah prayed that it might not rain for three years and it did not.

The imagery of the *Pomander* itself is of a sweet smelling object. Certain prayers are described as being like 'swete delicious wines' and prayer is 'an ambassador' and 'messenger'. Just as 'a thief flees when he hears the clamour and noise of resideants so does our ghostly enemy the devil when he hears the clamoure of prayer'. However, the author is well aware that the practice of prayer is not easy and that it is beset by many difficulties. He therefore encourages his readers to pray often and to persevere with their prayers. He assures his readers that if they do 'almyghty God though he deferre for a tyme (wyll) gyve us all thyng necessary if we call to hym

---

[34]   *Pomander*, ch. 5.
[35]   *Ibid.*, ch. 1.
[36]   *Ibid.*
[37]   *Ibid.*, ch. 2.
[38]   *Ibid.*, ch. 12, p. 1.
[39]   Ch. xiv.

with contynuance and perfourmance of prayer'.[40] The reader is not to be deterred by either time or place. The author takes a literal interpretation to support this claim. He points out that Jeremiah said his prayers whilst he was in prison and Daniel whilst among the lions. Jonas, even though he was in the belly of the fish, did not neglect his prayers.

Some of the most interesting chapters in the *Pomander* deal with the subject of distractions in prayer and their remedies. Various causes for these distractions are given which range from the seven deadly sins to the quality of life in society. In his references to contemporary life the author complains about those who eat delicate meats, indulge in drink and give themselves to sport. Blasphemy, swearing, clerical avarice and the sin of simony receive a special mention. The *Pomander* offers several remedies to combat these distractions. I would like to draw your attention to some of these because they reflect the spirituality of the time.[41]

The first refers to an exercise in church, and perhaps the author has in mind the leisured and learned laity for he assumes that the reader has time and opportunity to 'take holy water and kneel in some place where they intende to reste and pray'. It is a mental exercise relying upon the individual's ability to still his mind, ask God for forgiveness and thank him for his creation, redemption, and glorification. The author argues that such activity allows little spare for distractions. The *Pomander* continues, 'but if the persone be unlettered and moche encombred with wandrying cogitations of theyr herte than it is expedient for suche to have afore theyr eyes some devoute remembrance or object or some picture of the passion of Chryste or some saynt ... for that consideration ymages of saintes be set up in the churches as boks of laymen'. So his second remedy against distraction in prayer is to suggest that 'some useth agaynste such distractions lytell books in the whiche is conteyned pictures of the articles of the lyfe and passion of our Lorde Jesu'.[42] A *Pater*, an *Ave*, and a *Credo* are to be said for every article and this exercise is especially good for those who are unlearned. Thirdly, for those who do not possess such books the author recommends that they remember the said articles by the feasts of the year beginning with the Nativity and ending with the Resurrection and Ascension.

The chief aid recommended to combat distractions in prayer is use of the devotion of the Five Wounds of Our Lord.[43] The author suggests that the memory of Christ's Blessed Wound is the answer to vain and unprofitable thoughts. The *Pomander*'s interest in this spiritual exercise can

---

[40] The *Pomander* treatment of the profits of prayer is similar to Nicholas Love's in the *Mirror*: 'Reflections', p. 142.

[41] *Pomander*, ch. 8.

[42] Dr Jan Rhodes in her Ph.D. dissertation, 'Devotion on the Eve of the Reformation' (Durham, 1970) suggests that Bodleian Library, Gough Liturg. 19 may be such a book.

[43] D. Gray, 'The Five Wounds of Our Lord', *Notes and Queries* (March 1963), p. 82ff.; R. W. Pfaff, *New Liturgical Feasts in Later Medieval England* (Oxford, 1972); L. Gougaud, *Devotional and Ascetic Practices in the Middle Ages* (London, 1927).

further be illustrated by the fact that in the Redman edition of the *Pomander* deposited at John Ryland's Library, Manchester, there is a woodcut on the first page which is a drawing of the Risen Christ indicating a wound in his right side. The cult of the Five Wounds was popular in every sense of the word and the teaching that the wounds could act as a 'remedy' was commonplace in literature on that subject. But the author was not just presenting the reader with a popular devotion; he was setting out an aid to devotion which was intended to produce practical results. No doubt he had this in mind when later in the text he reminded his readers,

> Breke thy brede to hym that is hungry.
> Give hospitalite to the poore people that laboure in journey.
> And when thou seest a man that is naked gyve hym clothes.[44]

He concluded his treatise with this practical advice:

> Pryvetly put thyne almes into the bosome of the poore man and thà it wyll pray for the to God.[45]

Such advice is in keeping with a book which combines homely advice, practical hints and common sense with learning and experience of the practice of prayer.

The Pomander of Prayer did not survive in great numbers to be read time and again as the author intended. It was a treatise characteristic of its time with a spirituality which dwelt on the sacred humanity of Our Lord; it was traditional in its theology and obviously required a good deal of initiative from the reader. New prayer books were to appear such as Becon's which would provide set prayers for most occasions, and these were to win the market. Nevertheless it is interesting to see such a work being produced by a member of the most secluded of orders for the specific use of a busy, non-monastic and non-clerical group.

---

[44] *Pomander*, ch.14 (quoting Isaiah 58 v.7).
[45] *Ibid.*

DEVOTIONAL READING IN THE MONASTERY
AND IN THE LATE MEDIEVAL HOUSEHOLD

Ann M. Hutchison

In considering devotional reading in the monastery and in the late medieval household, I am particularly interested in the role of women. Many of the devotional compilations or translations of devotional texts appear to have been made for a particular woman, or group of women, either in orders or in the lay world. Among English monasteries known for the fostering of intellectual development, Syon Abbey, the Bridgettine house founded by Henry V, is perhaps the most prominent in the late medieval period. In addition, its connections with the Carthusians, which will be outlined below, make Syon a particularly appropriate choice for this conference. Originally Syon Abbey housed a double order, which included priests, deacons and lay brothers as well as nuns. The brothers lived in a separate part of the monastery, but the priests were there to take the services, preach sermons, and to assist the nuns with their education and devotions, while the lay brothers attended to the monastery as a whole. Though a strictly enclosed order, Syon formed important contacts with other religious houses as well as with pious members of the lay world, in particular with members of the Royal family and the court circle, and also with other households, during the years of its existence in England in the fifteenth and early sixteenth centuries. My main concern in this paper is with the guidance of the Bridgettine nuns of Syon Abbey and with those who followed their example in the outside world, with regard to the actual practice of reading; I shall also refer to some of the books they read.

Before turning to Syon Abbey itself, it is worth emphasising the complementary relationship that existed with Henry V's other major foundation, the Charterhouse of Jesus of Bethlehem at Sheen.[1] After 11 November 1431, when Syon moved a little further downstream from Twickenham to Isleworth, the new abbey stood almost directly across the Thames from the Carthusian house. As has been well documented, the

---

[1] According to Robert Persons (or Parsons), S.J., writing c.1595, the founder (i.e., Henry V) had ordained that worship in the two houses must continue without a break throughout day and night: 'so that where one monastery ended their office the other should begin, and so continue successively' ('A Sketch of the History of the Bridgettines of Syon written by Father Robert Parsons, S.J., About the Year 1595, edited from a MS. copy at Syon Abbey, Chudleigh' from Adam Hamilton, *The Angel of Syon* [Edinburgh and London: Sands & Co., 1905], p. 98). Referred to by A. Jefferies Collins in his edition of *The Bridgettine Breviary of Syon Abbey*, Henry Bradshaw Society 96 (Worcester: The Stanbrook Abbey Press, 1969), p. vii, n. 1.

Carthusians, a silent order whose work was primarily to preach the word of God with their hands,[2] were responsible for producing or providing many of the texts read at Syon. The following are some well known examples, but the list is by no means exhaustive. One of the manuscripts of the first English translation of the *Imitatio Christi*, now Hunterian MS 136, was written by one of the best-known of the Sheen scribes, William Darker (d.1513) for Elizabeth Gibbs, abbess of Syon (1497-1518).[3] Cambridge University Library MS Ff.6.33, also written by Darker,[4] contains an English translation of 'The rewyll of Seynt Sauioure', and though there is no *ex-libris* inscription, the manuscript must have formed part of the nuns' library, since the translation is of their rule. Darker's hand has also been identified in Lambeth Palace Library No. 546, Latin and English prayers and devotions written for Syon.[5] Annotations found in particular devotional texts, such as *The Scale of Perfection* by Walter Hilton and the *Incendium Amoris* by Richard Rolle seem to suggest, at least from one example, that the monks of Sheen may have provided spiritual direction to novices at Syon.[6] In *The Pomander of Prayer* (discussed by the Rev. Robert Horsfield above, pp. 205-13), the 'Exortacion' is by a brother of Syon, while the text itself is attributed to Sheen. This latter, which survives only in printed versions, is an especially interesting joint venture, since it seems to have been intended for a lay audience, rather than for either house.[7]

Though a substantial catalogue survives from the library of the brothers of Syon Abbey,[8] there is no evidence of a list of the contents of the nuns'

---

[2] See Guigo I, *Consuetudines*, PL 153, 693-95; quoted in Michael G. Sargent, *James Grenehalgh as Textual Critic*, vol. I, Analecta Cartusiana 85 (Salzburg, Austria: Institut für Anglistik und Amerikanistik, Universität Salzburg, 1984), pp. 16-17.

[3] M. G. Sargent, vol. I, p. 35.

[4] The copyist has been so identified by Dr A. I. Doyle. See James Hogg, *The Rewyll of Seynt Sauioure*, 2, Salzburger Studien zur Anglistik und Amerikanistik 6 (Salzburg, Austria: Institut für Anglistik und Amerikanistik, Universität Salzburg, 1978), p. iii.

[5] Hogg, p. iii; quoted from James Walsh and Edmund Colledge, '"The Cloud of Unknowing" and "The Mirror of Simple Souls" in the Latin Glossed Translations by Richard Methley of Mount Grace Charterhouse', *Archivio italiano per la storia della pietà*, at press.

[6] This case concerns James Grenehalgh, a monk of Sheen, who wrote textual comments and glosses in a number of manuscripts and printed books. On the profession of Joanna Sewell at Syon on 28 April 1500, he presented her with a copy of Wynken de Worde's 1494 print of Walter Hilton's *Scale of Perfection*, which he had inscribed and carefully annotated. Comments to Sewell and their combined monograms appear elsewhere, so much so in fact, that it can be argued that what must have begun as a pupil-teacher relationship was eventually considered excessive. In any case, Grenehalgh was removed from Sheen in 1507 or 1508. For a full discussion of the work and career of Grenehalgh see M. G. Sargent, *James Grenehalgh as Textual Critic*.

[7] A further, though less positive, connection could be added: that is, the fact that Richard Reynolds, a monk of Syon, was martyred along with three Carthusians on 4 May 1535 for refusing to acknowledge Royal Supremacy.

[8] Mary Bateson, ed., *Catalogue of the Library of Syon Monastery, Isleworth* (Cambridge: University Press, 1898).

library. We know from the Bridgettine Rule,[9] however, that reading was an important part of the daily life of the nuns. Whereas this is a rule in which poverty is stressed – 'therfor be it/ lefull to none to haue eny thyng propir: no/ manere thing. be it neuere so lityll. nor for to haue/ oon halpeny in possession. or towche it w^t/ hondys …' (ch. 1, ff. 42r-42v; Hogg, pp. 8-9) – and where even the number of service books is stringently regulated – 'Bookes also are to be had/ as many as be necessary to doo dyvyne office/ and moo in no wyse' (ch. 18, ff. 62v-63r; Hogg, pp. 49-50) – it is all the more impressive that an unlimited supply of books for study was permitted – 'Thoo bookes they shall/ haue as many as they wyll in whyche ys to/ lerne or to studye' (f. 63r; Hogg, p. 50). Moreover, the Additions to the Rule,[10] as has often been pointed out,[11] provide telling references to books and reading. First, under 'lyght defawtes' the negligence of the nun 'that hathe the kepyng of the bokes …' who might not provide appropriate books for the 'quyer, freytour, or chapter' (ch. II, 7 (Aungier, p. 252; Hogg, p. 1)) is listed. Under the same heading is included the making of 'any noyse of unreste' among other occasions 'in the freytour in tyme of redyng' (ch. II, 9 (Aungier, p. 252; Hogg, pp. 1-2)), and also the damaging or careless handling of books (ch. II, 13 (Aungier, p. 253; Hogg, p. 2)). Further on, under 'most greuous defautes', is the stealing, destroying, taking out or putting in of 'any thynge in the comen registyrs or comen bokes' without general approval (ch. V, 7 (Aungier, p. 261; Hogg, p. 15)). During his visitation, one of the bishop's prerogatives would be to examine 'If ther be an inuentory or register of the bokes of the library, and how they and other bokes of study be kepte and repayred' (ch. X, 18 (Aungier, p. 278; Hogg, p. 42)). In the chapter listing 'the places wher in silence is streytly to be kepte', the library is mentioned, though in this place the 'silence' is qualified: 'Also silence after some convenience, is to be kepte in the lybrary, whyls any suster is there alone in recordyng of her redynge' (ch. XIV (Aungier, p. 296; Hogg, p. 72)). Elsewhere, books are listed among the items the novice should be provided with (ch. XV (Aungier, p. 303; Hogg, p. 83)), and young sisters are enjoined to help their elders 'in beryng of heuy bokes' (ch. XLVII (Aungier, p. 365; Hogg, p. 154)).

The Additions for the sisters make no specific reference to the office of librarian, though there are ample references to duties connected with books and reading. It fell to the 'sexteyne' or sacristan, for example, to provide 'penners, pennes, ynke, ynkehornes, tables, and suche other as the abbes assygnethe her' (ch. XLVIII (Aungier, p. 367; Hogg, p. 155)); the 'chauntres' was responsible for 'alle the bokes … that longe to dyuyne seruyse, chapter, and freytour' and for ascertaining that 'they be corrected, and made of one

---

[9] Cambridge University Library MS Ff.6.33; printed in facsimile in James Hogg, *The Rewyll of Seynt Sauioure*, 2.
[10] See George James Aungier, *The History of the Antiquities of Syon Monastery* (London: J. B. Nichols & Son, 1840) and James Hogg, *The Syon Additions for the Sisters from the British Library MS. Arundel 146* in *The Rewyll of Seynt Sauioure*, 4.
[11] Most recently by Mary Carpenter Erler, 'Syon Abbey's Care for Books: Its Sacristan's Account Rolls 1506/7-1535/6', *Scriptorium* 39 (1985), 293-307.

acorde' (ch. XLV (Aungier, p. 361; Hogg, p. 149)), though this latter stipulation suggests that it was mainly the service books that were her responsibility; and the 'legister' was required to read 'distynctly and openly' in the refectory so 'that al may vnderstonde it' (ch. L (Aungier, pp. 374-375; Hogg, p. 161)).

Early documents connected with Syon Abbey give more particular evidence. R. J. Whitwell describes an agreement drawn up in 1482 between the fourth Abbess, Elizabeth Muston, and one Thomas Raille, the man who was contracted to report to the 'Chaunters of the Queres of the Bretherne and Systerne Sydes ...' as well as to 'the kepers of the libraris of the Bretherne and [Sys]terne Sydes there',[12] and be responsible for the repairing, binding and writing of books required. The ordinance is made specifically for Thomas Raille, and also for 'alle oþere þat shalle succede in that office' (p. 123), suggesting that the care and production of books was an ongoing activity at Syon.

Most recently, Dr Erler's careful analysis of sacristan's account rolls covering the period from 1506/7 to 1535/6 gives substantial evidence that Syon's reputation for books and learning is well deserved.[13] As Erler points out, the accounts suggest that during this period 'Syon is likely to have had a resident scribe and binder' (p. 298). In examining the purchase records of fine horn, which formed a protective cover for the Syon pressmark, Erler concludes that in the three-year period from 1528 to 1530 'an average of 30 books was ... processed', and she speculates that this number might represent a typical year's acquisition of books (p. 305). In general, she summarises, 'These regular and recurrent purchases of the sacristan ... indicate a constant attention to the maintenance of a great collection' (p. 305), and, 'Indeed the value of his account rolls lies in the unparalleled detail with which they present the traditional monastic activity of caring for books, in the final thirty years of English institutional monasticism' (p. 307). Interestingly, however, though her study confirms that Thomas Betson was the men's librarian, Erler has not been able to ascertain the identity of the librarian for the sisters' collection.

Nor is there any indication of how books were distributed amongst the nuns. It is possible that they followed the practice of Benedictine nunneries, such as Barking, which, as Phyllis Hodgson has remarked, 'prefigured Syon itself in the encouragement of learning'.[14] Barking, as an ordinal and customary drawn up in 1404 for Abbess Sibille Felton (Abbess 1394-1419) describes, held an annual book distribution on the first Monday of Lent after terce.[15] On the other hand, at Syon Abbey the emphasis placed on reading in the Rule, and in other documents such as those just mentioned, suggests that one book a year per nun would hardly be sufficient, especially since the

[12] 'An Ordinance for Syon Library, 1482', *English Historical Review* 25 (1910), 121.
[13] Erler, *Scriptorium* 39 (1985), 293-307.
[14] 'The Orchard of Syon and the English Mystical Tradition', *Proceedings of the British Academy* 50 (1964), 235.
[15] J. B. L. Tolhurst, ed., *The Ordinale and Customary of the Benedictine Nuns of Barking Abbey*, 2 vols., Henry Bradshaw Society 65-66 (London, 1927-28), 1, p. 67.

Bridgettines were, and are, an enclosed order whose time is intended to be spent in meditation and prayer.

A document that gives us special insight into the devotional life of the nuns of Syon Abbey is *The Myroure of oure Ladye*.[16] This work translates the service of the nuns from Latin and explains its meaning. It was written by one of the brothers of the order, and is divided into three parts. Two prologues introduce the work: the first describes the book and explains its purpose, while the second explains the translation and apologises for its shortcomings. In the first part of the work itself, the author, making explicit reference to St Bridget of Sweden, founder of the order, to their rule, and to Henry V, the order's founder in England, discusses the divine origin of their service – how it was dictated to St Bridget by an angel and then put together in Latin by St Bridget's confessor, Master Peter,* who himself was inspired in composing 'the songe' (p. 16), or musical notation, and eventually overseen by Master Alfonso da Vadaterra** (p. 20) – and provides a rationale of divine service generally. Part II begins with a short essay on the 'Deuoute redyng of holy Bokes' and then translates and explains the 'Hours' as they are said on each day of the week; and Part III consists of a translation of the Masses and Offices for special feasts as they were used at Syon Abbey.

The date of composition of *The Myroure of oure Ladye* is not known. It was certainly written after 1408, since the author refers to a constitution of Archbishop Arundel of that date which concerns the necessity of obtaining a licence from the bishop of the diocese before translating holy scripture into English (p. 71), and most probably after the enclosure of the order on 21 April 1420, since the text assumes that the service (and also the rule), is a routine matter for the nuns. In his edition of *The Bridgettine Breviary of Syon Abbey*, A. J. Collins notes that almost every Breviary now known is assigned, on the basis of handwriting, to the first decade or two after the Abbey's foundation which occurred in 1415.[17] Since Part II of *The Myroure* is primarily a translation of 'the entire text of the Breviary' – apart from the Psalms, for which the nuns are referred to Rolle's Psalter (p. xxxvi) – one might suppose that the author had one of these Latin Breviaries to hand.

Knowledge of the identity of the author would, of course, be helpful in establishing the date of composition, but unfortunately the work, as we have it, provides no specific clues. Nevertheless, we glean enough details to establish that this was a man of great learning, with a special understanding of the liturgy, who had a direct and intimate knowledge of the order – in fact, he speaks to the sisters as a brother of their order, and in a moving passage assures them that he is not laying down rules, but rather writing for their information (p. 52). Moreover, he had been in Rome, for he tells the sisters that he had often been in the Church of St Laurence (i.e., San Lorenzo

[16] J. H. Blunt, ed., *The Myroure of oure Ladye*, Early English Text Society, extra series 19 (London, 1873). Quotations from *The Myroure* are from this edition.

* Two priests named Petrus Olavi - the one a secular, the other the prior of the Cistercian house of Alvastra, accompanied her, translating, transcribing and collecting her revelations.

** Alphonse of Pecha.

[17] Collins, p. xli.

in Damaso) where he had seen the window through which St Bridget had looked into the Church and the altar upon which she saw 'the body of chryste eche day' as she 'saide her houres, & her prayers' (pp. 18-19). These hints have led Collins to propose two candidates: Thomas Fishbourne, who was elected the first Confessor-General of the order in 1420, or his contemporary, priest-brother, Simon Wynter (p. xxxix). Fishbourne died in 1428 and Wynter in 1448, and so if one accepts either of Collins' hypotheses, the work must certainly have been composed before 1448.

Only one manuscript of *The Myroure of oure Ladye* is known to have survived, and it exists in two parts: the first part is Aberdeen University MS 134, and the second is Bodleian MS Rawlinson C 941.[18] These two manuscripts were companion volumes written on paper sometime in the late fifteenth or early sixteenth century by Robert Tailour, who has signed the end of both parts and asked for the prayers of sister Elyzabeth Montoun (or Moutoun) for whom he copied the text. The identity of Robert Tailour has not been ascertained (he is not in the Syon 'Who's Who' compiled by Canon Fletcher,[19] nor is he in Emden, nor, according to Hargreaves (p. 269), has A. I. Doyle found any other reference to his work), and though we know the day of Sister Elyzabeth's death from the Syon Martiloge, the year has not been given, and so this surviving copy has so far been difficult to date with any degree of precision.[20]

In 1530, *The Myroure* was printed by Richard Fawkes at the request of the Lady Abbess and the Confessor-General of the time – Agnes Jordan and John Fewterer respectively – and at least seven copies of this edition are known to survive.[21] The text was edited by the Rev. John Henry Blunt for the EETS and published in 1873. Though he was lent the first half – but not all – of the one surviving manuscript (i.e., the Aberdeen MS, since the existence of the Rawlinson MS was not known until after the publication of the EETS volume – it was only discovered during the preparation of Part V, fasc. 2 of the Quarto Catalogue of Bodleian manuscripts, published in 1878), Blunt preferred to use the printed edition as the basis of his text, presumably because it was complete. A comparison of the manuscript and printed version reveals passages which diverge widely in some cases. The differences may arise from the fact that the Fawkes edition was prepared for a more general audience, as Hargreaves suggests (p. 276), or there may over time

[18] The manuscript parts are discussed by Henry Hargreaves, 'The Mirror of Our Lady', Aberdeen University Library MS. 134', *The Aberdeen University Review* 42 (1968), 267-280.

[19] The Syon Abbey 'Who's Who' is a series of hand-written notebooks documenting all those connected with Syon and compiled in the 1930s and 40s by Canon John Rory Fletcher; they are currently in the archives of Syon Abbey, South Brent, Devon. For a description of these notebooks, see Tore Nyberg, 'The Canon Fletcher Manuscripts in Syon Abbey', *Nordisk Tidskrift for Bok-och Biblioteksvasen* 47 (1960), 56-69.

[20] A. I. Doyle, however, has pointed out that the paper of the manuscript has a watermark used in Canterbury from c.1512-19; see Hargreaves, p. 268 and note.

[21] These can be found at the Cambridge University Library, the Bodleian, the British Library, Lambeth Palace, Bishop Cosin's Library, Durham, Peterborough Cathedral (now in the Cambridge University Library), and Warwick.

have been revisions and insertions; on the other hand, the differences may merely result from the fact that the copyist, Robert Tailour, was, as Hargreaves has called him, 'careless and unintelligent' (p. 278).[22] In any event, *The Myroure of oure Ladye* gives us insight from a very special perspective into the life and practices of the nuns at Syon Abbey.

In Part I, when he is speaking of the 'reuerence & deuocyon' with which the sisters ought to participate in divine service, the author reminds them of the injunction of the Pope: 'the Pope byddeth that this holy seruice shulde be sayde studyously' (Pt I, ch. 24, p. 63). Then he explains: 'For study is a grete and a vyolente applyeng of the harte to do a thynge wyth a greate & a feruent wyll. And therfore firste he sayth studyously and then deuoutly' (p. 63). Furthermore, he points out: 'And thys gostly study may not be done shortly. ne now done, and now lefte; but yt muste be contynued ful bysely and abydyngly, euery day, and euery houre & tyme of the day' (pp. 63-64). He emphasises the importance of this practice referring to the Rule:

> Therfore after our lorde Iesu cryste had sayde in hys holy rewle that neyther golde, ne syluer ne precyous stones shulde be oure tresure, but the grace of god shulde be oure rychesse; he sayde that thys treasure of grace must be kepte wyth contynuall studyes, *with* deuoute prayers, and *with* godly praisynges. Take hede what order our lorde kepeth in his wordes. Firste he saieth study, and then prayer, & then praysyng. For inwarde gostly study techeth to pray. and *con*tynuaunce of this study causeth to pray deuoutly. & deuoute prayer bryngeth gostly strenghte and comforte in the soulle wherby yt is lyfte vp and restyth, and delyteth in loue & praysynge of god. And whyle the soulle is thus occupyed; the treasure of grace ys kepte full seurely therin. And therfore thys gostly study to kepe the harte, ys youre chyefe laboure, thys ys youre moste charge and gretest bonde, this maketh the soule to be vertuous. and this causeth all the outwarde beryng to be relygious. (p. 64)

The author has thus provided the nuns with a rationale for their way of life, and he concludes by urging that they 'inwardly and bysely, & *con*tynewally trauayle in thys spyrytuall study', and in this endeavour he asks for their prayers on his own behalf (p. 65).

Immediately following in Part II is advice on how to read devoutly. These instructions on reading generally and on the reading of this particular book, form a sort of prologue to the heart of the work, the explanation and translation of their daily services. In this section 'Of Redynge', the author expands on the notion of study: 'Deuoute redyng of holy Bokes. ys called one of the partes of contemplacyon',[23] but in order to profit from reading,

---

[22] In the process of preparing a new edition of *The Myroure*, I hope to ascertain more clearly the causes of these differences.

[23] It is interesting to compare these remarks on reading with those of Guigo II in the *Scala claustralium*, translated as *The Ladder of Monks*. In reviewing the steps necessary for contemplation in the 'Recapitulation', for example, he says: 'Reading comes first, and is, as it were, the foundation; it provides the subject matter we must use for meditation', trans. Edmund Colledge, O.S.A. and James Walsh, S.J.

there are five things to keep in mind. First, it is important to choose books that are helpful and appropriate; second, the mind must be disposed to receive what is read or heard: 'For lyke as in prayer. man spekyth to god; so in redynge god spekyth to man. and therfore he oughte reuerently to be herde' (p. 66); third, it is important to 'laboure to vnderstande the same thynge that ye rede' (p. 67), and therefore when reading alone, one should read slowly and often go over the same passage until it is clearly understood – understanding is particularly important, he notes, for those whose duty it is to read aloud: 'They also that rede in the Couente. ought so bysely to ouerse theyr lesson before. & to vnderstonde yt; that they may poynte yt as it oughte to be poynted. & rede. yt sauourly & openly to the vnderstondinge of the heres' (p. 67); fourth, the chief purpose of reading is to inform oneself and to follow the precepts in one's own life – it is not, he emphasises, just for the sake of being learned; and fifth, it is necessary to have what he terms 'dyscressyon', that is, the ability to respond appropriately – sometimes with the intellect and sometimes with feeling – to what one is reading. Books, then, serve two basic functions: they educate, as does the first part of *The Myroure*, 'whyche enformeth you to vnderstande. & to knowe how ye oughte to be gouerned in saynge. & syngyng & redyng of your deuyne seruice' (p. 68); they also stir the feelings, to love and a desire for heaven in reading of its joys, or to dread and avoidance of sin in hearing of its miseries (p. 69). Moreover, the author cautions, in reading of this second kind, it is important to choose wisely: if one is despondent, one should read 'suche bokes as mighte sturre vp. hys affeccyons to comforte and to hope', and *vice versa*. The second part of *The Myroure*, he notes, fulfils both functions: it informs 'the vnderstondyng' by explaining the service and it stirs 'vp the affeccions' by means of the words of the service itself.

The author concludes this section with an explanation of how *The Myroure of oure Ladye* is to be used. Though this passage differs in the manuscript from the printed edition, since the method of presenting the text is different in each medium,[24] it is also corrupt in both existing sources. What is clear, however, is that Parts II and III of *The Myroure* are intended to be a supplement to, rather than a replacement of, the Latin texts of the Office and the Mass. For each part of each service, the author gives the first Latin word, or words, of the anthem, hymn, response, verse, and so forth, so that the nuns 'may know therby where yt begynneth' (p. 70), that is, so they will know the place in their breviaries. To make his point even more clearly, he uses the reading of the legend at Matins as an example. If at that time a nun might wish to have the English text to 'fede her mynde therewyth', she may do so, but, he firmly cautions, this is only 'to be vnderstonde of them that haue sayde theyre mattyns or redde theyr legende before. For else I wolde

(Kalamazoo, Michigan: Cistercian Publications, 1981), p. 79. See also George R. Keiser's essay on this work above, pp. 145-59.
[24] Originally the colour of the ink in the manuscript was to be varied so that the translation could be distinguished from the explanation. This is not the case, however, in the manuscript parts that survive. Similarly in the printed edition, the type face, rather than the colour of the print, is varied for the same reason.

not counsell them to leue the herynge of the latyn. for entendaunce of the englysshe' (p. 71).

As he explains the liturgy, the author's attention is focused on helping the nuns formulate their thoughts as they hear or say the familiar Latin words and phrases. An example drawn from his exposition of the *Pater noster* will demonstrate his method (and incidentally show how he envisions the devout reading will help): 'The exposycyon of thys holy prayer ye haue in dyuerse bokes. whiche yf ye study bysely to vnderstonde wyll gyue you cause to fynde grete comforte & deuocyon in the sayng therof. But I wyl telle yt you shortly lyke as ye may som what the better haue yt in mynde when ye say yt. yf ye wyll laboure theraboute' (p. 73).

In his very full description of 'The Sonday Seruyce', the author often includes some of the activities performed outside of the church. At the end of the day, for example, just before Compline, comes a time called 'Collacion', the time 'where ys redde some spyrytuall matter of gostly edyfycacion. to helpe to gather to gyther the scaterynges of the mynde. from all oute warde thynges' (p. 165). Though the reading of collation was adopted from the Rule of St Benedict, and was therefore standard monastic practice, the reference here gives further indication of the kind of reading done at Syon in that it stipulates that the books to be read at Collacion must be 'easy to vnderstande that all sowlles may be fedde therwyth and holpen thereby. to kepe themselfe in inwarde peace and stableness of mynde all the nyghte folowynge' (p. 165). This caution seems to suggest that the books read by the nuns were not always easy to understand.

The Myroure of oure Ladye, therefore, stands as an important witness to the value placed on spiritual or devotional reading at Syon Abbey, and, as the sources of the author's explanations indicate,[25] itself furnishes an example of the high degree of intellectual activity fostered in the monastery. The fact that *The Myroure* was printed in 1530 suggests its continuing use at Syon, and may also indicate a wider interest in this work in the world outside.[26]

Evidence from survivors in this same period, the fifteenth and early

[25] His explanations are taken, for example, from the Church Fathers, early English authorities such as Bede, theologians of the day, and the works of the mystics, including the Revelations of St Bridget herself.

[26] In a recent article, M. A. Hicks discusses the influence of *The Myroure* on Margaret, Lady Hungerford; 'The Piety of Margaret, Lady Hungerford (d.1478)', *Journal of Ecclesiastical History* 38 (1987), 19-38. Though Hicks presents convincing evidence concerning the influence of the Syon use on Margaret's mortuary chapel at Salisbury, I cannot agree with his assumption that 'her book of the use of the Brigettines of Syon' was, in fact, *The Myroure of oure Ladye* (pp. 23-24). Hicks makes this assumption on the mistaken belief that the nuns used *The Myroure* rather than the Latin breviary (p. 24), a view which, as I have argued above, is not supported by the remarks of the author of *The Myroure*. Hicks himself later states: 'The English translations in the *Myroure* cannot have been her sole source for these items [i.e., from the Syon use], as they do not represent accurately the tonal qualities of the Latin original, whose importance to Margaret is indicated by the predominance of versicles, hymns and anthems among her selected texts' (p. 26) – a point which further strengthens the evidence that Latin, rather than English, was used by the nuns at Syon.

sixteenth centuries, indicates that devotional books, or manuscripts collecting excerpts from writers, such as Suso, Rolle, Hilton and St Bridget
herself, proliferated. In one such compendium, Harley 1706, which once
belonged to Elizabeth, daughter of Sir Richard Scrope (who was married
first to William, Viscount Beaumont, and then to John de Vere, 13th Earl of
Oxford), there is an interesting rubric on spiritual reading. It occurs near the
end of the collection just after various poems of instruction, and reads as
follows:

> We schulde rede and vse bokes in to þis ende and entente: for formys
> of preysynge and preyynge to god, to oure lady, seynte marye, and to
> alle þe seyntes; þat we myȝte haue by þe forseyd vse of redynge
> vnderstondynge of god, of hys benyfetys, of hys lawe, of hys seruyce,
> or sume oþer goodly and gostely trowþis; or ellys þat we myȝte
> haue good affeccyon to ward god and hys seyntes, and hys seruyce to
> be gendryd and geten. (f. 212v)

Here, in a more elementary form, we have an expression of the same aims of
devotional reading as those expressed by the author of *The Myroure of oure
Ladye*: its purpose is, on the one hand, to educate by teaching forms of
prayer and/or by providing a meaning for these forms and for divine service
generally, and, on the other hand, to stir up feelings of love for God, his
saints and the eternal life. This is, as A. I. Doyle has termed it, a 'peculiarly
religious' notion of literature; that is, a literature which has become 'a
regular habit of mind and living, shared by solitaries and widows in vows,
... besides monks, nuns and friars, and accepted as something to be
emulated so far as possible by earnest seculars, clerks and layfolk'.[27] This
manuscript, which contains some Latin suffrages to Saint Ethelburga, and in
addition annotations 'which seem to imply more than ordinary lay learning
and interests' (p. 233), may, Doyle speculates, have once belonged to
Barking Abbey and have come from Barking into Elizabeth's possession.
She, in turn, seems to have possessed it 'from at least 1507 until the time of
her death in 1537' (p. 237), since it records both her married names. After her
death, it seems to have passed to her household, for the names of her nephew
and one of her women attendants are written in its margins in sixteenth-
century hands. Discovery of the provenance of many other such
manuscripts, or later printed editions of these texts, gives evidence of a well-
entrenched practice of a devotional mode of life.

The germ of this 'religious' way of life can, of course, be found in the
writings of the fourteenth-century mystics. Works such as 'The Mending of
Life' by Richard Rolle discuss the value of 'þinkynge & redynge holy
scripture'.[28] Similarly, Walter Hilton, in his *Epistle on Mixed Life*, written
perhaps initially for a worldly lord, and later adapted to a more general
audience, stresses the necessity of prayer and contemplation, even in a

---

[27] 'Books Connected with the Vere Family and Barking Abbey', *Transactions of the
Essex Archaeological Society* 25, new series, part II (1958), 231.
[28] Ralph Harvey, ed., *The Fire of Love and The Mending of Life or The Rule of
Living*, Early English Text Society, original series 106 (London, 1896), p. 121.

worldly life.[29] In addition, it is perhaps worth noting that in 1516 when Pynson printed the English version of the New Legend of England, he included a translation of the abridged life of St Bridget of Sweden, and also Hilton's treatise on the Mixed Life, even though it had been printed before, because, says Pynson, 'þe more a good thynge is knowen the better it is' and also because 'it may come to the knowledge of some men that otherwyse shulde neuer haue harde speke of it'.[30]

A well known example of a lay person who, as we learn from an account of her daily life, lived in such a manner, is Cicely, Duchess of York, mother of Edward IV and Richard III.[31] When she rose at seven in the morning, the account tells us, her chaplain was ready to say Matins of the day and Matins from the Little Office of Our Lady with her, followed by various other services throughout the day. He also read to her during her dinner, and among the works of 'holy matter' which she liked to hear were Hilton's *Mixed Life*, St Bonaventure, the *de infancia Salvatoris*, the Golden Legend, and the visions of St Maud (i.e., St Mechtild of Hackeborn, a figure frequently mentioned in *The Myroure of oure Ladye*) and St Katherine of Siena,[32] as well as the Revelations of St Bridget.[33] Not only was Cicely herself an example of a woman who followed the precepts of devout living, but the author of the account of her daily life may well have intended the account itself to be an example for other women in noble households to follow.[34]

The devout practices and interest in books of the mother of Henry VII, Lady Margaret Beaufort, are also well known; as Bishop John Fisher states in his 'mornynge remembrraunce': 'right studyous she was in bokes whiche she hadde in grete nombre both in Englysshe & in Frensshe, & for her exercyse & for the prouffyte of other she dyde translate dyuers maters of deuocyon out of Frensshe into Englysshe'.[35] Her daughter-in-law, Elizabeth of York, seems to have shared some of her tastes, in devout books, at least.[36]

[29] This treatise can be found in C. Horstmann, ed., *Yorkshire Writers*, 1 (London: Swan, Sonnenschein, 1895), pp. 264-92, and also in Dorothy Jones, *Minor Works of Walter Hilton* (London: Burns & Oates, 1929).

[30] From the 'Prologe' of Richard Pynson's edition of *The Kalendre of the newe Legende of Englande* (London, 1516), unpaginated.

[31] 'Orders and Rules of the House of the Princess Cecill, Mother of King Edward IV', *A Collection of Ordinances and Regulations for the Government of the Royal Household* (London: Society of Antiquaries, 1790), pp. 37-9.

[32] St Katherine's *Dialogue* was printed for the Syon nuns by Wynken de Worde in 1519 under the title of *The Orcherd of Sion*. For a modern edition see Phyllis Hodgson and Gabriel M. Liegey, eds., *The Orcherd of Syon*, Early English Text Society 258 (London, 1966).

[33] The account of Cicely's life is also quoted in W. A. Pantin, *The English Church in the Fourteenth Century* (Notre Dame, Indiana: University of Notre Dame Press, 1963), p. 254, and is cited in C. A. J. Armstrong, *England, France and Burgundy in the Fifteenth Century* (London: The Hambledon Press, 1983), p. 141.

[34] In support of this theory, Armstrong, for example, draws attention to the record's narrative style (p. 140).

[35] John E. B. Mayor, ed., *The English Works of John Fisher*, part I, Early English Text Society, extra series 27 (London, 1876), p. 292.

[36] In fact, Elizabeth's household records show that she received gifts from the Lady Abbess of Syon (i.e., Abbess Gibbs), which suggests a connection of some sort with

That interest in devotional books extended to women in the court circles is suggested in the account of Cicely, Duchess of York, who at supper related to those in her presence 'the reading that was had at dinner',[37] and again by the fact that a copy of Hilton's *Scale of Perfection*, printed by Wynken de Worde in 1494, was presented by Lady Margaret and Queen Elizabeth to Mary Roos, one of the ladies-in-waiting.[38] Though we have no direct evidence about the kind of life Mary Roos led, we do know that she kept the book throughout her life, since she, like Elizabeth Scrope, records her change of name, first when she marries Hugh Denys, and again when she marries Giles Capell.[39]

Somewhat earlier, Margaret, Duchess of Clarence, a woman with impressive courtly connections (i.e., she was the grandmother of Lady Margaret Beaufort), having been twice widowed, desired to live a celibate life 'away from worldly pomps'.[40] Entries in the Papal Registers from 1422 on attest to the extent of her piety. For a time, c.1428-1429, she went to live near Syon Abbey and petitioned the Pope for permission to allow the Brothers of Syon to bring her Holy Communion and to minister to her. Then, in 1429, she petitioned that permission be given to allow Simon Wynter, one of the Syon brothers, to move to a less arduous monastery. In the petition, the Duchess described Wynter as being zealous in the monastery and of great spiritual service to her. Indeed, George R. Keiser has recently shown from a colophon in a Yale manuscript of Latin and English devotional writings that Simon Wynter translated the life of St Jerome for the Duchess.[41] Among other things, this life is intended as a model for devout living, and it is of special interest to note that the point that the author makes of telling how St Jerome turned from the reading of 'bokys of Poetys & Philysophres' (f. 5v) to 'holy bokys' (f. 6r) echoes a similar point made by the author of *The Myroure of oure Ladye*.[42]

At a later stage in Syon's history, Richard Whytford, who became a

this monastery. See Nicholas Harris Nicolas, ed., *Privy Purse Expenses of Elizabeth of York: Wardrobe Accounts of Edward the Fourth. With a Memoir of Elizabeth of York, and Notes* (London: William Pickering, 1830), p. 13.

[37] Pantin, p. 254.

[38] This copy is now at Yale; see George R. Keiser, 'Patronage and Piety in Fifteenth-Century England: Margaret, Duchess of Clarence, Symon Wynter and Beinecke MS 317', *Yale University Library Gazette* (October 1985), 45.

[39] From the will of her first husband, who left property to both Syon and Sheen, we can deduce some connection with these houses, or, at the very least, an interest in their piety; see Michael G. Sargent, 'Walter Hilton's *Scale of Perfection*: the London Group Reconsidered', *Medium Aevum* 52 (1983), 207-208. For a full description of the presentation copy, see P. J. Croft, *Lady Margaret Beaufort, Countess of Richmond. Descriptions of Two Unique Volumes Associated with One of the First Patrons of Printing in England* (London: Bernard Quaritch, 1958).

[40] Fletcher, 'Who's Who', p. 66.

[41] Keiser, 'Patronage and Piety in Fifteenth-Century England', 32-46.

[42] In order to emphasise that the purpose of spiritual study is 'to kepe the Harte', the author tells the story of a meeting in the desert between 'hethen phylosophers' and 'relygyous fathers' in which the philosophers try to ascertain the essential differences in their seemingly identical ascetic way of life – unlike the heathen philosophers, the fathers know and trust in God, for only in God can the heart be kept (*Myroure*,

brother in 1507, wrote a practical treatise for the devout lay person who lived in more modest circumstances; this was called *A Werke for Housholders*. It was first published by Wynken de Worde in about 1530 (the same year in which Fawkes printed *The Myroure of oure Ladye*), because the copy he had sent to 'a pryuate persone' had been seen by 'certeyn deuout persones' who, Whytford says in his Preface, 'instantly required me to put it newly forth in commune'. This book provides instruction along lines similar to those of the author of *The Myroure*, but in simplified, more direct, form. Whytford is both realistic and practical in his presentation. He carefully explains the meanings of the *Pater Noster* and other prayers, and of the Creed, ten commandments, and so forth, and tells the householder, who could be a man or a woman, when and how these prayers should be said. When suggesting how the householder might make profitable use of Sunday, he recommends the reading of this book 'or suche other good englysshe bookes' to as large a company as could be gathered together.[43]

Though the 'good englysshe bookes' recommended to the householder would undoubtedly be simpler than the 'bokes of studye' possessed by the nuns of Syon, nevertheless, we can detect here the same impetus which generated the emphasis on devotional reading found in *The Myroure of oure Ladye*. In fact, the development of such an attitude to reading in the households of the late fifteenth and early sixteenth centuries might not be a new thing at all. We have only to think of Chaucer's *Retraction*, written just before the end of the fourteenth century. His decision to disown writings 'of worldly vanitees', or those 'that sownen into synne', and opt for 'bookes of legendes of seintes, and omelies, and moralitee, and devocion',[44] would have a familiar ring to devout readers of the later period.

pp. 64-65). Both works point to spiritual study as an important stage in the life of devotion.
[43]   As well as early printed copies by Wynken de Worde (London, 1530, 1533, etc.) and by Robert Redman (London, 1537), *A Werke for Housholders* has been reissued by James Hogg in the *Appendices* of *Richard Whytford's 'The Pype or Tonne of the Lyfe of Perfection'*, 5, Salzburger Studien zur Anglistik und Amerikanistik (Salzburg, Austria: Institut für Anglistik und Amerikanistik, Universität Salzburg, 1979), pp. 1-62.
[44]   F. N. Robinson, ed., *The Complete Works of Geoffrey Chaucer*, 2nd edition (Boston: Houghton Mifflin, 1957), p. 265.

PICTURES IN PRINT:
LATE FIFTEENTH- AND EARLY SIXTEENTH-CENTURY ENGLISH RELIGIOUS BOOKS FOR LAY READERS

Martha W. Driver

Printing increased the number and availability of books, and readership, or at least ownership, of books was made possible for a broad number of people for the first time. Consideration of the introduction of printing and its effect on potential audiences for early printed books raises a number of questions; these concern printing's impact on the growth of literacy in England, lay readership of books formerly read predominantly by religious, and the role of book illustration and layout in promoting literacy among laymen. This paper falls into five sections: first, there will be a brief discussion of the function of illustration in early printed books; second, an inquiry into lay readership of printed religious books and how to determine it; next, a look at the role of illustration in printed Books of Hours, produced for the English market; fourth, an examination of what I call the conventional, or associative, image which links texts with similar contents, usually religious and devotional handbooks, saints' lives, and miscellanies; finally, I will consider Bridgettine texts which are linked by the same or similar woodcuts. Pictures were an integral part of the early printed book in England, and as I hope to demonstrate here, a vital part of the reading process. The illustrated books I will discuss, mainly English translations from French and Latin works, reflect the pre-Reformation groundswell of religious interest and enthusiasm, and play a central role in the movement from lay ignorance to lay literacy.[1]

Of woodblock illustration, it is generally (and incorrectly) said that the early printers did not pay much attention to it, placing whatever woodblocks they had to hand in the forme. In 1925, Henry Plomer criticised Wynkyn de Worde, the foreman who inherited William Caxton's shop and

---

[1] While the role of images in encouraging literacy has been generally ignored by recent scholarship, Miriam Chrisman includes a chapter, 'Illustrated Books for the Layman, 1490-1529', in her *Lay Culture, Learned Culture: Books and Social Change in Strasbourg 1480-1599* (Yale University Press, 1982), which serves as a useful introduction to this subject. The basic catalogue of English woodcut illustration in this period is Edward Hodnett's *English Woodcuts, 1480-1535* (1935; repr. Oxford University Press, 1973). STC numbers for books are taken from the *RSTC: A Short-Title Catalogue of Books Printed in England, Scotland, and Ireland, 1475-1640*, first compiled by A. W. Pollard, G. R. Redgrave, second edition begun by W. A. Jackson and F. S. Ferguson, completed by Katharine E. Pantzer (London: The Bibliographical Society, 1976 and 1986). STC numbers are cited in the explanatory notes. I have also cited locations of books in library collections when this information has been omitted by or is not usually included in *RSTC*.

ran it successfully for forty-four years after Caxton's death, for just this. Plomer said de Worde did not 'trouble himself as to whether the blocks or ornaments he used were suitable to the text or type of book he was printing. Anything that happened to be on the shelves at the time was inserted.'[2] This fallacy, that printers cared little for the illustrations in their books, is repeated, becomes more broadly accepted, and in a 1975 exhibition catalogue we read that 'Fifteenth-century printers often made little attempt to ensure a close correspondence between text and illustration. Instead they used whatever blocks they happened to have in stock, repeating them in book after book, and making them do duty variously captioned, for several scenes within the same work.' But this statement, from *MS to Print, Tradition and Innovation in the Renaissance Book*, edited by A. I. Doyle, Elizabeth Rainer, and D. B. Wilson, is not altogether false. Pictures *are* often repeated in early printed books. They do not, however, always appear haphazardly. Printers were well aware of the correspondence between pictures and text, and pictures were often repeated with an eye to linking and/or introducing similar texts. I shall demonstrate this shortly.

Determining lay readership of printed religious books, the second main thread of this essay, is far more complex and difficult. Basically, this problem can be split into two (sometimes overlapping) parts: first, there is the intended audience, and second, the actual readers of the text. Actual readers can be further divided into primary, or those who read the books first, and secondary, those readers, often layfolk, who read them later.

When Sir Richard Sutton, steward of Syon Monastery, commissioned de Worde to print *The Orcharde of Syon*,[3] the revelations of St Catherine of Siena, who was the intended audience? De Worde's colophon says Sutton, finding the text 'in a corner by it selfe, wyllynge of his great charyte it sholde come to lyghte, that many relygyous and deuoute soules myght be releued and haue conforte therby, he hathe caused at his great coste, this booke to be prynted'. Just who these 'relygyous and deuoute soules' were, whether layfolk or religious, is not specifically stated. But, it is almost a certainty that the nuns at Syon Abbey were among that number; it is known, for example, that de Worde printed sixty copies of *The Image of Loue* expressly for the Bridgettine nuns at Syon.[4] And reading, private and public,

[2] Henry R. Plomer, *Wynkyn de Worde and His Contemporaries from the death of Caxton to 1535* (London: Grafton & Company, 1925), p. 61.

[3] I have examined copies of *The Orcharde of Syon* (STC 4815), printed by de Worde in 1519, in the British Library, the Spencer Collection of the New York Public Library, and in the collection of the Marquess of Bath, Longleat House, Wiltshire (this copy is not cited in *RSTC*). Formerly owned by book collector Beriah Botfield (1807-63), the Longleat copy is printed on vellum; its woodcuts were illuminated with gouache, gold leaf, and watercolour in the sixteenth century, probably soon after the volume issued from the press. On the leaf facing the original title-page appears Botfield's coat of arms, the colours and style of which cleverly imitate those of the sixteenth century. The Longleat copy was cleaned and rebound in the nineteenth century.

[4] James Moran, in *Wynkyn de Worde: Father of Fleet Street* (2nd edn, London: Wynkyn de Worde Society, 1976), p. 41, includes this rather curious account of de Worde's printing of the *Image of Love* (STC 21471.5): in 1524 de Worde was 'one of

was encouraged at Syon, which had one of the largest pre-Reformation libraries, its volumes numbering close to fourteen hundred. A chapter in *The Mirror of Our Lady*, a Book of Hours and masses used at Syon, emphasises the private reading of books, which should be read and reread 'twyes or thryes' for comprehension.[5] And, as Mary Erler reminds us in her recent article, 'Syon Abbey's Care for Books: Its Sacristan's Account Rolls 1506/7-1535/6', the Rule specified that the novice own or 'acquire certain books at her entrance', one of which might have been *The Orcharde of Syon*.[6] In the case of *The Image of Love*, an edition of sixty, or if every man and woman at Syon was to own a copy, of eighty-five, is fairly small for the first half of the sixteenth century, but not unheard of.[7] And, besides the primary audience for such a work, there are the secondary readers, who are usually lay.

The copy of *The Orcharde of Syon* in the Spencer collection of the New York Public Library was owned first by 'Syster elyzabeth Stryckland professed in Syon', according to the inscription on the flyleaf. A second entry on the flyleaf states that 'Ryc(hard) assheton off Mydlton knyght executor unto my lady stryckland decessed have gyffen thys boke unto my lady wyffe ... in the xxiiii yere off the Reyne of our sufferan kyng henre viii', that is, in 1542. According to an article by Sr Mary Denise, 'The Orchard of Syon: An Introduction', Sr Elizabeth Stryckland died in 1540.[8] At her death, Richard Assheton, executor of her will, came into possession of her copy of *Orcharde of Syon*, giving it to his wife. The book then passed into the Sacheverall family, 'katherin Sacheverell' having written her name

those warned by Bishop Tunstall against importing Lutheran books into England. ... A year later he was again summoned before the bishop with John Gough to answer a charge of having published a work called *The Image of Love*. De Worde confessed that he was one of those present in the previous year and that since that date he had printed *The Image of Love*, which was alleged to contain heresy, and had sent sixty copies to the nuns of Syon and had sold as many more. The two men were warned not to sell any more and to get back those they had already sold.'
[5] *The Mirror of Our Lady* (STC 17542) circulated first in manuscript and later in an edition printed by Richard Fawkes in 1530. See Ann Hutchison's essay in this volume for a more specific description of reading practices at Syon.
[6] Mary Carpenter Erler, 'Syon Abbey's Care for Books: Its Sacristan's Account Rolls 1506/7-1535/6', *Scriptorium* (1985), p. 295.
[7] A. S. G. Edwards, in 'Wynkyn de Worde and Patronage' (forthcoming), comments 'in 1525 we find de Worde printing sixty copies of *The Image of Love* for the Bridgettine nuns at Syon, a hefty and presumably profitable job lot'. Actually, if Moran's account is correct (see note 4), de Worde's statement that he 'had sent sixty copies to the nuns of Syon and had sold as many more' implies an edition of 120 copies. Print runs are difficult to calculate, and little work has been done on the production of English presses. Rudolph Hirsch, in *Printing, Selling and Reading 1450-1550*, 2nd edn (Wiesbaden, 1974), discusses the size of editions on the Continent: 'By 1470 editions of 400 copies were coming off the presses.' (p.66) Citing Konrad Haebler's work, Hirsch further comments, 'Editions of 100 are known; Haebler calls these rightly 'most modest.' With this low is to be contrasted an edition of 2,300 copies of the *Decretals* of Gregory IX, issued twice within four years by the Venetian printer Baptista de Tortis (1491).'
[8] Sr Mary Denise, RSM, 'The Orchard of Syon: An Introduction', *Traditio*, vol. xiv (1958), p. 275 n. 5.

on folio three; she then gave the book to her son, 'Fr. Sacheuerell' in 1556, according to a note on folio 1. These several inscriptions in the Spencer copy of *The Orcharde of Syon* demonstrate the movement from religious to lay readers (and, perhaps, depending on how 'Fr. Sacheverell' is interpreted, back again), which is typical for many early printed books.[9]

Volumes primarily intended for the pious, or for the nun or priest, often fell into other hands later. On a flyleaf of a Book of Hours now in the Pierpont Morgan library, which was printed in Paris for Antoine Vérard c.1503, is this inscription in an early seventeenth-century hand: 'This Book was Brought from west Court itt is A Papist Book as I suppose and not To be made Use of.'[10] The Morgan copy of Richard Fawkes' edition of *Mirror of Our Lady* has page after page of virulent anti-Catholic marginalia written in the same hand.[11] One wonders why this early seventeenth-century reader did not simply destroy his copy – and is immediately grateful he did not do so. In the copy of Caxton's *Golden Legend* in the Rare Book Room of the New York Public Library, all references to the pope have been obliterated by brown ink, and cross-hatchings appear throughout several saints' lives, including that of Thomas à Beckett.[12] The question of lay readership and preservation of Catholic texts in the period following Henry's break with Rome is an interesting and large one, which I can only touch on here.

Yet another way to determine readership of a printed work, and its popularity, is by reprints, especially those occurring in quick succession. For example, de Worde prints the *Ordinary of Chrysten Men* in 1502, then reprints it in 1506.[13] This illustrated religious handbook for the laity was translated by Andrew Chertsey from the very popular French work *L'art de bien vivre et de bien mourir*. Between the Chertsey translations of 1502 and 1506, de Worde publishes yet another translation of *L'art de bien vivre* under the title *The craft to liue well and to dye well*. Three editions of this

[9] According to the *Dictionary of English Usage*, the abbreviation 'Fr' may stand for friar, father, or *frater*. The use of the surname is typical in more formal usage.
[10] PML 590. The writing continues, rather confusedly, 'As is one or 2 more which I can not find.'
[11] Anti-Catholic marginalia and commentary written in one seventeenth-century hand occur throughout the Morgan *Mirror of Our Lady*, and I think merit further examination. For example, on the title-page is written: 'A Glass wherein may bee seene ye Idollatry & Impiety superstition & Irreligion of ye Church of Roome & of ye Followers of ye pope.' Beneath the woodcut of Bridget on the verso of the title-page occurs this comment: 'you may take notice yt ye Idolatous (*sic*) pappists yt pretend to own ye scripture and yt they might impose upon ye Ignorant'. Beside the hymn *Rubens rosa* (to the Virgin Mary), the gloss says, 'This hymn is filled with their blasphemy and Idolatry.' And after the colophon occurs this particularly paranoid commentary: 'This booke though it bee long sinne yt use of it was in ye monastery of Sion yet papists doie kepe for another day and then we may see which an abominable seruice will bee obtruded uppon thee people.'
[12] The copy of Caxton's 1483 *Golden Legend* (STC 24873) in the Rare Book Room of the New York Public Library lacks several of its opening leaves; others are fragmentary. The woodcut illustrating the murder of Beckett is missing altogether. However, the copy at Longleat House (again not cited in *RSTC*), which I have also examined, is intact; many of its cuts are handcoloured.
[13] STC 5198; STC 5199.

work in four years indicate that it is making money, and presumably, being read by its intended audience. Another very popular work among the laity, the *Kalender of Shepherds*, went through eight printings in Paris and Geneva between 1493 and 1500, before appearing in English translation in 1503. A miscellany of shepherd's lore, tables for finding dates of moveable feasts, descriptions of the torments of purgatory, and explications of the Ten Commandments, Lord's Prayer, and Creed, the *Shepherd's Kalender* was then reprinted in England by Richard Pynson in 1506, by de Worde in 1508, 1511, and 1528, and by a variety of other printers until 1631. And, judging from their reprint history, the writings of Richard Whytforde, the self-proclaimed 'wretch of Syon', were bestsellers in the late fifteenth and early sixteenth centuries. Whytforde's works were published by a number of contemporary printers, among them Robert Redman, Robert Wyer, Thomas Godfray, Robert Copland, and Wynkyn de Worde. Several of Whytforde's handbooks, most notably *The golden pystle* and *A Werke for housholders*, went into simultaneous editions, printings issued the same year, often by two or more printers. This implies there was a great clamour for Whytforde's works, which probably went well beyond the religious market. This is true also for John Mirk's *Festial*, the numerous editions of which 'argue for a wider than clerical interest'.[14]

As I have shown, lay readership of religious books can be determined by observing signatures and marginalia in the books themselves, and more generally, by the large number of reprints, which attest to a book's saleability and popularity. Other methods to ascertain who's reading what include looking at dedicatory prologues and prefaces, wills, and contemporary accounts of reading practice among the laity.

For example, *A mornyng remembraunce*, printed by de Worde in 1509, is John Fisher's eulogy of Margaret Beaufort, Countess of Richmond and Derby, which recounts her reading habits in rather great detail:

> right studyous she was in bokes whiche she hadde in grete nombre
> bothe in Englysshe & in Frensshe/& for her exercyse & for þe
> prouffyte of other she dyde translate dyuers maters of deuocyon out of
> Frensshe in to Englysshe. Ful often she complayned þt in her youthe
> she had not gyuen her to þe understondynge of latyn wherin she had a
> lytell perceyuynge specyally of þe rubrysshe of þe ordynall for þe
> sayeng of her seruyse whiche she dyde wel understande.

[14] The Longleat copy of de Worde's 1505 *The craft to liue well and to dye well* (STC 792) is not cited in *RSTC*. The *Kalender of Shepherds* was printed in an odd English dialect in Paris by Vérard (STC 22407), reprinted by Pynson with an improved text in 1506 (STC 22408), and became one of de Worde's basic bestsellers, a stock in trade; he reprinted it in 1508 (STC 22409; the *RSTC* dating of 1516 is incorrect as have pointed out elsewhere), 1511 (STC 22409.5), and 1528 (STC 22411). For more background on Whitford and Mirk, see Margaret Aston, *Lollards and Reformers: Images and Literacy in Late Medieval Religion* (Hambleton Press, 1984). See also James Hogg's essay, 'Richard Whytford's A Dayly Exercyse and Experyence of Death', in *Zeit, Tod, und Ewigkeit in der Renaissance Literatur* (Universität Salzburg, Institut für Anglistik und Amerikanistik, 1987), and Robert Horsfield's essay in this volume.

Margaret's ignorance of Latin, except for the rubrics of the Ordinall, must have been particularly tedious, given her daily religious practices. According to *A mornyng remembraunce*, Margaret awoke a little after 5.00 a.m. each day, when:

> she began certayne deuocyons/& so after theym w^t one of her gentylwomen þe matynes of our lady/whiche kepte her to then she came in to her closet/where then w^t her chapelayne she sayde also matyns of þe daye. And after þt dayly herde .iiii. or .v. masses upon her knees/soo contynuynge in her prayers & deuocions unto þe hour of dyner ... Dayly her dyryges & commendacyons she wolde saye. And her euensonges before souper bothe of þe daye & of our lady/ besyde many other prayers & psalters of Dauyd thrugh out þe yere ...

However, as Fisher informs us, 'for medytacyon she had dyuers bokes in Frensshe wherwith she wolde occupy herselfe whan she was wery of prayer'.[15] Though fluent in French and English, Lady Margaret Beaufort, mother of Henry VII, patronness of printers, including Caxton and de Worde, pious, powerful, and intellectual, had no Latin.[16]

And, apparently, this bilingual literacy in both French and English, and the ignorance of Latin, was typical among less privileged layfolk as well. With his *Dialogues in French and English*, printed in 1480, Caxton cashed in on what was apparently a real need for a French-English conversation book.[17] Richard Pynson's version, *A Boke to lerne to speke french*, printed in 1500, was intended for merchants and their apprentices.[18] This little volume contains short dialogues, and lists of numbers, money values, types of merchandise, for example, wine and corn, the parts of the body, and the days of the week. The book closes with a sample letter 'A prentyse writeth to his mayster: first in englisshe, and after in frenche.' Pynson's French conversation book is representative of a new genre and a new type of literacy

[15] STC 10891.

[16] Margaret's reputation as a woman of letters and also her lack of literacy in Latin are both well known. Michael Jones and Malcolm Underwood, in *History Today* (August 1985), pp. 27-28, discuss her various activities: 'She translated from French into English the fourth book of the *Imitation of Christ*. ... Margaret also commissioned Wynkyn de Worde to print Walter Hilton's *Ladder of Perfection*, and Richard Pynson printed her English version of a French translation of the *Speculum Aureum Peccatorum*, a product of Carthusian piety, as *The Mirror of God for the Sinful Soul*. Her own ignorance of Latin, beyond that sufficient to understand the order of worship, forced her to rely on scholars to complement her work. The French version of *The Mirror of Gold* was "checked and corrected by many clerks, doctors and masters of divinity" before she turned it into English.' George Keiser, in 'Patronage and Piety in Fifteenth-Century England: Margaret, Duchess of Clarence, Symon Wynter and Beinecke MS 317', *Yale University Gazette* 60, discusses the 'ongoing Lancastrian, perhaps specifically Beaufort, tradition of support for Syon, and, by implication, for Syon's contributions to vernacular devotional literature'.

[17] STC 24865; these are discussed by H. S. Bennett in his *English Books & Readers 1475 to 1557*, 2nd edn (Cambridge, 1970), pp. 93f.

[18] STC 24867; de Worde also published an edition, in 1497, titled *Here begynneth a lytell treatyse for to lerne Englysshe and Frensshe ... Soo that I maye doo my marchaundyse* (STC 24866).

– what Malcolm Parkes calls 'pragmatic literacy',[19] or learning to read and write to improve business and trade. And, pragmatic literacy was geared toward the vernacular.

Many religious books, however, were still printed in Latin. A case in point is the Book of Hours, or Primer, which was traditionally read by the laity, yet written in Latin. In fact, Margaret Beaufort's daily series of prayers as described by Fisher seems to mirror the contents of the Book of Hours, from the 'matynes of our lady' to the 'dyryges & commendacyons' which typically were included at the end of a Book of Hours. Perhaps in the pre-print era, the laity could ponder Books of Hours, read the rubrics, study the pictures. But, in an age of vernacular literacy, stress begins to be placed on comprehension of text. For example, the translator of *The Arte for to deye well*, printed by de Worde in 1505, says: 'I haue loked on this boke/& consyderyng that to all people of goodnes it is profytable/& that all people understondes not the latyn, I haue wyll to translate it ... in to englysshe ... to thende that al good crystens may read.'[20] And, in the dialogue between the clerk and lord at the start of the *Polychronicon*, the lord rather bluntly says: 'for to make a sermon of holy wryte all in latyn to men that can Englysshe and noo latyn/it were a lewde dede/for they be neuer the wyser'.[21] If the laity could not read Latin, or did not, at any rate, understand what was read, what is of value in a printed Book of Hours? Why are they so popular, and why do they remain so? Here I wish briefly to redefine the Book of Hours, or primer, as a text for the nonliterate in Latin, and to examine, again briefly, the parallel activities of reading pictures and reading text.

The first printed Book of Hours is generally agreed to be that published by Antoine Vérard in Paris in 1486, with blanks for pictures intended to be painted by hand.[22] This modest volume was quickly followed by hundreds of printed Books of Hours, many produced in Paris for Sarum, or Salisbury, use, that is, for the English market. Like their manuscript counterparts, printed Books of Hours illustrated specific portions of text, often using ornate wood- or metalcuts in place of miniatures. For example, the beginning of Matins, in the Hours of the Virgin, was introduced in both manuscript and printed Hours by an Annunciation scene. A page (Plate 1) from a Book of Hours printed at Paris by Thielman Kerver in 1503 is mostly metalcut; note the minimal text and the four separate borderblocks surrounding the image. Another Annunciation scene (Plate 2), also indicating the start of Matins, appears in a Book of Hours published by Vérard on 21 July, 1510; this also has minimal text, four borderblocks, and a

---

[19]   See Malcolm Parkes' discussion in his classic essay, 'The Literacy of the Laity', in *The Mediaeval World*, ed. Daiches and Thorlby (London, 1973), pp. 555–577.
[20]   This is incorporated into *The arte or crafte to lyue well* (STC 792); the copy I examined at Longleat House is not listed in STC.
[21]   The 1527 edition of the *Polychronicon*, de Worde's reprint of Higden in the Longleat library, is dated in *RSTC* as 1528 (STC 10002) and may be another edition entirely.
[22]   John Harthan, *Books of Hours and Their Owners*, 2nd edn (Thames and Hudson, 1982), p. 169.

partly obliterated woodcut capital *D*.[23] Vérard used the same metalcut earlier in a vellum Book of Hours printed in 1500 (Plate 3). In this case, the metalcut has been painted over to resemble a manuscript miniature. The block border is missing and the text omitted. These have been replaced by a hand-painted architectural border in red and gold; other details of the original metalcut, for example, the lily in the pot and the angel hosts in the background, have been painted out.

In both manuscript and printed Books of Hours, the Sequences, or Gospel passages on the coming of Christ, occur just after the Calendar, at the start of the volume. While manuscripts usually show John the Evangelist on Patmos to signal the beginning of passages from the Gospel of St John, the illustration in printed books tends to be more gruesome. John is more often shown tortured before the Porta Latina in Rome. A luxurious version of this scene (Plate 4), again hand-painted to resemble a manuscript miniature, occurs in the Book of Hours produced for Pigouchet in Paris in 1498, now in the John Carter Brown library at Brown University in Providence.

The Annunciation and some representations of John are typical text markers in both manuscript and printed Books of Hours. But, with printing, more scenes are added to the conventional picture cycle. These include the Jesse Tree (Plate 5), signifying the Church Militant and Triumphant, and Bathsheba bathing as David looks on, an image often accompanied in printed books by a companion illustration of the death of Bathsheba's husband, Uriah the Hittite, in battle.[24] More pictures mean more ways to organise, divide, and minimise text, useful for the reader who has less than a firm grasp of Latin.

Another introduction which quickly becomes conventional in printed Books of Hours is the narrative cycle in the borders. These borders sometimes enhance the text, but more often serve to divert the reader's attention away from it. A Book of Hours, dated 1515, in the John Carter Brown library at Brown University, for example, has metalcuts with Latin captions. These bordercuts, illustrating the showing and devouring of the Book from Chapter 10 of Revelation (Plate 6), rather incongruously appear in the text of the Psalms. And, in the 1503 Book of Hours printed for Kerver, bordercuts of the Fifteen Last Things recur in three cycles throughout the volume. The picture captions in this example (Plate 7) are French. There is an earlier Book of Hours in the Morgan library, printed for Kerver in 1497 by Jean Philippe, which has the same bordercuts but the rubrics are Latin. This switch to the vernacular seven years later seems significant.

John Harthan, writing about manuscript Books of Hours, comments that 'the main purpose of Books of Hours was to provide every class of the laity from kings and royal dukes down to prosperous burghers and their wives with personal prayerbooks. All literate people, and even some who could

[23] This has been reproduced from John Macfarlane's catalogue, *Antoine Vérard* (Bibliographical Society, 1900 for 1899), plate LIII.
[24] Harthan, p. 170.

Plate 1   Annunciation. Book of Hours. Paris, Thielmann Kerver, 1503
(courtesy of the Academy of Medicine, New York)

Plate 2 Annunciation. Book of Hours. Paris, Antoine Vérard, 1510
(reproduced from John Macfarlane, Antoine Vérard, Bibliographical Society,
Bibliographical Society, 1900 for 1899, pl. LIII)

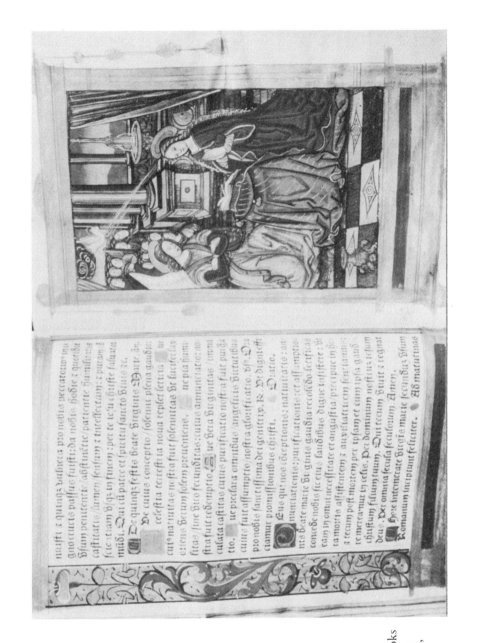

Plate 3 Annunciation.
Book of Hours. Paris,
Antoine Vérard, c.1500
(courtesy of the Rare Books
and Manuscripts Division,
New York Public Library,
Astor, Lenox and Tilden
Foundations)

Plate 4 The Martyrdom of John the Evangelist. Book of Hours. Paris, Philippe Pigouchet, 1498 (courtesy of the John Carter Brown Library at Brown University, Providence, RI)

Plate 5   Jesse Tree. Book of Hours. Paris, Pigouchet, 1498
(courtesy of the John Carter Brown Library at Brown University,
Providence, RI)

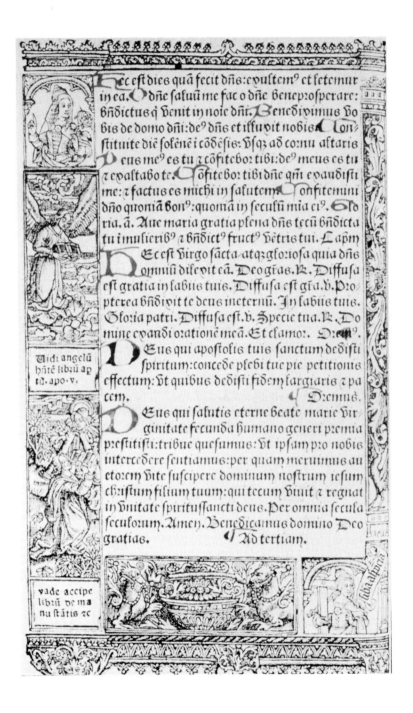

Plate 6　The Showing and Devouring of the Book. Book of Hours.
Paris, np, c.1515 (courtesy of the John Carter Brown Library at
Brown University, Providence, RI)

Plate 7 Fifteen Last
Things and Last Judgment.
Book of Hours. Paris,
Thielmann Kerver, 1503
(courtesy of the Academy
of Medicine)

Plate 8 Astrological Man. Book of Hours. Paris, Gvillavme & Godart, 1520?
(courtesy of the John Carter Brown Library at Brown University, Providence, RI)

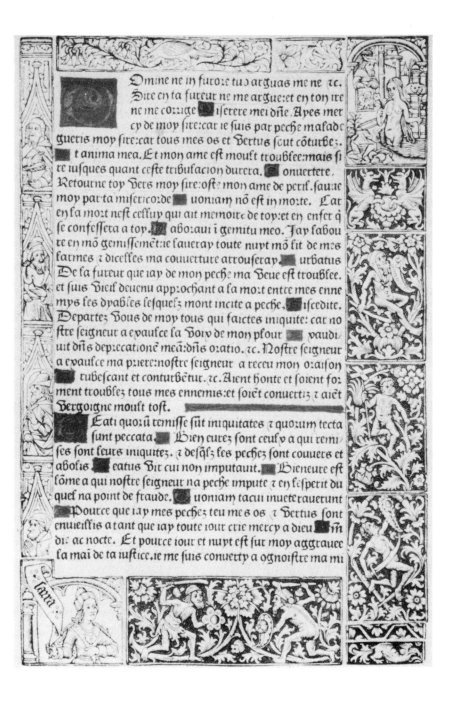

Ðmine ne in furoze tuo arguas me ne zc.
Ðie en ta fureur ne me argue:et en ton ire
ne me corrige ⬛ iserere mei dñe. Apes met
cy de moy sire:car ie suis par peche malade
guetis moy sire:car tous mes os et vertus scut cóturbe;.
⬛ t anima mea. Et mon ame est moust troublee:mais si
te iusques quant ceste tribulacion durera. ⬛ onuertere.
Retourne toy vers moy sire:oste mon ame de peril.sauue
moy par ta misericozde ⬛ uoniam nó est in mozte. Car
en sa mozt nest cessuy qui ait memoire de toy:et en enfer q
se confesseta a toy. ⬛ abozaui i gemitu meo. Jay sabou
te en mó gemissemét:ie saueray toute nupt mó sit de mes
farmes i dicesses ma couuctture atrouferay ⬛ urbatus
De sa fureur que iay de mon peche ma veue est troublee.
et suis vieil deuenu approchant a sa mozt entre mes enne
mys ses dyables fesquelz mont incite a peche. ⬛ iscedite.
Departe; vous de moy tous qui faictes iniquite: car no
stre seigneur a epaufce sa voix de mon plour ⬛ paudi
uit dñs depzecationé meá:dñs ozatio. zc. Noftre seigneur
a epaufce ma pziere:noftre seigneur a receu mon ozaison
⬛ tubefcant et conturbétur. zc. Aient honte et soient foz
ment troublez tous mes ennemis:et soiet conuertiz i aiét
vergoigne mouft toft. ▬▬▬▬
⬛ Eati quozú temiffe sút iniquitates i quozum tecta
sunt peccata. ⬛ Bien eurez font ceulx a qui remi
fes font leurs iniquitez. i defqf; fes pechez font couuers et
abofis ⬛ eatus vir cui non imputauit. ⬛ Bieneure eft
lóme a qui noftre seigneur na peche impute i en fefperit du
quel na point de fraude. ⬛ uoniam tacui inueterauerunt
⬛ Pource que iay mes pechez teu mes os i vertus font
enuieiffis a tant que iay toute iour crie mercy a dieu ⬛ ñ
diz ac nocte. Et pource iour et nupt eft fur moy aggrauee
fa mai de ta iuftice.ie me fuis conuetty a ognoiftre ma mi

Plate 9 David and Bathsheba Borderpiece. Book of Hours. Paris, Philippe Pigouchet, 1498 (courtesy of the John Carter Brown Library at Brown University, Providence, RI)

Domine ne in furore.

Frendes this daye I
shall not declare vnto
you ony parte of the
epystle oz gospel/whi
che perauenture you
doo abyde foz to here
at this tyme. But at the desyze and in
staunce of them (whome I may not
cōtrary in ony thȳge whiche is bothe
accozdynge to my duty ⁊ also to theyz
soules helth) I haue taken vpon me shoztly to declare
the fyzst penytēcyall psalme/wherin I beseche almygh
ty god foz his grete mercy and pyte soo to helpe me this
daye by his grace that whatsoeuer I shall say may fyzst
be to his pleasure to the pzofyte of myn owne wzetched
soule/and also foz the holsome comfozte to all synners/
whiche be repentaūt foz theyz synnes and hath tourned
themselfe with all theyz hole herte ⁊ mynde vnto god
the way of wyckednesse and synne vtterly forsake. But
oz we go to ẏ declaracyon of this psalme/ it shall be pzo
fytable and conuenyent to shewe who dyde wzyte this
psalme/foz what occasyon he wzote it/and what fruyte
pzofyte/and helpe he obteyned by the same Dauyd the
sone of Jesse a man syngulerly chosen of almyghty god
and endued with many grete benefytes/afterwarde he
synned full greuously agaynste god and his lawe/ and
foz the occasyon of his grete offence/ he made this holy
        vii.psal.   aa.ii.

Plate 10   David and Bathsheba. *The Seuen penytencyall psalmes of Dauid.*
London, Wynkyn de Worde, 1509 (courtesy of the Rare Books and Manuscripts
Division, New York Public Library, Astor, Lenox and Tilden Foundations)

Plate 11 Assembly of Saints. *Legenda Aurea*. Westminster, William Caxton, 1483 (reproduced by permission of the Marquess of Bath, Longleat House, Warminster, Wiltshire)

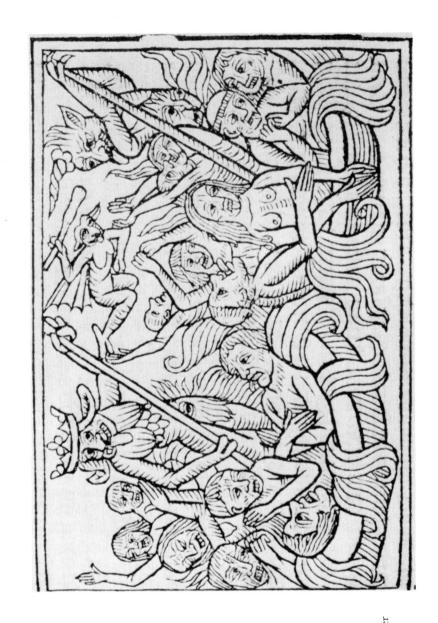

Plate 12 Fate of the Lecherous. *Ordinarye of Chrysten Men.* London, Wynkyn de Worde, 1506 (courtesy of the John Carter Brown Library at Brown University, Providence, RI)

Plate 13 Fate of the Envious. *Le Compost et Kalendrier des Bergiers.*
Paris, Guy Marchant, 1493 (reproduced courtesy of the Spencer Collection,
New York Public Library, Astor, Lenox and Tilden Foundations)

Plate 14   Fate of the Lecherous. *Kalendayr of the Shyppars*. Paris,
Antoine Vérard, 1503 (reproduced from H. O. Sommer, facsim., London, 1892)

Plate 15 Title Page. *Ordinarye of Chrysten Men*. London, Wynkyn
de Worde, 1506 (courtesy of the John Carter Brown Library at Brown
University, Providence, RI)

❋:꧁꧂ ꧁꧂ ꧁꧂ ꧁꧂ ꧁꧂ ꧁꧂ ꧁꧂ ꧁꧂ ❋

Greuoufly dyeth he that hathe not lerned too
deye/lerne thenne to dye pf thou fhall conne
lyue/foz no man fhall can lyue/that hath not
lerned to dye/and he is by ryght called a cay
tyf that can not lyue ne that knoweth not to
dye/pf thou wyll lyue frely and furelye lerne to deye by
felye/pf thou faye how fhall it bee lerned. J fhall now
telle to the. Thou oughteft to knowe that this lyf nys
but deth. Foz deth is a departynge/this knoweth euery

Plate 16 How-to-Die-Well. *Boke Named the Royall*. London, Wynkyn
de Worde, 1507 (courtesy of the Rare Books and Manuscripts Division,
New York Public Library, Astor, Lenox and Tilden Foundations)

Plate 17 *Ars moriendi*, c.1475 (courtesy of the Rare Books and Manuscripts Division, New York Public Library, Astor, Lenox and Tilden Foundations)

Plate 18 Title Page. *Boke Named the Royall*. London, Wynkyn de Worde, 1507 (courtesy of the Rare Books and Manuscripts Division, New York Public Library, Astor, Lenox and Tilden Foundations)

Plate 19 *Ars moriendi*, c.1475 (courtesy of the Rare Books and Manuscripts Division, New York Public Library, Astor, Lenox and Tilden Foundations)

Plate 20 St Catherine of Siena. *The Orcharde of Syon*. London, Wynkyn de Worde, 1519 (courtesy of the Spencer Collection, New York Public Library, Astor, Lenox and Tilden Foundations)

Plate 21 Frontispiece. *The Orcharde of Syon*. London, Wynkyn de Worde, 1519 (courtesy of the Spencer Collection, New York Public Library, Astor, Lenox and Tilden Foundations)

Plate 22   Illuminated Endleaf. *The Orcharde of Syon*. London,
Wynkyn de Worde, 1519 (reproduced by permission of the Marquess of Bath,
Longleat House, Warminster, Wiltshire)

¶ Here begynneth the
boke called the Pype/oʒ Tonne/of the
lyfe of perfection. The reaſon oʒ cauſe
wherof dothe playnely | appere
in the pʒoceſſe.

Plate 23 St Bridget. *The Pype or Tonne of the Lyfe of Perfection.*
London, Robert Redman, 1532 (reproduced courtesy of the Beinecke Rare Book
and Manuscript Library, Yale University)

Die godlike reuelacii ... de
gher vrouwe sinte Birgitten.
den leuen ende passie ons heeren
ihesu xpristi eñ sijnre lieuer moe-
der Marien.

Plate 24 St Bridget. *Revelations*. Antwerp, Gerard Leeu, 1491 (reproduced
courtesy of Princeton University Library)

not read, aspired to own one.'[25] With printing, the Book of Hours circulated more widely than its manuscript counterpart, becoming more readily available and affordable. The size of the traditional picture cycle is increased; the text seems to diminish, and the narrative illustrations, as well as the grotesque and allegorical figures in the borders, offer the reader a variety of diversions. In England, the Book of Hours may have been a schoolbook as well as a prayerbook, called a Primer, according to some sources, 'because it was the *Primus liber* of the medieval schoolboy',[26] but it was also a text that became subtly revised and edited as its audience broadened. One has only to recall the bilingual talents of such diverse people as Margaret Beaufort and Pynson's merchant, and their mutual ignorance of Latin, to comprehend the challenge printers faced. Always the province of laymen, primers were to reach a larger audience of lay readers, who were largely ignorant of Latin, through the new medium of printing. The question was how to make them accessible to a wider audience while retaining orthodoxy of text.

What I have observed, having looked at printed Books of Hours at the Pierpont Morgan Library, the New York Public Library, and in the libraries at Princeton, Harvard, and Brown, is that vernacular elements are slipped in, rather like the captions on the 15 Last Things bordercuts. De Worde, in his 1494 Book of Hours, includes English rubrics and instructions for use of text, and some English titles in his Table of Contents; he also manages to conceal, very adequately, four English prayers in his predominantly Latin text.[27] Antoine Vérard then follows de Worde's lead in the Book of Hours he published for Sarum use. A bit later, in early sixteenth-century primers, there is a tendency to cluster short texts in English or French either at the end of the volume, near the Table of Contents, or at the front, near the Calendar. The Calendar itself seems like a kind of 'free zone', where vernacular verses on the ages of man accompany pictures of the Labours of the Months, where there are occasional rebuses and wordplay (these occur, for example, in an edition printed by Gile Couteau in 1513 now at the Pierpont Morgan Library), and where Astrological Man (Plate 8) usually appears, often along with French or English verses as he does in this example from a Book of Hours printed in Paris in 1520, now in the John Carter Brown Library. The printer François Regnault was particularly inventive in incorporating vernacular works into his Latin primers, as Mary Erler has pointed out in her recent article on the *Maner to Lyue Well*.[28] In his primer of 1527, Regnault replaces the usual Latin captions beneath the typical full-page illustrations with four-line verses in English.[29] For example, accompanying the illustration of John boiled in his pot are the lines:

[25]   Harthan. See also 'Books for Everybody', in Christopher de Hamel's *A History of Illuminated Manuscripts* (Godine, 1986).
[26]   Edwyn Birchenough, 'The Prymer in English', *The Library*, 4th series 18 (1938), p. 177.
[27]   STC 15875.
[28]   Mary C. Erler, 'The Maner to Lyue Well and the Coming of English to François Regnault's Primers of the 1520s and 1530s', *The Library* (1984).
[29]   STC 15954.

Hovv saynt iohan dyde vvryte in vvyldernesse/
The apocalyps and of tokens vuondrous/
Whiche in the ayre he herde and sewe expresse/
With myracles terryble and monstrvous

The object of these vernacular incursions into the Latin printed primer was to help the reader with little or no Latin through the text. The vernacular portions tend to be tied to layout, as in the rubrics or the instructions, or to pictures, which divide and organise the text. In the case of printed Books of Hours, illustration and vernacular text are clearly linked. Pictures act as guides through the text. They may also serve as diversions from a barely comprehensible text, or as invitations to read the text, invitations to literacy.

This may be their function as well in vernacular religious texts for lay readers. Pictures seem to link the same or similar subjects in a number of different texts; they are being used conventionally or associatively. For example, a borderblock of Bathsheba in her bath (Plate 9) illustrates a Psalms text in a Book of Hours printed for Pigouchet in 1498. A copy of the Bathsheba cut (Plate 10) illustrates *The Seuen penytencyall psalmes of David*, a collection of John Fisher's sermons, printed by de Worde in 1509. This image occurs at the start of text and is the only pictorial woodcut in the book. The same woodcut is used by de Worde to illustrate the life of David in his 1527 edition of Voragine's *Golden Legend*.[30] Are these woodcuts being reused merely for convenience or for economic reasons? Or is there a conscious linking and identification of subject and text?

Another example, 'The Trinity Adored by the Assembly of Saints' (Plate 11), first appears as the prefatory woodcut in a copy of Voragine's *Golden Legend*, which was translated by William Caxton and printed by him in 1483. The woodcut recurs as the frontispiece to de Worde's editions of the *Golden Legend*, those which appeared in 1493, 1498, and 1527, linking them with Caxton's earlier bestseller. And, between de Worde's re-editions, the same woodcut is used, again as a frontispiece, in the first edition of John of Tynemouth's *Nova legenda Angliae*, printed by de Worde in 1516. By reusing the image, de Worde is connecting John's work, which describes the lives of English saints, with his (and Caxton's) earlier editions of the *Golden Legend*, an effective marketing technique. And, in all these editions, 'The Assembly of Saints' woodcut identifies and introduces the idea of the text to the reader.[31]

Another aspect of what I call the conventional or associative image is the

---

[30] STC 10903; STC 24880.

[31] Copies of the 1493 de Worde edition (STC 24875) and the 1498 edition (STC 24876) are in the Pierpont Morgan Library; de Worde's edition of 1527 (STC 24880) is the Spencer collection of the New York Public Library. The *Nova Legenda Angliae* (STC 4601) is listed under Capgrave in the *RSTC*, but is no longer attributed to him. The *RSTC* does not cite the copy in the Annmary Brown Memorial at Brown University (though it does refer to the copy in the Houghton, from which the illustration is taken). For further discussion of 'The Assembly of Saints' and other woodcuts in Caxton's *Golden Legend*, see Pamela Sheingorn's essay, 'The Woodcuts in Caxton's Golden Legende' in *From Manuscript to Printed Book*, ed. Horrall and Driver (forthcoming).

use and reuse of pictures to illustrate the same or similar *contents* in a variety of texts. For example, this woodcut (Plate 12) illustrates a passage on the pains of purgatory in the *Ordinarye of Chrysten Men*, one of the popular devotional handbooks printed by de Worde in 1502 and again in 1506. Though rather unassuming, if not downright crude, the woodcut has powerful associations. It is a copy of one of a fixed set of images used to illustrate the pains of purgatory in other contemporary miscellanies and handbooks. Another one of the set (Plate 13) illustrates the fate of the envious in purgatory in a French copy of the *Kalender of Shepherds*, published by Guy Marchant in 1500. Some other cuts in this series which appear in the 1503 English *Kalendayr of the Shyppars*, printed for Vérard in Paris, represent the fate of the proud, souls tortured on racks; the fate of the gluttonous, showing souls being forcefed toads and other creatures; and finally, the prototype for our woodcut in *The Ordinary of Chrysten Men* (Plate 14), which illustrates the fate of lecherous.[32] These picture cycles of the torments of purgatory appeared in numerous contemporary French and English books, some of which were probably known to the literate layman. These include Marchant's *Le Compost et Kalendrier des Bergiers*, printed in 1493, and Vérard's 1503 *Kalendayr*, and his *Art of good lywyng and good deyng*, also printed in English in 1503. De Worde himself prints the entire picture cycle in his *Craft to Live Well* of 1505 and in *The arte or craft to deye Well*, published in 1506. In *The Ordinarye of Chrysten Men* (Plate 12), the image is again acting as a signal to the reader and as a powerful invitation to read the text.

Another evocative image (Plate 15) appears on the verso of the final folio of the 1506 *Ordinary of Chrysten Men*. It occurs also in *Boke Named the Royall* (Plate 16), yet another religious prose manual for layfolk. One of the few known collaborations between de Worde and his rival Richard Pynson, *Boke Named the Royall*, was reprinted from Caxton's translation of the *Somme le Roi*, which appeared c.1486-87 under the title *Ryal Book*.[33] De Worde liked the book enough to reprint it in 1507, though his collaboration with Pynson may indicate a fear of financial risk or failure. *Boke Named the Royal* is a quarto, about two hundred folios long, and is not as ambitious an undertaking as the *Golden Legend*, for example. But it does have a large number of illustrations.

The *Somme le Roy*, the manuscript source for *Boke named the Royall*, had a well established picture cycle of fifteen illuminations before the end of the thirteenth century. Caxton includes seven pictures in his *Ryal Book*, which introduce some of the chapters, but divide the book less effectively than the

---

[32] Vérard's edition (STC 22407) has been reproduced in facsimile by H. O. Sommer (London, 1892).

[33] I looked at copies of *Boke Named the Royall* (STC 21430), the de Worde/Pynson collaboration, in the New York Public Library; the NYPL copy has de Worde's name in the colophon, while Pynson's name appears in the colophon of the STC microfilm (STC 21430a). Copies of Caxton's *Ryal Book* (STC 21429) were examined in the Morgan Library and in the John Carter Brown Library. De Worde and Pynson also collaborated on the *Golden Legend* (see Hodnett, p. 21) and possibly on a single-sheet woodcut with links to Syon Abbey, which is described by Hind (p. 738).

manuscript miniatures do. But, de Worde, in his reprint, almost doubles the number of pictures in the traditional cycle, expanding the illustrations from fifteen to twenty-seven. In this case, again, pictures make the text more accessible and easier to understand. The number of illustrations in *Boke Named the Royall* indicates that de Worde and/or Pynson intended that it reach a larger audience of lay readers than it ever had before.

One of two woodcuts illustrating the how-to-die-well text in *Boke Named the Royall* (Plate 16) is drawn, perhaps indirectly, from the final image in blockbook *Ars moriendi*, which began to be produced around 1460 in Germany and Holland, and quickly became popular throughout Europe. I reproduce here one example from a blockbook dated c.1475 (Plate 17). After studying this image in several blockbooks, incunables, and facsimiles, I was amused to find that the demons always curse the same way as they depart, though the order in which they do so in the de Worde woodcut is reversed (as is the image; see Plate 16). Inversion of image and captions is clear evidence of copying (and, in this case, appropriate demon behaviour).

Another *Ars moriendi* cut, which occurs in both the *Ordinary* and *Boke Named the Royall*, is that of the patient kicking his doctor (Plate 18), representing the temptation to impatience, one of the early stages of death, where the sick 'ben madde wexen woode and becometh demoniacles impacyentes'. Here, the woodcut serves as the title page to *Boke Named the Royall*. De Worde may have used a blockbook source for this image (Plate 19) or found it in French copies, in *L'art de bien vivre* or the *Art of good lywyng and good deyinge*, published by Vérard.[34] The deathbed scene and the patient kicking his physician also both appear in de Worde's *Craft to Live Well*, of 1505, and in his *The arte or craft to lyue well & dye well*, of 1506. In de Worde's *Ars moriendi*, a brief volume consisting of nine leaves printed in 1506, the deathbed scene is the sole woodcut in the volume.

Ars moriendi images were both common and popular in early printed religious books for the laity, and de Worde's reuse of them should not be chalked up sheerly to economics, expediency, or unimaginative copying of what had come before. Instead, these are images with a history, with associations. Behind them lies a consciousness of *Ars moriendi* blockbooks and manuscript miniatures, for example, those which occur in the Litany and Office of the Dead in Books of Hours, and they will remain popular for some time, reaching their peak with Holbein's *Dance of Death* series.[35] These

---

[34] This text accompanies the same woodcut of the patient kicking his doctor in de Worde's *Arte for to Deye Well* (included in his *Craft to Lyue Well*, 1505), fol. lvi^v. Vérard's edition of the *Art of good lywyng and good deyinge* (STC 791) was published in 1503.

[35] In *Small Books and Pleasant Histories: Popular Fiction and its Readership in Seventeenth-century England* (Methuen, 1981), Margaret Spufford discusses the continued potency of *Ars moriendi* images in the seventeenth and eighteenth centuries: 'The most striking thing about the religious chapbooks is their domination, both in words and woodcuts, by the skeletal figure of Death. Death has been removed, in the English chapbooks, from its place as a separate tonic in popular culture, stemming from the medieval Dance of Death, and has become a pedagogue. ... The main themes of popular sermons may have changed less at the Reformation

images were immediately recognisable to contemporary readers, identifying and introducing the content of the text. In this case, we might say that familiarity breeds literacy.

A final example of the conventional, or associative, image occurs, I think, in the work I mention first in this paper, *The Orcharde of Syon*. The illustrations here are quite unusual in style, and are unlike pictures de Worde uses elsewhere. Their imagery is dense and compacted; the figure outlines are thick and black. Woodcuts introduce each book of text. The title woodcut (Plate 20) shows St Catherine of Siena kneeling at her desk, heart in hand, receiving her revelations from God.[36]

The cuts in *Orcharde of Syon* are by one artist and are clearly not English in style. They look closest to Spanish woodcuts of the period, and I suspect the artist might possibly have been a nun of Spanish or possibly Italian origin living at Syon, given the book making and binding activities going on there in the late fifteenth and early sixteenth centuries.[37] In any case, these woodcuts were made expressly for this volume. De Worde reuses only one of the set of eight, for the title cut in his *Dyetary of ghostly helthe* of 1527.

A particularly confusing image in *Orcharde of Syon* occurs at the beginning and end of the text. I reproduce here the opening woodcut from the volume in the Spencer Collection of the New York Public Library (Plate 21), and, for comparison, the painted woodcut which appears at the end of the copy at Longleat House (Plate 22). In her *Traditio* article, Sr Mary Denise says this represents 'St. Bridget of Sweden surrounded by the community of nuns which she founded'.[38] This interpretation fits generally with Bridgettine iconography. In five manuscripts of the late fourteenth or early fifteenth century, Bridget is shown seated on a throne

than is at first supposed, ... The surviving chapbooks from the 1650s on may only indicate the spread of a theme in cheap print that had been familiar orally for five centuries, or, on the other hand, they may indicate its growing hold on the popular imagination. In the chapbooks, however, the images of Death and Judgement do seem to predominate, and to be stressed at the expense of other Christian imagery. ... The *danse macabre* does not seem to have lost its hold on the popular imagination' (p. 138).

[36] *The Orcharde of Syon* cuts are distinctive in their style and handling of subject matter, with several scenes occurring simultaneously. St Catherine is always present as her vision progresses around her. For example, the illustration introducing Part Three of text shows the Bridge, a central image in Catherine's revelations (and in the *Orcharde of Syon* woodcuts), on which shrouded souls hop their way heavenward. In the copy of the *Orcharde of Syon* owned by the Marquess of Bath, the painting of woodcuts is contemporary as demonstrated by a painted-over page mending at the start of Book Four. Illuminated borders have been added to the woodcut illustrations and the opening page of text.

[37] See Erler, *Scriptorium* (1985); George Keiser, 'The Progress of Purgatory: Visions of the Afterlife in Later Middle English Literature'; James Hogg, 'Richard Whytford's *A Dayly exercyse and Experyence of Dethe*', in *Zeit, Tod und Ewigkeit in der Renaissanceliteratur* (1987); the essays by Robert Horsfield and Ann Hutchison in this volume. Ann Hutchison suggested in passing that the nun-artist might have been associated with the Spanish court of Katharine of Aragon.

[38] Denise, p. 273. In a note, she says, 'Churton believed that this cut represented St Catharine' (n. 18).

surrounded on either side by nuns, and often by priests and monks as well.[39]

She is also shown this way in one of the woodcuts illustrating the 1492 Lübeck edition of her Revelations, which were designed and cut by a lay brother at Wadstena, the monastery endowed by St Bridget in 1344, and in a woodcut produced c.1490 in Augsburg, now in the Ashmolean museum, which has the inscription: 'Thus gave Bridget the rules of salvation to the sisters and brothers.'[40] An illustration similar in its layout and presentation (though vastly superior in skill), designed by the young Albrecht Dürer, appears in the edition of Bridget's Revelations published in 1502 by Dürer's godfather, Anton Koberger.[41] However, in all these woodcuts, Bridget is holding books or scrolls in both hands, giving her Rule and writings to her Order; in the miniatures and woodcuts (excepting Dürer's), there is always a crown at her feet. But, the central figure here (Plate 21) holds a heart, an attribute of St Catherine of Siena, and her feet trample a dragon. St Catherine is usually shown wearing the Dominican habit,[42] holding a heart and a book, and wearing a crown of thorns, as she is in the *Orcharde* woodcut. This blurring of identity again argues that the artist of the *Orcharde of Syon* woodcuts was intimately connected with Syon, imposing a familiar model, St Bridget, on a new subject, St Catherine.[43]

And this influence also seems to work in reverse. The title cut in *Orcharde of Syon* (Plate 20) with its bold lines, heavy borders and rather dense

[39] See Carl Nordenfalk, 'Saint Bridget of Sweden as Represented in Illuminated Manuscripts', in *De Artibus Opuscula XL: Essays in Honor of Erwin Panofsky*, ed. Millard Meiss (New York, 1961), pp. 371-393, pls. 122-127; *Lexikon der christlichen Ikonographie*, ed. Kirschbaum, vol. 5; Isak Collijn, *Handskifter Urkunder Och Bocker Rorande Birgitta Och Vadstena* (1918).

[40] This is reproduced as fig. 4b in Aston (Ashmolean Museum, Oxford, p. 132).

[41] See figs. 128 and 141 (St Bridget divides her work amongst nuns and monks; St Bridget gives her works to the Emperor, Kings, and Princes) in *The Complete Woodcuts of Albrecht Dürer*, ed. Willi Kurth, transl. Silvia M. Welsh, 2nd edn (New York: Dover Publications Inc.).

[42] Contemporary descriptions of the habits of the orders of Bridget and Catherine of Siena are included in *The original & sprynge of all sectes & orders by whome whan or were they beganne. Tr. out of hye Dutch* (STC 18849a), printed in 1537. The description of the nuns of St Catherine says: 'They weare garmentes lyke blacke or preacher freres. Theyr cloke and vayle are blacke, theyr cote is whyte. They dyffer muche from all other orders in ceremonies, saue only in the Psalter þᵉ whiche they bable without understandynge ...' Their Psalter, presumably, was in Latin. Of the Bridgettines, this comment: 'Theyr clothing is a graye cote wᵗ a graye cloke thero (*sic*), and a reed crosse in a whyte cyrkle. They may weare no lynnen, after the tenoure of theyre rule.'

[43] The closest example I have found to the image in the *Orcharde of Syon* is an Italian panel painting by Cosimo Rosselli in the National Gallery of Scotland, Edinburgh, which shows St Catherine seated in a niche, surrounded by saints, her feet on a dragon, giving the book of her Rule to kneeling members of the second Order of St Dominic, and the scroll of regulations to kneeling members of the third Order. This painting, however, seems to have remained in Florence until it was acquired by Charles Butler around 1885. See the catalogue of the National Gallery of Scotland, Edinburgh, and reproduction in George Kaftal, *St. Catherine in Tuscan Painting* (Oxford, 1949); Berenson cites this painting only briefly in his *Italian Pictures of the Renaissance* (Oxford, 1932).

imagery is the most direct source for this image (Plate 23) of St Bridget.[44] The thickness of line, busy-ness of image, and heavy borders argue that the artist knew and was perhaps consciously echoing the illustrations in *Orcharde of Syon*, though in this case, the artist is, I think, connected with de Worde's shop. Interestingly, both the Bridget cut and the *Orcharde of Syon* cuts were first used in 1519, the Bridget appearing in a Book of Hours printed by de Worde. Other probable models for this scene (Plate 24) also show Bridget at her desk, an angel looking over her shoulder, and the twin images of the Virgin and child, and co-Passion, which shows God the Father suffering with Christ. This woodcut illustrates the title-page of the Dutch edition of Bridget's revelations, printed by Gerard Leeu in 1491.[45] Another, perhaps more direct source, comes from the 1481 edition of Bridget's writings published in Nuremberg.[46] But, in style, the de Worde woodcut of St Bridget looks most like the cuts in *Orcharde of Syon*.

The Bridget woodcut (Plate 23) appears in eighteen books between 1519 and 1534, and is popular not only with de Worde but with other early English printers, Richard Pynson, Robert Redman, and Richard Fawkes among them. Writing in his catalogue of English woodcuts, Edward Hodnett comments that one of the cuts in William Bonde's *Pylgrimage of Perfection* is 'de Worde's useful St Bridget, a borrowing that is even harder to explain than most'.[47] But, once the idea of the conventional, or associative, image is applied, the use of the Bridget woodcut becomes quite clear.

The St Bridget woodcut appears in seven editions of books written by Richard Whytforde, the self-styled 'wretch of Syon'. That is a first clue. The cut also appears on the title-page of *Mirror of Our Lady*, produced for Agnes Jordan, abbess of Syon, in 1530 by Richard Fawkes. William Bonde, the author mentioned by Hodnett, describes himself as a 'Brother of Syon' in both editions of *A deuoute Epistle or Treatyse for them that ben*

[44] This woodcut is reproduced from the copy of Richard Whitforde's *The Pype or Tonne of the lyfe of perfection* (STC 25421), printed by Robert Redman in 1532, in the Beinecke Library, Yale University. The cut is first used by de Worde in his Book of Hours, published 1519, and continues to appear through 1534. See Hodnett, 457, fig. 54. The Beinecke *Pype* was formerly owned by the Marquess of Bath, Longleat House.

[45] This copy of the *Revelacien van S. Birgitten*, published in Antwerp by Gerard Leeu in 1491 and now in the Rare Book Room of Princeton University, has been damaged.

[46] The 1481 Bridget woodcut is reproduced in Richard S. Field *Fifteenth Century Woodcuts & Metalcuts From the National Gallery of Art* (Washington, DC, 1965), fig. 210. Field describes it this way: 'To the upper right above the Virgin and Child is the SPQR of Rome, referring to her pilgrimage to that city in 1349; at the bottom left are the arms of Bavaria (Wittelsbach) and at the lower right those of the Counts Oettingen in whose territory the Brigittine monastery of Maria-Maihingen was located. The cross on both her own mantel and that of the monk alludes to her voyage and death in Jerusalem in 1372.' The woodcut appeared in a book entitled *Von der Bewerung und Bestettigung der Offenbarungen St. Birgitten*, published in Nüremberg by Zeninger in 1481.

[47] Hodnett, p. 46. Hodnett mentions de Worde's St Bridget woodcut throughout his Introduction (pp. 54, 65, 68-69 *passim*).

tymorouse and fearfull in conscience.[48] The Bridget cut occurs once again in *The Directory of Conscience, a profytable treatise to such that be Tymorous or ferfull in Conscyence*, which, given the title, sounds suspiciously like Bonde's *Deuoute Epistle*, though no author is mentioned in the text (*RSTC* attributes it to William Bonde).[49] Published by Lawrence Andrew in 1527, *The Directory* is, however, briefer than the *Epistle*; has, according to the title, been 'compyled by one of the fathers of Syon'; and is attributed in the prologue to 'a deuout fader of Syon' and 'louyngly & tenderly endyted to one of the Systers of Syon'.

Yet another work with the Bridget woodcut is the *Myrrour or Glasse of Christes Passion*, published by Redman in 1534. This has a preface signed by the translator, John or Johan Fewterer, the general confessor at Syon. Then, there are four works without clear textual evidence linking them to Syon. These are three Sarum primers, printed by de Worde in 1519, 1523, and 1526, and a brief text called the *Dyetary of ghostly helthe*. Since the *Dyetary* is directed to 'my good sisters', discusses activities such as reading aloud at meals, and includes the Bridget woodcut, it too may be linked convincingly to Syon. And, after finding all these examples of books clearly connected to Syon both by text and by woodcut, I must conclude that the Primers are connected also.[50]

The fact that St Bridget appears in all these works, published over a period of fifteen years by a number of printers, is clearly no coincidence. This is, instead, an example of the associative image in its broadest sense. The Bridget woodcut links these texts and points to their common source – Syon Abbey. The woodcut functions simultaneously as a kind of imprimatur and trademark, assuring the reader of the authenticity of the book's contents and inviting him once again to read the text.

The early days of printing in England were transitional in more ways than one: with the transition from manuscript to print, the number and availability of books increased. Woodcuts were not employed haphazardly; rather, pictures encouraged literacy among laymen and insured financial survival for printers like Wynkyn de Worde and Richard Pynson. Pictures function as the key to the text, emblematic of a second vital and exciting transition made possible by printing: the movement from lay ignorance to lay literacy. Analysis of picture patterns (in this case, the use of the associative image) in the early English Renaissance book is a first step in discovering how lay readers read religious books and the role of pictures in this process.

---

[48]   STC 3275, 3276.
[49]   STC 3274.5.
[50]   STC 6833, 6844.